BLUE PERIOD 12

TSUBASA YAMAGUCHI

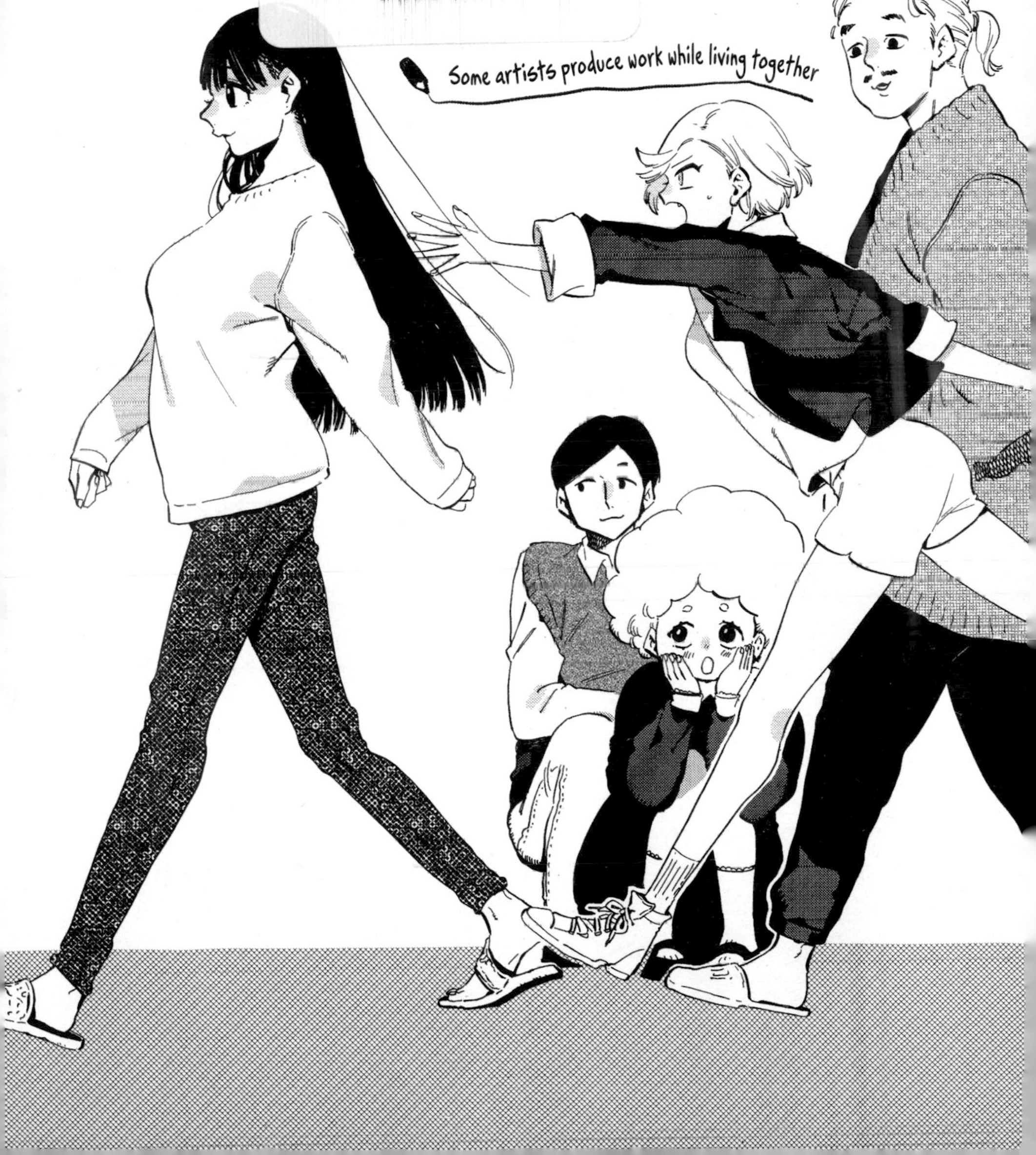
Some artists produce work while living together

CHARACTERS

Yotasuke Takahashi

After quitting the prep school that he and Yatora had been attending, he studied on his own and passed TUA's exams on his first attempt. His talent, skills, and unsociable character inspire Yatora to be a better artist.

Maki Kuwana

A former prep-school classmate of Yatora's. She failed her entrance exams but is still striving to get into an art school. She's been studying sculpture at prep school, but...

Yatora Yaguchi

After getting hooked on the joy of making art, he studied to get into Tokyo University of the Arts, the most competitive of all Japanese art colleges, and passed on his first attempt. He's a hardworking normie.

Yakumo Murai

An all-around knowledgeable guy who is constantly redefining what it means to be "the strongest." He's taken a liking to Yatora.

Haruka Hashida

He used to attend the same prep school as Yatora. He's currently attending Tama Art University.

TABLE OF CONTENTS

[STROKE 48] MY LEAST FAVORITE FOOD IS KETCHUP SPAGHETTI — 3

[STROKE 49] WHERE'S THE WALKTHROUGH SITE THAT'LL SHOW ME HOW TO BEAT THIS DEATHLOOP OF WORRY — 35

[STROKE 50] ONE OF THOSE SITUATIONS WHERE I TOOK THE HEAT AND KEPT MY COOL — 83

[STROKE 51] STRAY 2.0: STUDENT EDITION — 101

[STROKE 52] WHEN THE GROUND SOFTENS, YOU QUICKLY GET STUCK — 147

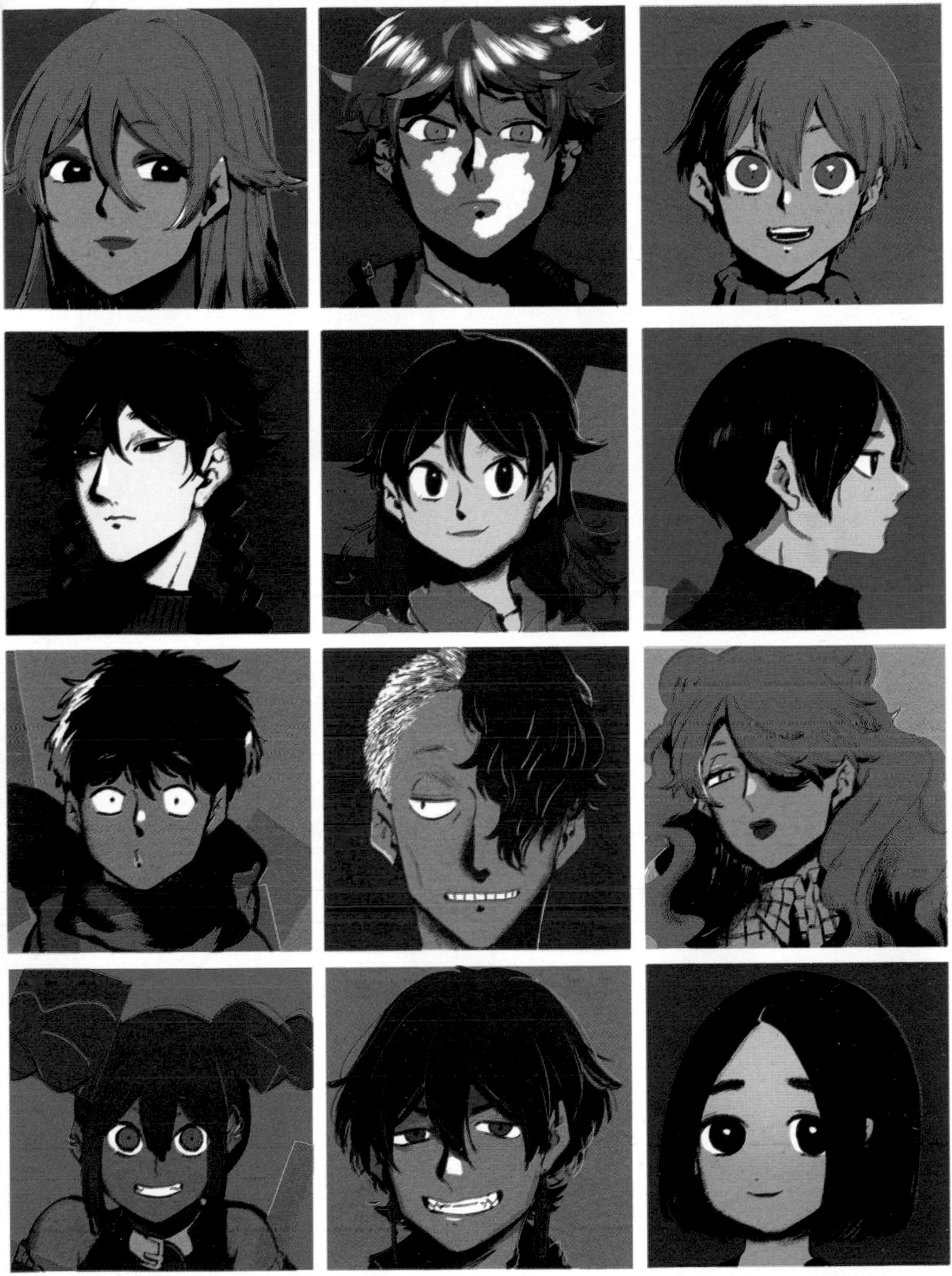

STROKE 48 MY LEAST FAVORITE FOOD IS KETCHUP SPAGHETTI

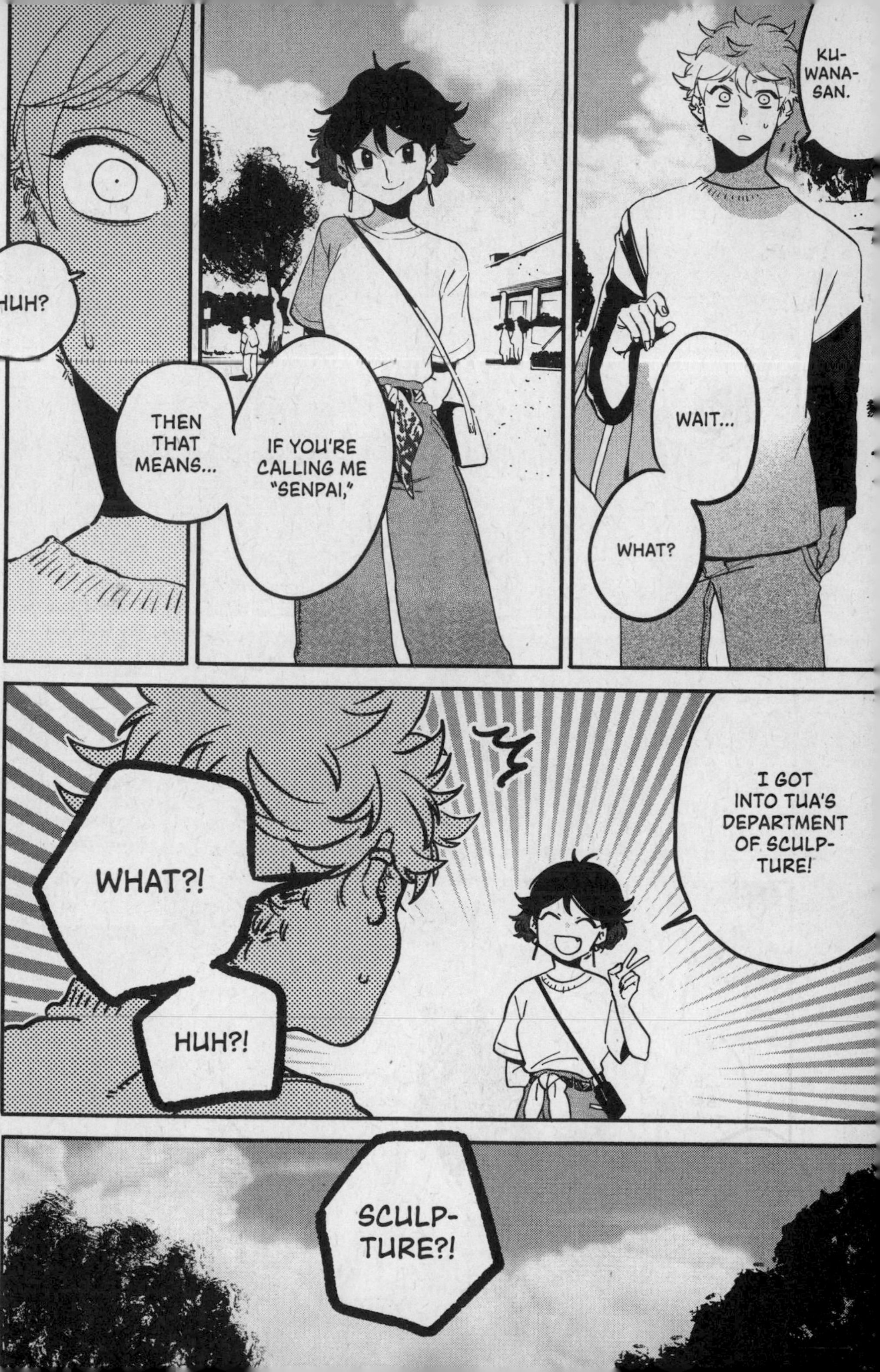
KU-WANA-SAN.
WAIT...
WHAT?
IF YOU'RE CALLING ME "SENPAI,"
THEN THAT MEANS...
HUH?
I GOT INTO TUA'S DEPARTMENT OF SCULP-TURE!
WHAT?!
HUH?!
SCULP-TURE?!

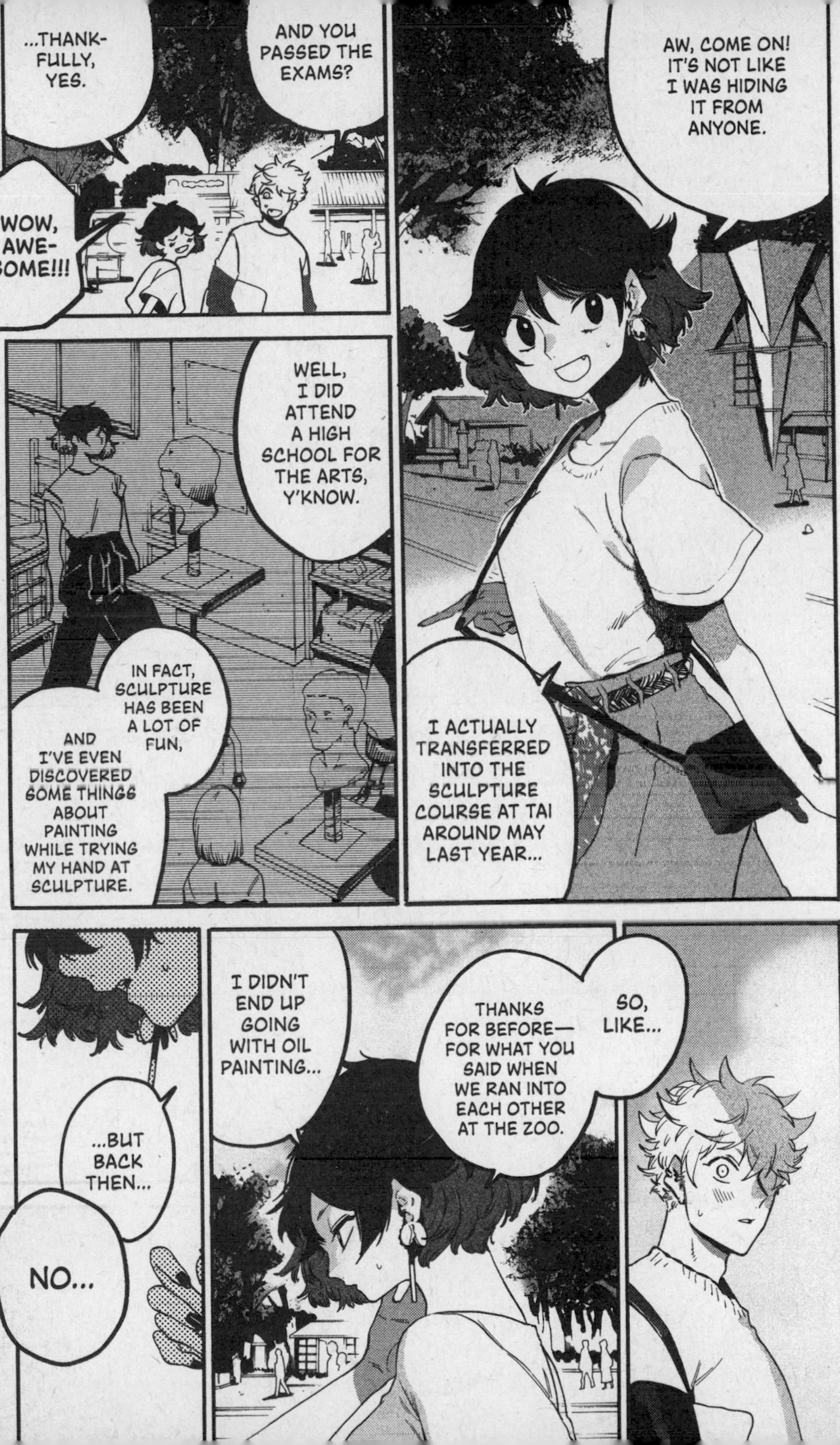
AW, COME ON! IT'S NOT LIKE I WAS HIDING IT FROM ANYONE.
I ACTUALLY TRANSFERRED INTO THE SCULPTURE COURSE AT TAI AROUND MAY LAST YEAR...
AND YOU PASSED THE EXAMS?
...THANK-FULLY, YES.
WOW, AWE-SOME!!!
WELL, I DID ATTEND A HIGH SCHOOL FOR THE ARTS, Y'KNOW.
IN FACT, SCULPTURE HAS BEEN A LOT OF FUN,
AND I'VE EVEN DISCOVERED SOME THINGS ABOUT PAINTING WHILE TRYING MY HAND AT SCULPTURE.
SO, LIKE...
THANKS FOR BEFORE— FOR WHAT YOU SAID WHEN WE RAN INTO EACH OTHER AT THE ZOO.
I DIDN'T END UP GOING WITH OIL PAINTING...
...BUT BACK THEN...
NO...

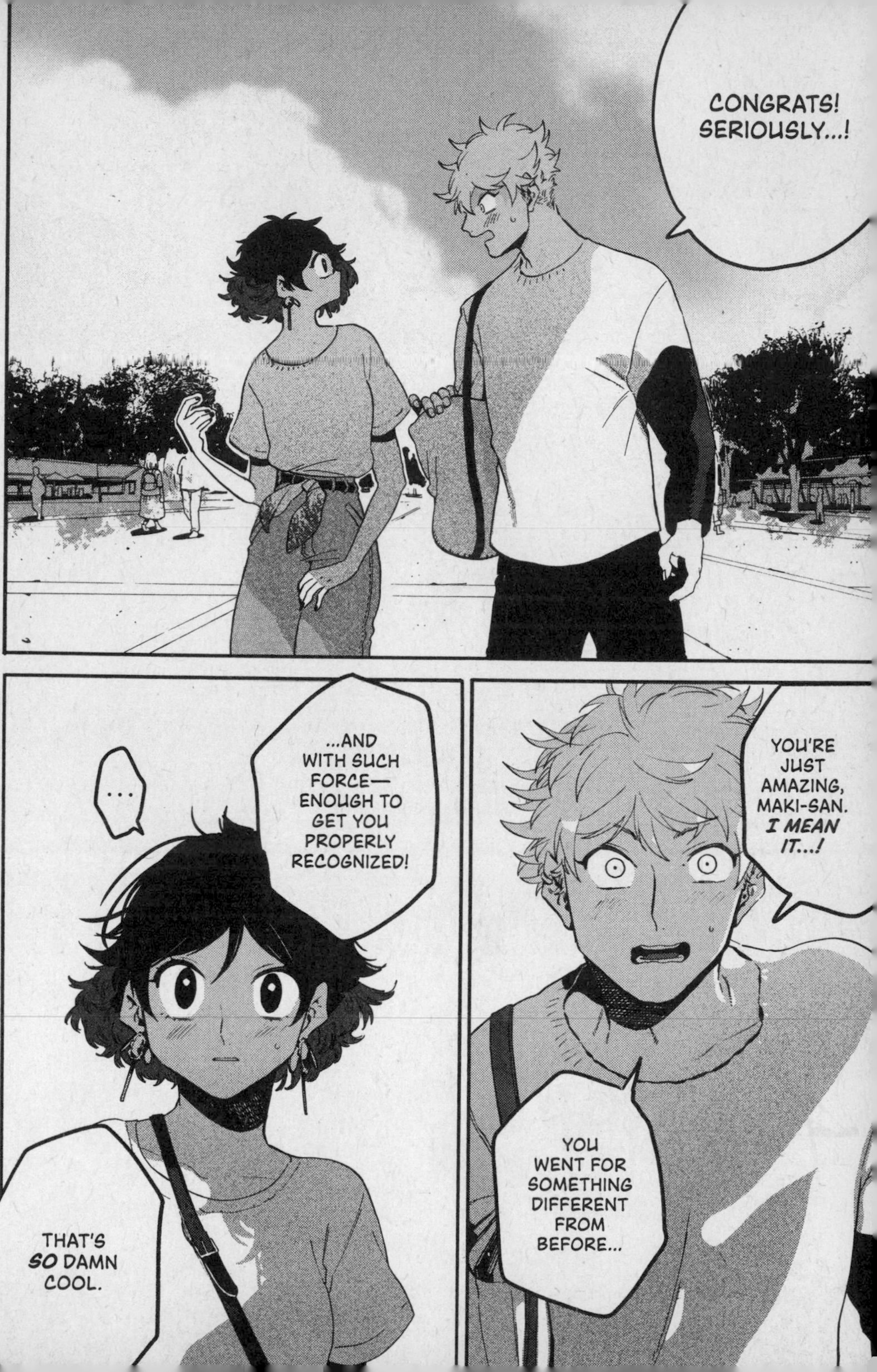
CONGRATS! SERIOUSLY...!
YOU'RE JUST AMAZING, MAKI-SAN. I MEAN IT...!
YOU WENT FOR SOMETHING DIFFERENT FROM BEFORE...
...AND WITH SUCH FORCE—ENOUGH TO GET YOU PROPERLY RECOGNIZED!
...
THAT'S SO DAMN COOL.

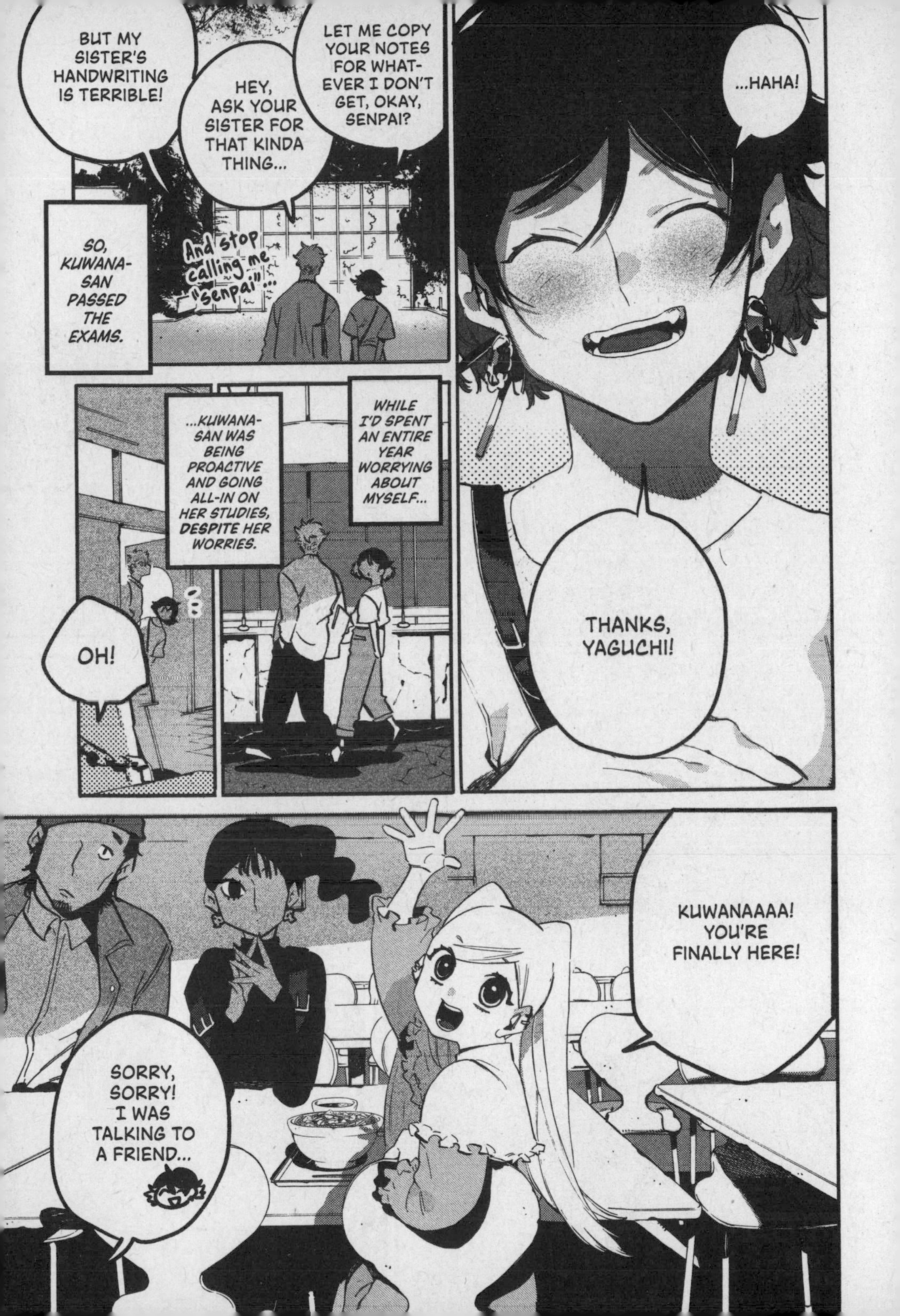
...HAHA!
THANKS, YAGUCHI!
LET ME COPY YOUR NOTES FOR WHAT-EVER I DON'T GET, OKAY, SENPAI?
HEY, ASK YOUR SISTER FOR THAT KINDA THING...
BUT MY SISTER'S HANDWRITING IS TERRIBLE!
And stop calling me "senpai"...
SO, KUWANA-SAN PASSED THE EXAMS.
WHILE I'D SPENT AN ENTIRE YEAR WORRYING ABOUT MYSELF...
...KUWANA-SAN WAS BEING PROACTIVE AND GOING ALL-IN ON HER STUDIES, DESPITE HER WORRIES.
OH!
KUWANAAAA! YOU'RE FINALLY HERE!
SORRY, SORRY! I WAS TALKING TO A FRIEND...

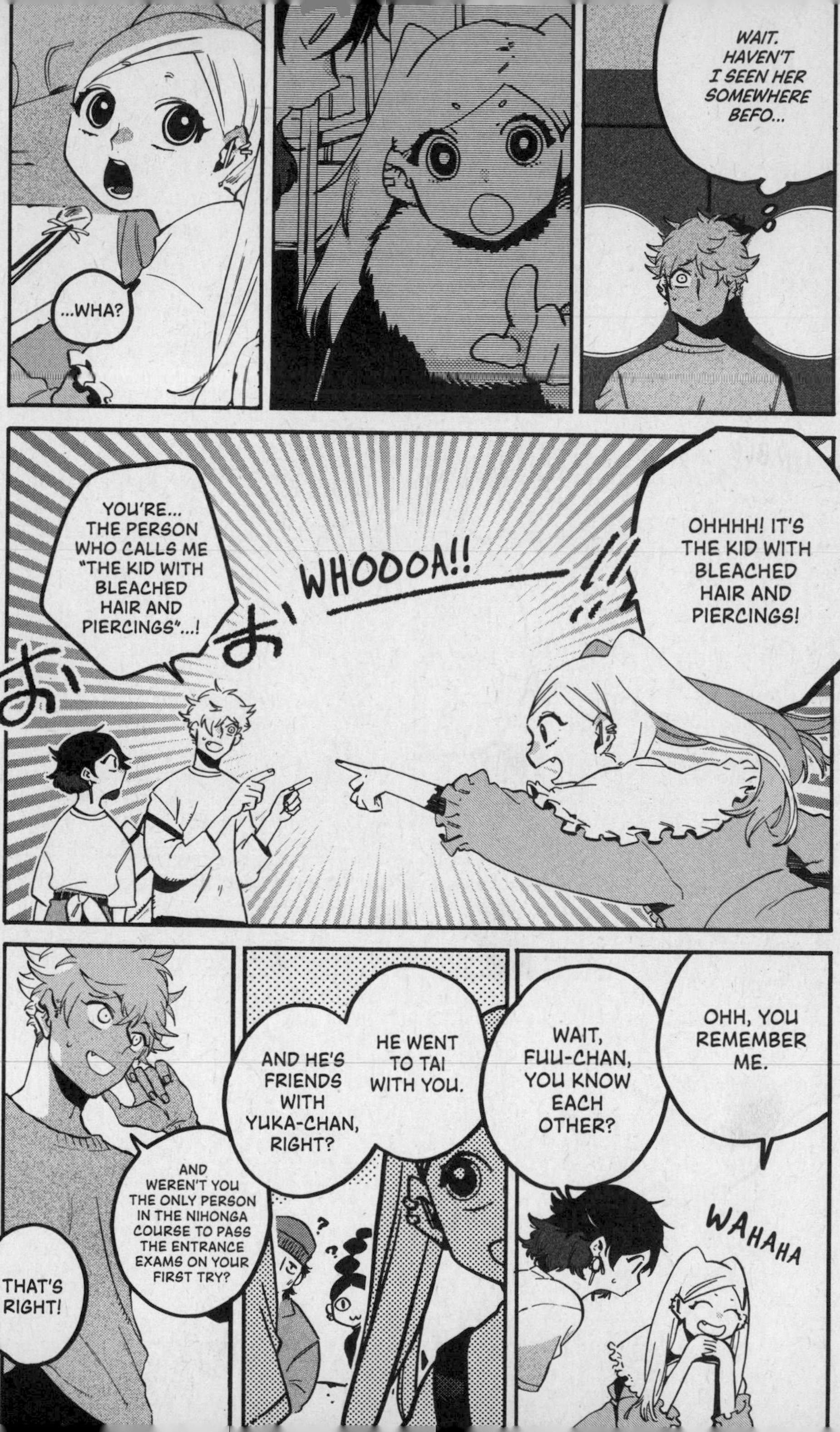
WAIT. HAVEN'T I SEEN HER SOMEWHERE BEFO...
...WHA?
OHHHH! IT'S THE KID WITH BLEACHED HAIR AND PIERCINGS!
WHOOOA!!
おお
YOU'RE... THE PERSON WHO CALLS ME "THE KID WITH BLEACHED HAIR AND PIERCINGS"...!
OHH, YOU REMEMBER ME.
WAIT, FUU-CHAN, YOU KNOW EACH OTHER?
WAHAHA
HE WENT TO TAI WITH YOU.
AND HE'S FRIENDS WITH YUKA-CHAN, RIGHT?
AND WEREN'T YOU THE ONLY PERSON IN THE NIHONGA COURSE TO PASS THE ENTRANCE EXAMS ON YOUR FIRST TRY?
THAT'S RIGHT!

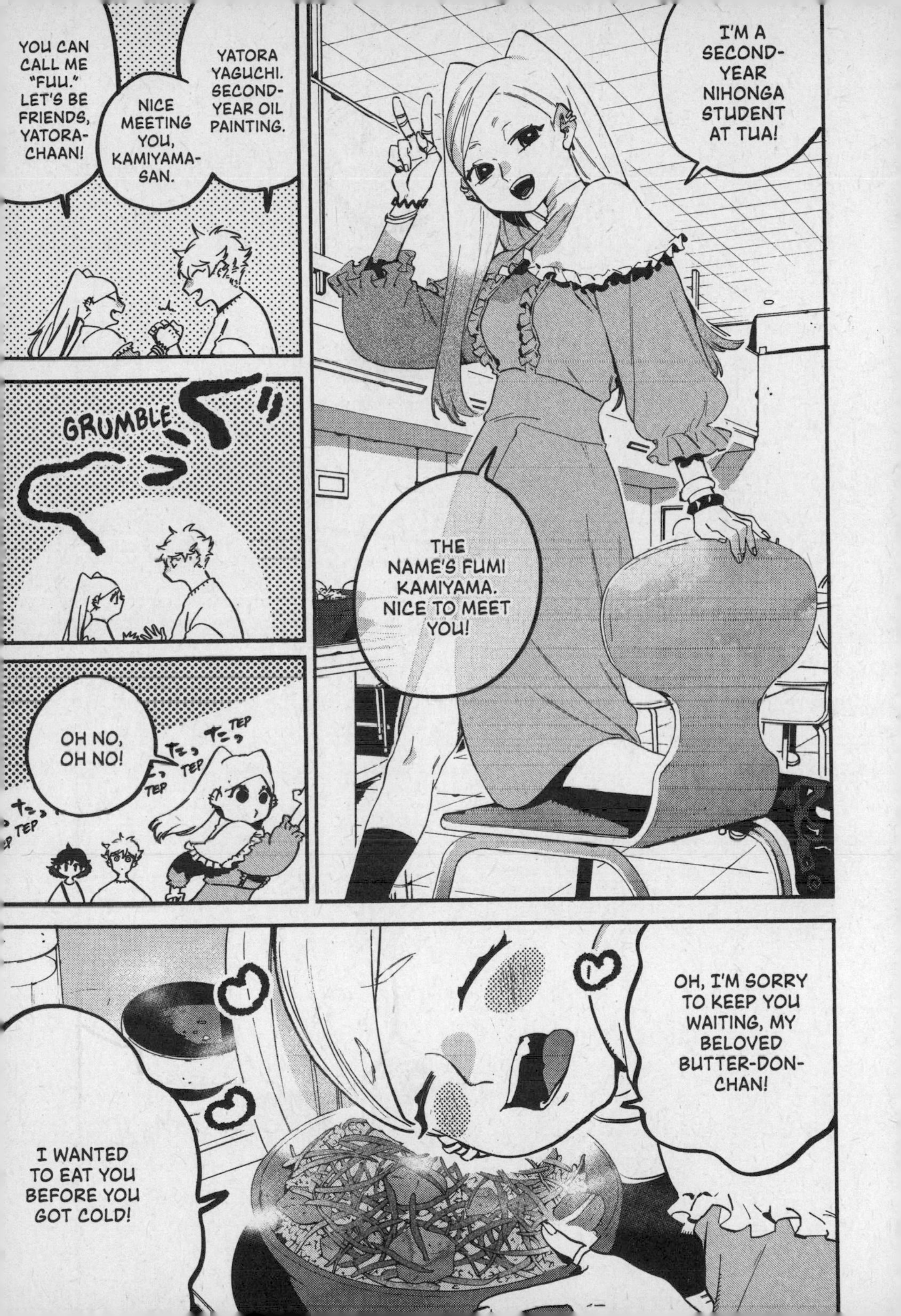
I'M A SECOND-YEAR NIHONGA STUDENT AT TUA!
THE NAME'S FUMI KAMIYAMA. NICE TO MEET YOU!
YATORA YAGUCHI. SECOND-YEAR OIL PAINTING.
NICE MEETING YOU, KAMIYAMA-SAN.
YOU CAN CALL ME "FUU." LET'S BE FRIENDS, YATORA-CHAAN!
GRUMBLE
TEP TEP TEP TEP
OH NO, OH NO!
OH, I'M SORRY TO KEEP YOU WAITING, MY BELOVED BUTTER-DON-CHAN!
I WANTED TO EAT YOU BEFORE YOU GOT COLD!

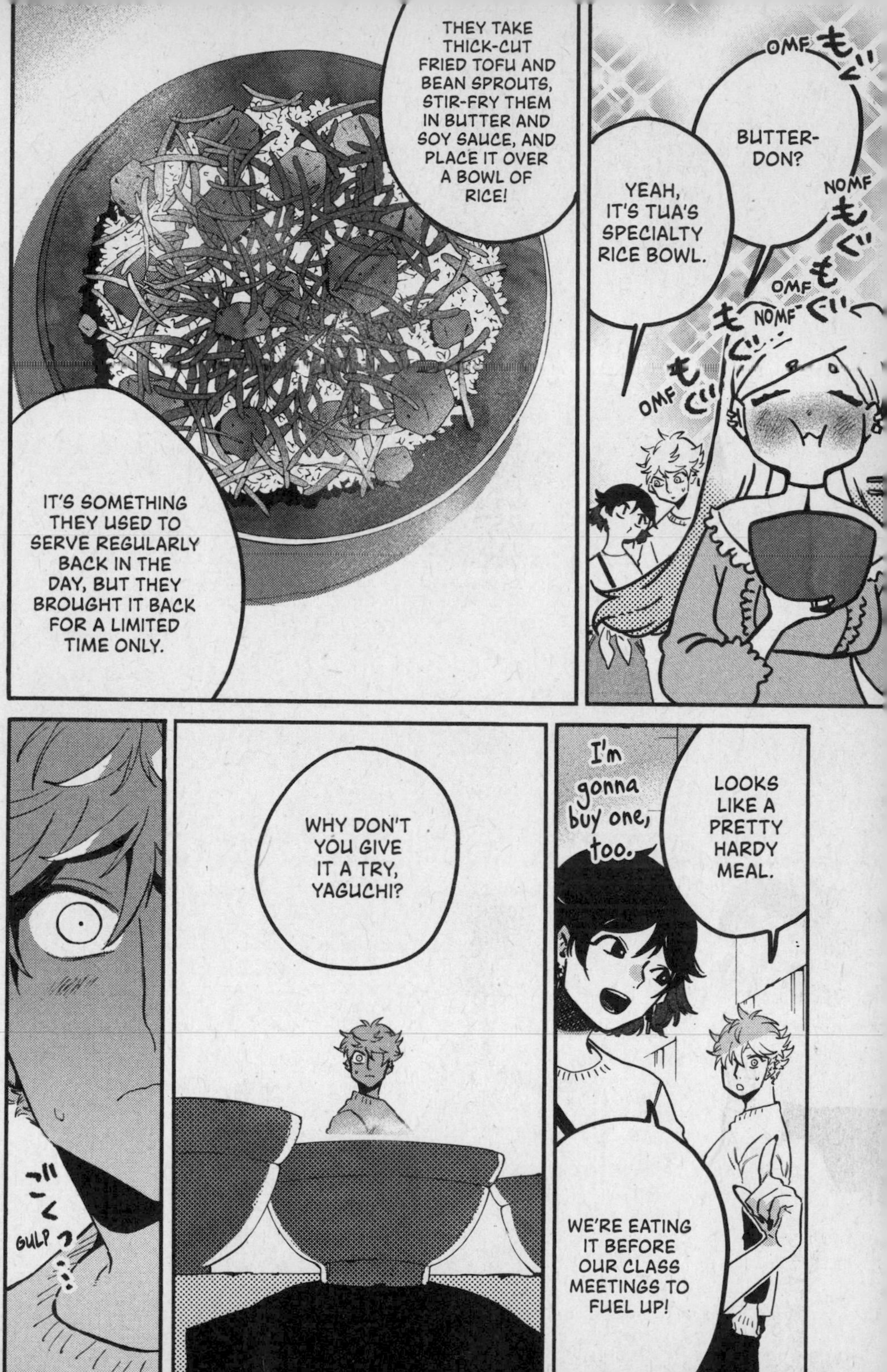

OMF
BUTTER-DON?
NOMF
YEAH, IT'S TUA'S SPECIALTY RICE BOWL.
OMF
NOMF
OMF
THEY TAKE THICK-CUT FRIED TOFU AND BEAN SPROUTS, STIR-FRY THEM IN BUTTER AND SOY SAUCE, AND PLACE IT OVER A BOWL OF RICE!
IT'S SOMETHING THEY USED TO SERVE REGULARLY BACK IN THE DAY, BUT THEY BROUGHT IT BACK FOR A LIMITED TIME ONLY.
LOOKS LIKE A PRETTY HARDY MEAL.
I'm gonna buy one, too.
WE'RE EATING IT BEFORE OUR CLASS MEETINGS TO FUEL UP!
WHY DON'T YOU GIVE IT A TRY, YAGUCHI?
GULP

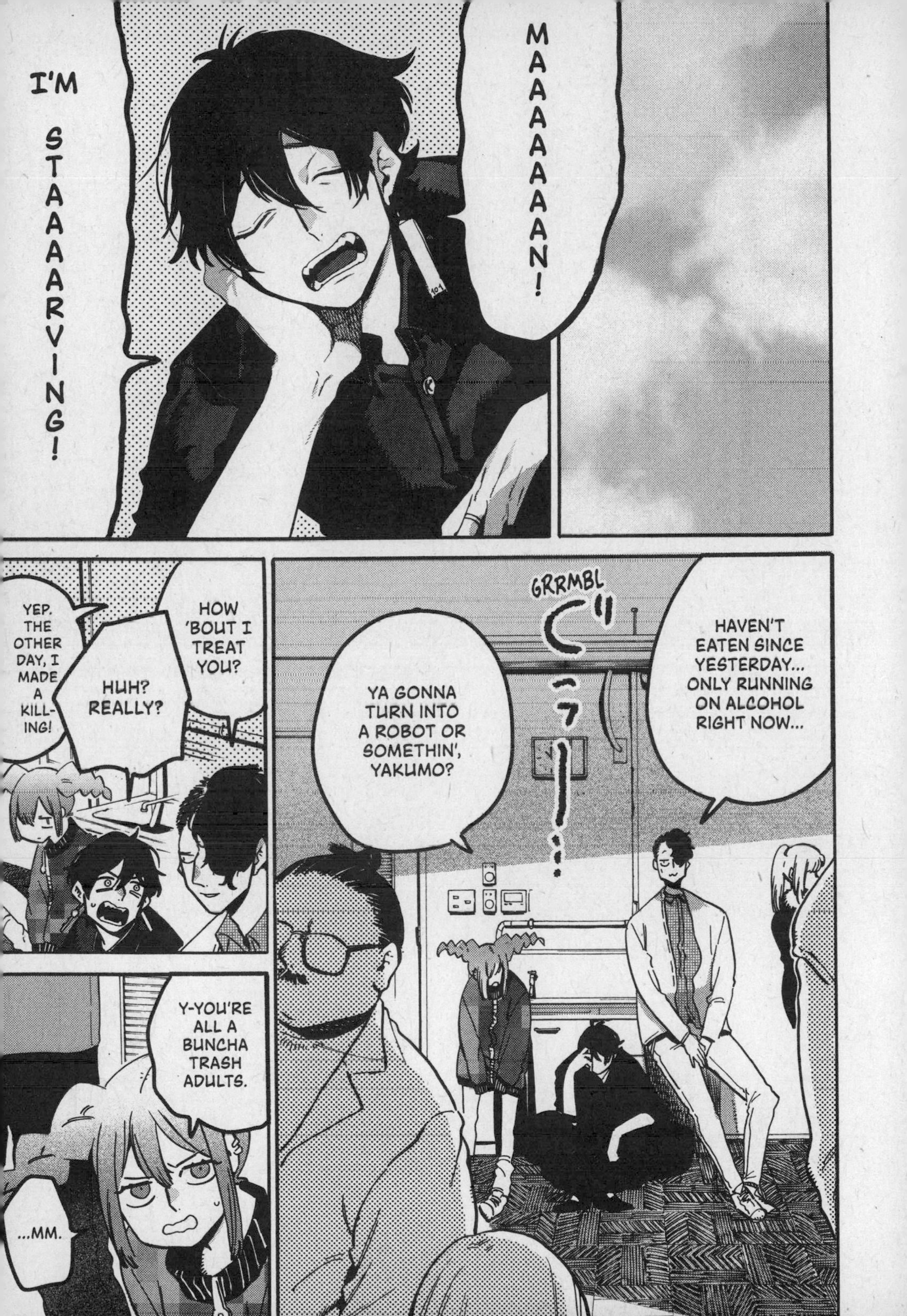
MAAAAAAAAN!
I'M STAAAARVING!
HAVEN'T EATEN SINCE YESTERDAY... ONLY RUNNING ON ALCOHOL RIGHT NOW...
GRRMBL
YA GONNA TURN INTO A ROBOT OR SOMETHIN', YAKUMO?
HOW 'BOUT I TREAT YOU?
HUH? REALLY?
YEP. THE OTHER DAY, I MADE A KILL-ING!
Y-YOU'RE ALL A BUNCHA TRASH ADULTS.
...MM.

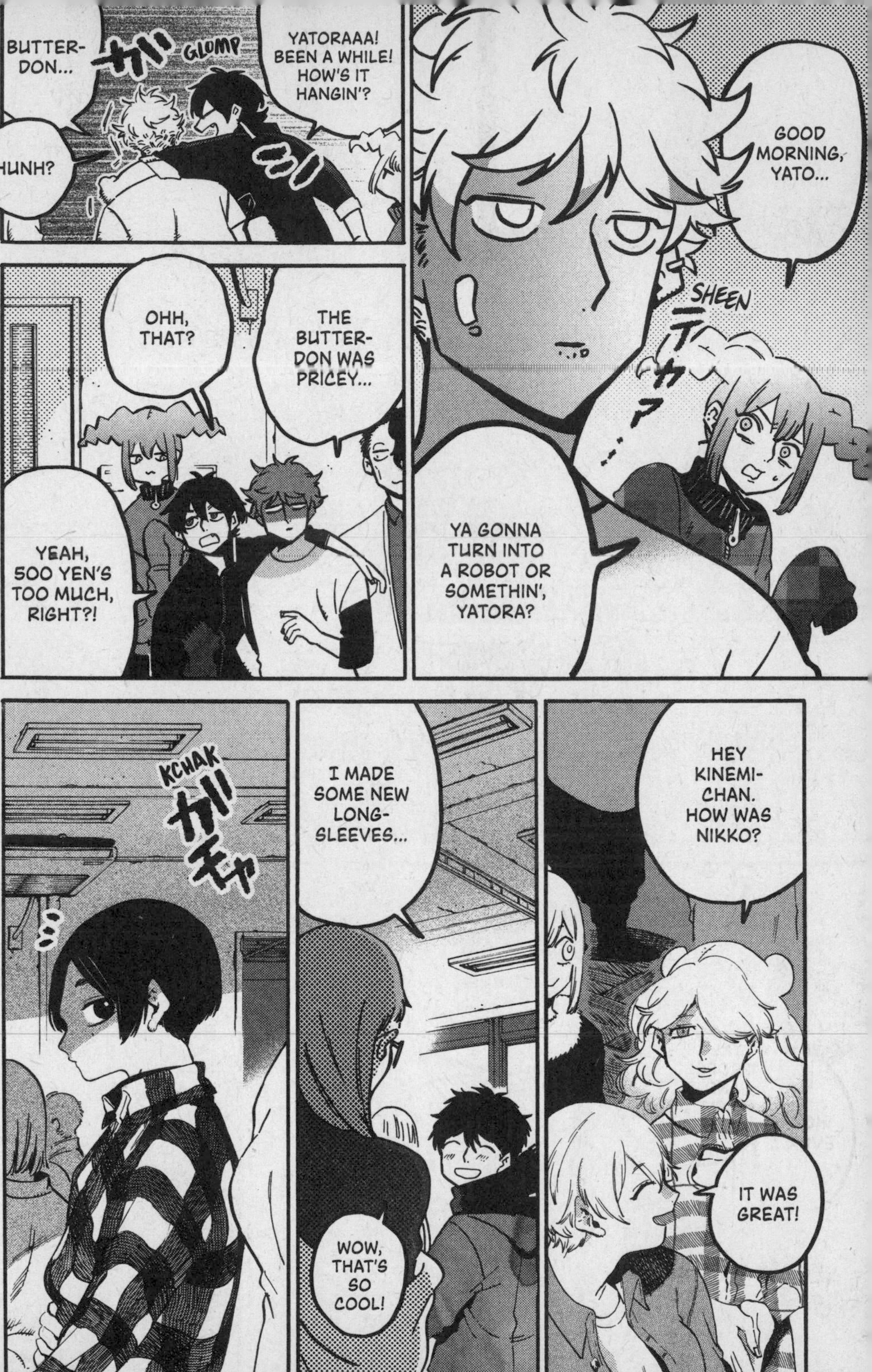
GOOD MORNING, YATO...
SHEEN
YA GONNA TURN INTO A ROBOT OR SOMETHIN', YATORA?
YATORAAA! BEEN A WHILE! HOW'S IT HANGIN'?
GLOMP
BUTTER-DON...
HUNH?
THE BUTTER-DON WAS PRICEY...
OHH, THAT?
YEAH, 500 YEN'S TOO MUCH, RIGHT?!
HEY KINEMI-CHAN. HOW WAS NIKKO?
IT WAS GREAT!
I MADE SOME NEW LONG-SLEEVES...
WOW, THAT'S SO COOL!
KCHAK

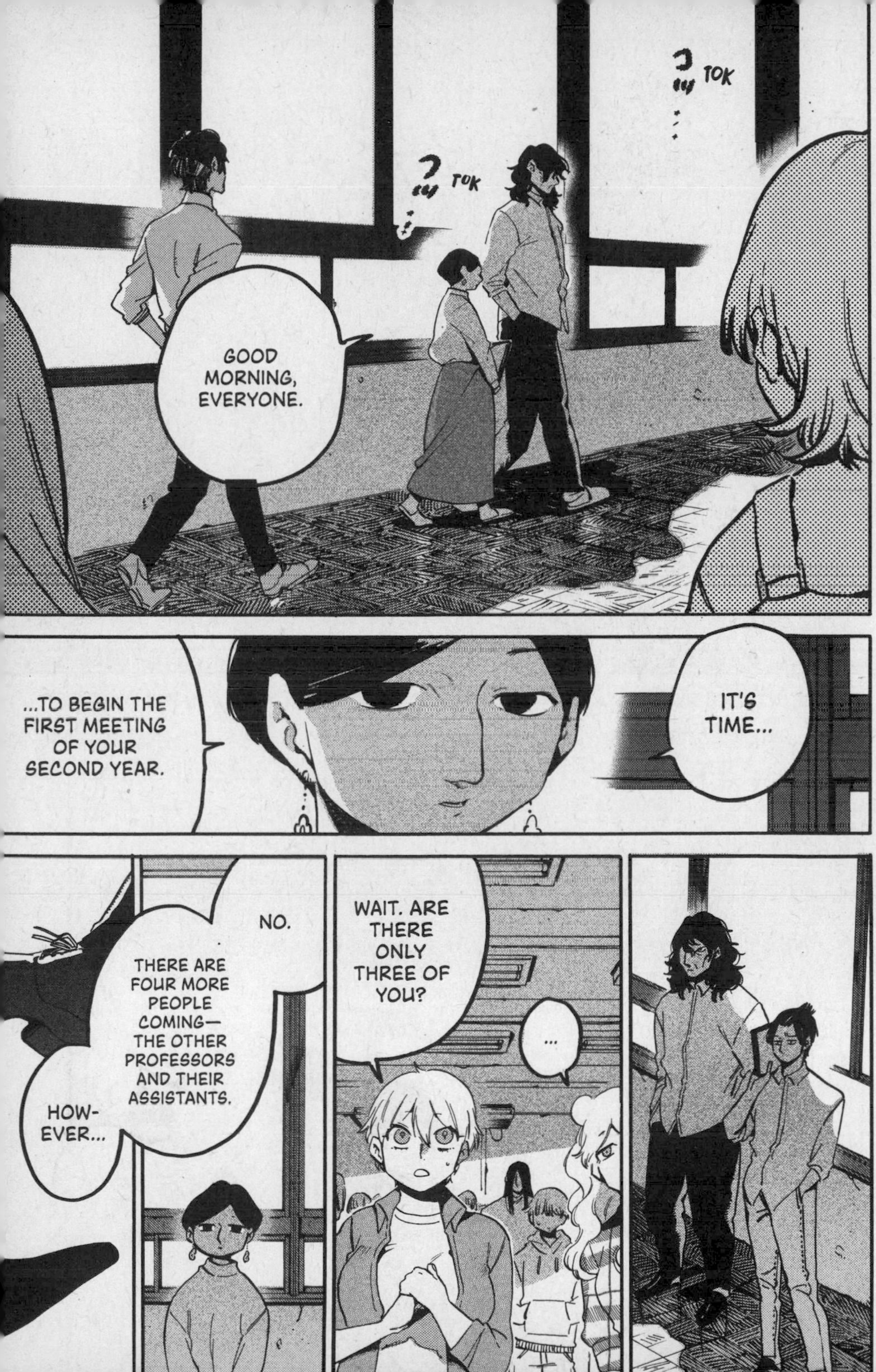
TOK
?
TOK
GOOD MORNING, EVERYONE.
IT'S TIME...
...TO BEGIN THE FIRST MEETING OF YOUR SECOND YEAR.
WAIT. ARE THERE ONLY THREE OF YOU?
...
NO.
THERE ARE FOUR MORE PEOPLE COMING—THE OTHER PROFESSORS AND THEIR ASSISTANTS.
HOW-EVER...

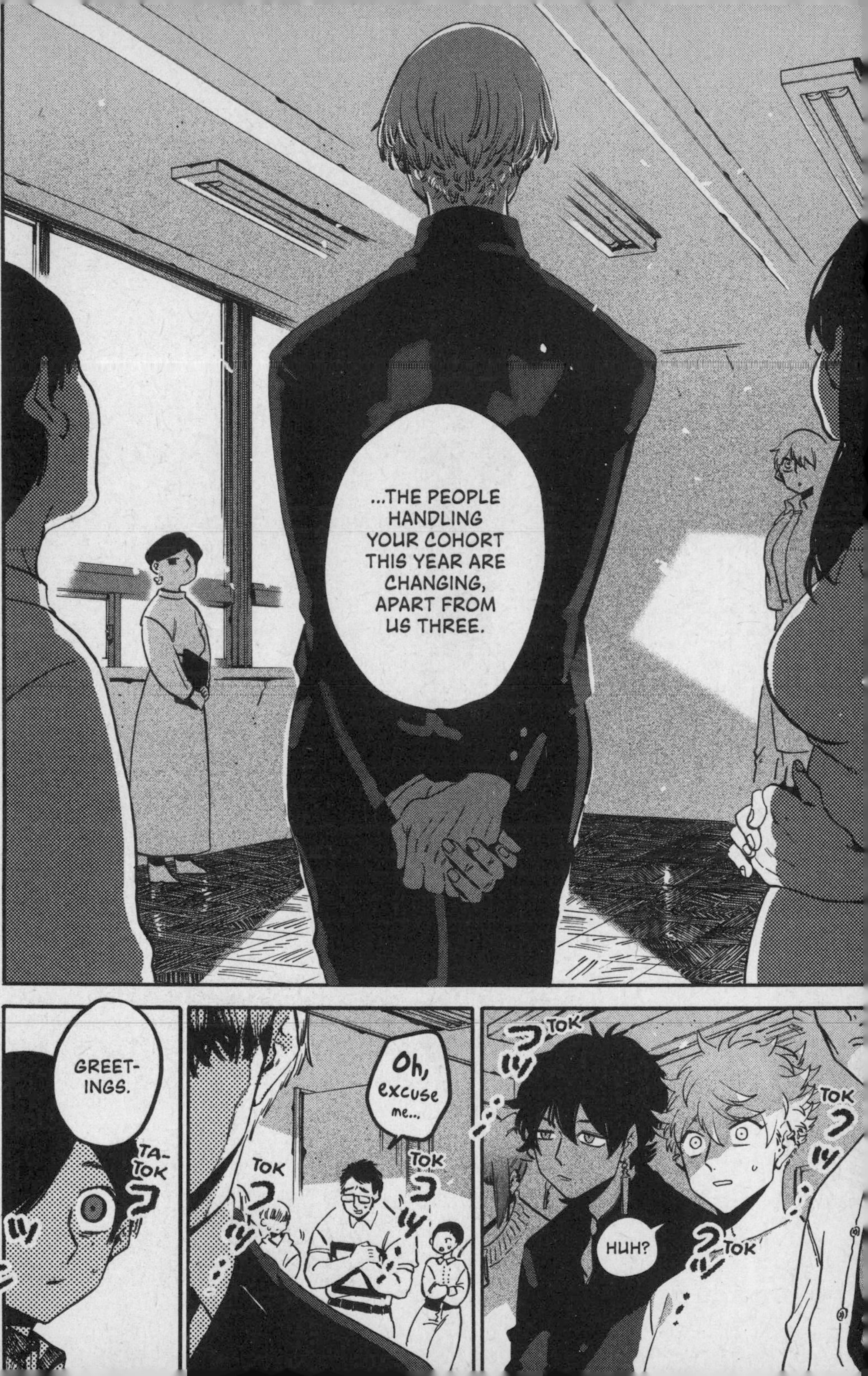
...THE PEOPLE HANDLING YOUR COHORT THIS YEAR ARE CHANGING, APART FROM US THREE.
TOK
TOK
HUH?
TOK
Oh, excuse me...
TOK
TOK
GREET-INGS.
TA-TOK

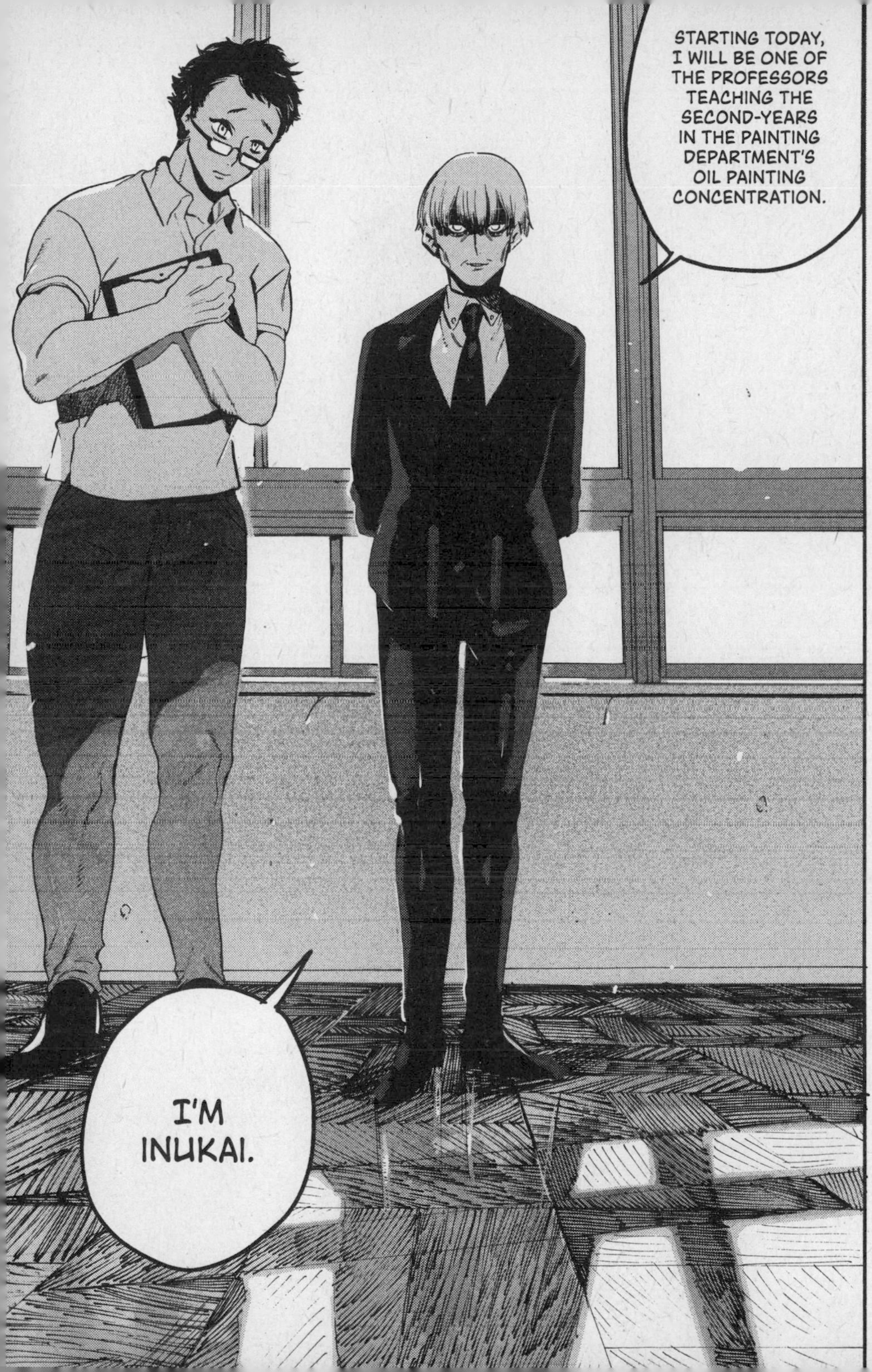
STARTING TODAY, I WILL BE ONE OF THE PROFESSORS TEACHING THE SECOND-YEARS IN THE PAINTING DEPARTMENT'S OIL PAINTING CONCENTRATION.
I'M INUKAI.

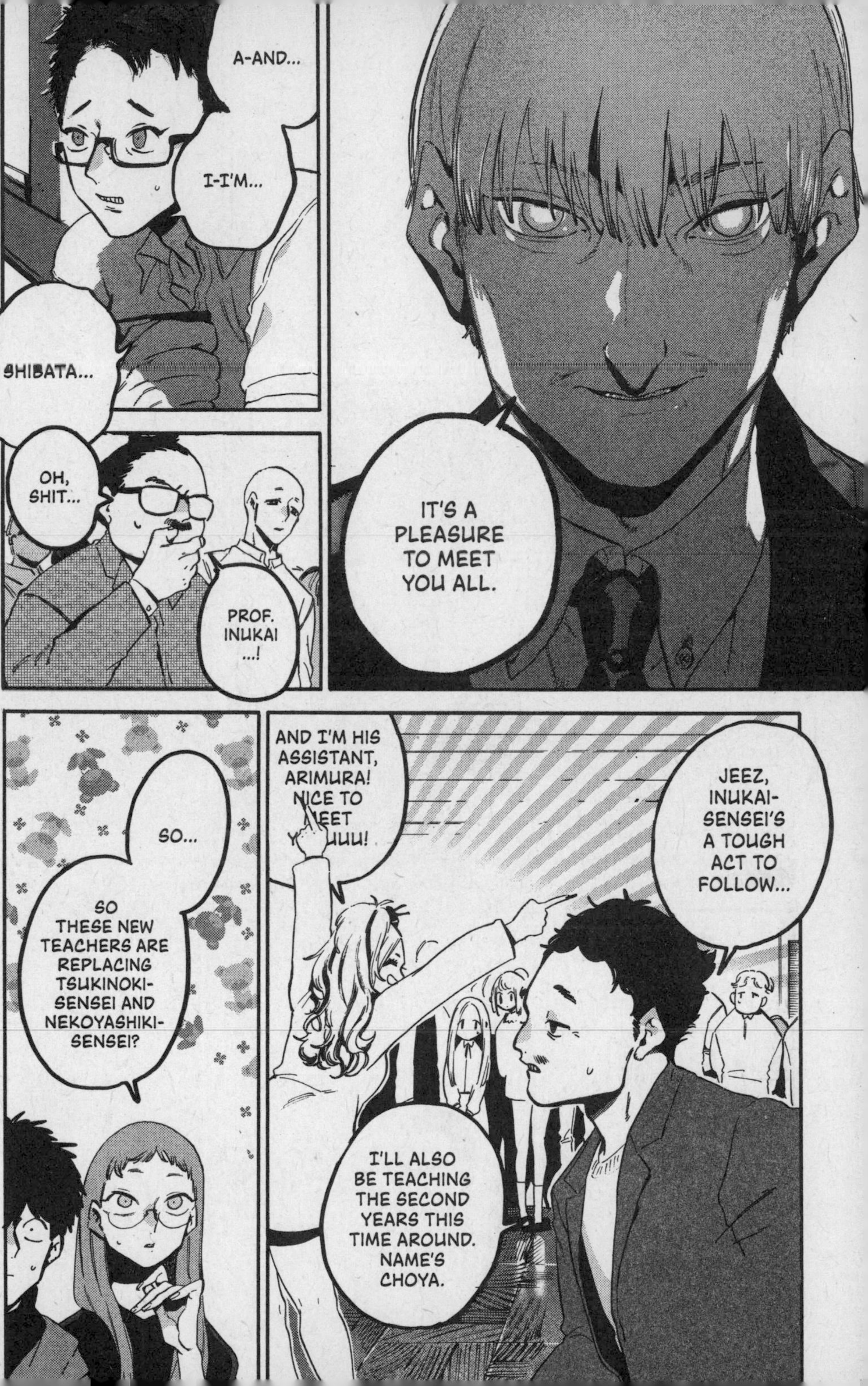
IT'S A PLEASURE TO MEET YOU ALL.
A-AND...
I-I'M...
SHIBATA...
OH, SHIT...
PROF. INUKAI ...!
JEEZ, INUKAI-SENSEI'S A TOUGH ACT TO FOLLOW...
AND I'M HIS ASSISTANT, ARIMURA! NICE TO MEET YOUUU!
I'LL ALSO BE TEACHING THE SECOND YEARS THIS TIME AROUND. NAME'S CHOYA.
SO...
SO THESE NEW TEACHERS ARE REPLACING TSUKINOKI-SENSEI AND NEKOYASHIKI-SENSEI?

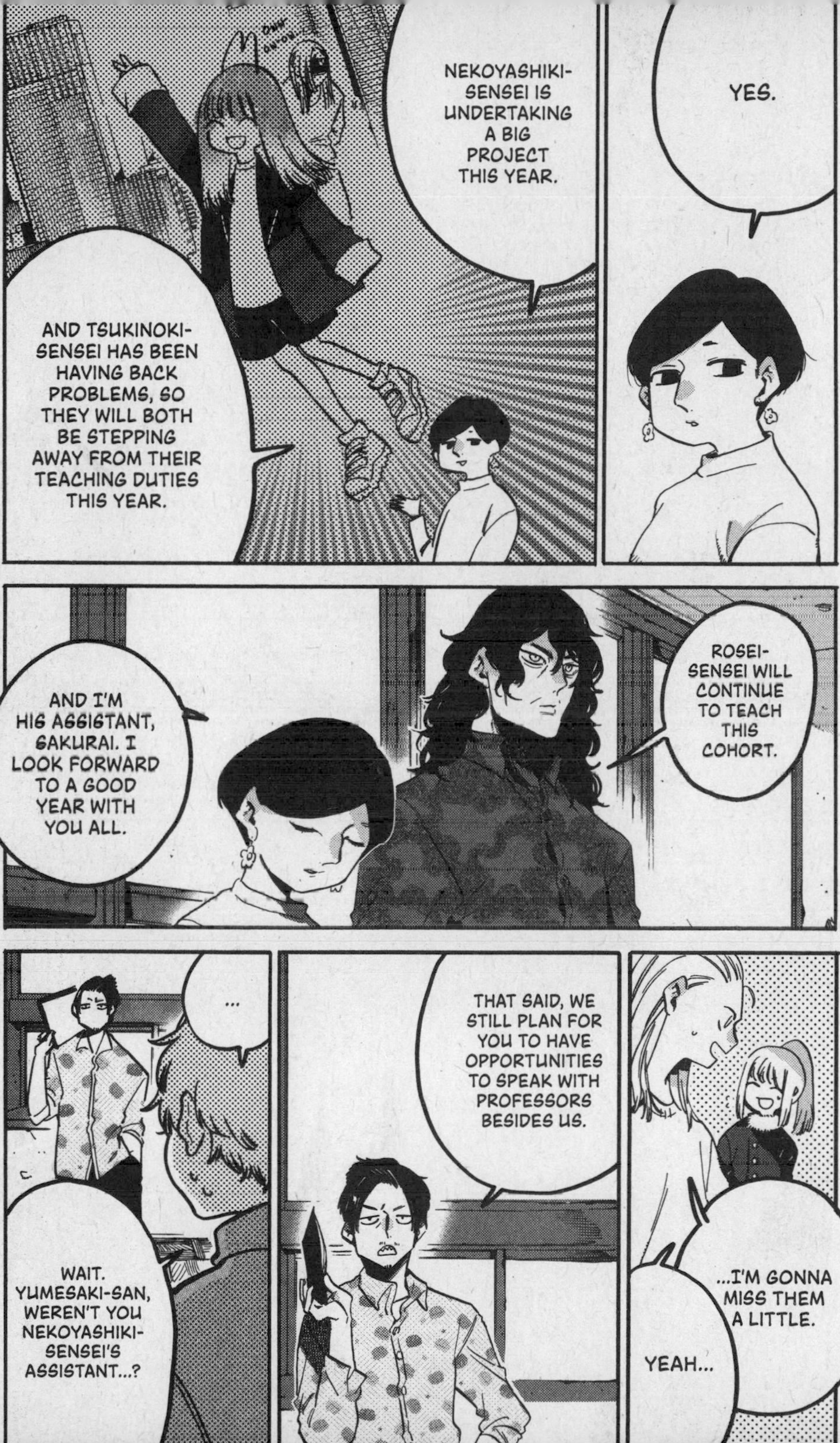
YES.
NEKOYASHIKI-SENSEI IS UNDERTAKING A BIG PROJECT THIS YEAR.
AND TSUKINOKI-SENSEI HAS BEEN HAVING BACK PROBLEMS, SO THEY WILL BOTH BE STEPPING AWAY FROM THEIR TEACHING DUTIES THIS YEAR.
ROSEI-SENSEI WILL CONTINUE TO TEACH THIS COHORT.
AND I'M HIS ASSISTANT, SAKURAI. I LOOK FORWARD TO A GOOD YEAR WITH YOU ALL.
...I'M GONNA MISS THEM A LITTLE.
YEAH...
THAT SAID, WE STILL PLAN FOR YOU TO HAVE OPPORTUNITIES TO SPEAK WITH PROFESSORS BESIDES US.
...
WAIT. YUMESAKI-SAN, WEREN'T YOU NEKOYASHIKI-SENSEI'S ASSISTANT...?

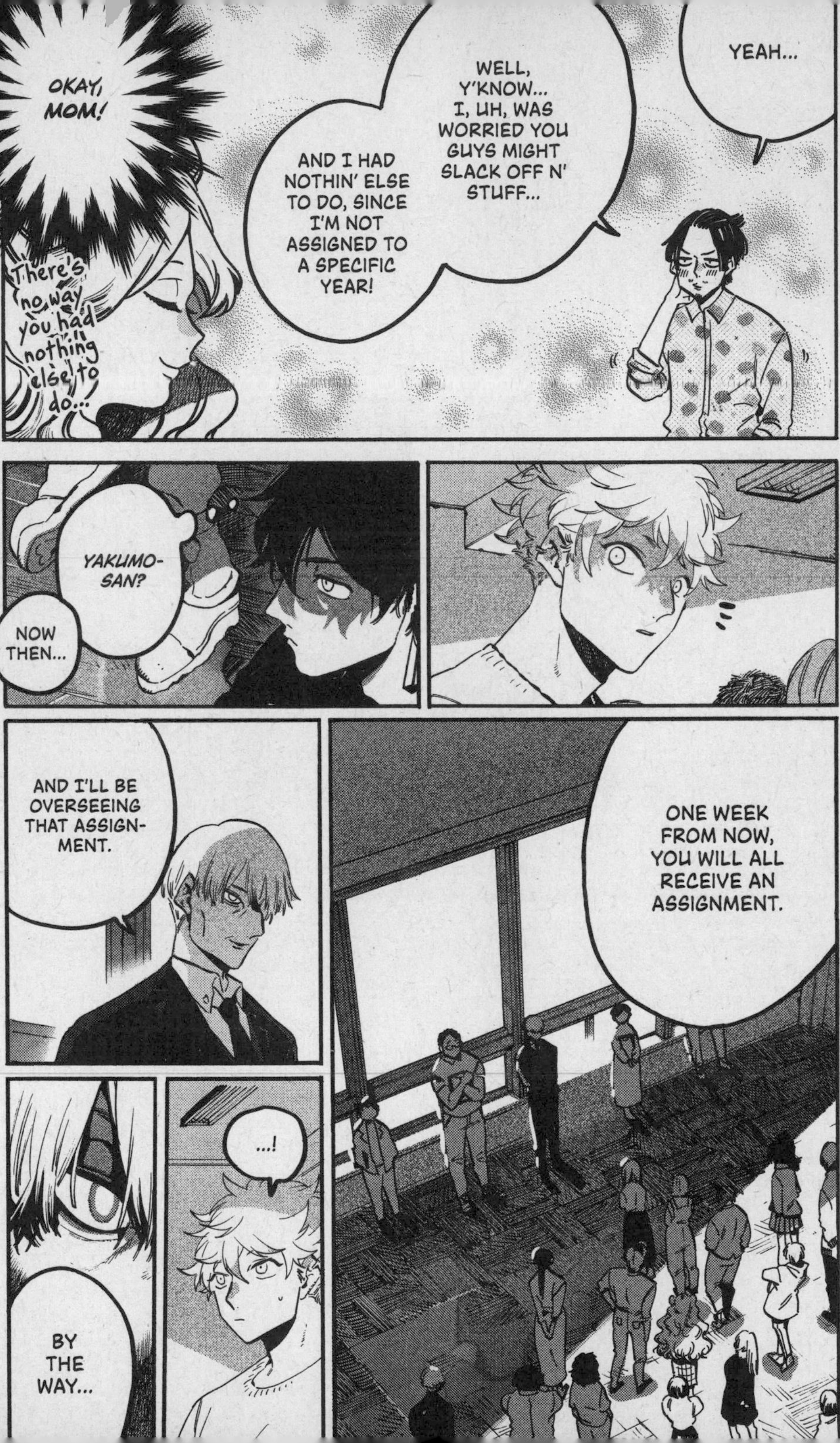
YEAH...
WELL, Y'KNOW... I, UH, WAS WORRIED YOU GUYS MIGHT SLACK OFF N' STUFF...
AND I HAD NOTHIN' ELSE TO DO, SINCE I'M NOT ASSIGNED TO A SPECIFIC YEAR!
OKAY, MOM!
There's no way you had nothing else to do...
YAKUMO-SAN?
NOW THEN...
ONE WEEK FROM NOW, YOU WILL ALL RECEIVE AN ASSIGNMENT.
AND I'LL BE OVERSEEING THAT ASSIGN-MENT.
...!
BY THE WAY...

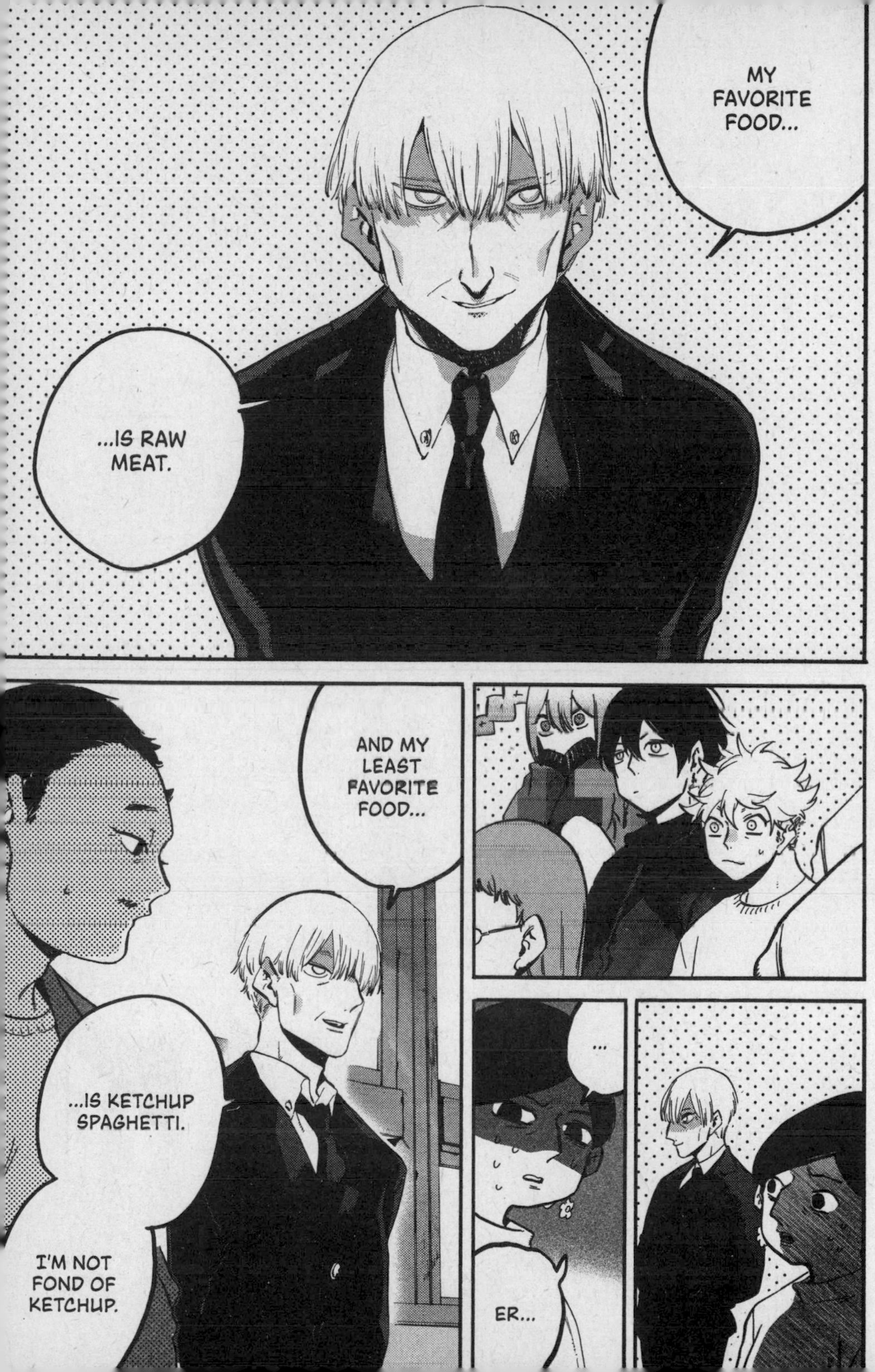
MY FAVORITE FOOD...
...IS RAW MEAT.
...
ER...
AND MY LEAST FAVORITE FOOD...
...IS KETCHUP SPAGHETTI.
I'M NOT FOND OF KETCHUP.

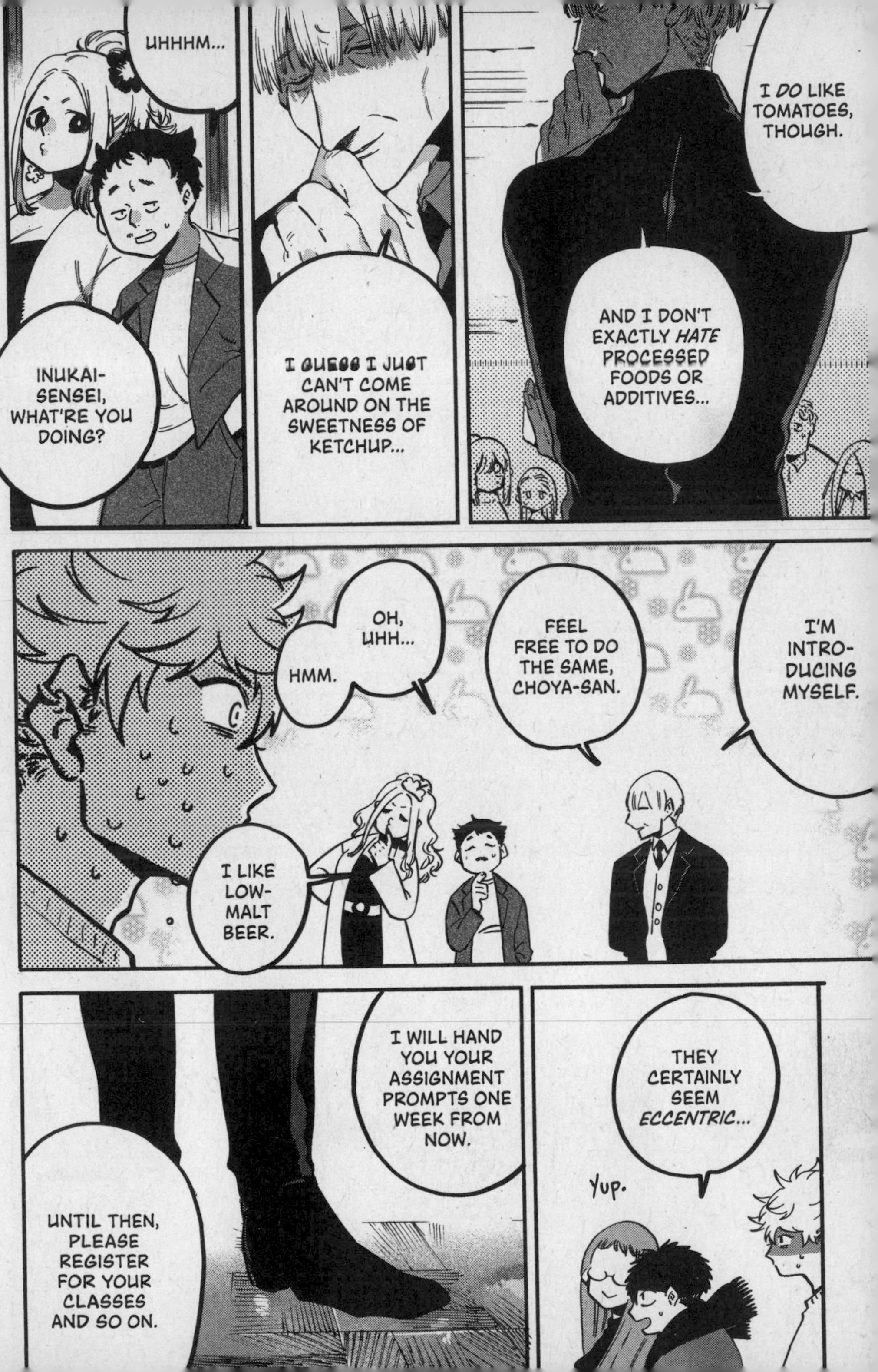
I *DO* LIKE TOMATOES, THOUGH.
AND I DON'T EXACTLY *HATE* PROCESSED FOODS OR ADDITIVES...
I GUESS I JUST CAN'T COME AROUND ON THE SWEETNESS OF KETCHUP...
UHHHM...
INUKAI-SENSEI, WHAT'RE YOU DOING?
I'M INTRO-DUCING MYSELF.
FEEL FREE TO DO THE SAME, CHOYA-SAN.
OH, UHH... HMM.
I LIKE LOW-MALT BEER.
THEY CERTAINLY SEEM *ECCENTRIC*...
Yup.
I WILL HAND YOU YOUR ASSIGNMENT PROMPTS ONE WEEK FROM NOW.
UNTIL THEN, PLEASE REGISTER FOR YOUR CLASSES AND SO ON.

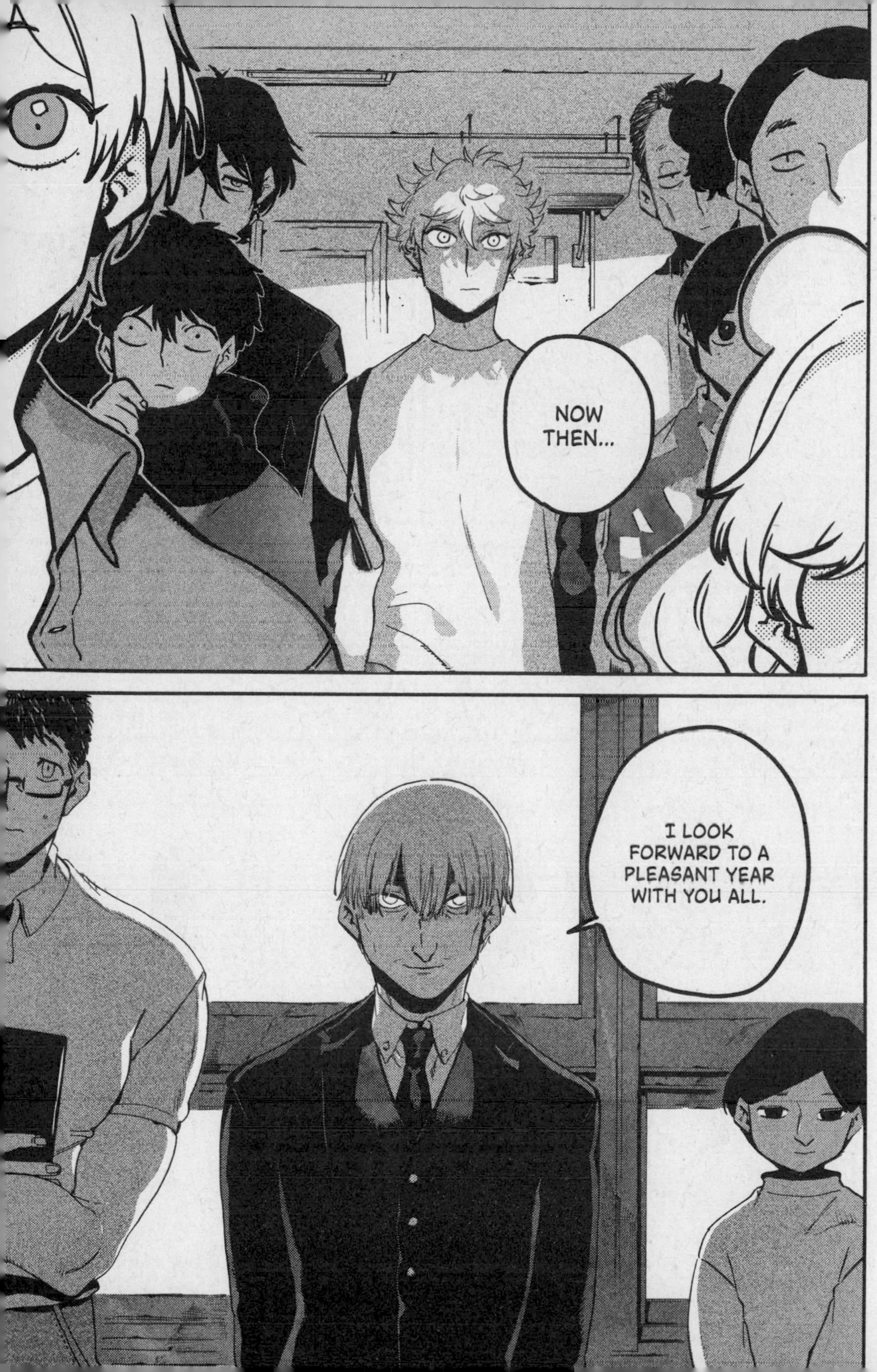
NOW THEN...
I LOOK FORWARD TO A PLEASANT YEAR WITH YOU ALL.

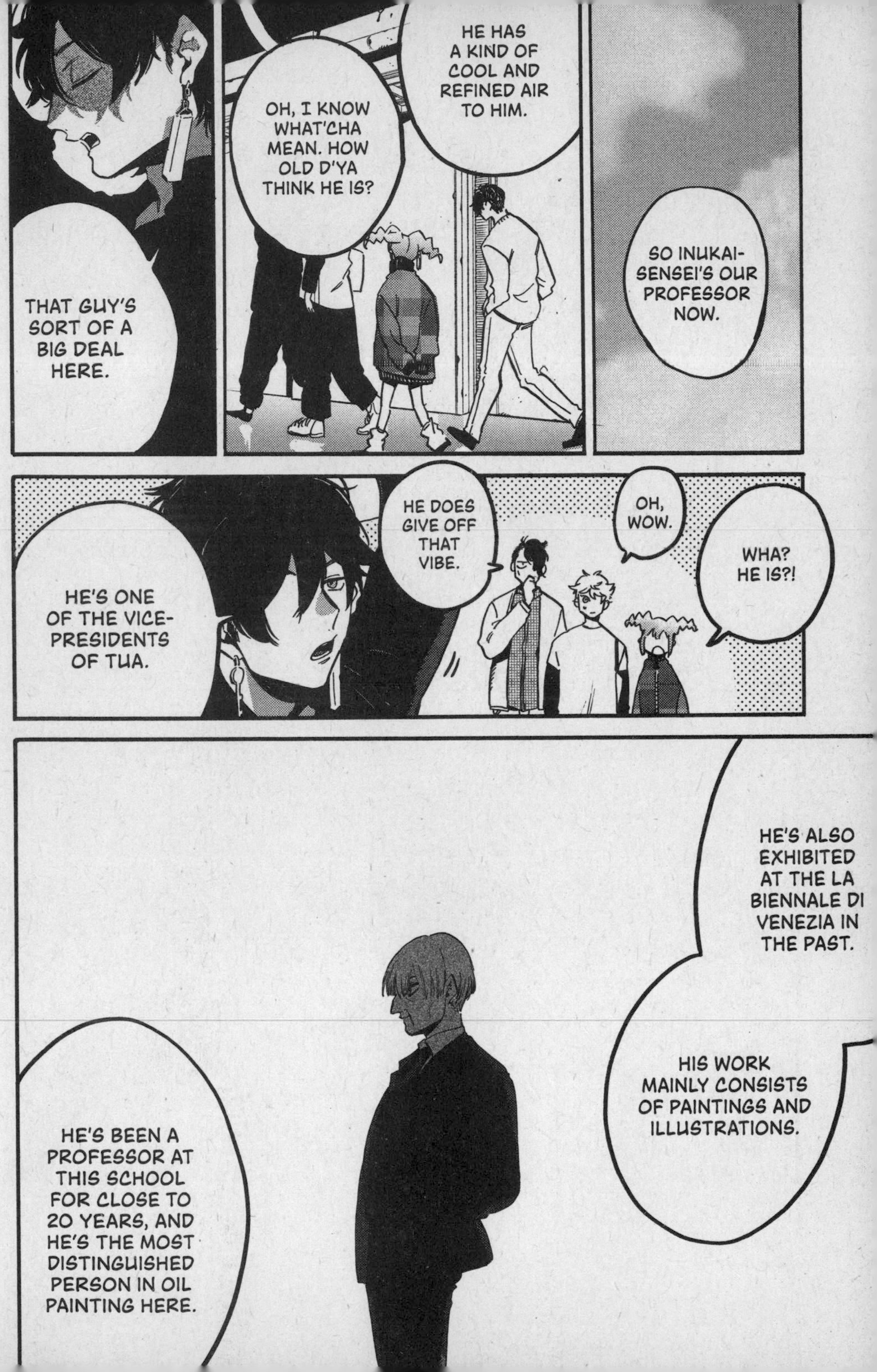
SO INUKAI-SENSEI'S OUR PROFESSOR NOW.
HE HAS A KIND OF COOL AND REFINED AIR TO HIM.
OH, I KNOW WHAT'CHA MEAN. HOW OLD D'YA THINK HE IS?
THAT GUY'S SORT OF A BIG DEAL HERE.
HE'S ONE OF THE VICE-PRESIDENTS OF TUA.
WHA? HE IS?!
OH, WOW.
HE DOES GIVE OFF THAT VIBE.
HE'S ALSO EXHIBITED AT THE LA BIENNALE DI VENEZIA IN THE PAST.
HIS WORK MAINLY CONSISTS OF PAINTINGS AND ILLUSTRATIONS.
HE'S BEEN A PROFESSOR AT THIS SCHOOL FOR CLOSE TO 20 YEARS, AND HE'S THE MOST DISTINGUISHED PERSON IN OIL PAINTING HERE.

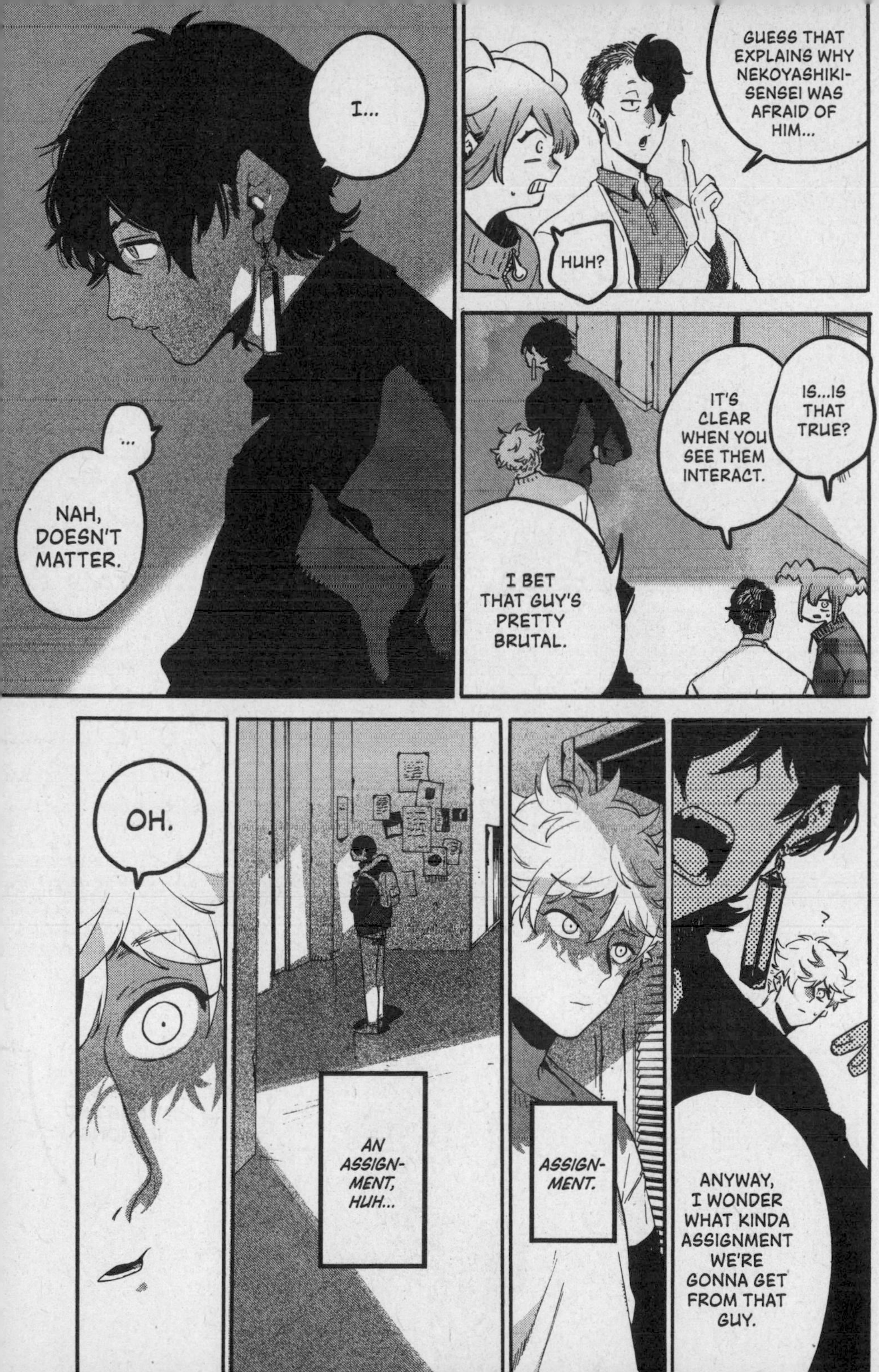
GUESS THAT EXPLAINS WHY NEKOYASHIKI-SENSEI WAS AFRAID OF HIM...
HUH?
IS...IS THAT TRUE?
IT'S CLEAR WHEN YOU SEE THEM INTERACT.
I BET THAT GUY'S PRETTY BRUTAL.
I...
...
NAH, DOESN'T MATTER.
?
ANYWAY, I WONDER WHAT KINDA ASSIGNMENT WE'RE GONNA GET FROM THAT GUY.
ASSIGN-MENT.
AN ASSIGN-MENT, HUH...
OH.

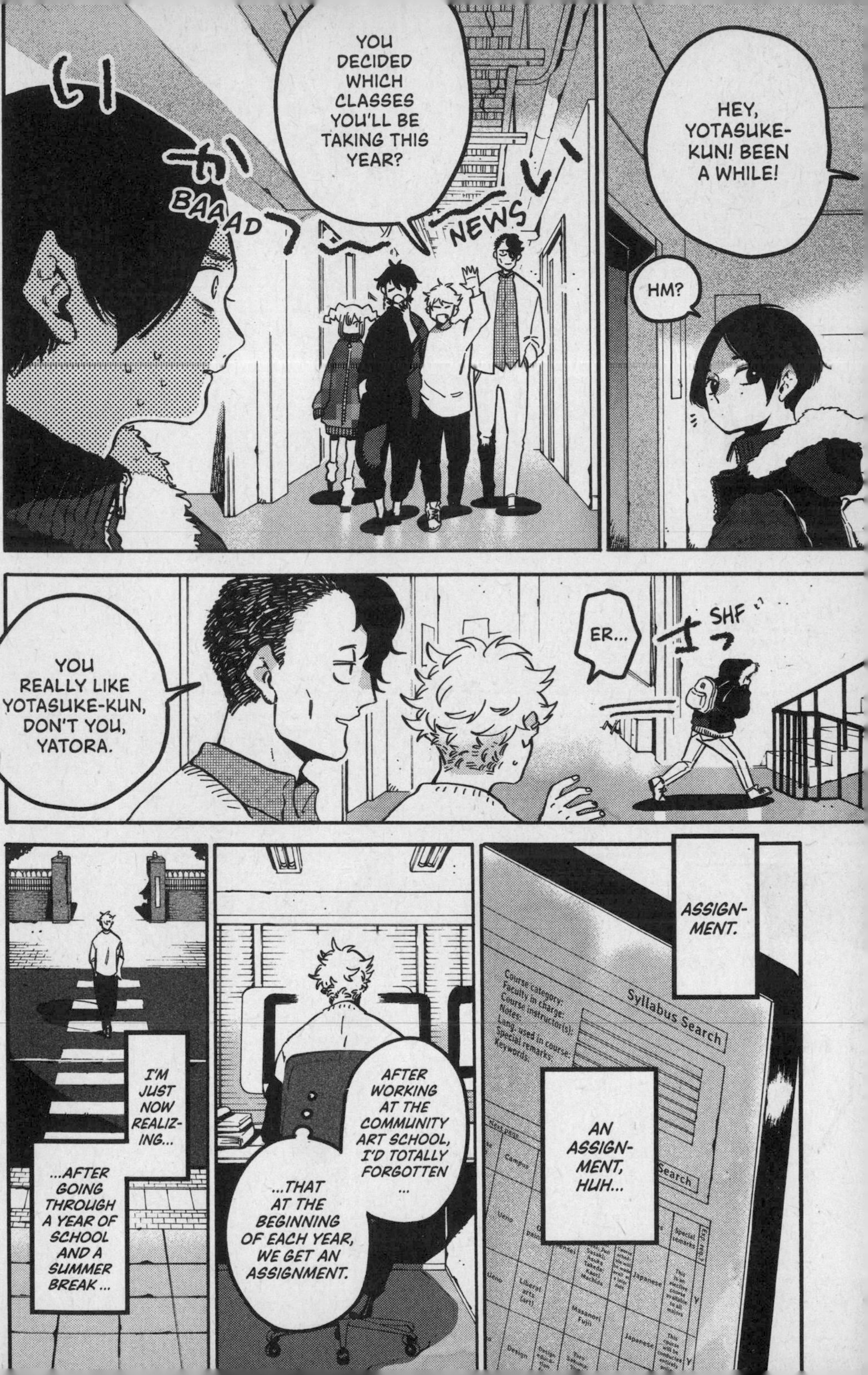
HEY, YOTASUKE-KUN! BEEN A WHILE!
HM?
YOU DECIDED WHICH CLASSES YOU'LL BE TAKING THIS YEAR?
BAAAD NEWS
ER...
SHF
YOU REALLY LIKE YOTASUKE-KUN, DON'T YOU, YATORA.
ASSIGNMENT.
Syllabus Search
Course category:
Faculty in charge:
Course instructor(s):
Notes:
Lang. used in course:
Special remarks:
Keywords:
AN ASSIGNMENT, HUH...
AFTER WORKING AT THE COMMUNITY ART SCHOOL, I'D TOTALLY FORGOTTEN ...
...THAT AT THE BEGINNING OF EACH YEAR, WE GET AN ASSIGNMENT.
I'M JUST NOW REALIZING...
...AFTER GOING THROUGH A YEAR OF SCHOOL AND A SUMMER BREAK ...

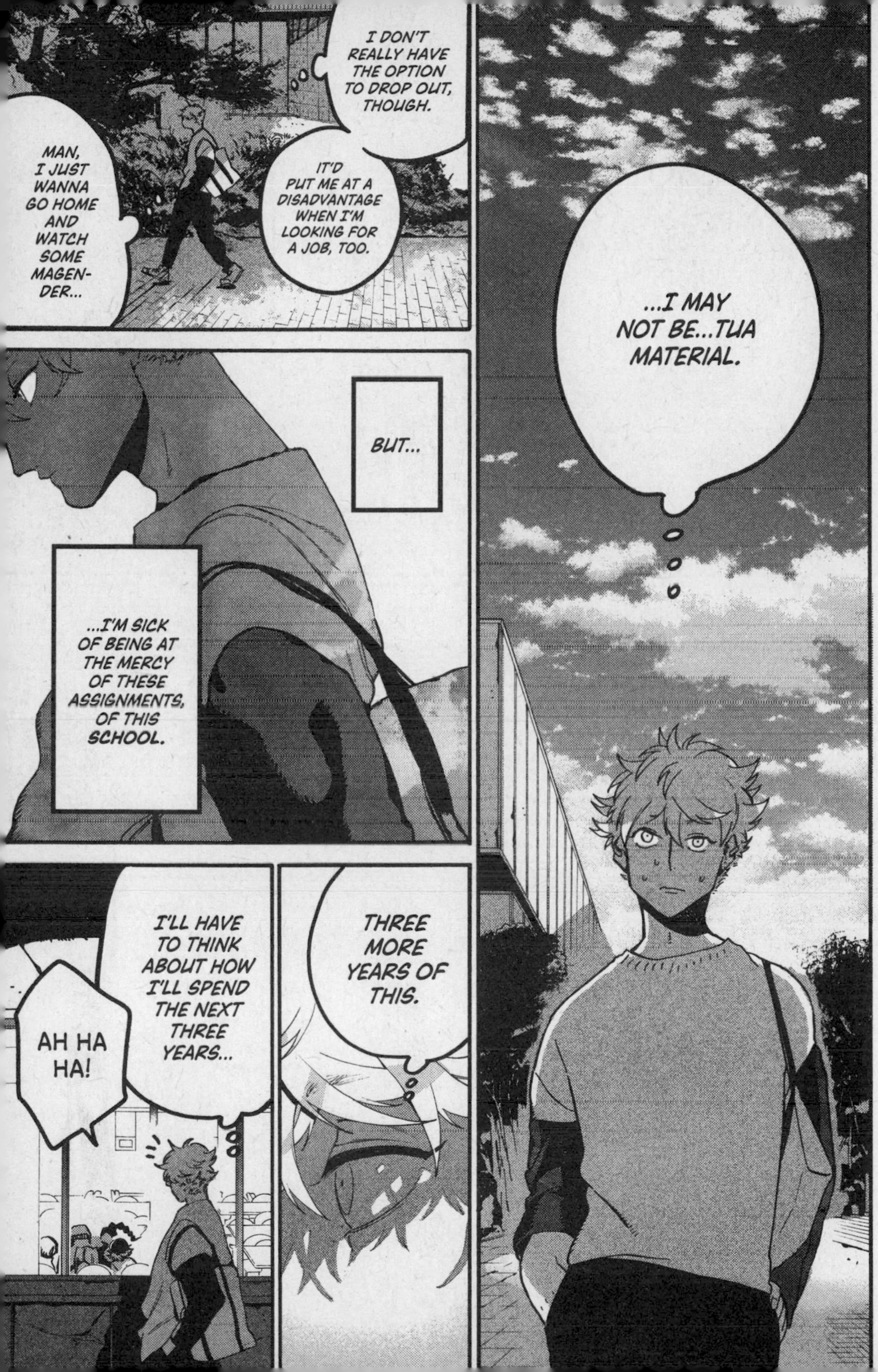

...I MAY NOT BE...TUA MATERIAL.
I DON'T REALLY HAVE THE OPTION TO DROP OUT, THOUGH.
IT'D PUT ME AT A DISADVANTAGE WHEN I'M LOOKING FOR A JOB, TOO.
MAN, I JUST WANNA GO HOME AND WATCH SOME MAGEN-DER...
BUT...
...I'M SICK OF BEING AT THE MERCY OF THESE ASSIGNMENTS, OF THIS SCHOOL.
THREE MORE YEARS OF THIS.
I'LL HAVE TO THINK ABOUT HOW I'LL SPEND THE NEXT THREE YEARS...
AH HA HA!

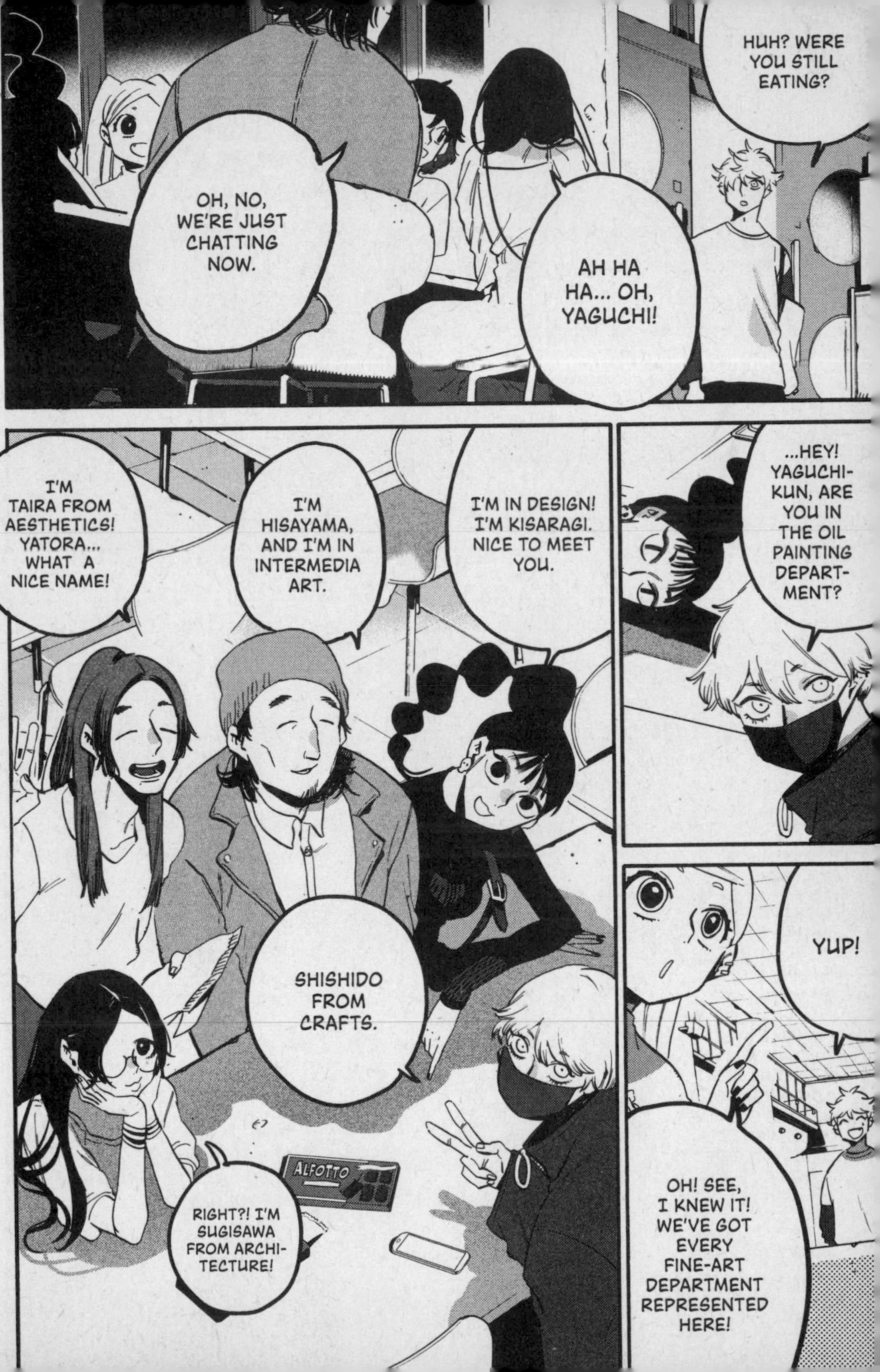
HUH? WERE YOU STILL EATING?
AH HA HA... OH, YAGUCHI!
OH, NO, WE'RE JUST CHATTING NOW.
...HEY! YAGUCHI-KUN, ARE YOU IN THE OIL PAINTING DEPART-MENT?
YUP!
OH! SEE, I KNEW IT! WE'VE GOT EVERY FINE-ART DEPARTMENT REPRESENTED HERE!
I'M IN DESIGN! I'M KISARAGI. NICE TO MEET YOU.
I'M HISAYAMA, AND I'M IN INTERMEDIA ART.
I'M TAIRA FROM AESTHETICS! YATORA... WHAT A NICE NAME!
SHISHIDO FROM CRAFTS.
RIGHT?! I'M SUGISAWA FROM ARCHI-TECTURE!
ALFOTTO

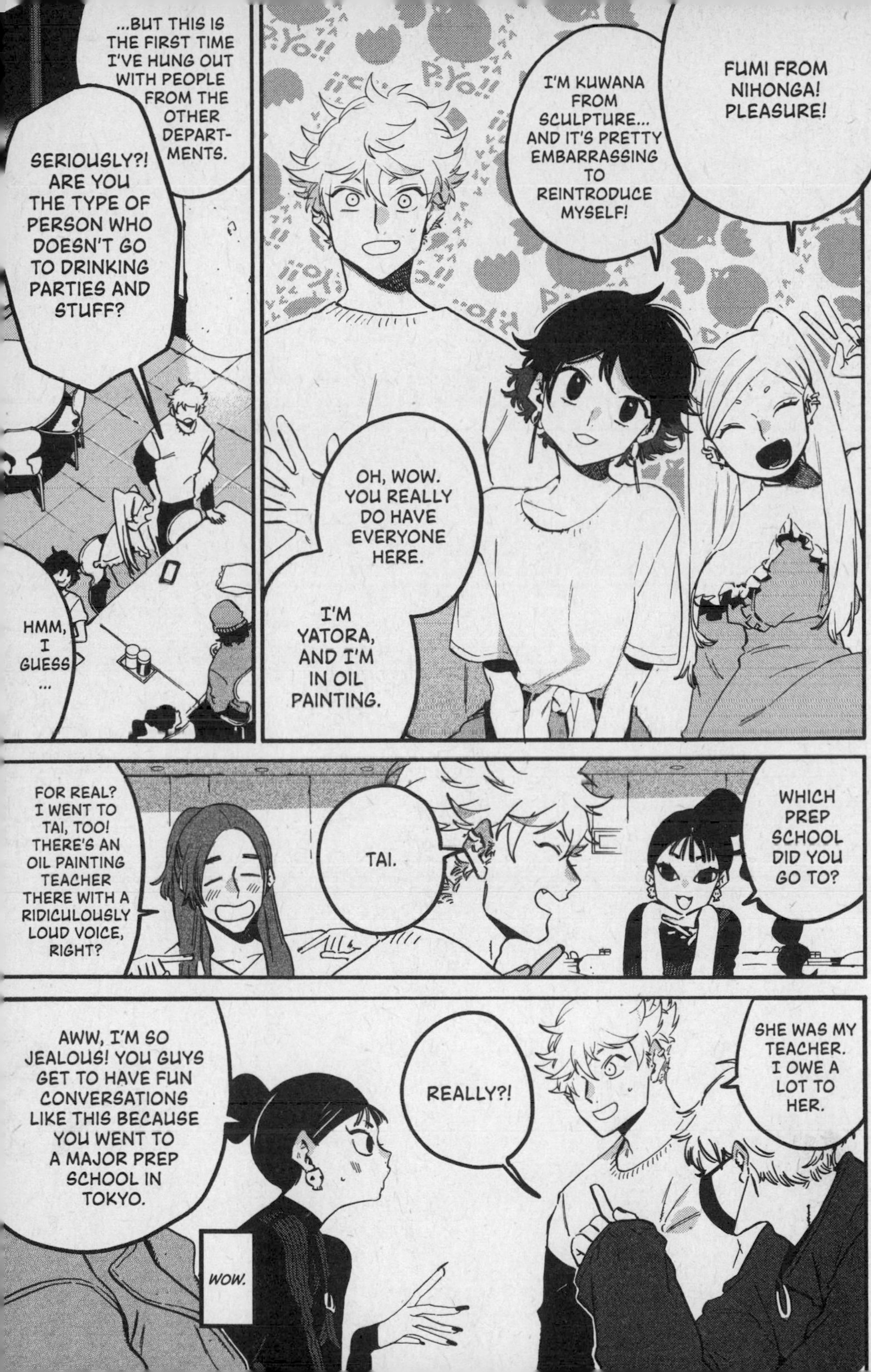
FUMI FROM NIHONGA! PLEASURE!
I'M KUWANA FROM SCULPTURE... AND IT'S PRETTY EMBARRASSING TO REINTRODUCE MYSELF!
OH, WOW. YOU REALLY DO HAVE EVERYONE HERE.
I'M YATORA, AND I'M IN OIL PAINTING.
...BUT THIS IS THE FIRST TIME I'VE HUNG OUT WITH PEOPLE FROM THE OTHER DEPARTMENTS.
SERIOUSLY?! ARE YOU THE TYPE OF PERSON WHO DOESN'T GO TO DRINKING PARTIES AND STUFF?
HMM, I GUESS...
WHICH PREP SCHOOL DID YOU GO TO?
TAI.
FOR REAL? I WENT TO TAI, TOO! THERE'S AN OIL PAINTING TEACHER THERE WITH A RIDICULOUSLY LOUD VOICE, RIGHT?
SHE WAS MY TEACHER. I OWE A LOT TO HER.
REALLY?!
AWW, I'M SO JEALOUS! YOU GUYS GET TO HAVE FUN CONVERSATIONS LIKE THIS BECAUSE YOU WENT TO A MAJOR PREP SCHOOL IN TOKYO.
WOW.

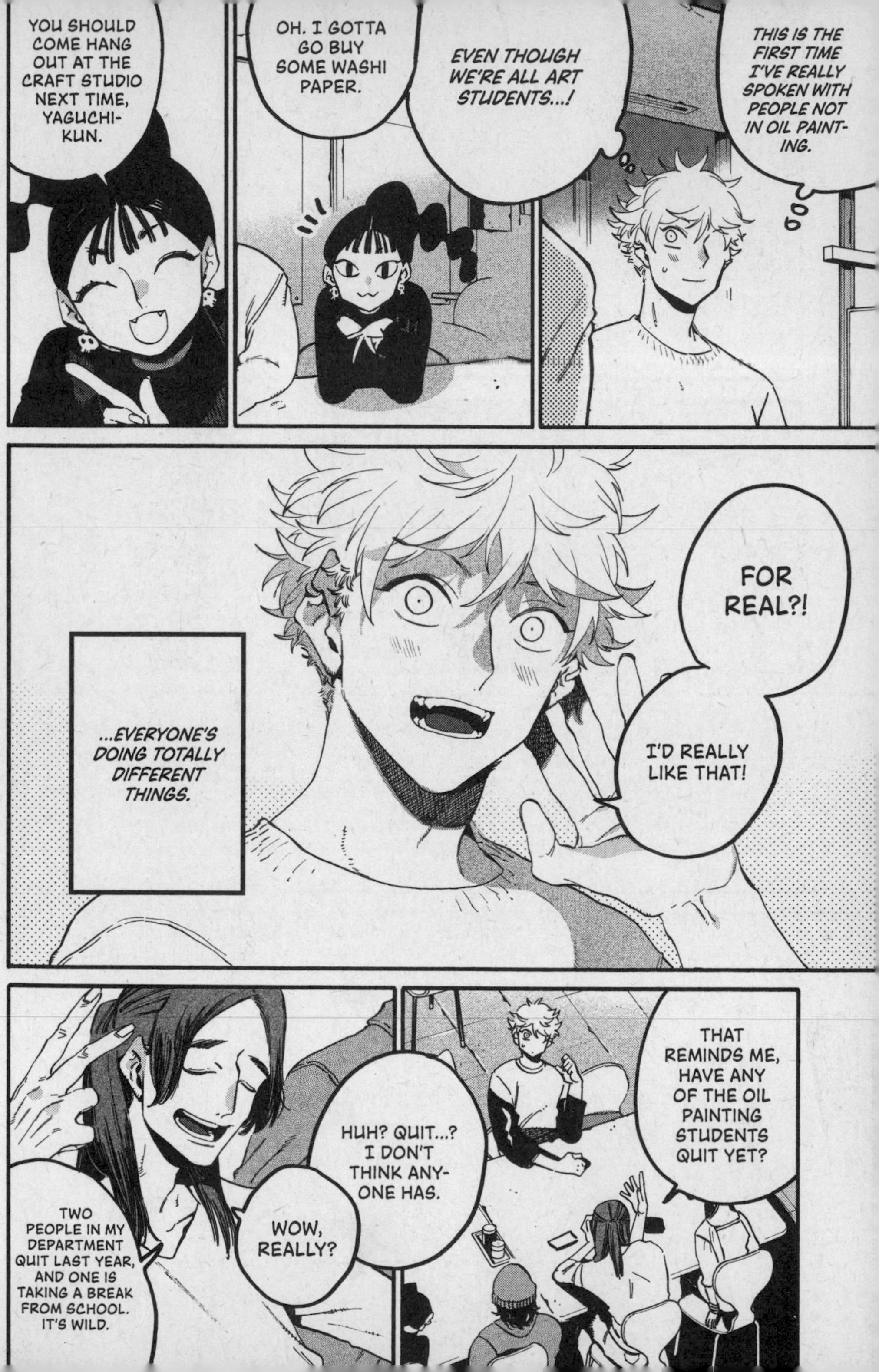
THIS IS THE FIRST TIME I'VE REALLY SPOKEN WITH PEOPLE NOT IN OIL PAINTING.
EVEN THOUGH WE'RE ALL ART STUDENTS...!
OH. I GOTTA GO BUY SOME WASHI PAPER.
YOU SHOULD COME HANG OUT AT THE CRAFT STUDIO NEXT TIME, YAGUCHI-KUN.
FOR REAL?!
I'D REALLY LIKE THAT!
...EVERYONE'S DOING TOTALLY DIFFERENT THINGS.
THAT REMINDS ME, HAVE ANY OF THE OIL PAINTING STUDENTS QUIT YET?
HUH? QUIT...? I DON'T THINK ANYONE HAS.
WOW, REALLY?
TWO PEOPLE IN MY DEPARTMENT QUIT LAST YEAR, AND ONE IS TAKING A BREAK FROM SCHOOL. IT'S WILD.

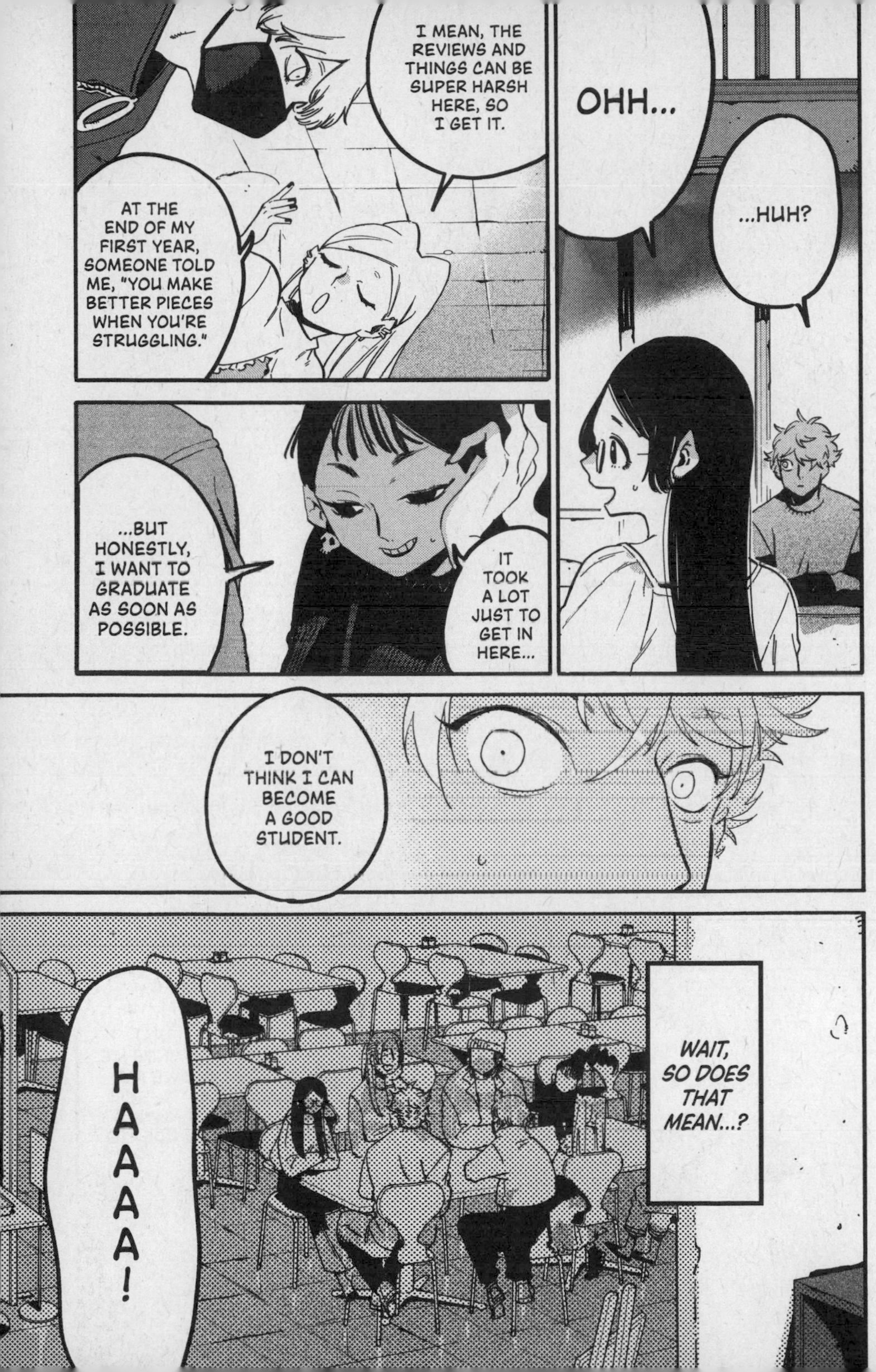
OHH...
...HUH?
I MEAN, THE REVIEWS AND THINGS CAN BE SUPER HARSH HERE, SO I GET IT.
AT THE END OF MY FIRST YEAR, SOMEONE TOLD ME, "YOU MAKE BETTER PIECES WHEN YOU'RE STRUGGLING."
IT TOOK A LOT JUST TO GET IN HERE...
...BUT HONESTLY, I WANT TO GRADUATE AS SOON AS POSSIBLE.
I DON'T THINK I CAN BECOME A GOOD STUDENT.
WAIT, SO DOES THAT MEAN...?
HAAAA!

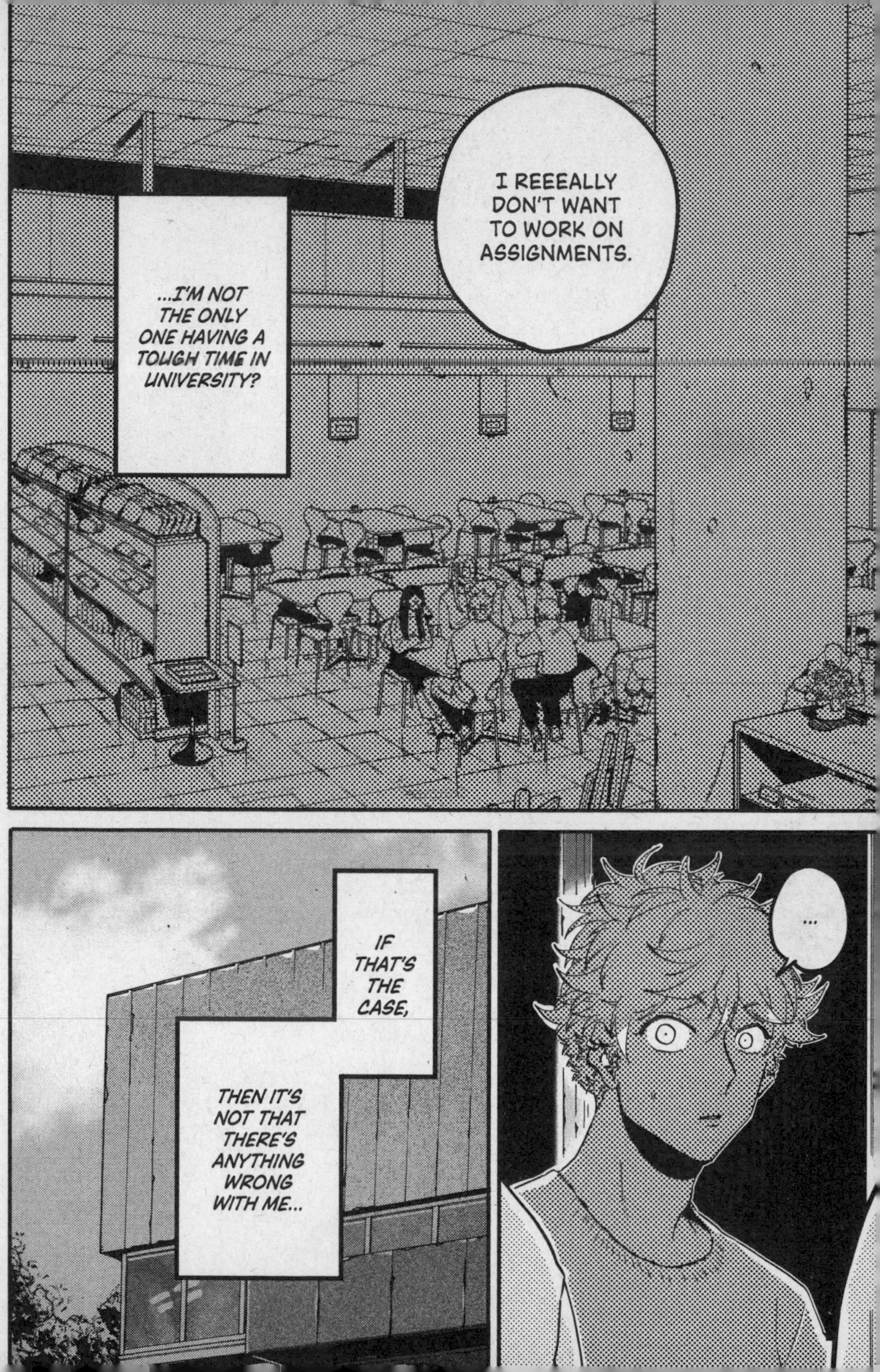
I REEEALLY DON'T WANT TO WORK ON ASSIGNMENTS.
...I'M NOT THE ONLY ONE HAVING A TOUGH TIME IN UNIVERSITY?
...
IF THAT'S THE CASE,
THEN IT'S NOT THAT THERE'S ANYTHING WRONG WITH ME...

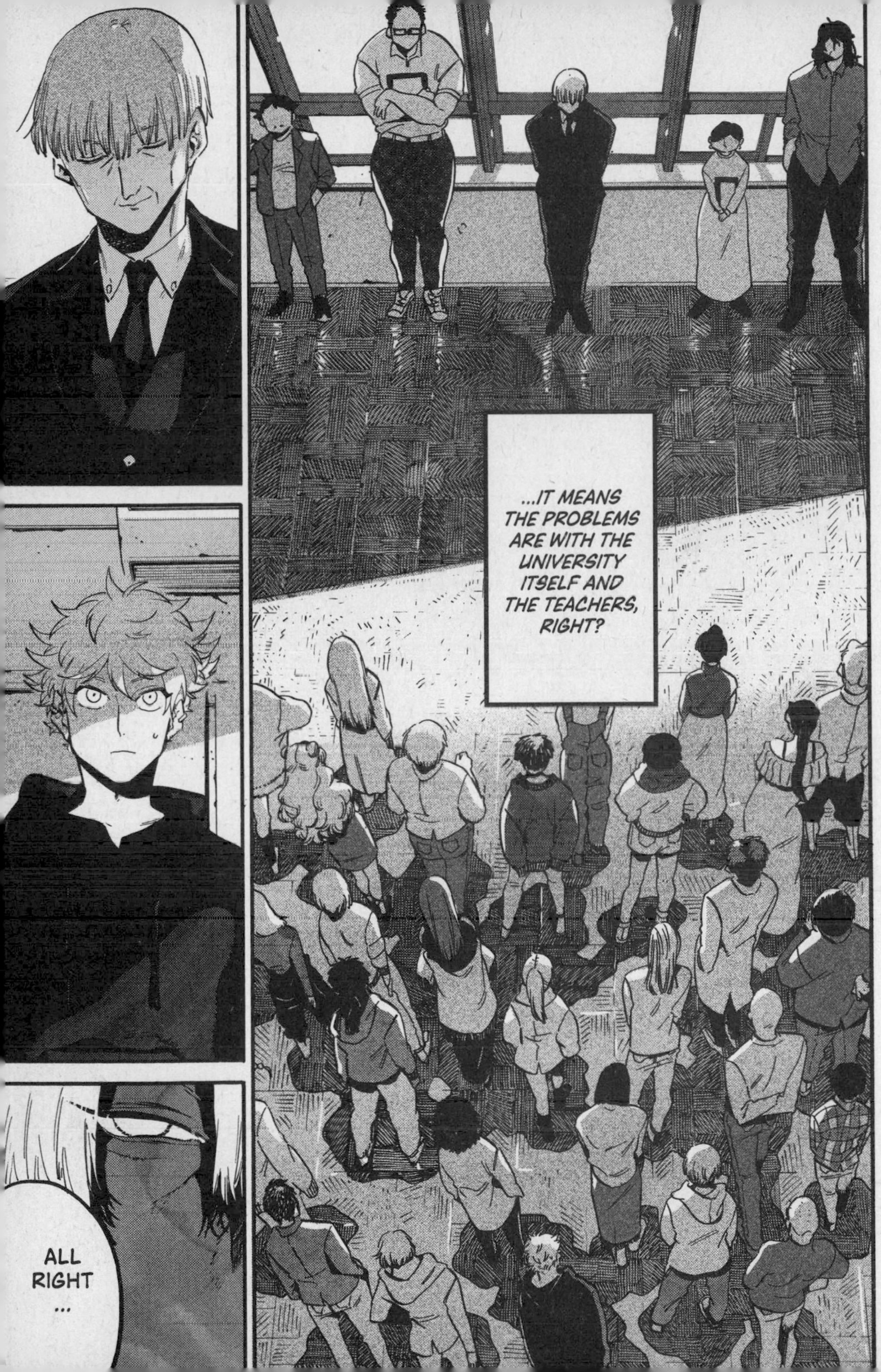
...IT MEANS THE PROBLEMS ARE WITH THE UNIVERSITY ITSELF AND THE TEACHERS, RIGHT?
ALL RIGHT ...

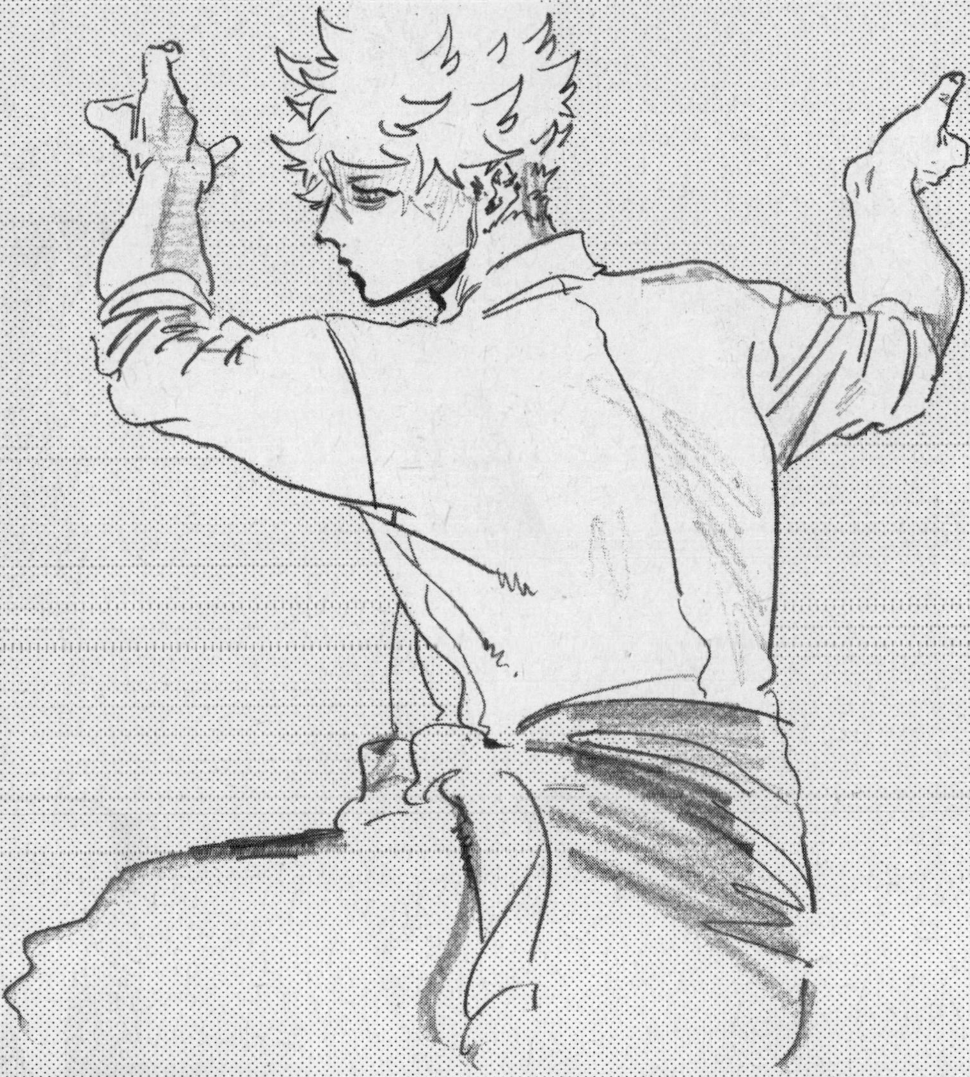

STROKE 49

WHERE'S THE WALKTHROUGH SITE THAT'LL SHOW ME HOW TO BEAT THIS DEATHLOOP OF WORRY

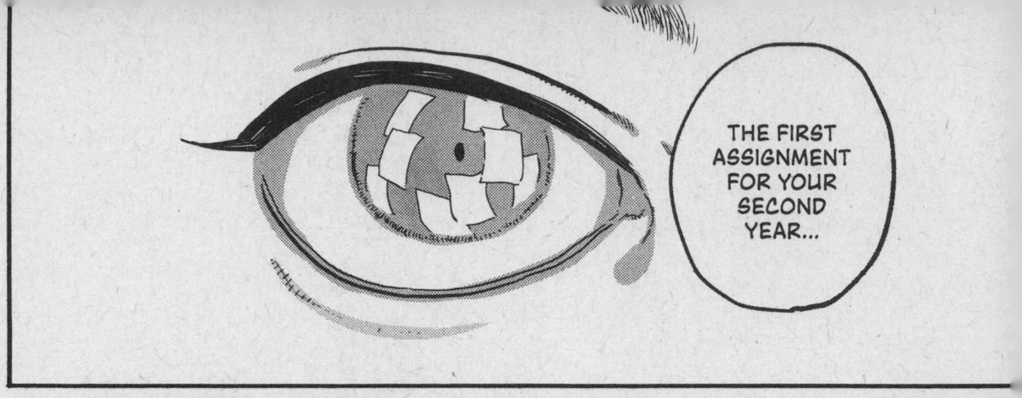
THE FIRST ASSIGNMENT FOR YOUR SECOND YEAR...
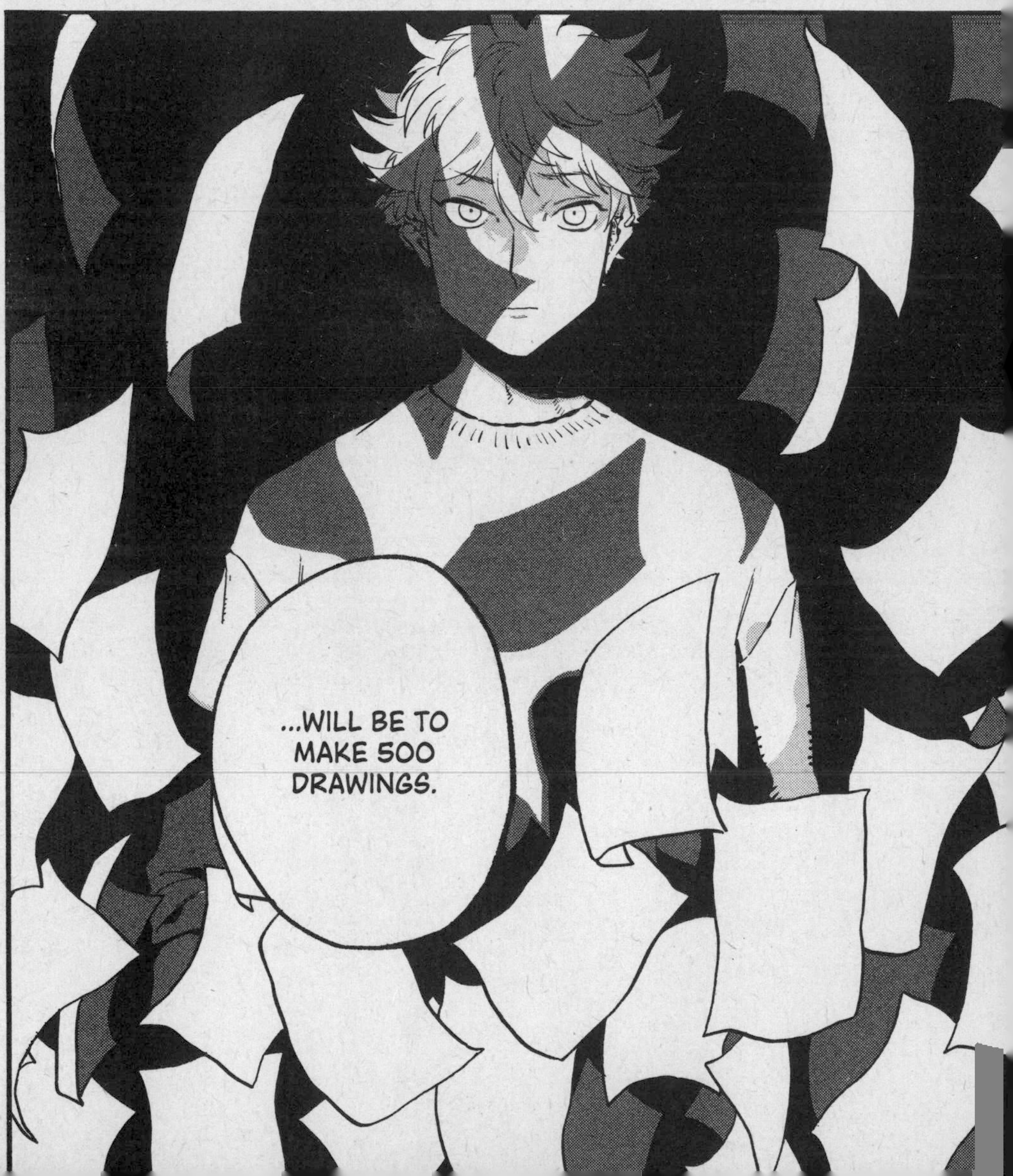
...WILL BE TO MAKE 500 DRAWINGS.

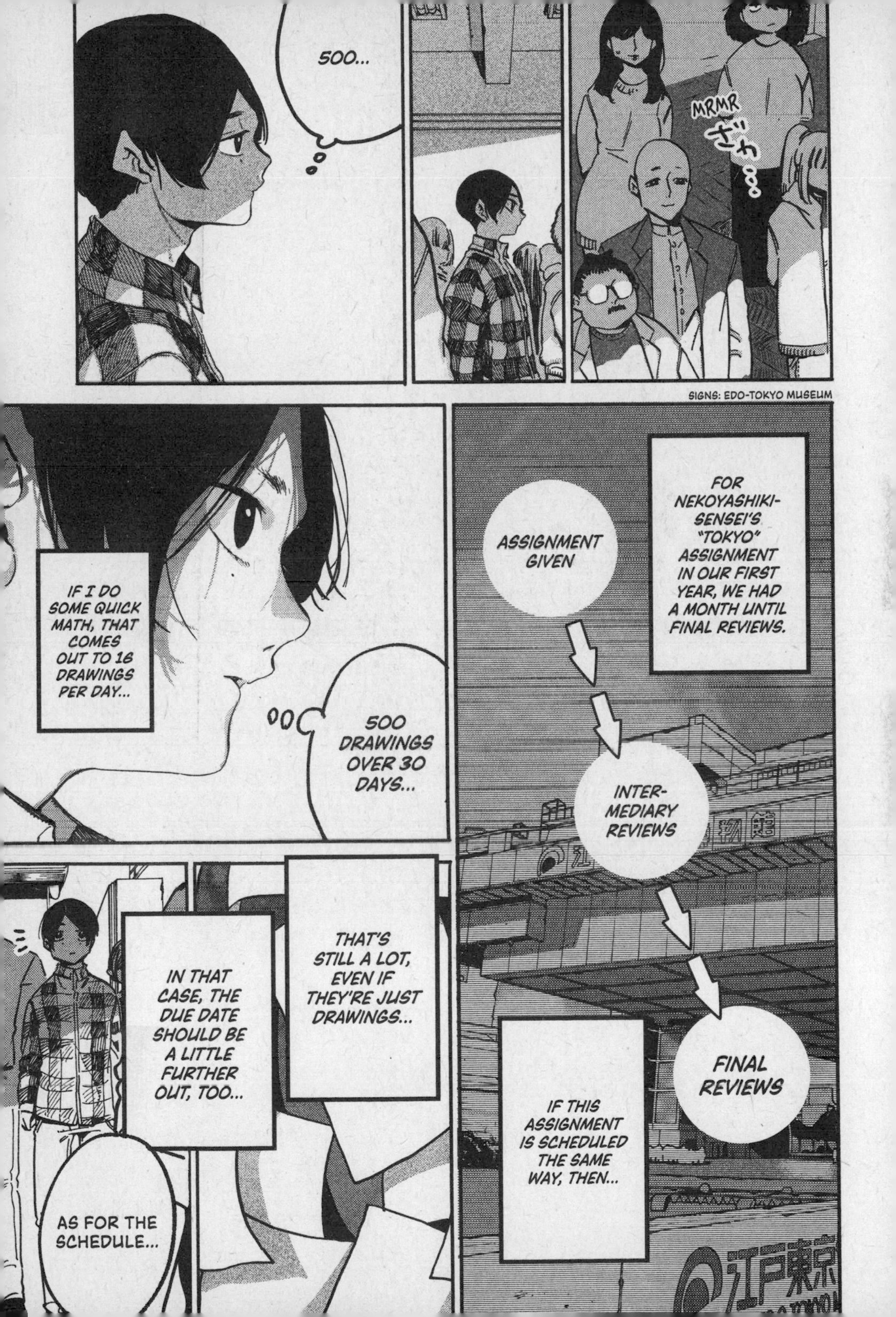
MRMR
ざわ…
500...
SIGNS: EDO-TOKYO MUSEUM
FOR NEKOYASHIKI-SENSEI'S "TOKYO" ASSIGNMENT IN OUR FIRST YEAR, WE HAD A MONTH UNTIL FINAL REVIEWS.
ASSIGNMENT GIVEN
INTER-MEDIARY REVIEWS
FINAL REVIEWS
IF THIS ASSIGNMENT IS SCHEDULED THE SAME WAY, THEN...
500 DRAWINGS OVER 30 DAYS...
IF I DO SOME QUICK MATH, THAT COMES OUT TO 16 DRAWINGS PER DAY...
THAT'S STILL A LOT, EVEN IF THEY'RE JUST DRAWINGS...
IN THAT CASE, THE DUE DATE SHOULD BE A LITTLE FURTHER OUT, TOO...
AS FOR THE SCHEDULE...

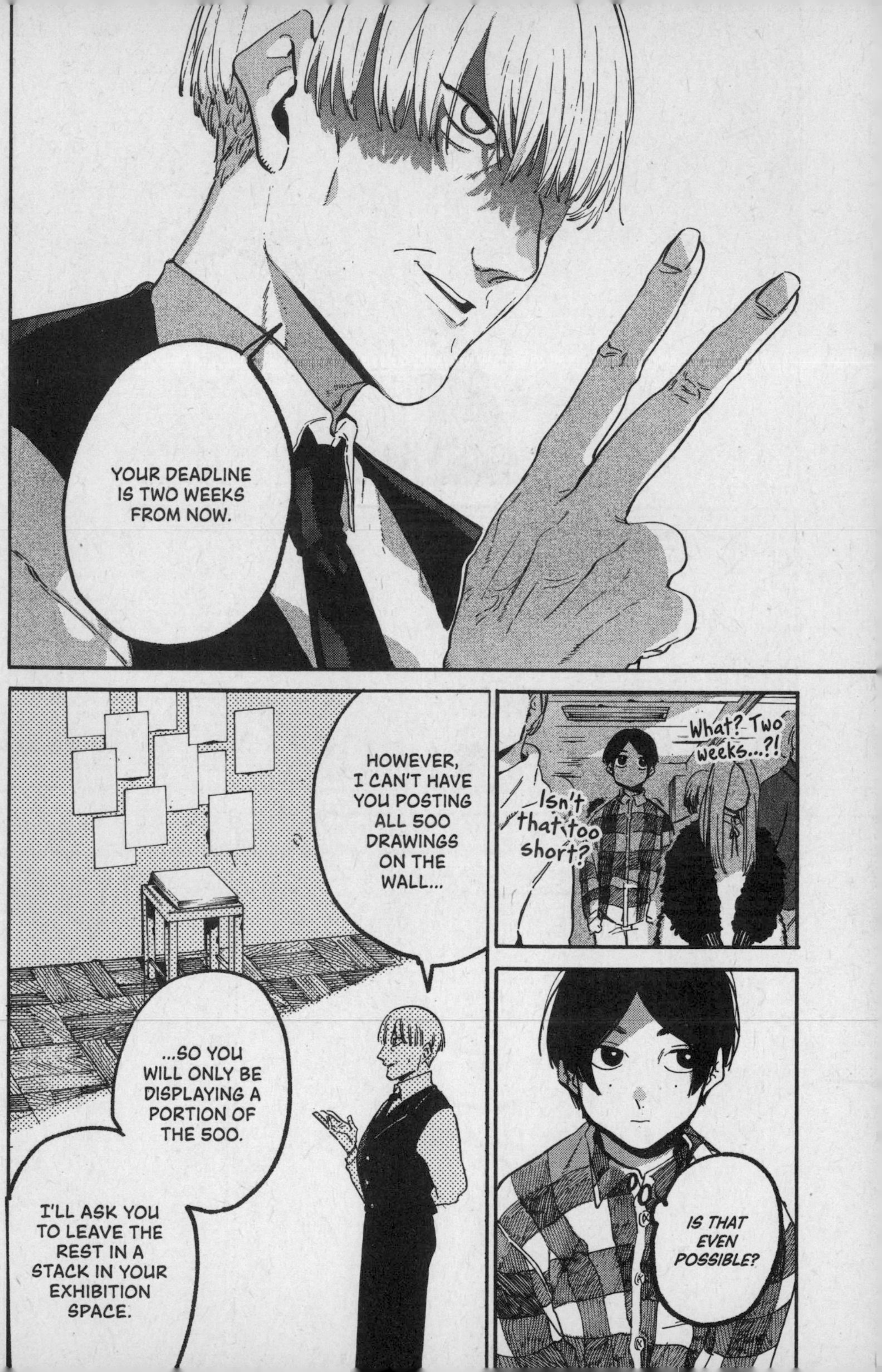
YOUR DEADLINE IS TWO WEEKS FROM NOW.
What? Two weeks...?!
Isn't that too short?
IS THAT EVEN POSSIBLE?
HOWEVER, I CAN'T HAVE YOU POSTING ALL 500 DRAWINGS ON THE WALL...
...SO YOU WILL ONLY BE DISPLAYING A PORTION OF THE 500.
I'LL ASK YOU TO LEAVE THE REST IN A STACK IN YOUR EXHIBITION SPACE.

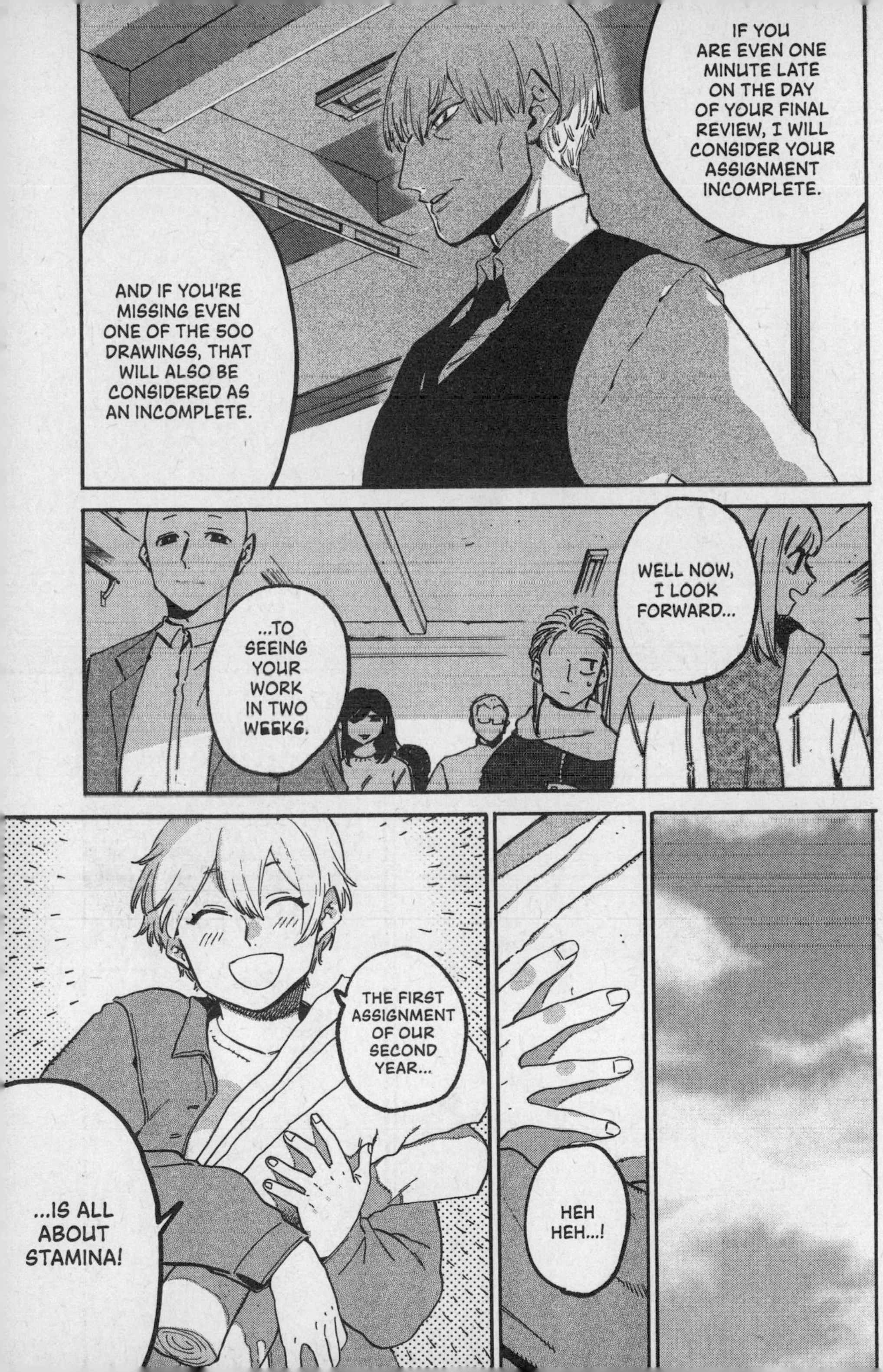
IF YOU ARE EVEN ONE MINUTE LATE ON THE DAY OF YOUR FINAL REVIEW, I WILL CONSIDER YOUR ASSIGNMENT INCOMPLETE.
AND IF YOU'RE MISSING EVEN ONE OF THE 500 DRAWINGS, THAT WILL ALSO BE CONSIDERED AS AN INCOMPLETE.
WELL NOW, I LOOK FORWARD...
...TO SEEING YOUR WORK IN TWO WEEKS.
HEH HEH...!
THE FIRST ASSIGNMENT OF OUR SECOND YEAR...
...IS ALL ABOUT STAMINA!

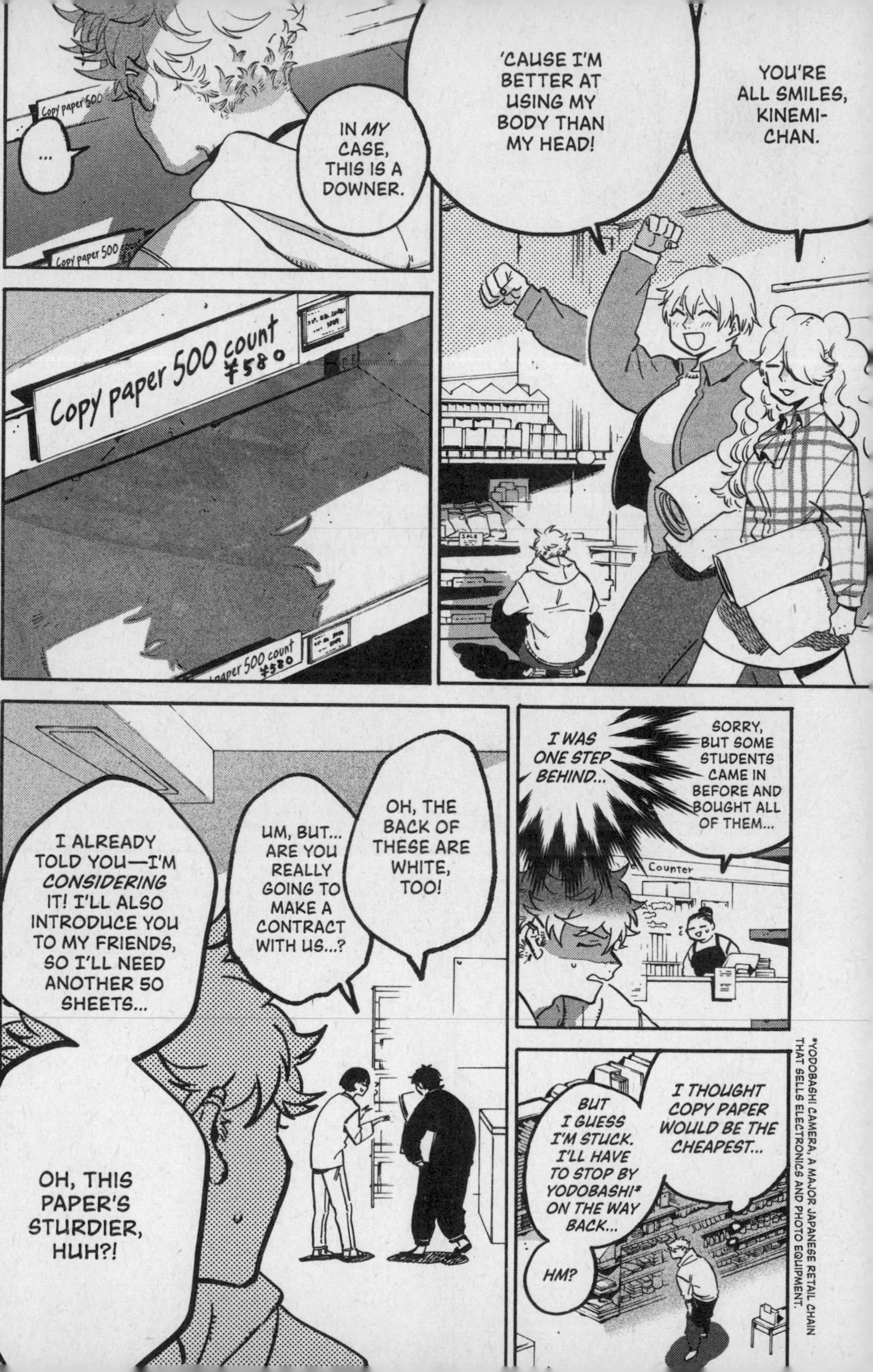
YOU'RE ALL SMILES, KINEMI-CHAN.
'CAUSE I'M BETTER AT USING MY BODY THAN MY HEAD!
IN *MY* CASE, THIS IS A DOWNER.
...
Copy paper 500
Copy paper 500 count
Copy paper 500 count ¥580
paper 500 count ¥580
SORRY, BUT SOME STUDENTS CAME IN BEFORE AND BOUGHT ALL OF THEM...
I WAS ONE STEP BEHIND...
Counter
I THOUGHT COPY PAPER WOULD BE THE CHEAPEST...
BUT I GUESS I'M STUCK. I'LL HAVE TO STOP BY YODOBASHI ON THE WAY BACK...*
HM?
OH, THE BACK OF THESE ARE WHITE, TOO!
UM, BUT... ARE YOU REALLY GOING TO MAKE A CONTRACT WITH US...?
I ALREADY TOLD YOU—I'M *CONSIDERING* IT! I'LL ALSO INTRODUCE YOU TO MY FRIENDS, SO I'LL NEED ANOTHER 50 SHEETS...
OH, THIS PAPER'S STURDIER, HUH?!

*YODOBASHI CAMERA, A MAJOR JAPANESE RETAIL CHAIN THAT SELLS ELECTRONICS AND PHOTO EQUIPMENT.

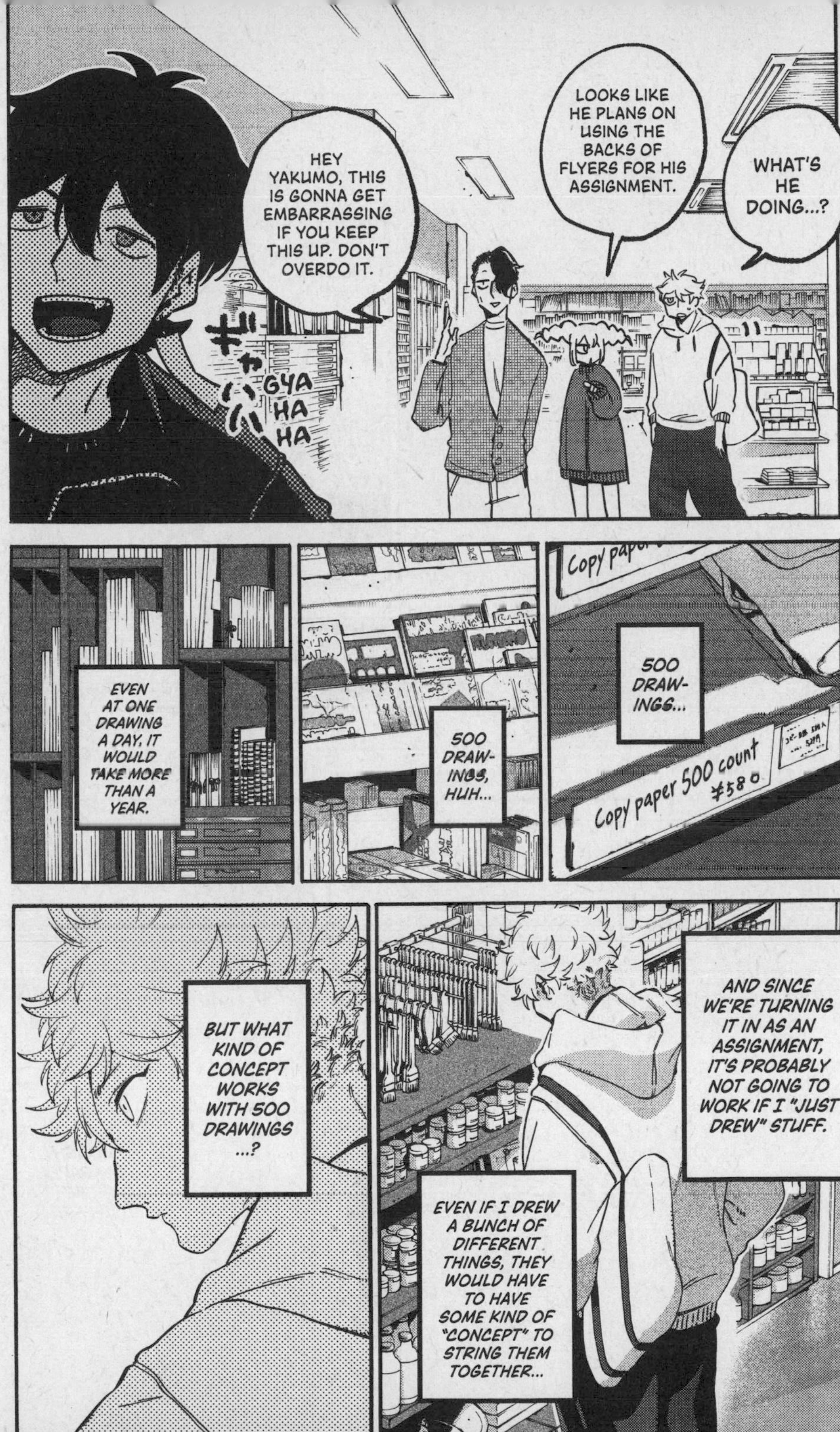
WHAT'S HE DOING...?
LOOKS LIKE HE PLANS ON USING THE BACKS OF FLYERS FOR HIS ASSIGNMENT.
HEY YAKUMO, THIS IS GONNA GET EMBARRASSING IF YOU KEEP THIS UP. DON'T OVERDO IT.
GYA HA HA
500 DRAWINGS...
Copy paper 500 count
¥580
500 DRAWINGS, HUH...
EVEN AT ONE DRAWING A DAY, IT WOULD TAKE MORE THAN A YEAR.
AND SINCE WE'RE TURNING IT IN AS AN ASSIGNMENT, IT'S PROBABLY NOT GOING TO WORK IF I "JUST DREW" STUFF.
EVEN IF I DREW A BUNCH OF DIFFERENT THINGS, THEY WOULD HAVE TO HAVE SOME KIND OF "CONCEPT" TO STRING THEM TOGETHER...
BUT WHAT KIND OF CONCEPT WORKS WITH 500 DRAWINGS ...?

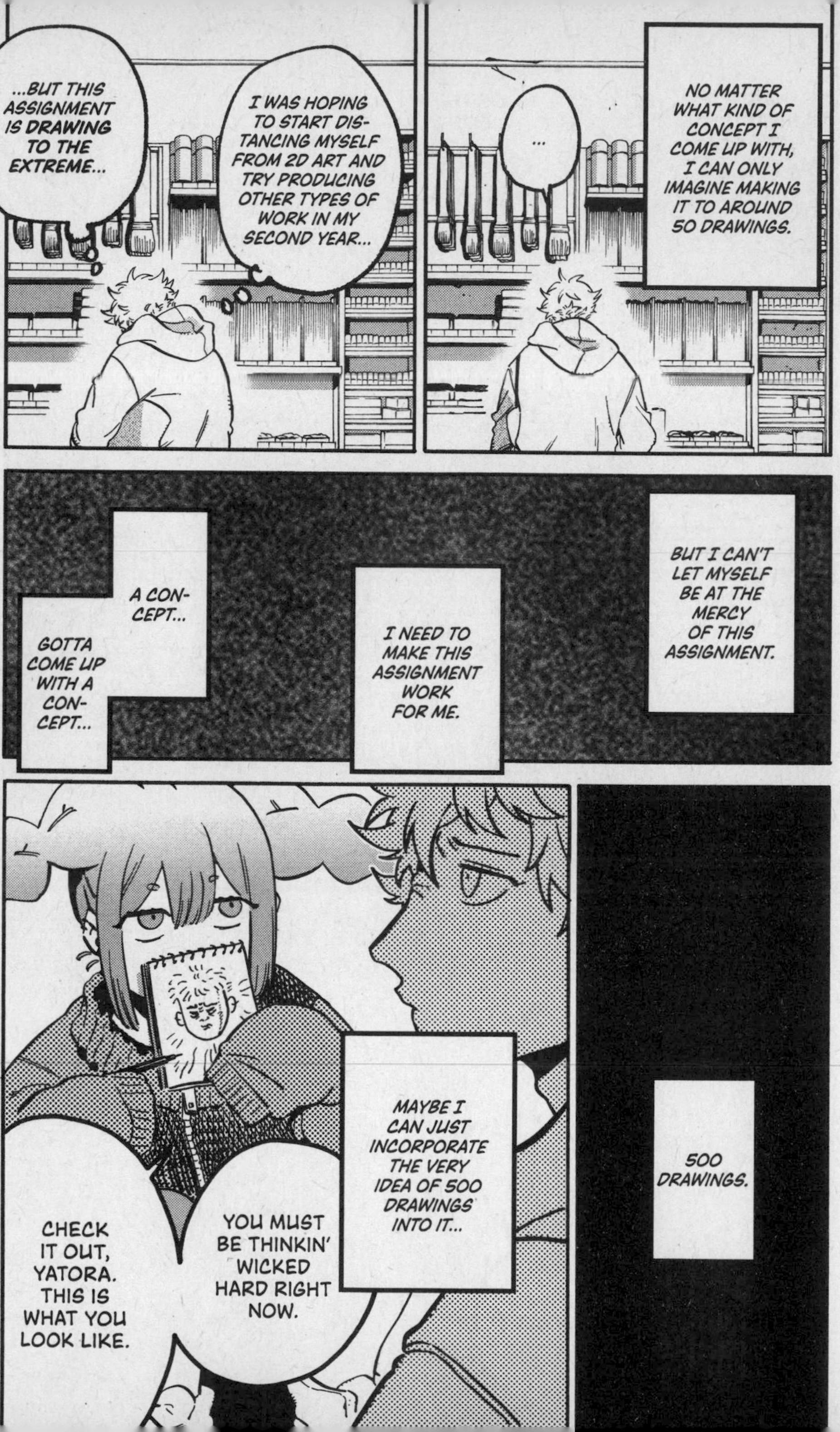
NO MATTER WHAT KIND OF CONCEPT I COME UP WITH, I CAN ONLY IMAGINE MAKING IT TO AROUND 50 DRAWINGS.
...
I WAS HOPING TO START DISTANCING MYSELF FROM 2D ART AND TRY PRODUCING OTHER TYPES OF WORK IN MY SECOND YEAR...
...BUT THIS ASSIGNMENT IS DRAWING TO THE EXTREME...
BUT I CAN'T LET MYSELF BE AT THE MERCY OF THIS ASSIGNMENT.
I NEED TO MAKE THIS ASSIGNMENT WORK FOR ME.
A CONCEPT...
GOTTA COME UP WITH A CONCEPT...
500 DRAWINGS.
MAYBE I CAN JUST INCORPORATE THE VERY IDEA OF 500 DRAWINGS INTO IT...
YOU MUST BE THINKIN' WICKED HARD RIGHT NOW.
CHECK IT OUT, YATORA. THIS IS WHAT YOU LOOK LIKE.

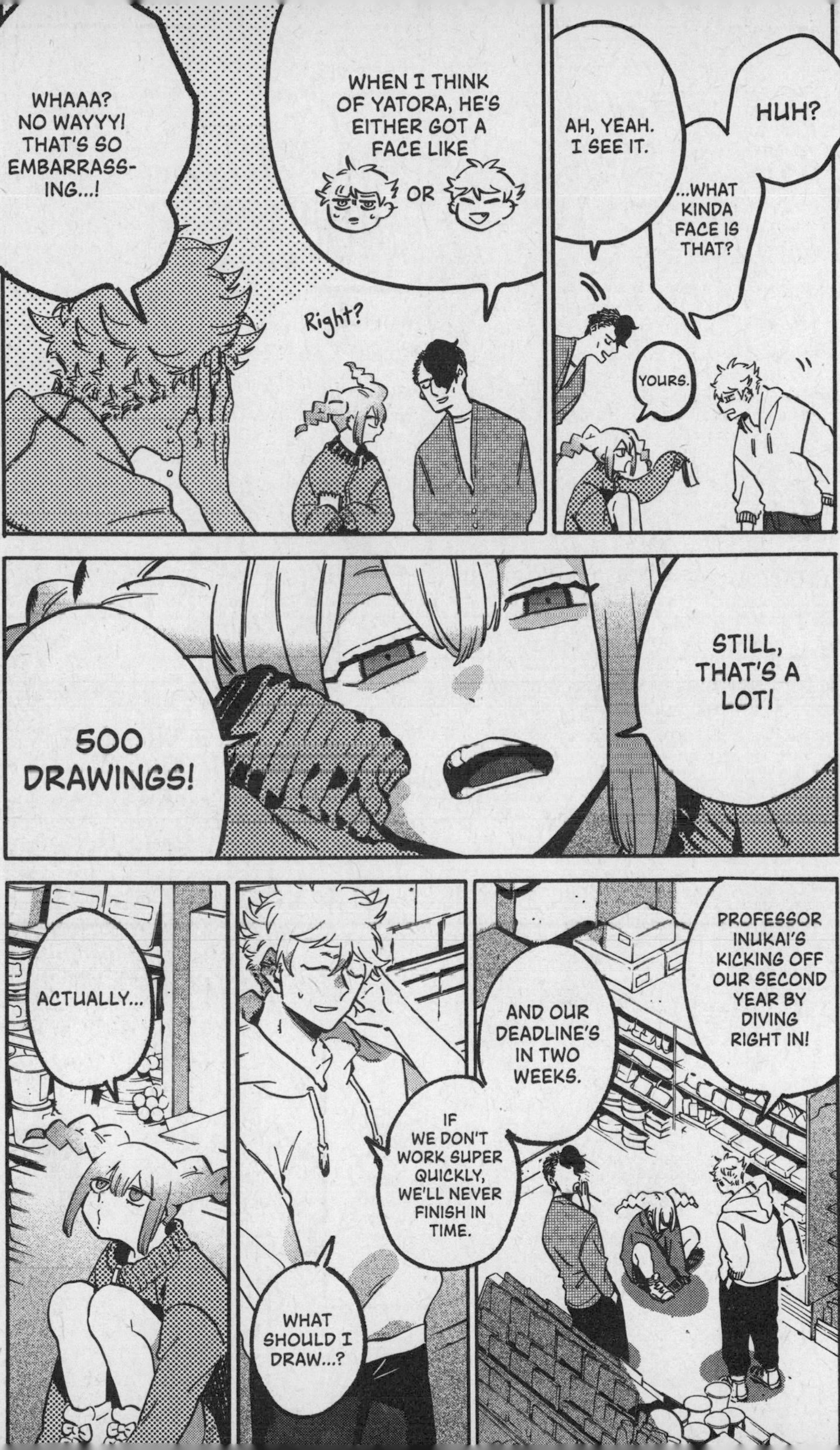
AH, YEAH. I SEE IT.
HUH?
...WHAT KINDA FACE IS THAT?
YOURS.
WHEN I THINK OF YATORA, HE'S EITHER GOT A FACE LIKE OR
Right?
WHAAA? NO WAYYY! THAT'S SO EMBARRASS-ING...!
STILL, THAT'S A LOT!
500 DRAWINGS!
PROFESSOR INUKAI'S KICKING OFF OUR SECOND YEAR BY DIVING RIGHT IN!
AND OUR DEADLINE'S IN TWO WEEKS.
IF WE DON'T WORK SUPER QUICKLY, WE'LL NEVER FINISH IN TIME.
WHAT SHOULD I DRAW...?
ACTUALLY...

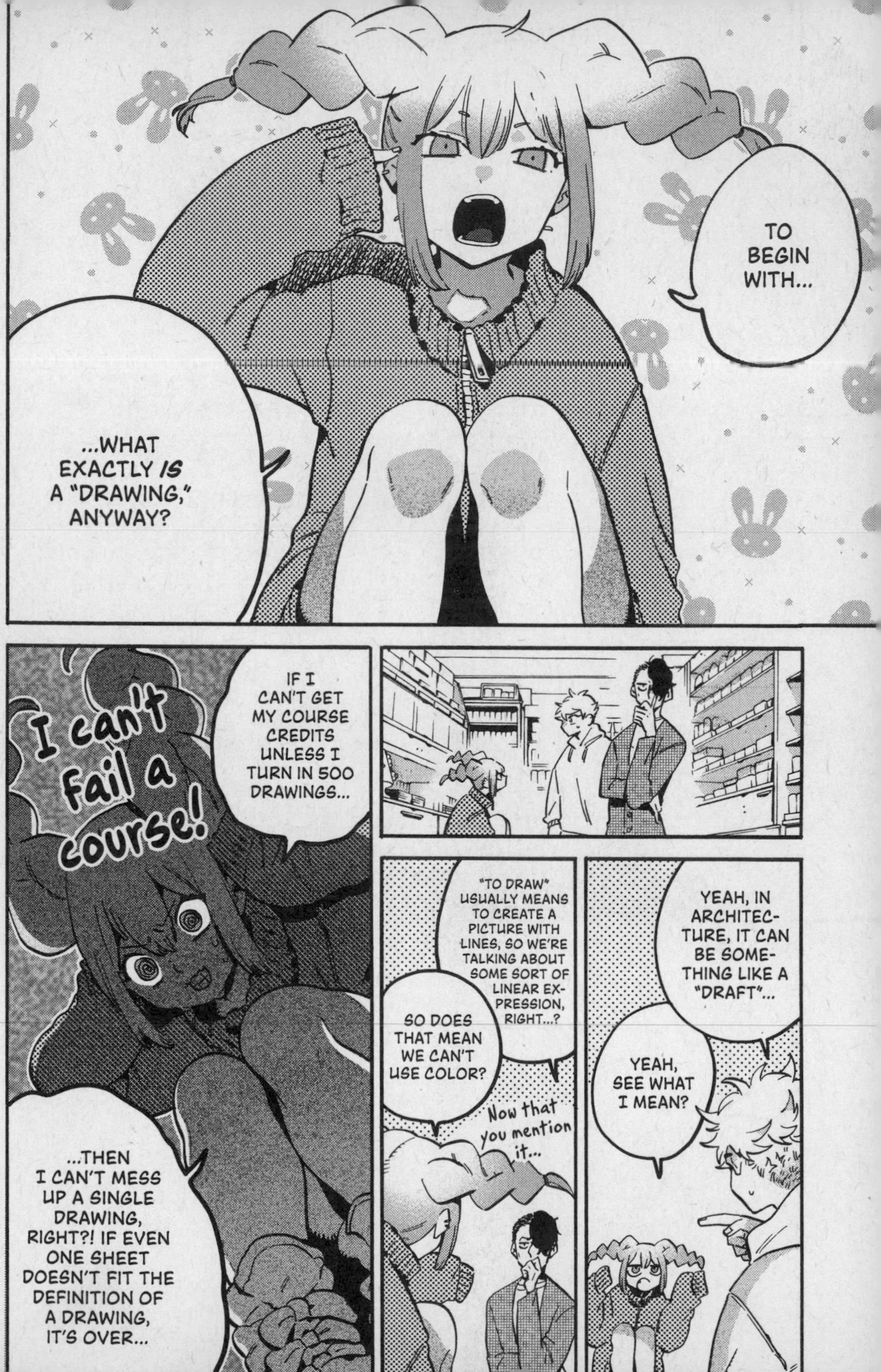
TO BEGIN WITH...
...WHAT EXACTLY *IS* A "DRAWING," ANYWAY?
YEAH, IN ARCHITEC-TURE, IT CAN BE SOME-THING LIKE A "DRAFT"...
YEAH, SEE WHAT I MEAN?
"TO DRAW" USUALLY MEANS TO CREATE A PICTURE WITH LINES, SO WE'RE TALKING ABOUT SOME SORT OF LINEAR EX-PRESSION, RIGHT...?
SO DOES THAT MEAN WE CAN'T USE COLOR?
Now that you mention it...
IF I CAN'T GET MY COURSE CREDITS UNLESS I TURN IN 500 DRAWINGS...
I can't fail a course!
...THEN I CAN'T MESS UP A SINGLE DRAWING, RIGHT?! IF EVEN ONE SHEET DOESN'T FIT THE DEFINITION OF A DRAWING, IT'S OVER...

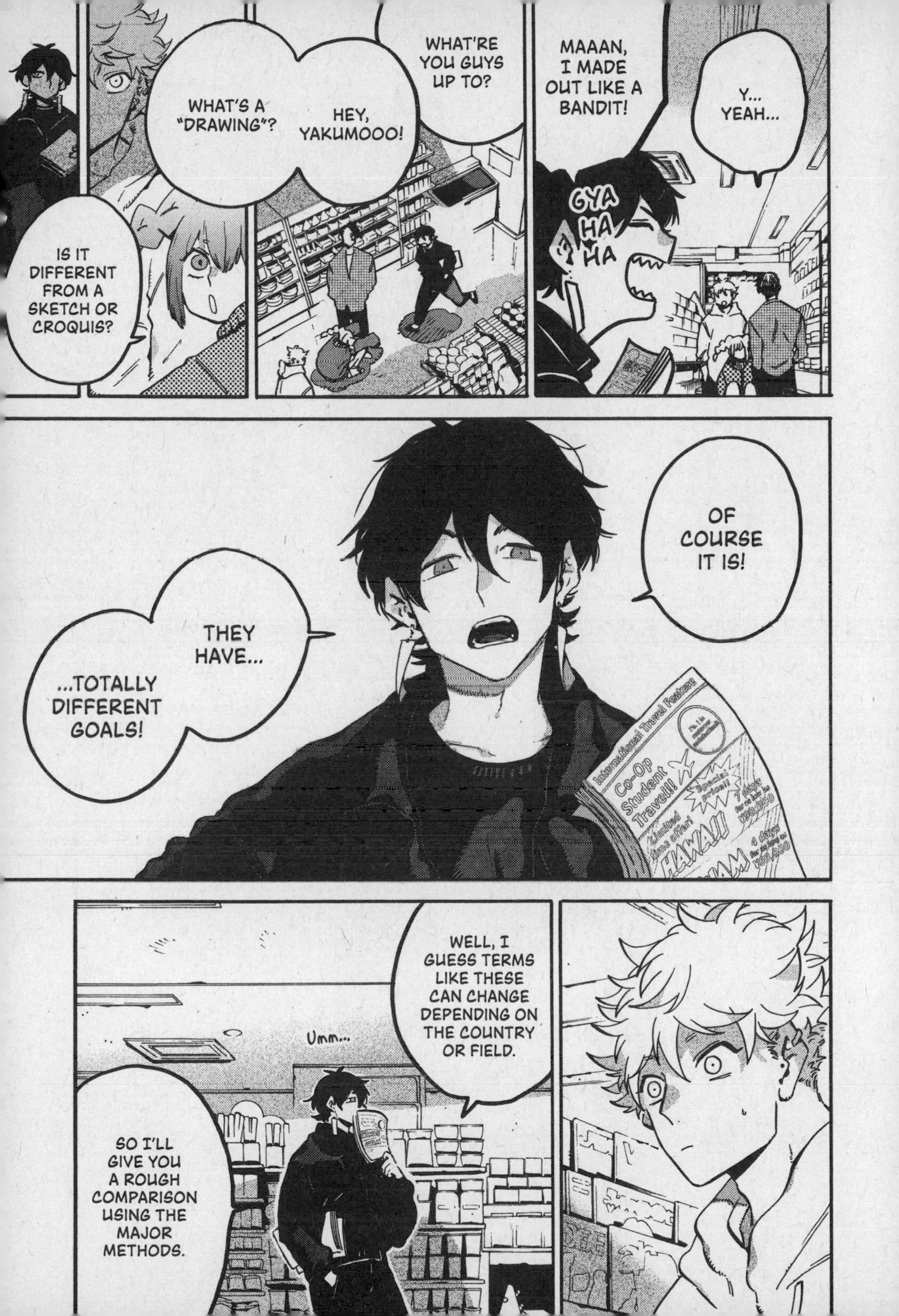
Y... YEAH...
MAAAN, I MADE OUT LIKE A BANDIT!
GYA HA HA
WHAT'RE YOU GUYS UP TO?
HEY, YAKUMOOO!
WHAT'S A "DRAWING"?
IS IT DIFFERENT FROM A SKETCH OR CROQUIS?
OF COURSE IT IS!
THEY HAVE...
...TOTALLY DIFFERENT GOALS!
International Travel Feature
Co-Op Student Travel!!
Special price!!
Limited time offer!
HAWAII
WELL, I GUESS TERMS LIKE THESE CAN CHANGE DEPENDING ON THE COUNTRY OR FIELD.
Umm...
SO I'LL GIVE YOU A ROUGH COMPARISON USING THE MAJOR METHODS.

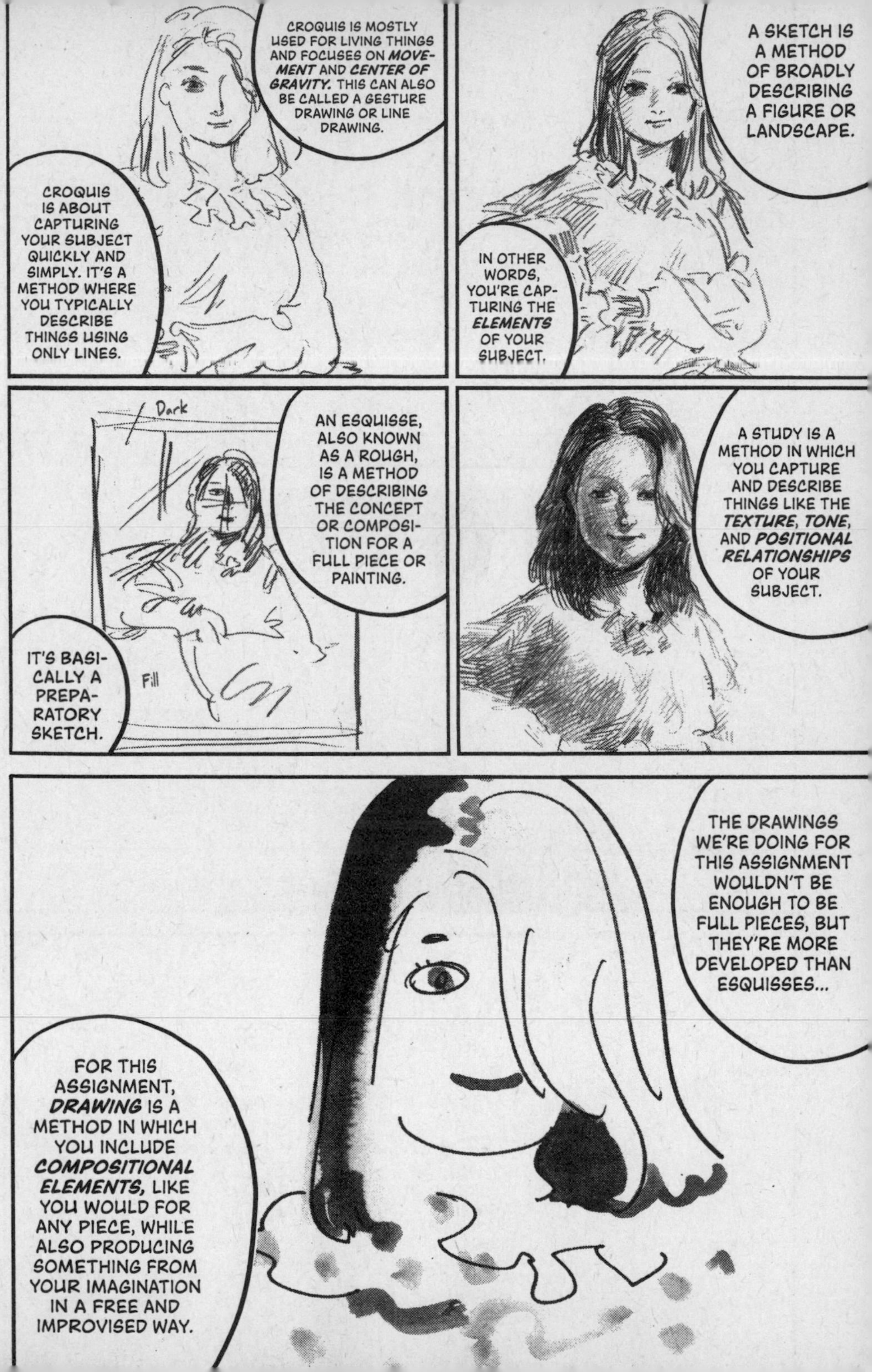
A SKETCH IS A METHOD OF BROADLY DESCRIBING A FIGURE OR LANDSCAPE.
IN OTHER WORDS, YOU'RE CAPTURING THE ELEMENTS OF YOUR SUBJECT.
CROQUIS IS MOSTLY USED FOR LIVING THINGS AND FOCUSES ON MOVEMENT AND CENTER OF GRAVITY. THIS CAN ALSO BE CALLED A GESTURE DRAWING OR LINE DRAWING.
CROQUIS IS ABOUT CAPTURING YOUR SUBJECT QUICKLY AND SIMPLY. IT'S A METHOD WHERE YOU TYPICALLY DESCRIBE THINGS USING ONLY LINES.
A STUDY IS A METHOD IN WHICH YOU CAPTURE AND DESCRIBE THINGS LIKE THE TEXTURE, TONE, AND POSITIONAL RELATIONSHIPS OF YOUR SUBJECT.
AN ESQUISSE, ALSO KNOWN AS A ROUGH, IS A METHOD OF DESCRIBING THE CONCEPT OR COMPOSITION FOR A FULL PIECE OR PAINTING.
Dark
Fill
IT'S BASICALLY A PREPARATORY SKETCH.
THE DRAWINGS WE'RE DOING FOR THIS ASSIGNMENT WOULDN'T BE ENOUGH TO BE FULL PIECES, BUT THEY'RE MORE DEVELOPED THAN ESQUISSES...
FOR THIS ASSIGNMENT, DRAWING IS A METHOD IN WHICH YOU INCLUDE COMPOSITIONAL ELEMENTS, LIKE YOU WOULD FOR ANY PIECE, WHILE ALSO PRODUCING SOMETHING FROM YOUR IMAGINATION IN A FREE AND IMPROVISED WAY.

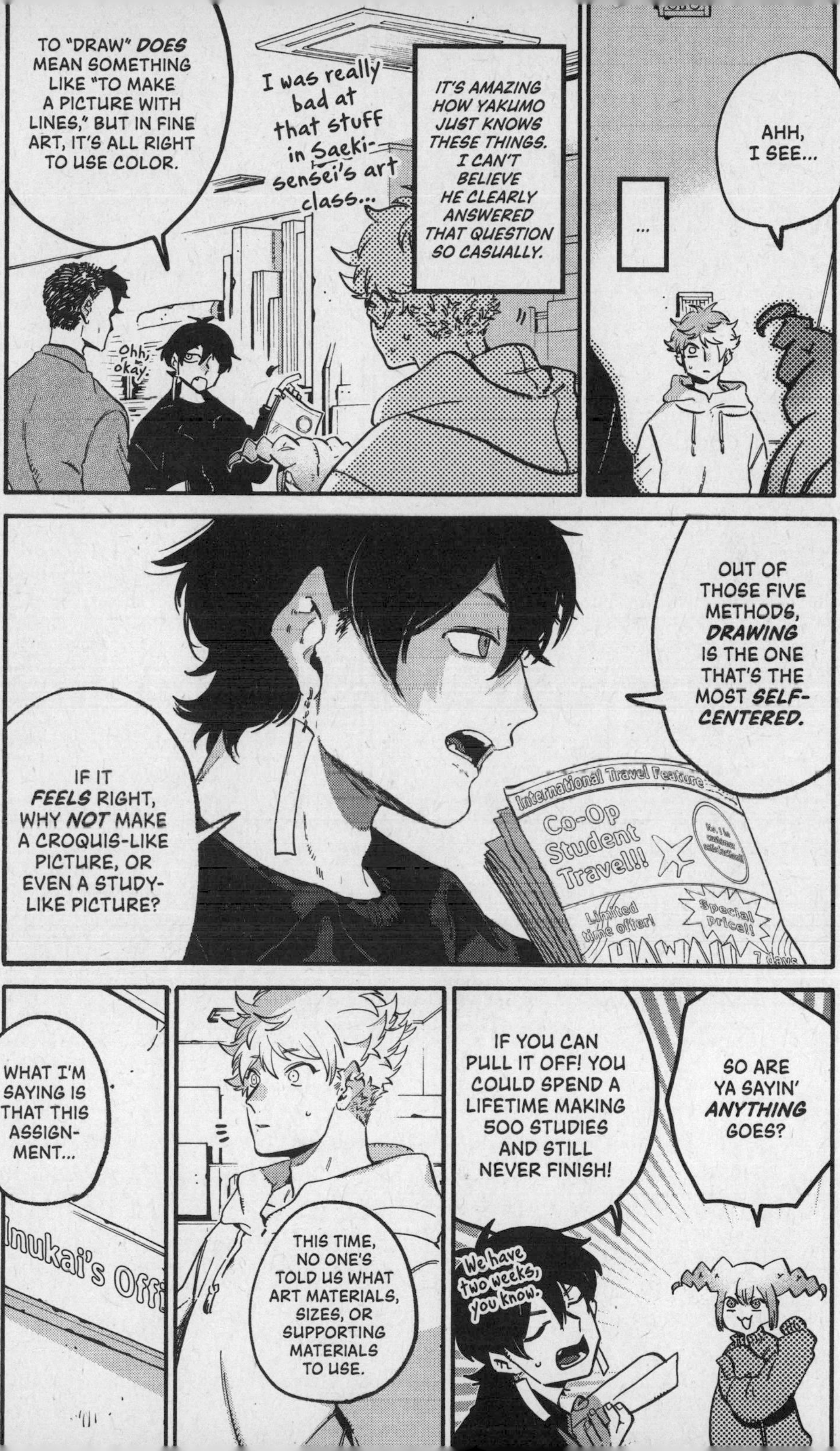
AHH, I SEE...
...
IT'S AMAZING HOW YAKUMO JUST KNOWS THESE THINGS. I CAN'T BELIEVE HE CLEARLY ANSWERED THAT QUESTION SO CASUALLY.
I was really bad at that stuff in Saeki-sensei's art class...
TO "DRAW" DOES MEAN SOMETHING LIKE "TO MAKE A PICTURE WITH LINES," BUT IN FINE ART, IT'S ALL RIGHT TO USE COLOR.
Ohh, okay.
OUT OF THOSE FIVE METHODS, DRAWING IS THE ONE THAT'S THE MOST SELF-CENTERED.
IF IT FEELS RIGHT, WHY NOT MAKE A CROQUIS-LIKE PICTURE, OR EVEN A STUDY-LIKE PICTURE?
International Travel Feature
Co-Op Student Travel!!
Limited time offer!
Special price!!
SO ARE YA SAYIN' ANYTHING GOES?
IF YOU CAN PULL IT OFF! YOU COULD SPEND A LIFETIME MAKING 500 STUDIES AND STILL NEVER FINISH!
We have two weeks, you know.
THIS TIME, NO ONE'S TOLD US WHAT ART MATERIALS, SIZES, OR SUPPORTING MATERIALS TO USE.
WHAT I'M SAYING IS THAT THIS ASSIGNMENT...
Inukai's Offi

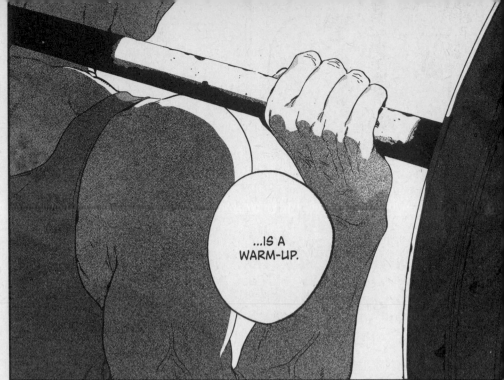

...IS A WARM-UP.

I FEEL JUST AS NERVOUS KNOCKING ON THIS DOOR NOW AS I DID WHEN I WAS A STUDENT...

HAAH...

WHA?

I'm doing it?

...GO AHEAD, YUMESAKI-SAN.

IF IT DOESN'T HAPPEN IN THAT ORDER, THERE WILL BE TROUBLE.

SLIIINK

"KNOCK TWICE."

"YES. COME IN."

"KA-CHAK."

Trouble how? IS INUKAI-SENSEI SOME SORTA URBAN LEGEND?

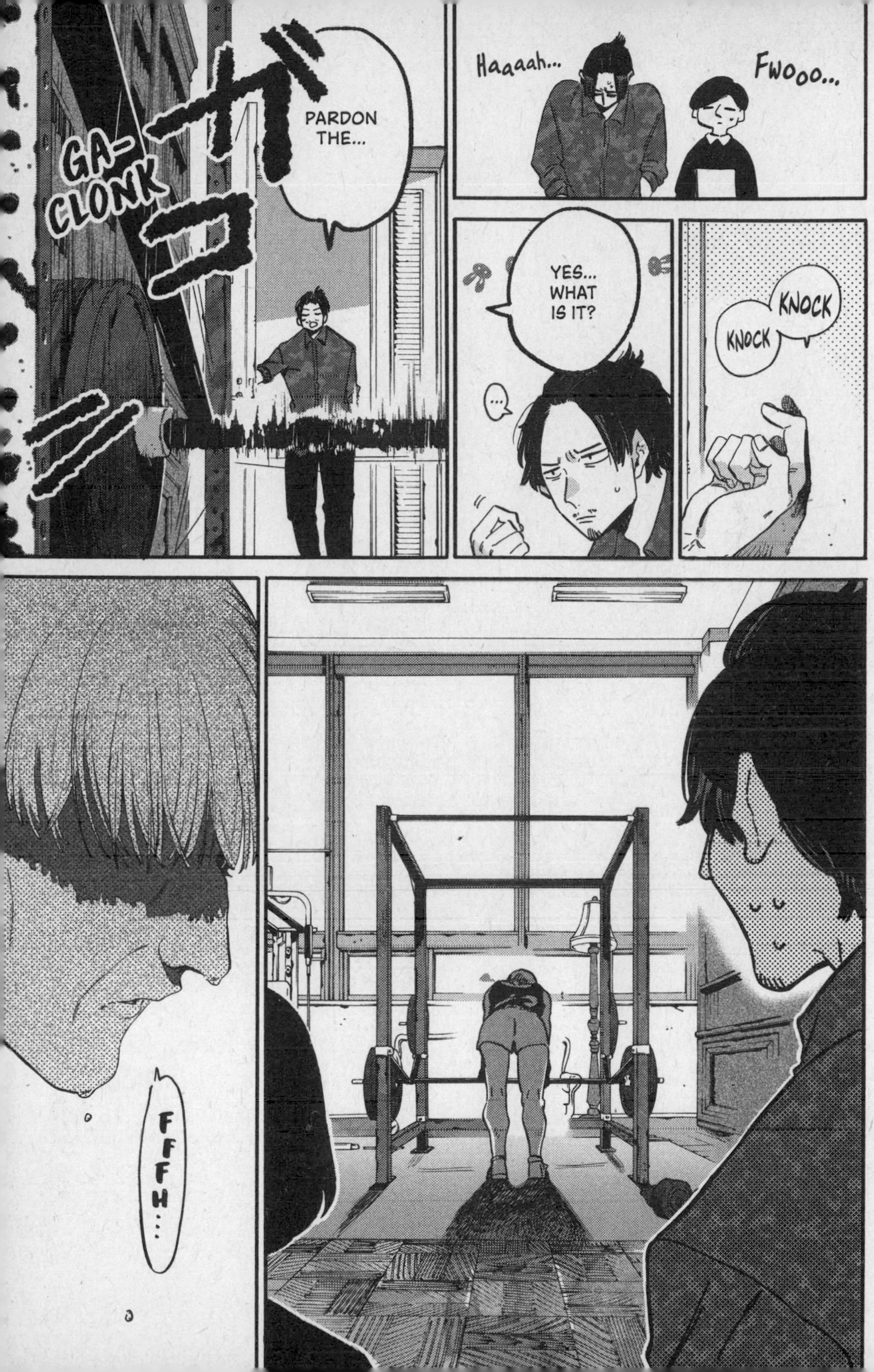
Fwooo...
Haaaah...
KNOCK
KNOCK
YES... WHAT IS IT?
...
PARDON THE...
GA-CLONK
FFFH...

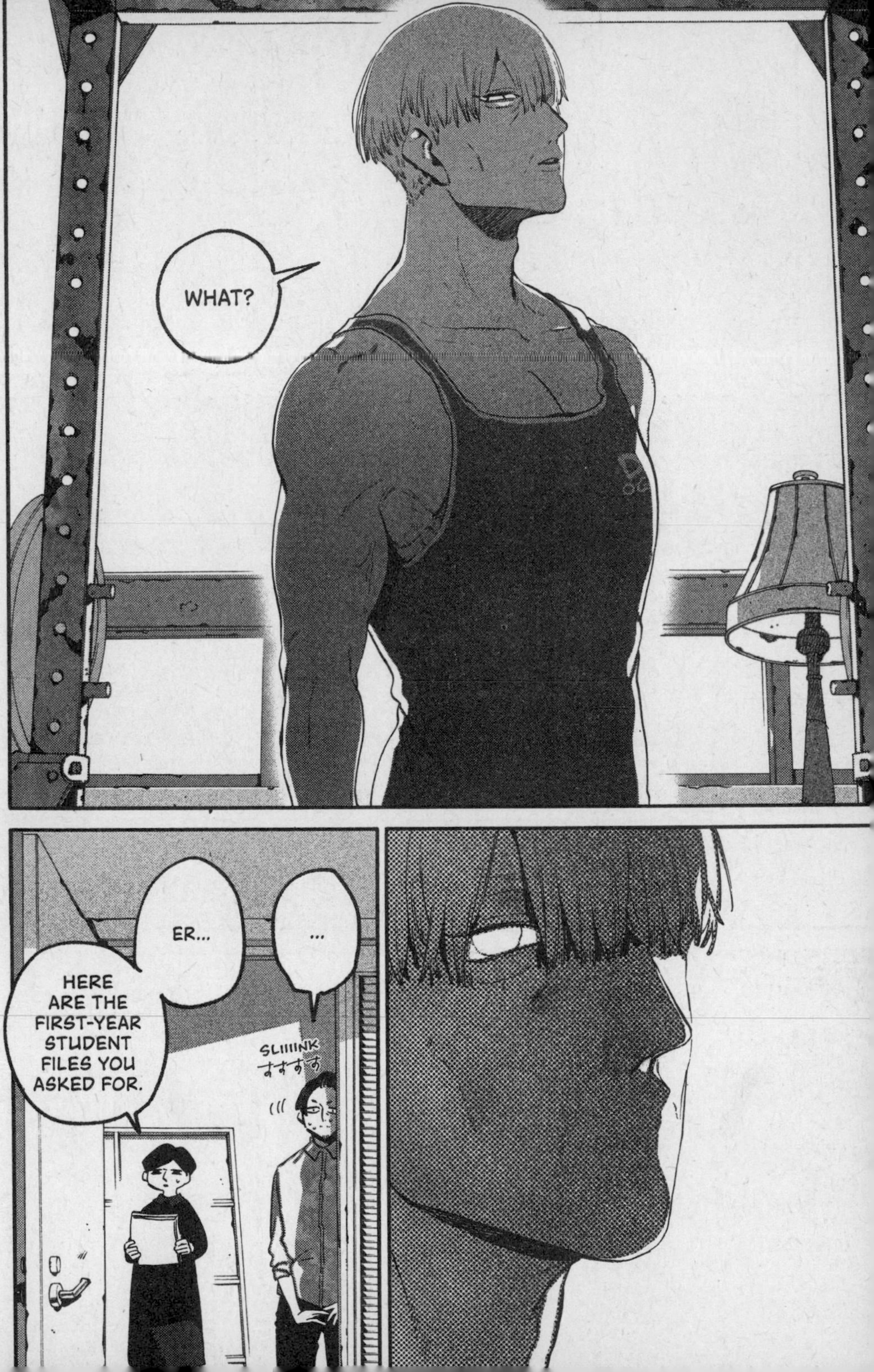
WHAT?
...
ER...
HERE ARE THE FIRST-YEAR STUDENT FILES YOU ASKED FOR.
SLIIIINK
すすすす

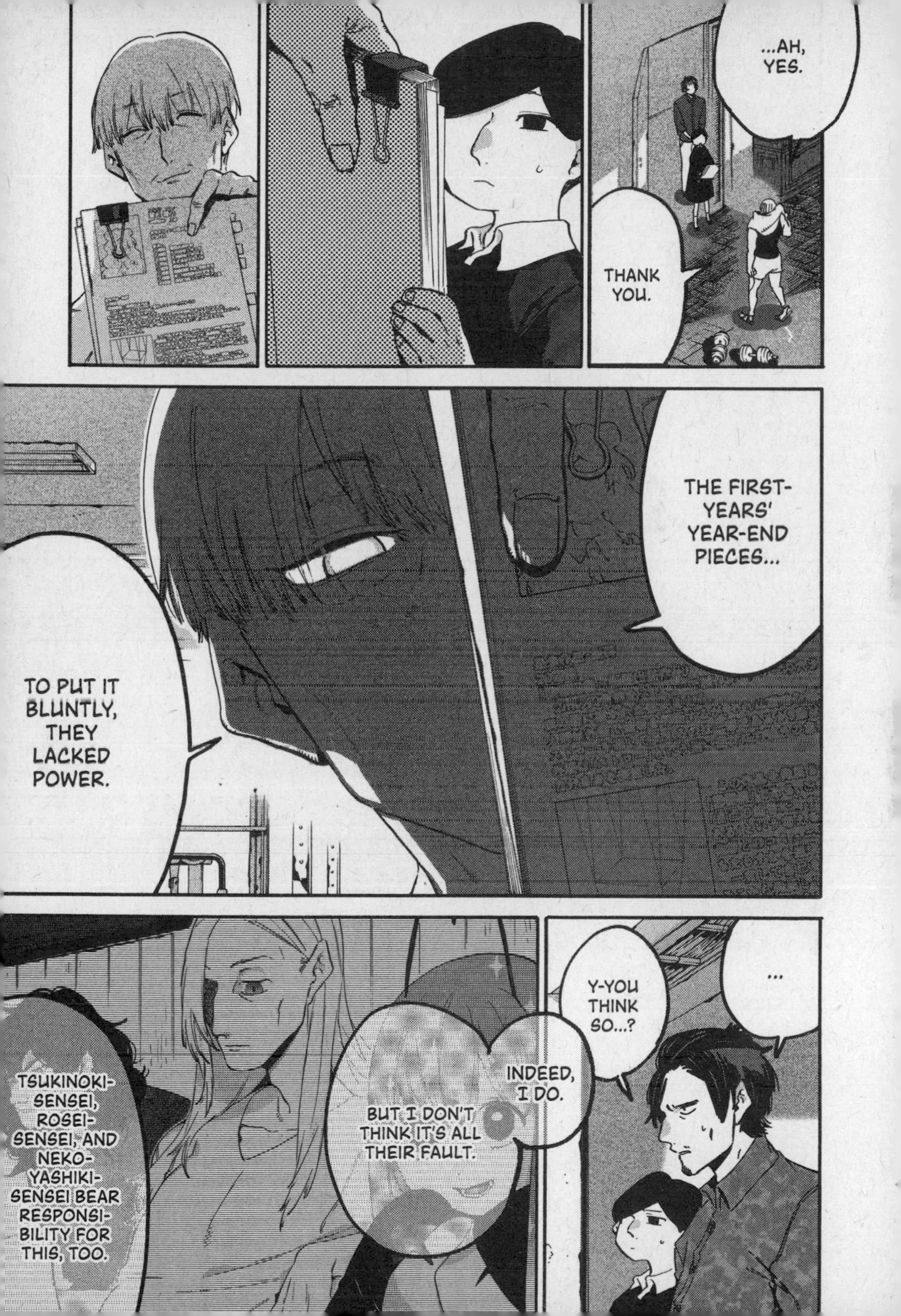
...AH, YES.
THANK YOU.
THE FIRST-YEARS' YEAR-END PIECES...
TO PUT IT BLUNTLY, THEY LACKED POWER.
...
Y-YOU THINK SO...?
INDEED, I DO.
BUT I DON'T THINK IT'S ALL THEIR FAULT.
TSUKINOKI-SENSEI, ROSEI-SENSEI, AND NEKO-YASHIKI-SENSEI BEAR RESPONSI-BILITY FOR THIS, TOO.

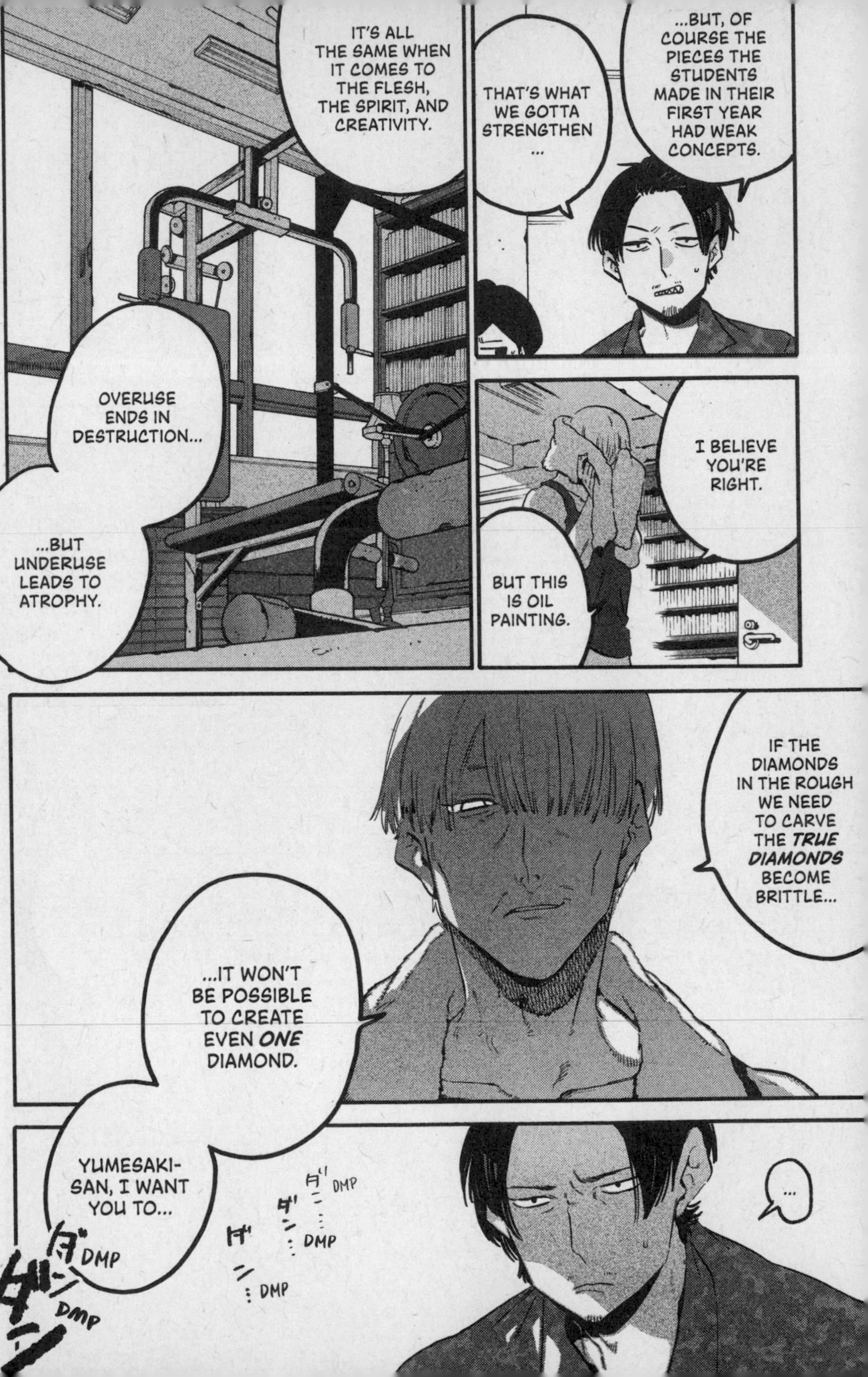
...BUT, OF COURSE THE PIECES THE STUDENTS MADE IN THEIR FIRST YEAR HAD WEAK CONCEPTS.
THAT'S WHAT WE GOTTA STRENGTHEN ...
I BELIEVE YOU'RE RIGHT.
BUT THIS IS OIL PAINTING.
IT'S ALL THE SAME WHEN IT COMES TO THE FLESH, THE SPIRIT, AND CREATIVITY.
OVERUSE ENDS IN DESTRUCTION...
...BUT UNDERUSE LEADS TO ATROPHY.
IF THE DIAMONDS IN THE ROUGH WE NEED TO CARVE THE *TRUE DIAMONDS* BECOME BRITTLE...
...IT WON'T BE POSSIBLE TO CREATE EVEN *ONE* DIAMOND.
...
YUMESAKI-SAN, I WANT YOU TO...
ダ DMP
ダ DMP
ダ DMP
ダ DMP
ダン DMP

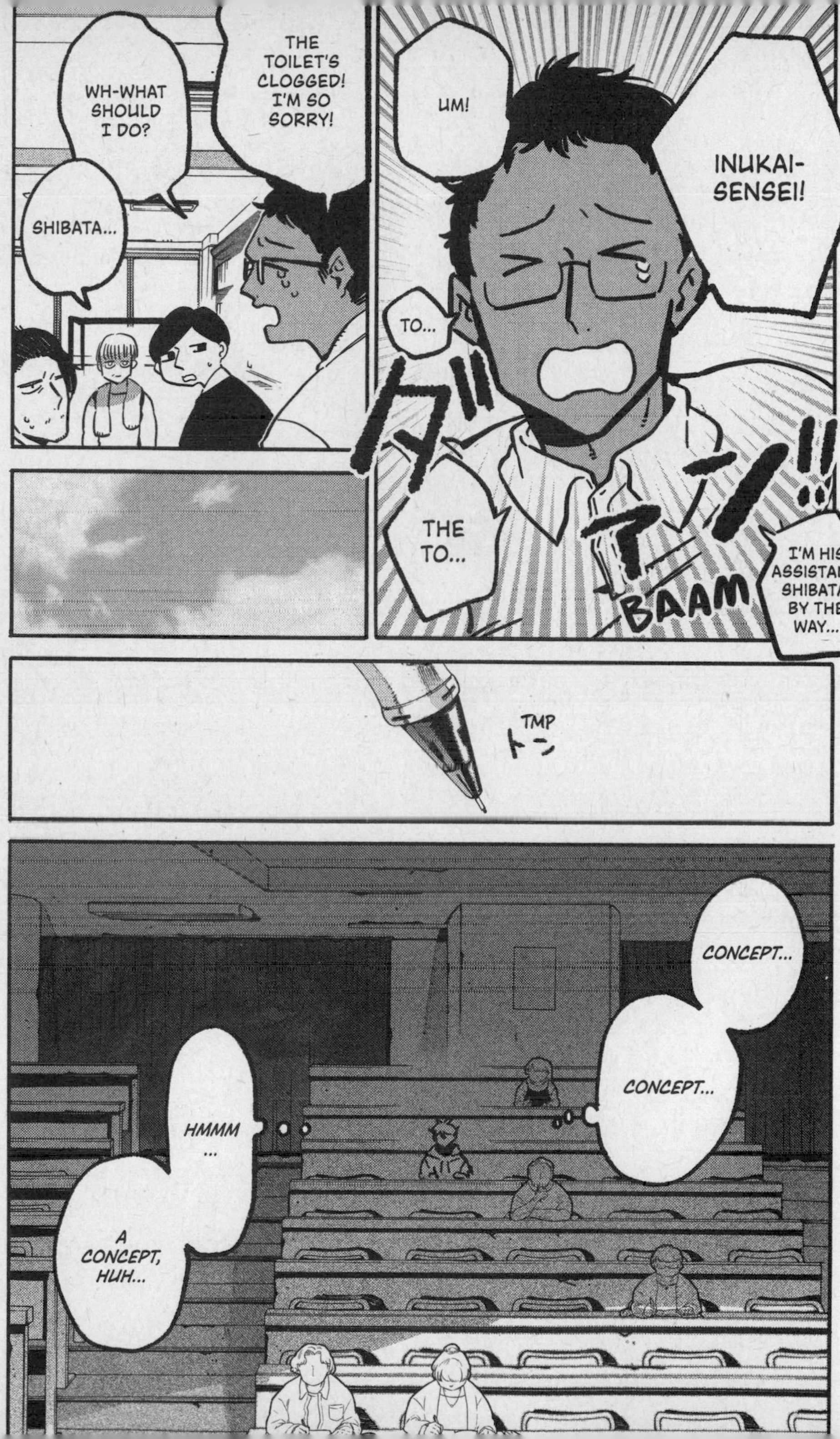
INUKAI-SENSEI!
UM!
TO...
THE TO...
BAAM
I'M HIS ASSISTANT, SHIBATA, BY THE WAY...
THE TOILET'S CLOGGED! I'M SO SORRY!
WH-WHAT SHOULD I DO?
SHIBATA...
TMP
トン
CONCEPT...
CONCEPT...
HMMM...
A CONCEPT, HUH...

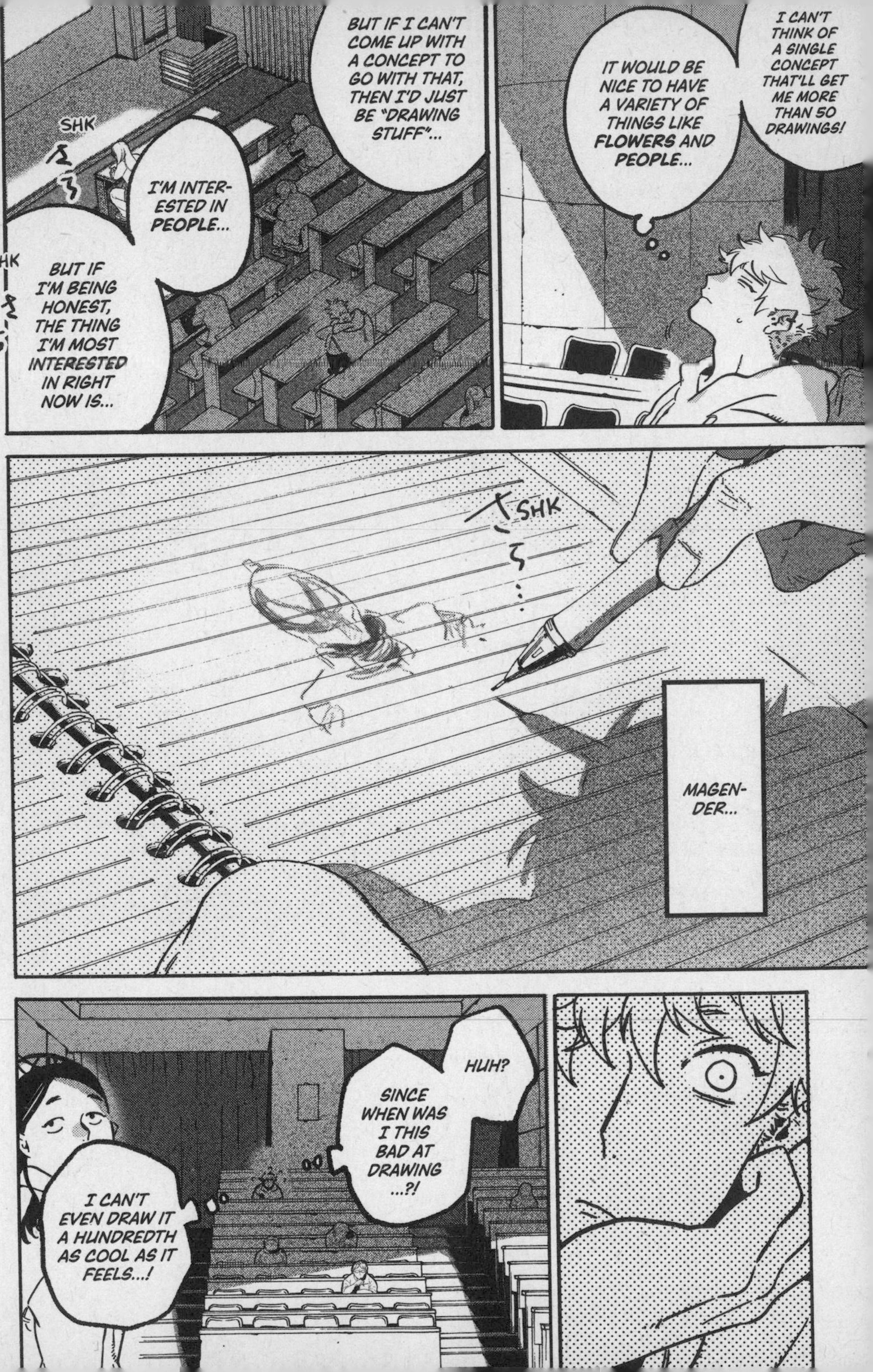
I CAN'T THINK OF A SINGLE CONCEPT THAT'LL GET ME MORE THAN 50 DRAWINGS!
IT WOULD BE NICE TO HAVE A VARIETY OF THINGS LIKE FLOWERS AND PEOPLE...
BUT IF I CAN'T COME UP WITH A CONCEPT TO GO WITH THAT, THEN I'D JUST BE "DRAWING STUFF"...
SHK
I'M INTER-ESTED IN PEOPLE...
SHK
BUT IF I'M BEING HONEST, THE THING I'M MOST INTERESTED IN RIGHT NOW IS...
SHK
MAGEN-DER...
HUH?
SINCE WHEN WAS I THIS BAD AT DRAWING ...?!
I CAN'T EVEN DRAW IT A HUNDREDTH AS COOL AS IT FEELS...!

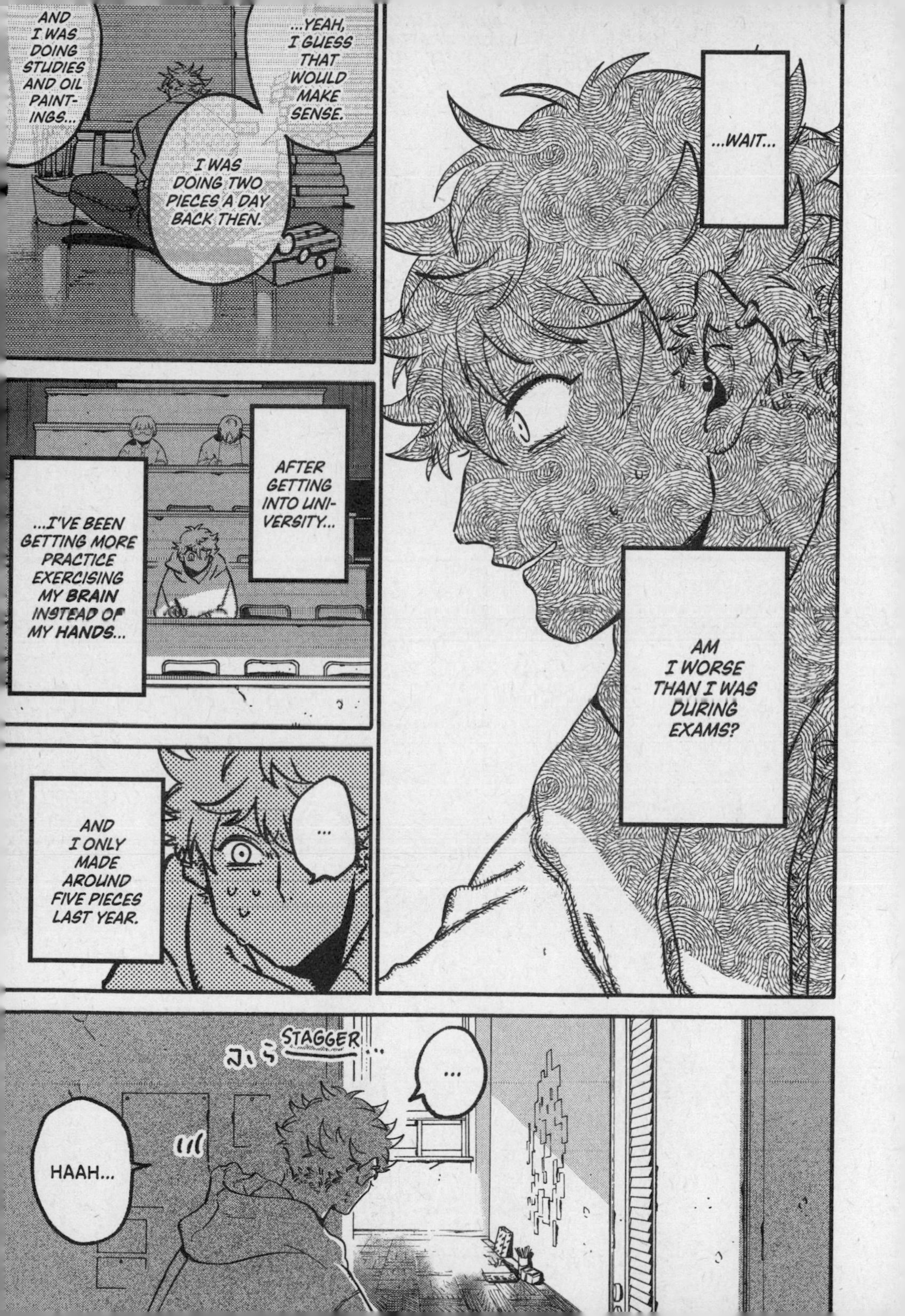
...WAIT...
AM I WORSE THAN I WAS DURING EXAMS?
...YEAH, I GUESS THAT WOULD MAKE SENSE.
AND I WAS DOING STUDIES AND OIL PAINTINGS...
I WAS DOING TWO PIECES A DAY BACK THEN.
AFTER GETTING INTO UNIVERSITY...
...I'VE BEEN GETTING MORE PRACTICE EXERCISING MY BRAIN INSTEAD OF MY HANDS...
...
AND I ONLY MADE AROUND FIVE PIECES LAST YEAR.
...
STAGGER...
ふら
HAAH...

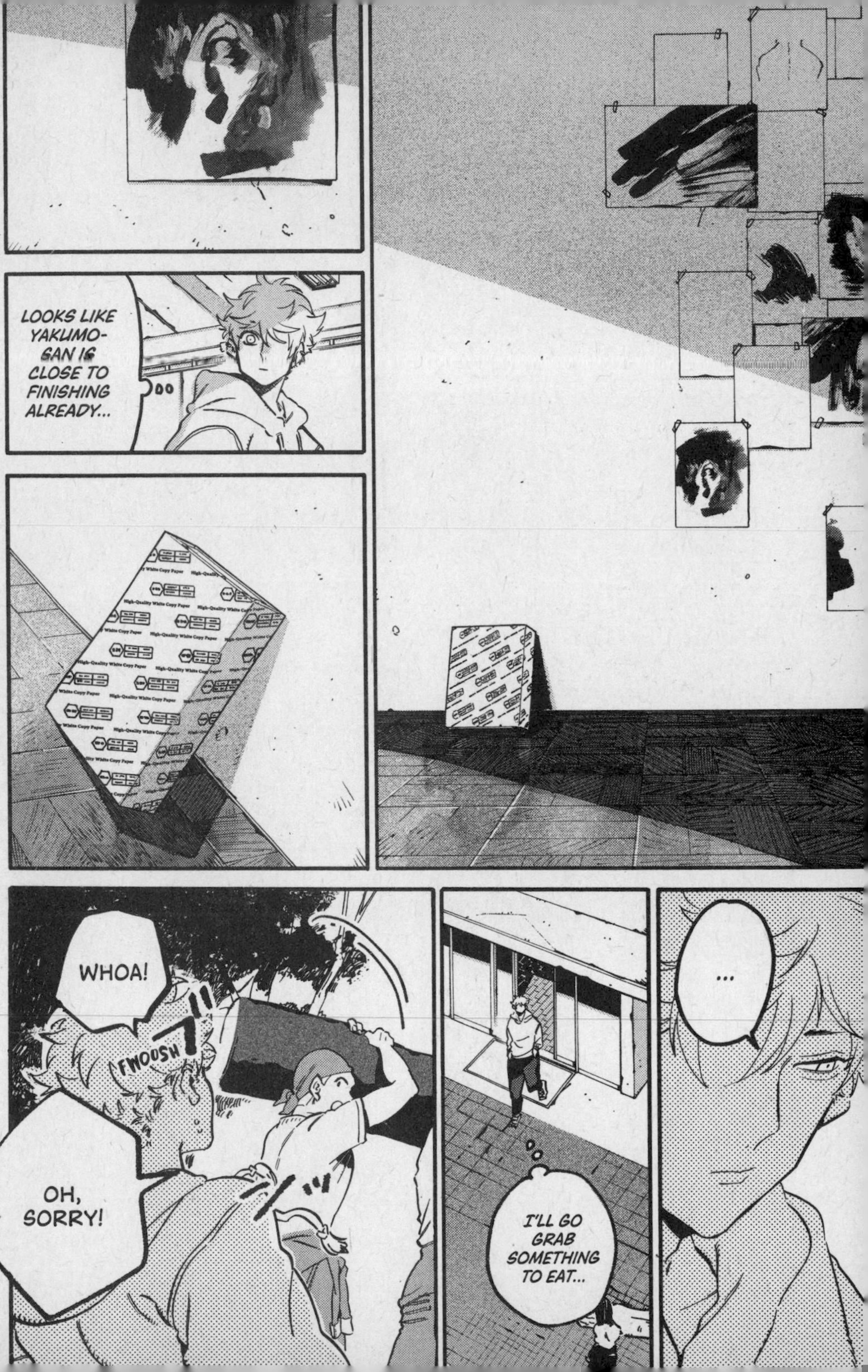
LOOKS LIKE YAKUMO-SAN IS CLOSE TO FINISHING ALREADY...
...
I'LL GO GRAB SOMETHING TO EAT...
WHOA!
FWOOSH
OH, SORRY!

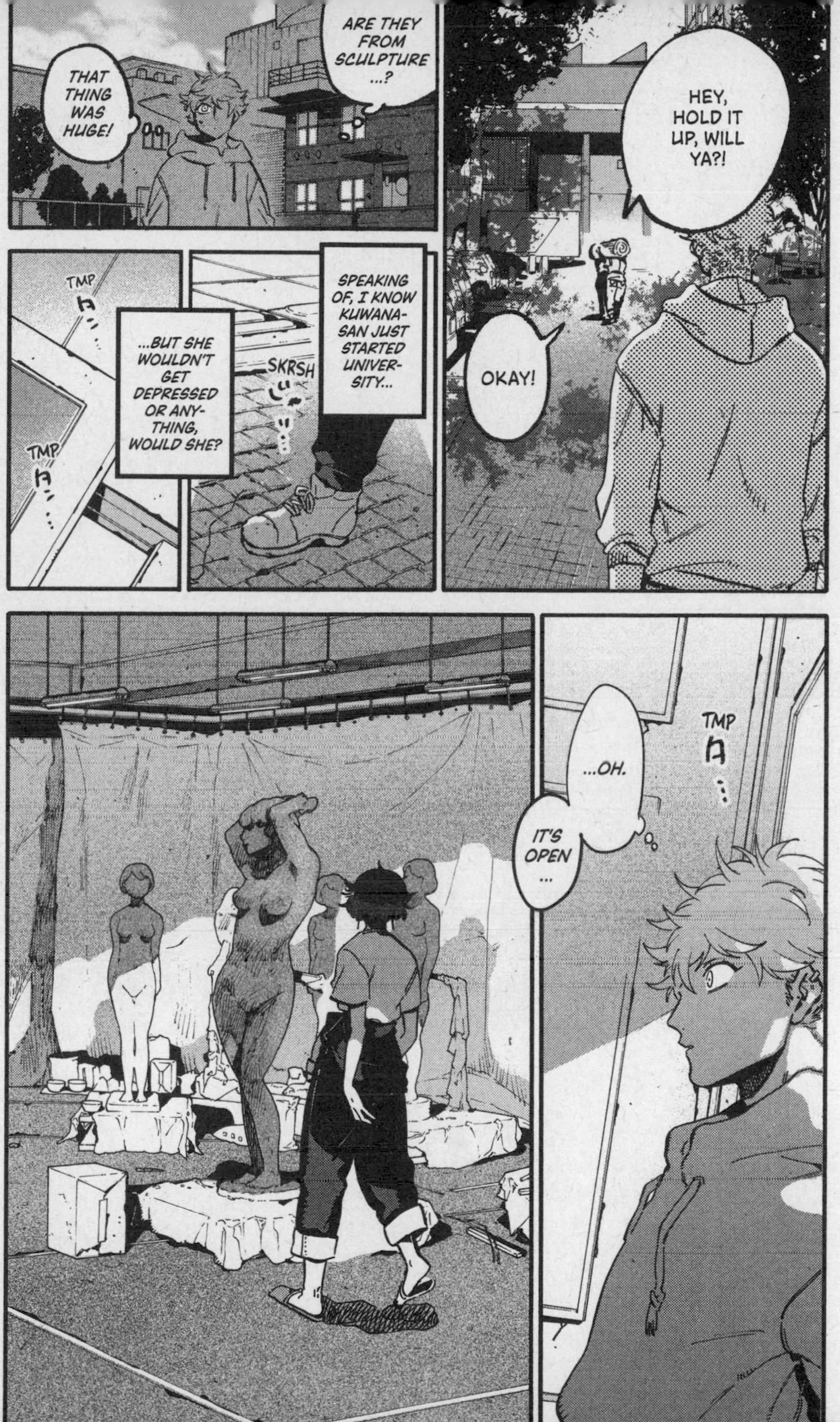
HEY, HOLD IT UP, WILL YA?!
OKAY!
THAT THING WAS HUGE!
ARE THEY FROM SCULPTURE ...?
SPEAKING OF, I KNOW KUWANA-SAN JUST STARTED UNIVER-SITY...
SKRSH
...BUT SHE WOULDN'T GET DEPRESSED OR ANY-THING, WOULD SHE?
TMP
TMP
TMP
...OH.
IT'S OPEN ...

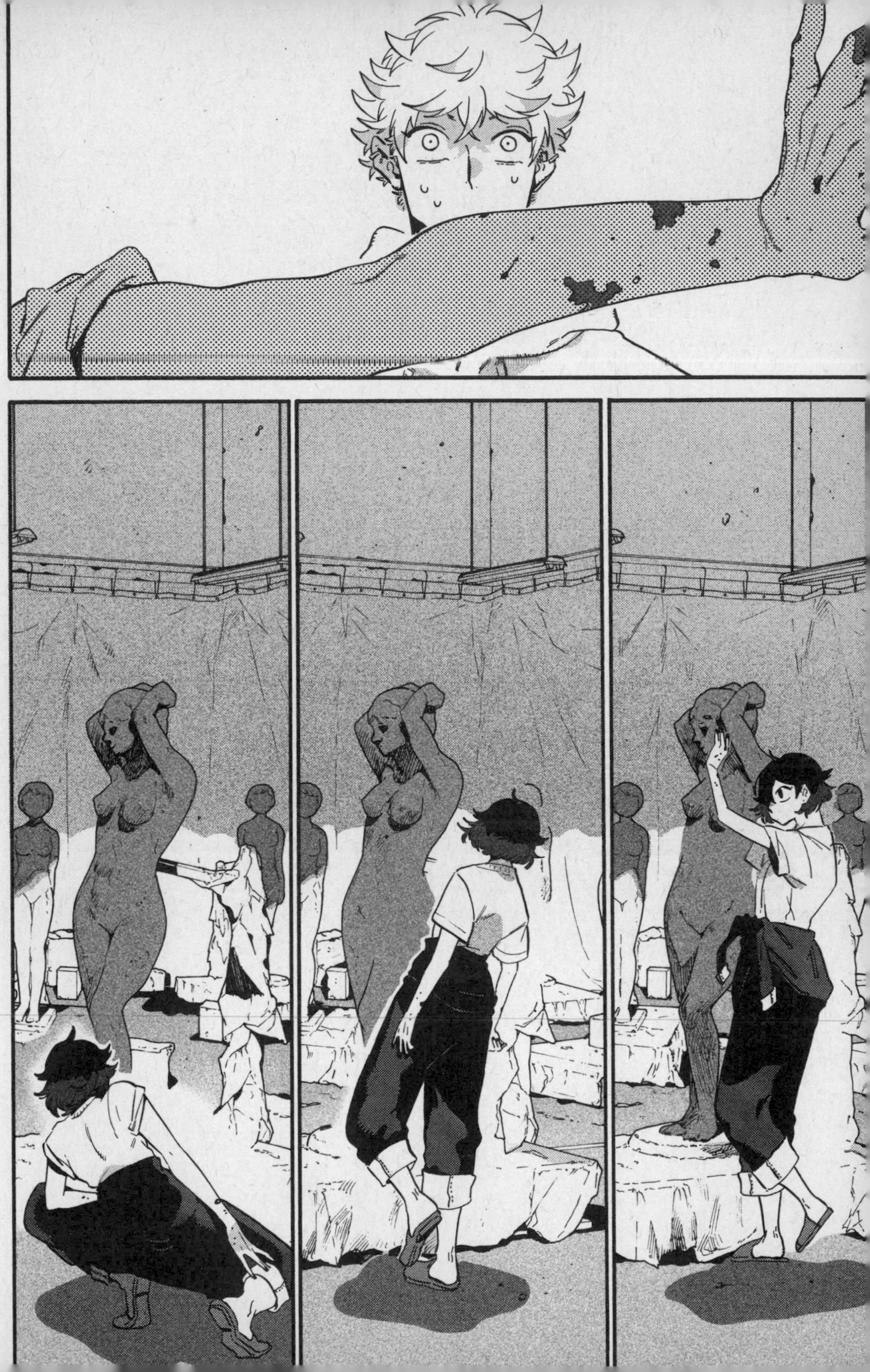

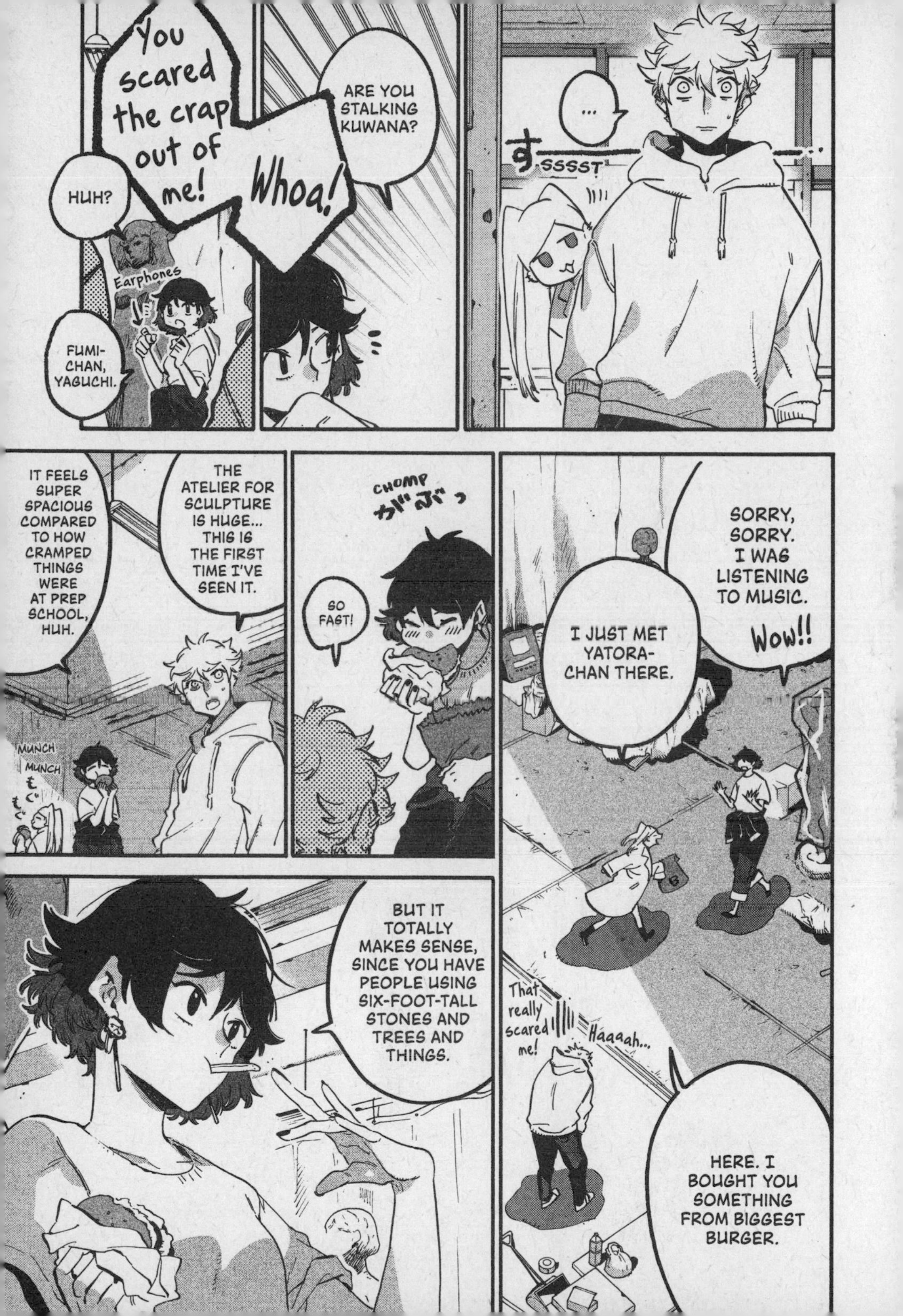
...
す SSSST
ARE YOU STALKING KUWANA?
Whoa!
You scared the crap out of me!
HUH?
Earphones
FUMI-CHAN, YAGUCHI.
SORRY, SORRY. I WAS LISTENING TO MUSIC.
Wow!!
I JUST MET YATORA-CHAN THERE.
That really scared me!
Haaaah...
HERE. I BOUGHT YOU SOMETHING FROM BIGGEST BURGER.
CHOMP がぶっ
SO FAST!
THE ATELIER FOR SCULPTURE IS HUGE... THIS IS THE FIRST TIME I'VE SEEN IT.
IT FEELS SUPER SPACIOUS COMPARED TO HOW CRAMPED THINGS WERE AT PREP SCHOOL, HUH.
MUNCH MUNCH もぐもぐ
BUT IT TOTALLY MAKES SENSE, SINCE YOU HAVE PEOPLE USING SIX-FOOT-TALL STONES AND TREES AND THINGS.

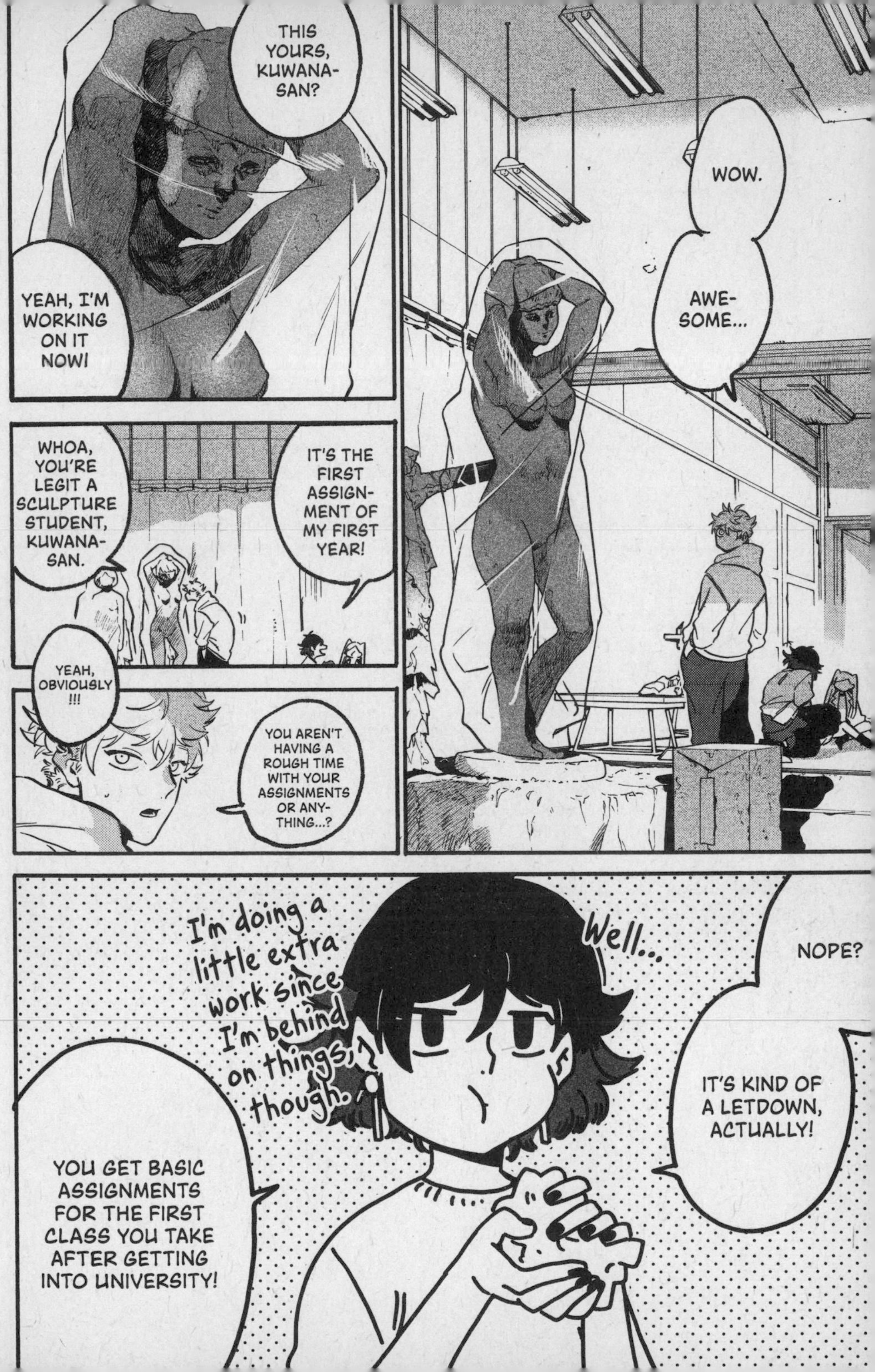
WOW.
AWE-SOME...
THIS YOURS, KUWANA-SAN?
YEAH, I'M WORKING ON IT NOW!
IT'S THE FIRST ASSIGN-MENT OF MY FIRST YEAR!
WHOA, YOU'RE LEGIT A SCULPTURE STUDENT, KUWANA-SAN.
YEAH, OBVIOUSLY!!!
YOU AREN'T HAVING A ROUGH TIME WITH YOUR ASSIGNMENTS OR ANY-THING...?
NOPE?
IT'S KIND OF A LETDOWN, ACTUALLY!
Well...
I'm doing a little extra work since I'm behind on things, though.
YOU GET BASIC ASSIGNMENTS FOR THE FIRST CLASS YOU TAKE AFTER GETTING INTO UNIVERSITY!

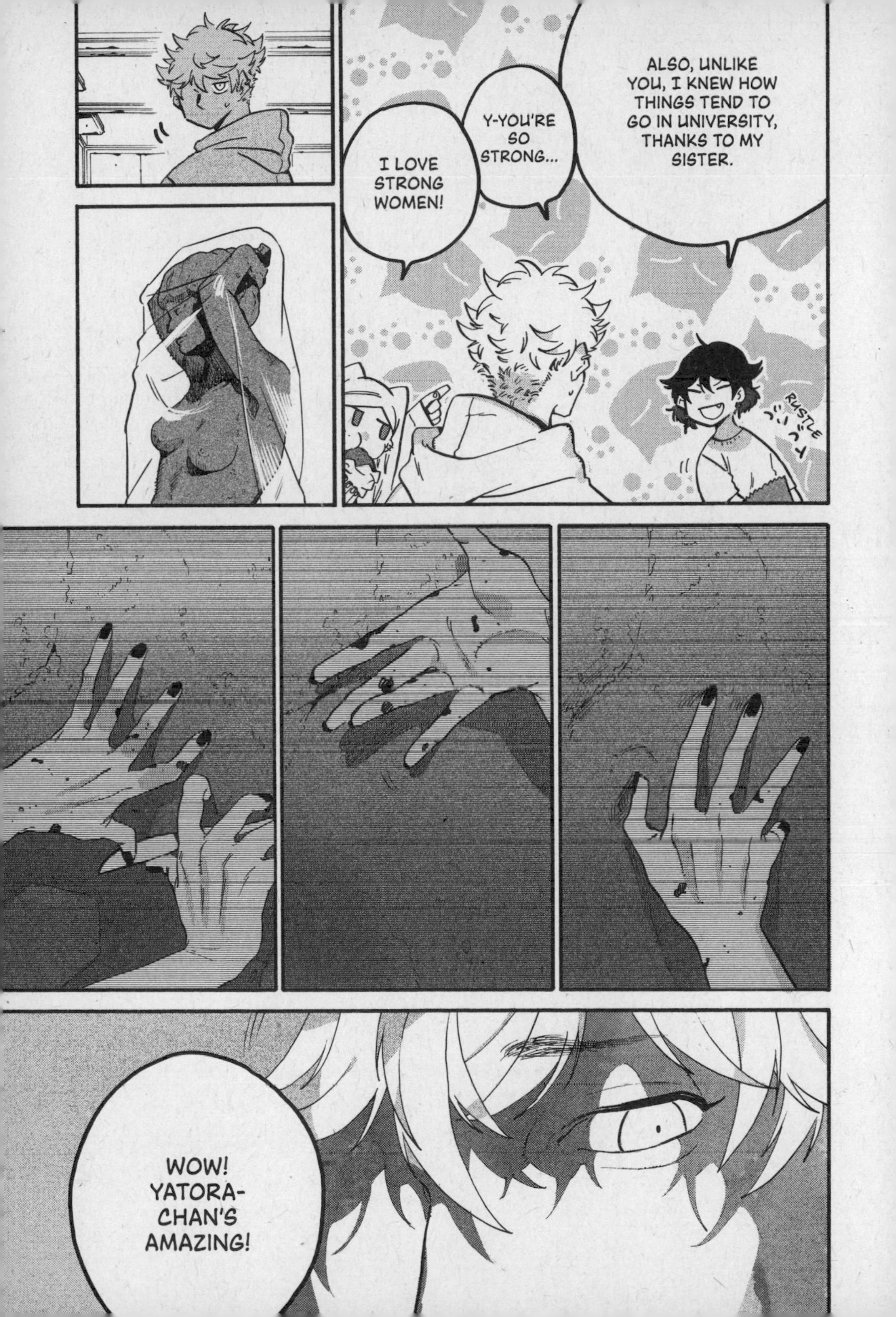
ALSO, UNLIKE YOU, I KNEW HOW THINGS TEND TO GO IN UNIVERSITY, THANKS TO MY SISTER.
Y-YOU'RE SO STRONG...
I LOVE STRONG WOMEN!
RUSTLE
WOW! YATORA-CHAN'S AMAZING!

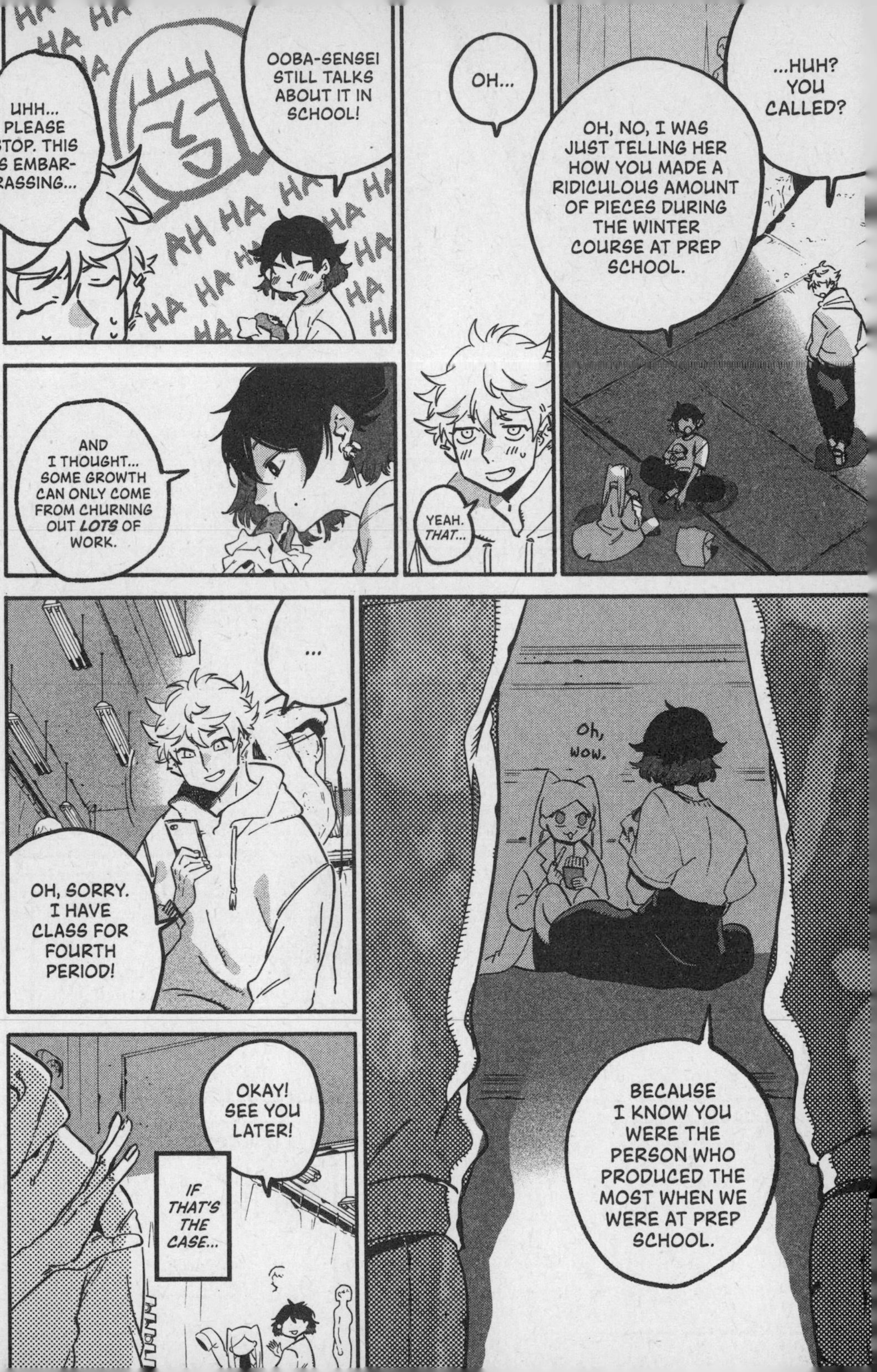
...HUH? YOU CALLED?
OH, NO, I WAS JUST TELLING HER HOW YOU MADE A RIDICULOUS AMOUNT OF PIECES DURING THE WINTER COURSE AT PREP SCHOOL.
OH...
YEAH. *THAT*...
OOBA-SENSEI STILL TALKS ABOUT IT IN SCHOOL!
UHH... PLEASE STOP. THIS IS EMBARRASSING...
HA HA HA HA AH HA HA HA HA HA HA HA HA HA
AND I THOUGHT... SOME GROWTH CAN ONLY COME FROM CHURNING OUT *LOTS* OF WORK.
Oh, wow.
BECAUSE I KNOW YOU WERE THE PERSON WHO PRODUCED THE MOST WHEN WE WERE AT PREP SCHOOL.
...
OH, SORRY. I HAVE CLASS FOR FOURTH PERIOD!
OKAY! SEE YOU LATER!
IF THAT'S THE CASE...

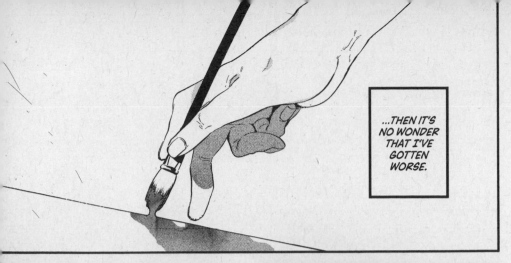

...THEN IT'S NO WONDER THAT I'VE GOTTEN WORSE.

BECAUSE I HAVEN'T BEEN MAKING ART.

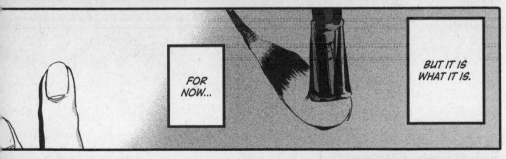

FOR NOW...

BUT IT IS WHAT IT IS.

HEY!

...500 DRAW-INGS.

...SO I CAN MAKE...

I HAVE TO THINK OF SOME-THING...

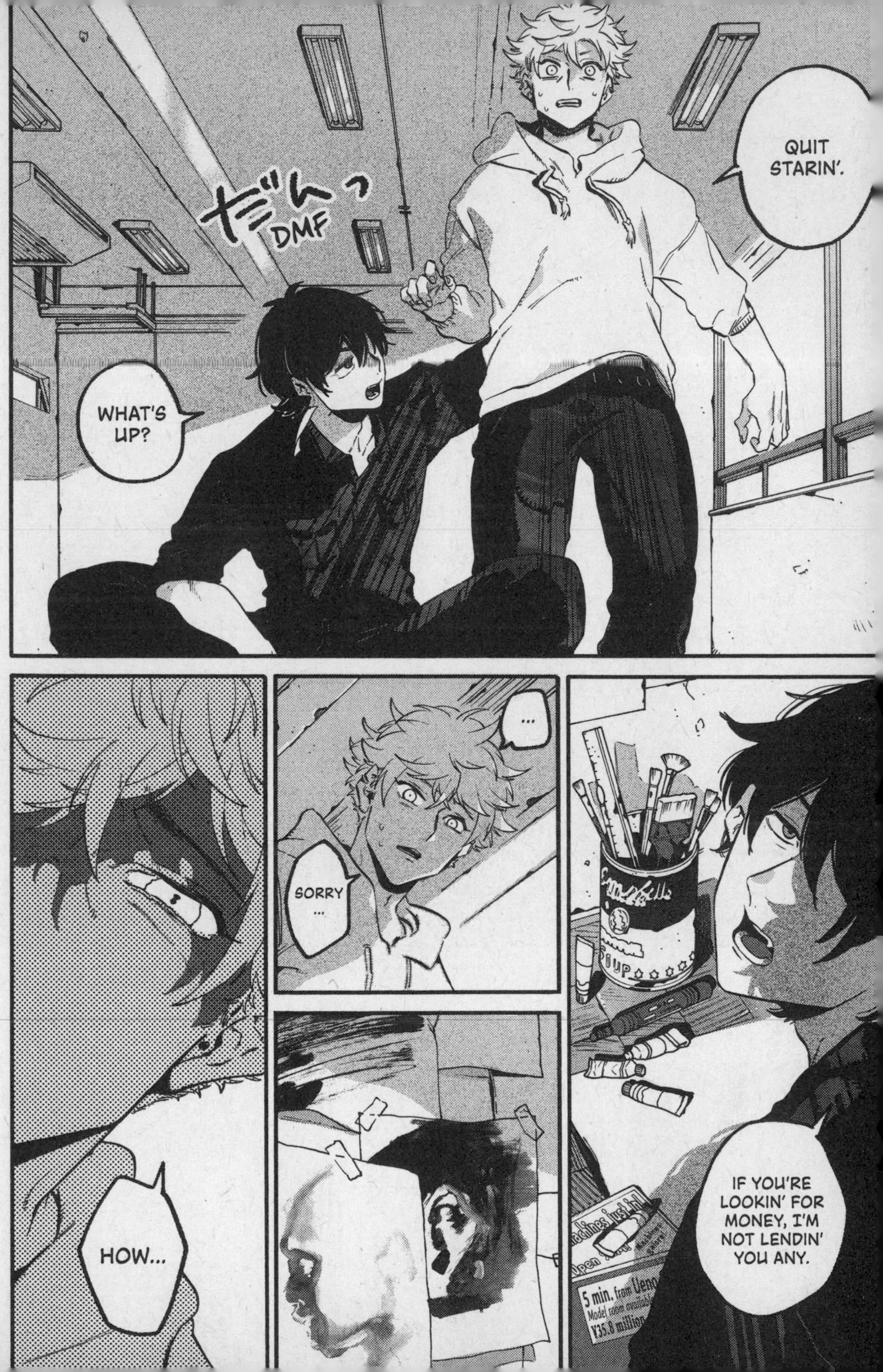
QUIT STARIN'.
だんっ
DMF
WHAT'S UP?
IF YOU'RE LOOKIN' FOR MONEY, I'M NOT LENDIN' YOU ANY.
...
SORRY ...
HOW...

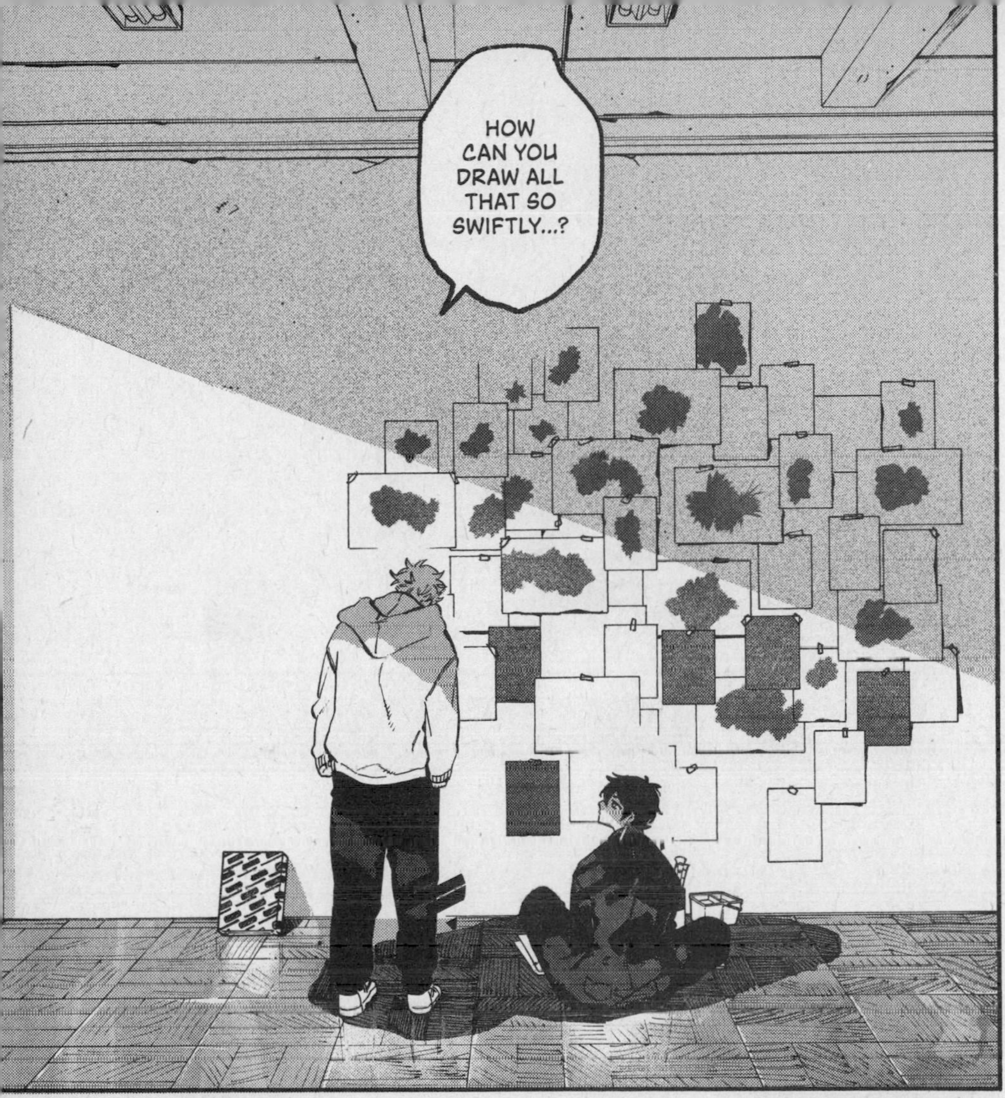
HOW CAN YOU DRAW ALL THAT SO SWIFTLY...?
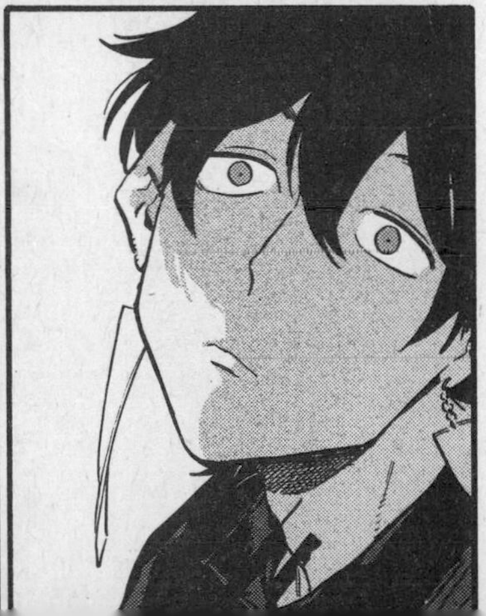
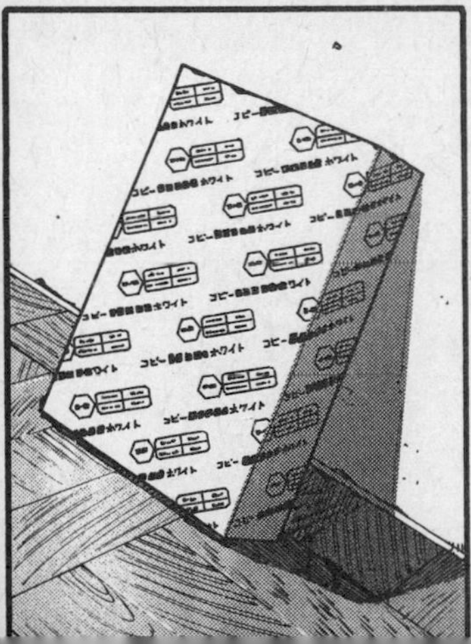
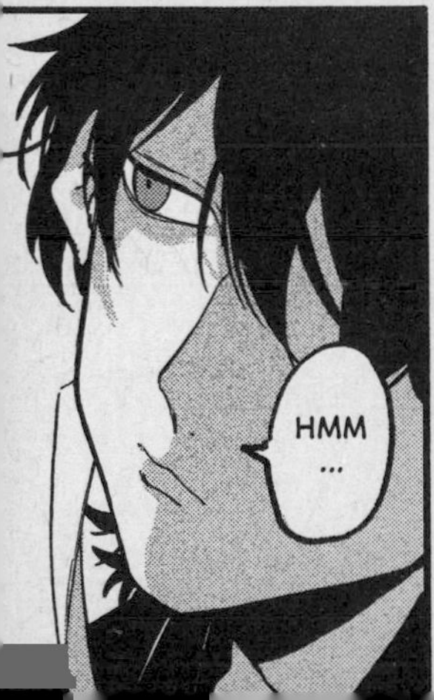
HMM ...

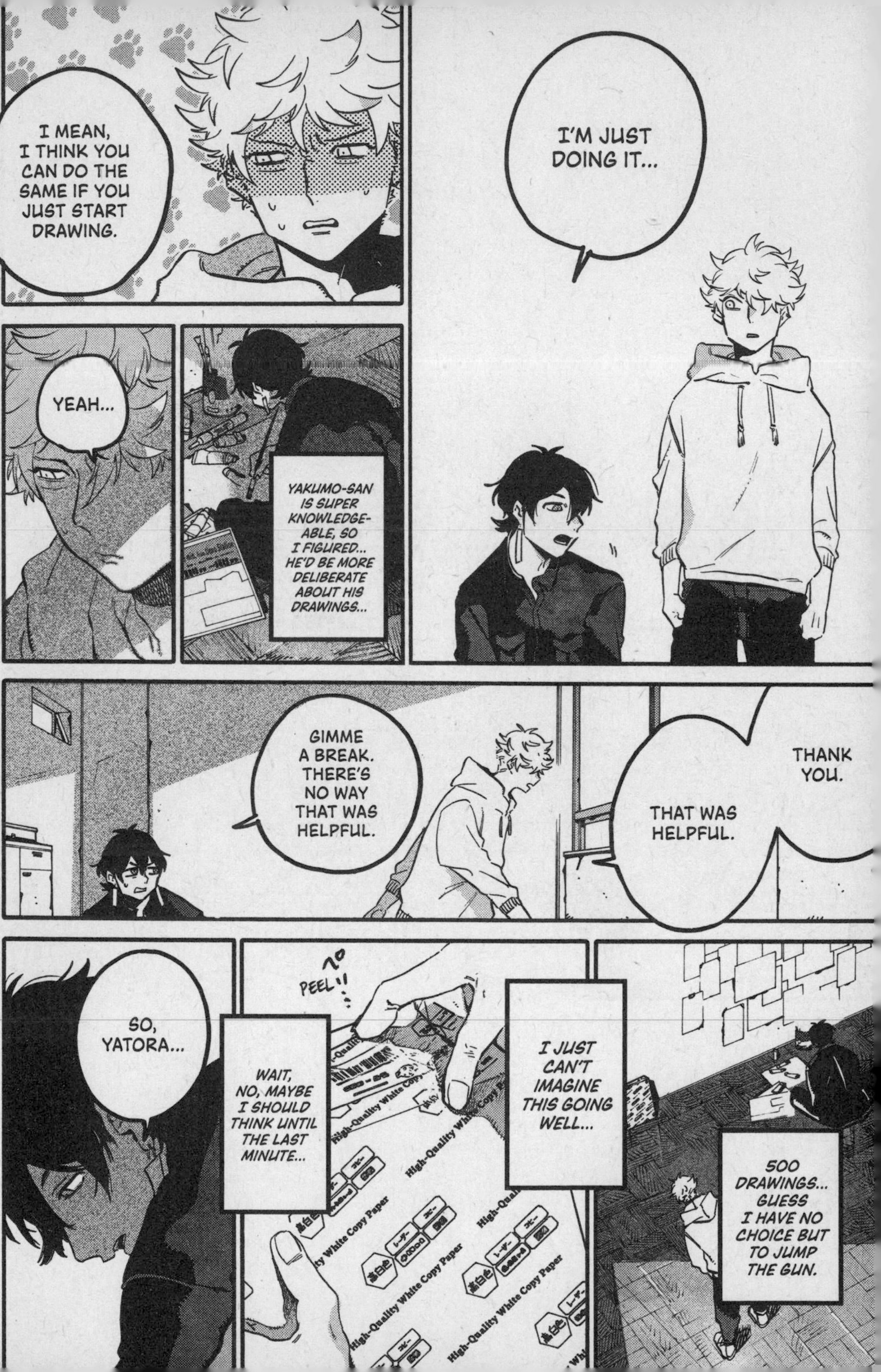
I'M JUST DOING IT...
I MEAN, I THINK YOU CAN DO THE SAME IF YOU JUST START DRAWING.
YAKUMO-SAN IS SUPER KNOWLEDGE-ABLE, SO I FIGURED... HE'D BE MORE DELIBERATE ABOUT HIS DRAWINGS...
YEAH...
THANK YOU.
THAT WAS HELPFUL.
GIMME A BREAK. THERE'S NO WAY THAT WAS HELPFUL.
500 DRAWINGS... GUESS I HAVE NO CHOICE BUT TO JUMP THE GUN.
I JUST CAN'T IMAGINE THIS GOING WELL...
PEEL
WAIT, NO, MAYBE I SHOULD THINK UNTIL THE LAST MINUTE...
High-Quality White Copy Paper
SO, YATORA...

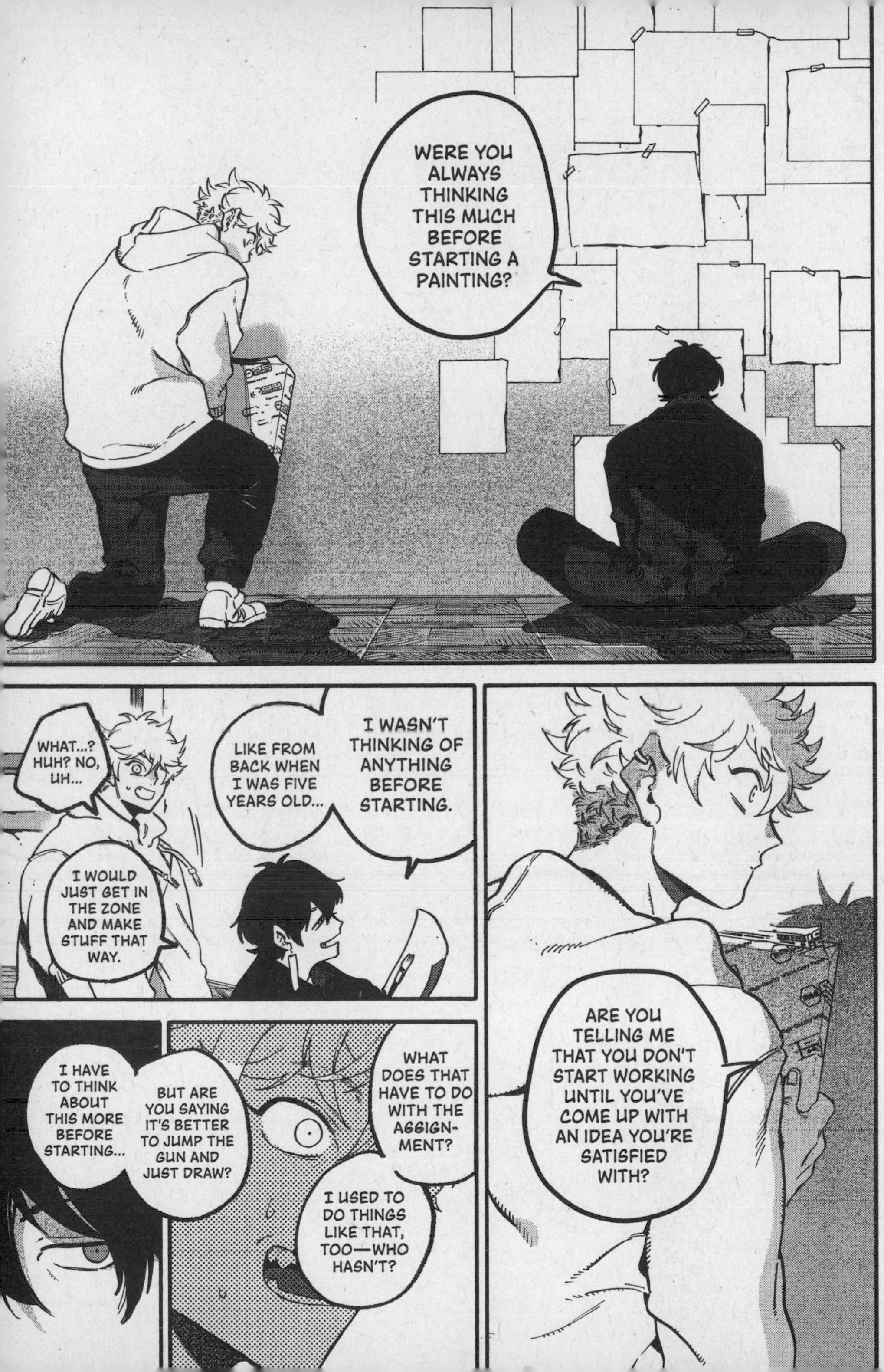
WERE YOU ALWAYS THINKING THIS MUCH BEFORE STARTING A PAINTING?
ARE YOU TELLING ME THAT YOU DON'T START WORKING UNTIL YOU'VE COME UP WITH AN IDEA YOU'RE SATISFIED WITH?
I WASN'T THINKING OF ANYTHING BEFORE STARTING.
LIKE FROM BACK WHEN I WAS FIVE YEARS OLD...
WHAT...? HUH? NO, UH...
I WOULD JUST GET IN THE ZONE AND MAKE STUFF THAT WAY.
WHAT DOES THAT HAVE TO DO WITH THE ASSIGN-MENT?
BUT ARE YOU SAYING IT'S BETTER TO JUMP THE GUN AND JUST DRAW?
I USED TO DO THINGS LIKE THAT, TOO—WHO HASN'T?
I HAVE TO THINK ABOUT THIS MORE BEFORE STARTING...

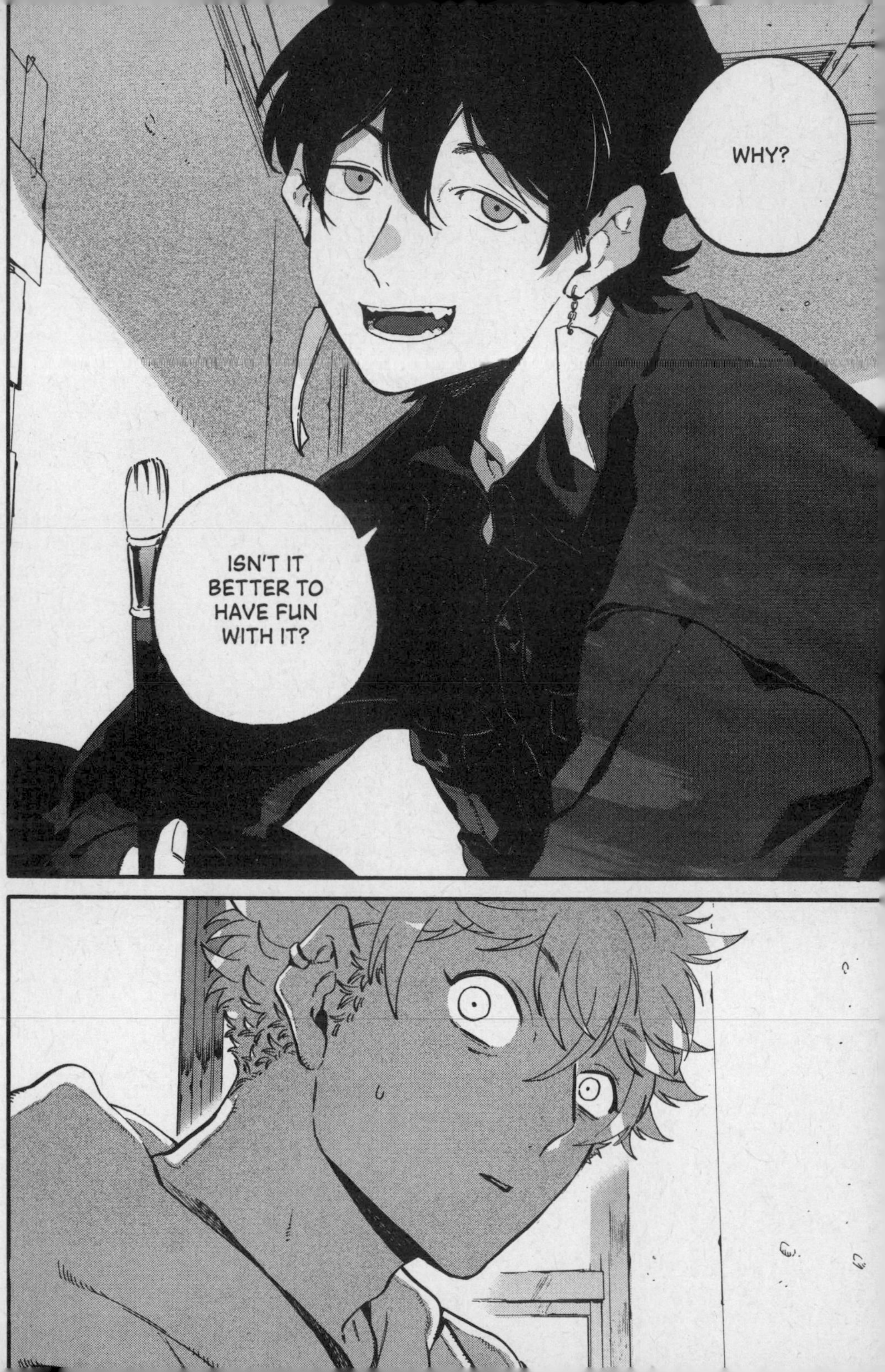
WHY?
ISN'T IT BETTER TO HAVE FUN WITH IT?

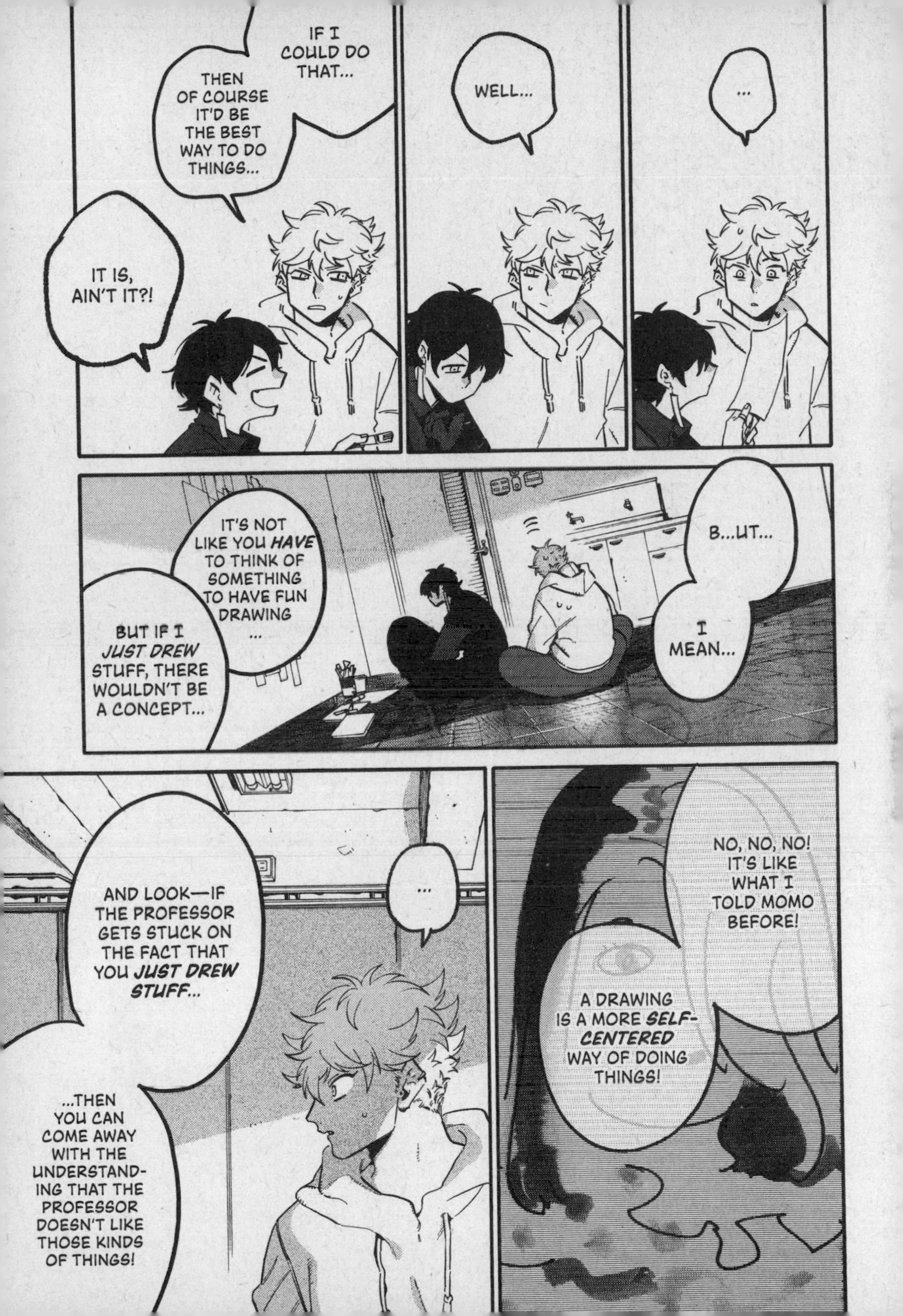
...
WELL...
IF I COULD DO THAT...
THEN OF COURSE IT'D BE THE BEST WAY TO DO THINGS...
IT IS, AIN'T IT?!
B...UT...
I MEAN...
IT'S NOT LIKE YOU *HAVE* TO THINK OF SOMETHING TO HAVE FUN DRAWING...
BUT IF I *JUST DREW* STUFF, THERE WOULDN'T BE A CONCEPT...
NO, NO, NO! IT'S LIKE WHAT I TOLD MOMO BEFORE!
A DRAWING IS A MORE ***SELF-CENTERED*** WAY OF DOING THINGS!
...
AND LOOK—IF THE PROFESSOR GETS STUCK ON THE FACT THAT YOU ***JUST DREW STUFF***...
...THEN YOU CAN COME AWAY WITH THE UNDERSTANDING THAT THE PROFESSOR DOESN'T LIKE THOSE KINDS OF THINGS!

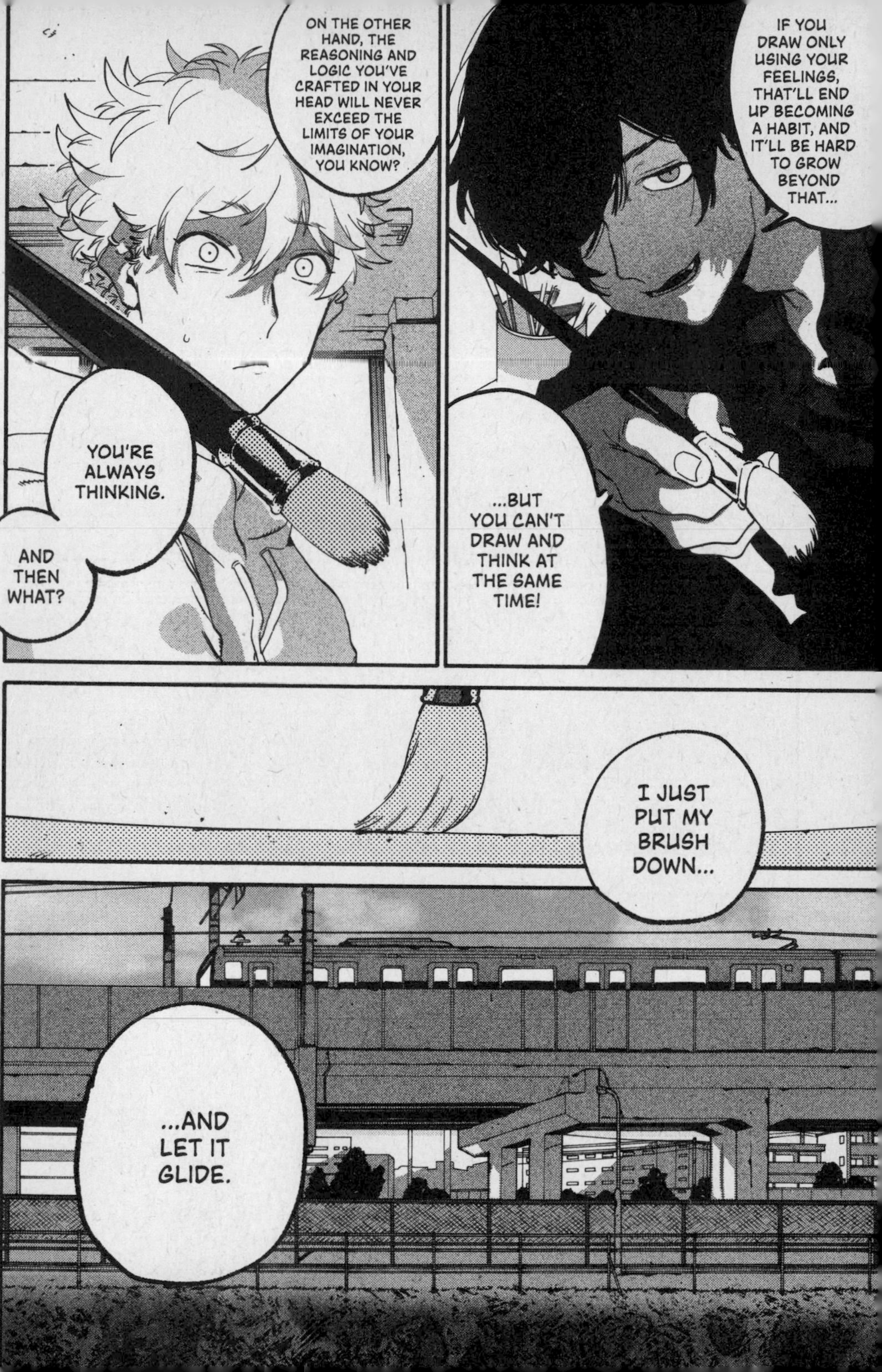
IF YOU DRAW ONLY USING YOUR FEELINGS, THAT'LL END UP BECOMING A HABIT, AND IT'LL BE HARD TO GROW BEYOND THAT...
...BUT YOU CAN'T DRAW AND THINK AT THE SAME TIME!
ON THE OTHER HAND, THE REASONING AND LOGIC YOU'VE CRAFTED IN YOUR HEAD WILL NEVER EXCEED THE LIMITS OF YOUR IMAGINATION, YOU KNOW?
YOU'RE ALWAYS THINKING.
AND THEN WHAT?
I JUST PUT MY BRUSH DOWN...
...AND LET IT GLIDE.

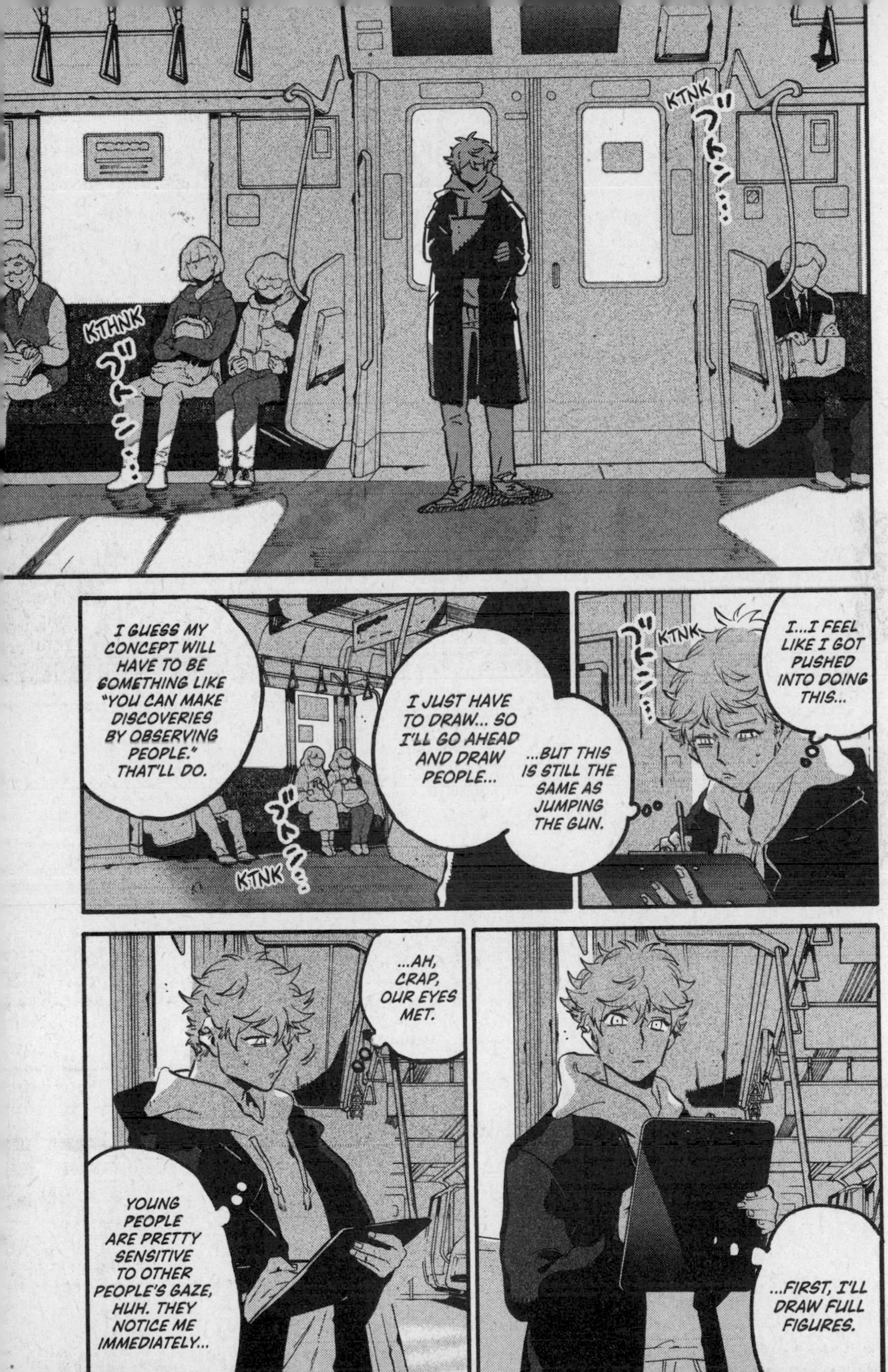

KTNK
KTHNK
KTNK
I...I FEEL LIKE I GOT PUSHED INTO DOING THIS...
I JUST HAVE TO DRAW... SO I'LL GO AHEAD AND DRAW PEOPLE...
...BUT THIS IS STILL THE SAME AS JUMPING THE GUN.
I GUESS MY CONCEPT WILL HAVE TO BE SOMETHING LIKE "YOU CAN MAKE DISCOVERIES BY OBSERVING PEOPLE." THAT'LL DO.
KTNK
...FIRST, I'LL DRAW FULL FIGURES.
...AH, CRAP, OUR EYES MET.
YOUNG PEOPLE ARE PRETTY SENSITIVE TO OTHER PEOPLE'S GAZE, HUH. THEY NOTICE ME IMMEDIATELY...

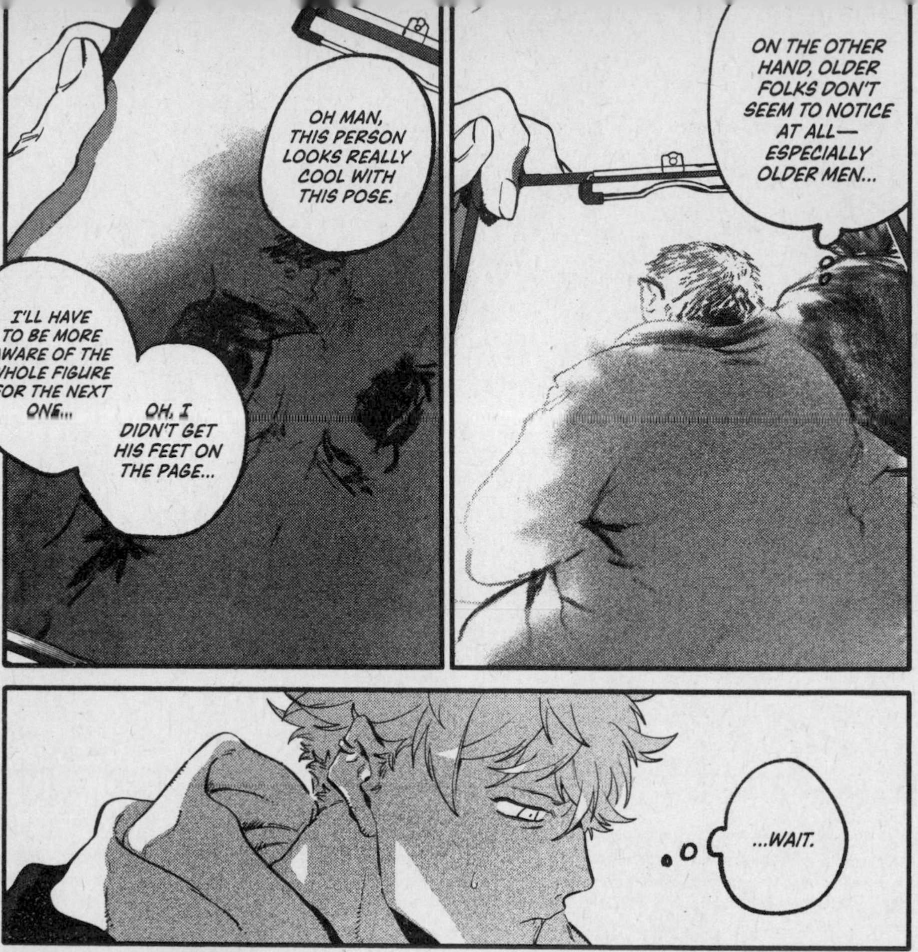
ON THE OTHER HAND, OLDER FOLKS DON'T SEEM TO NOTICE AT ALL— ESPECIALLY OLDER MEN...
OH MAN, THIS PERSON LOOKS REALLY COOL WITH THIS POSE.
OH, I DIDN'T GET HIS FEET ON THE PAGE...
I'LL HAVE TO BE MORE AWARE OF THE WHOLE FIGURE FOR THE NEXT ONE...
...WAIT.

ART: TAMANA MOTEKI

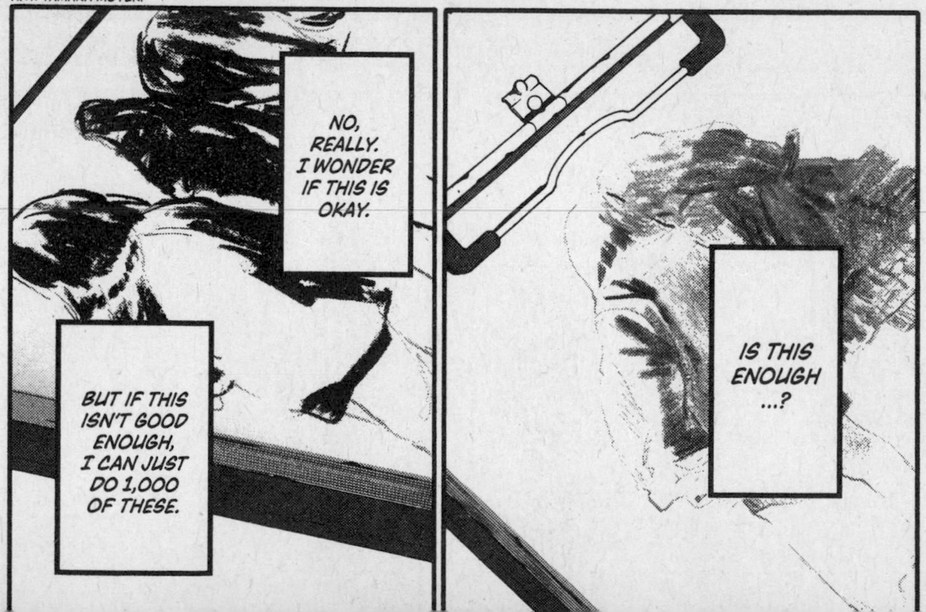
IS THIS ENOUGH ...?
NO, REALLY. I WONDER IF THIS IS OKAY.
BUT IF THIS ISN'T GOOD ENOUGH, I CAN JUST DO 1,000 OF THESE.

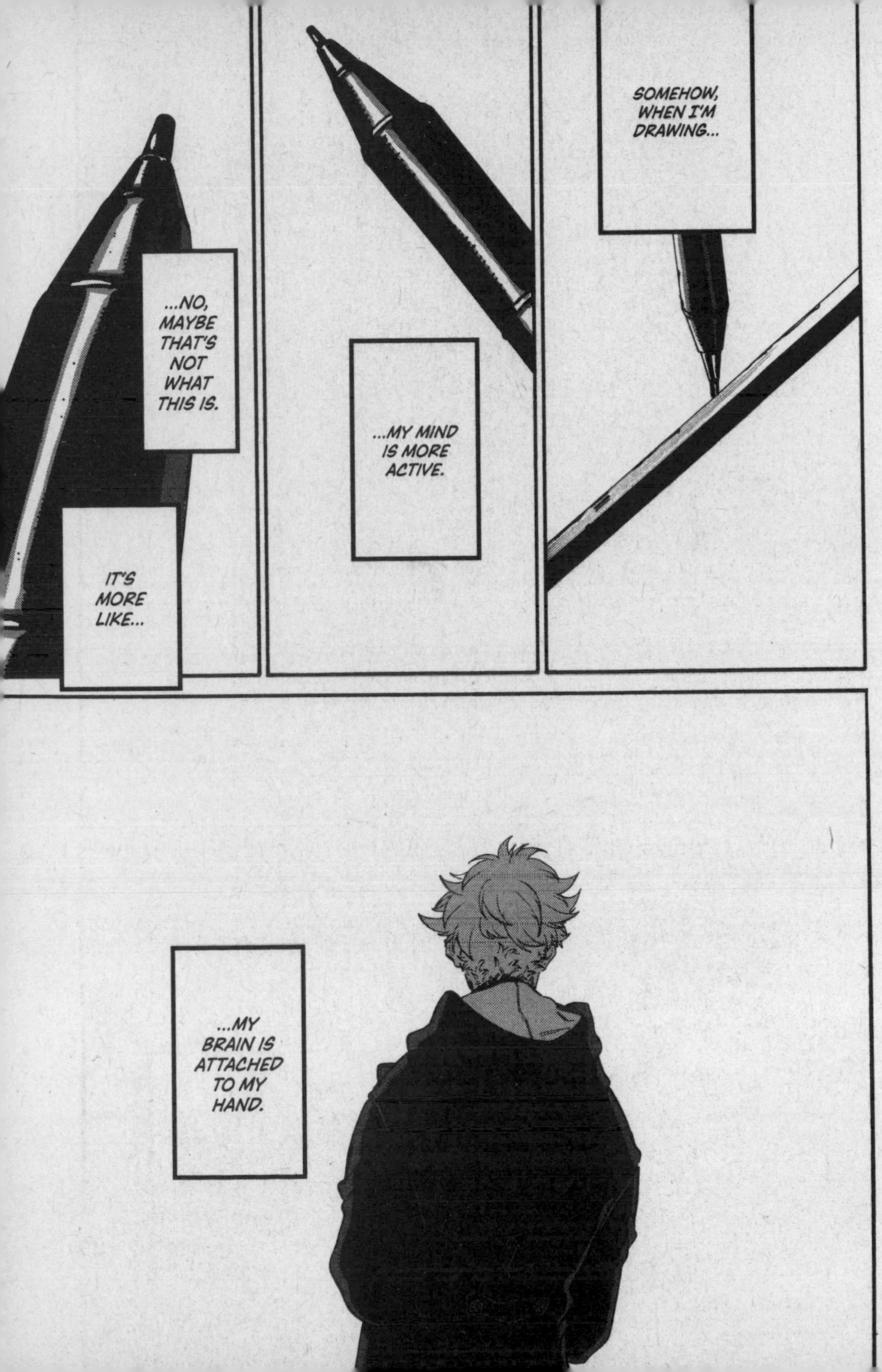
SOMEHOW, WHEN I'M DRAWING...
...MY MIND IS MORE ACTIVE.
...NO, MAYBE THAT'S NOT WHAT THIS IS.
IT'S MORE LIKE...
...MY BRAIN IS ATTACHED TO MY HAND.

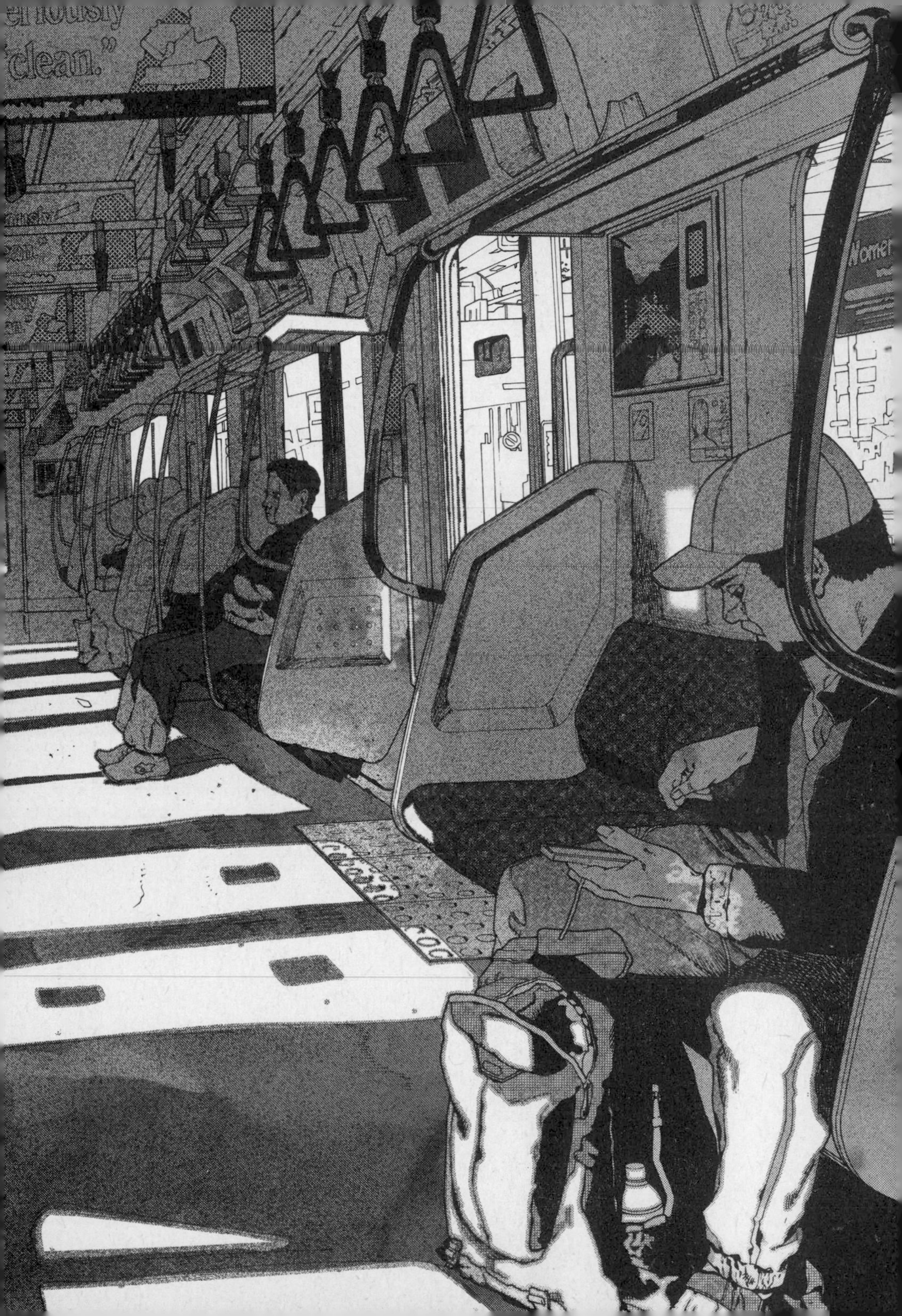
"clean."

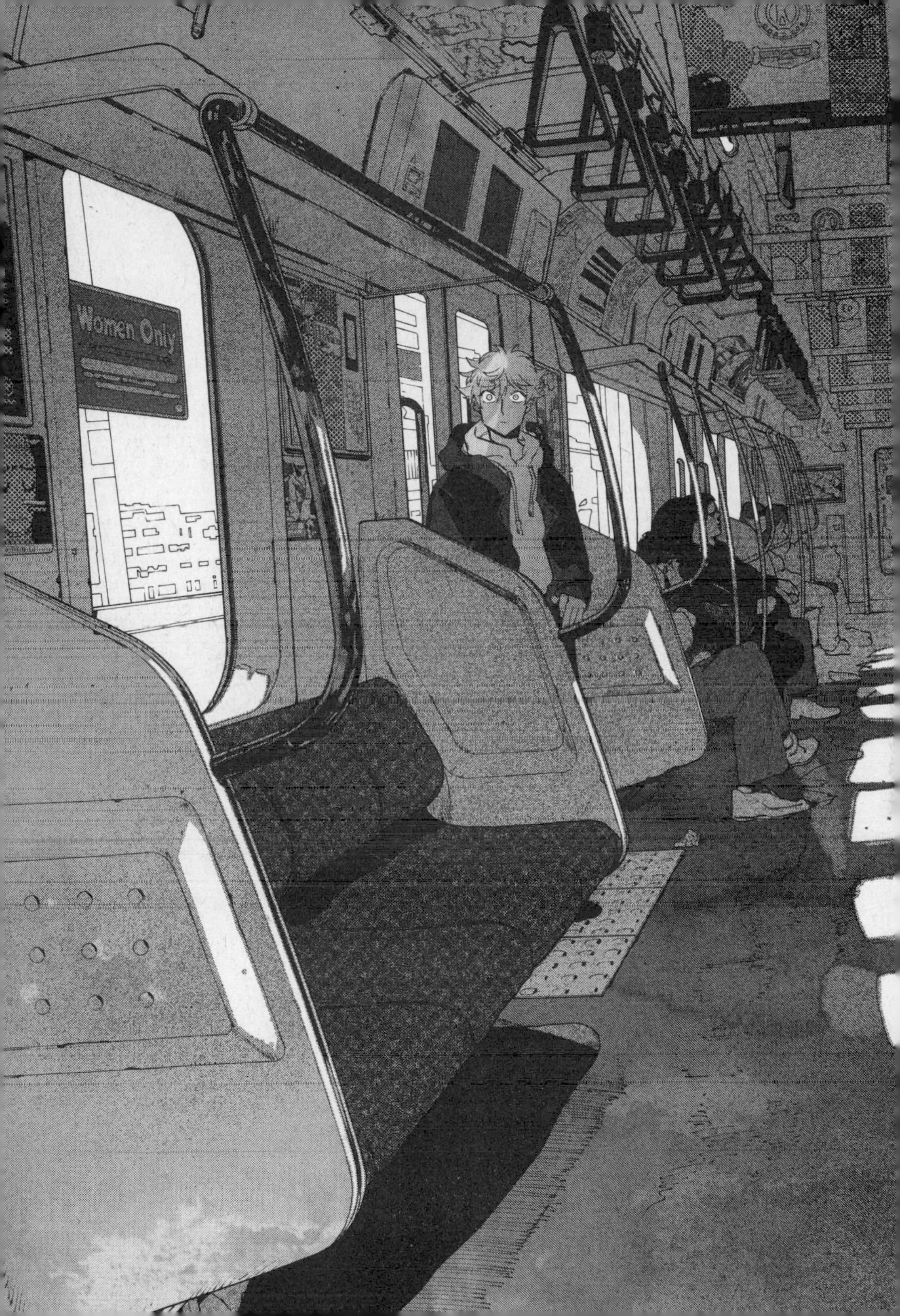
Women Only

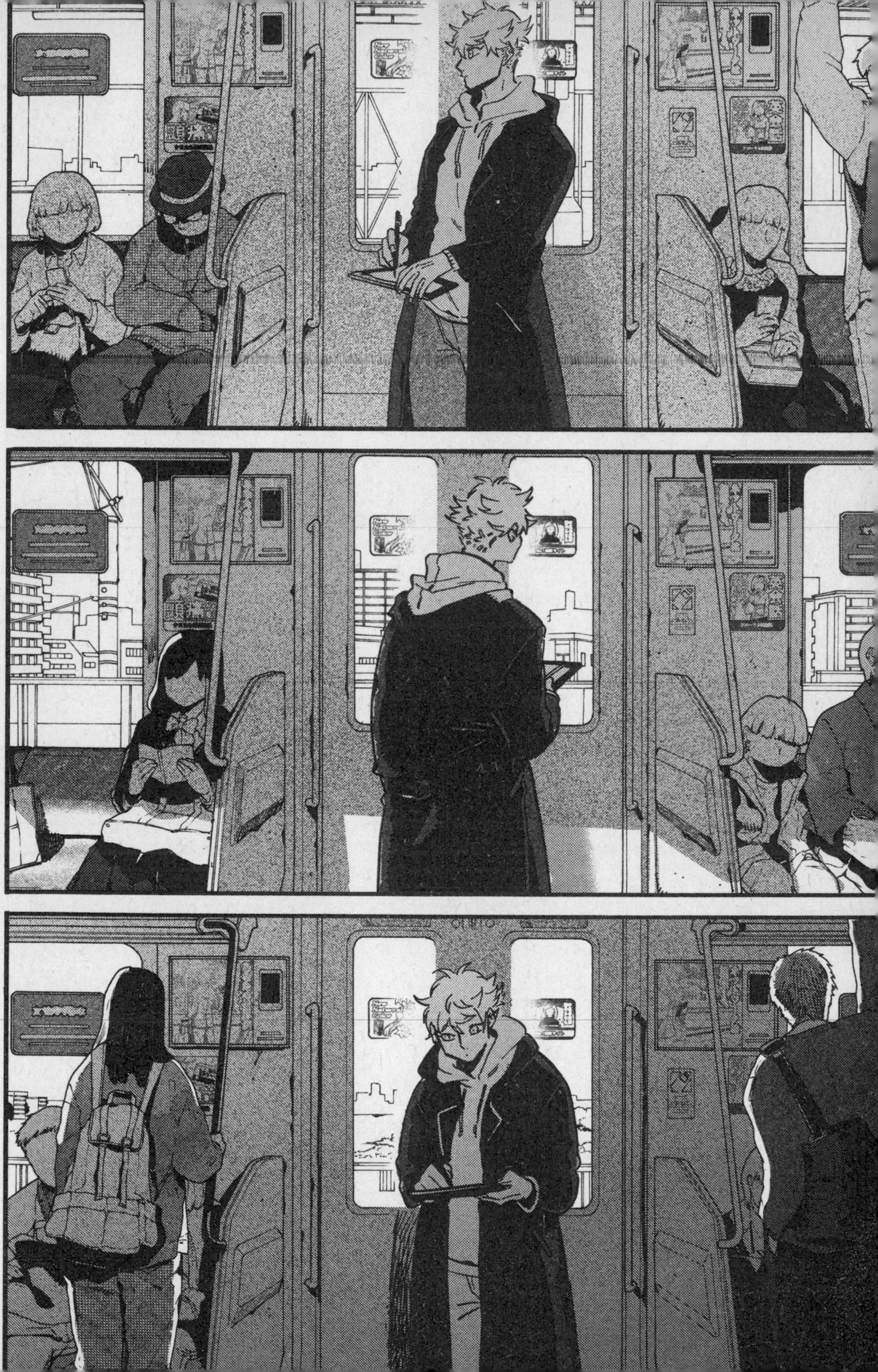

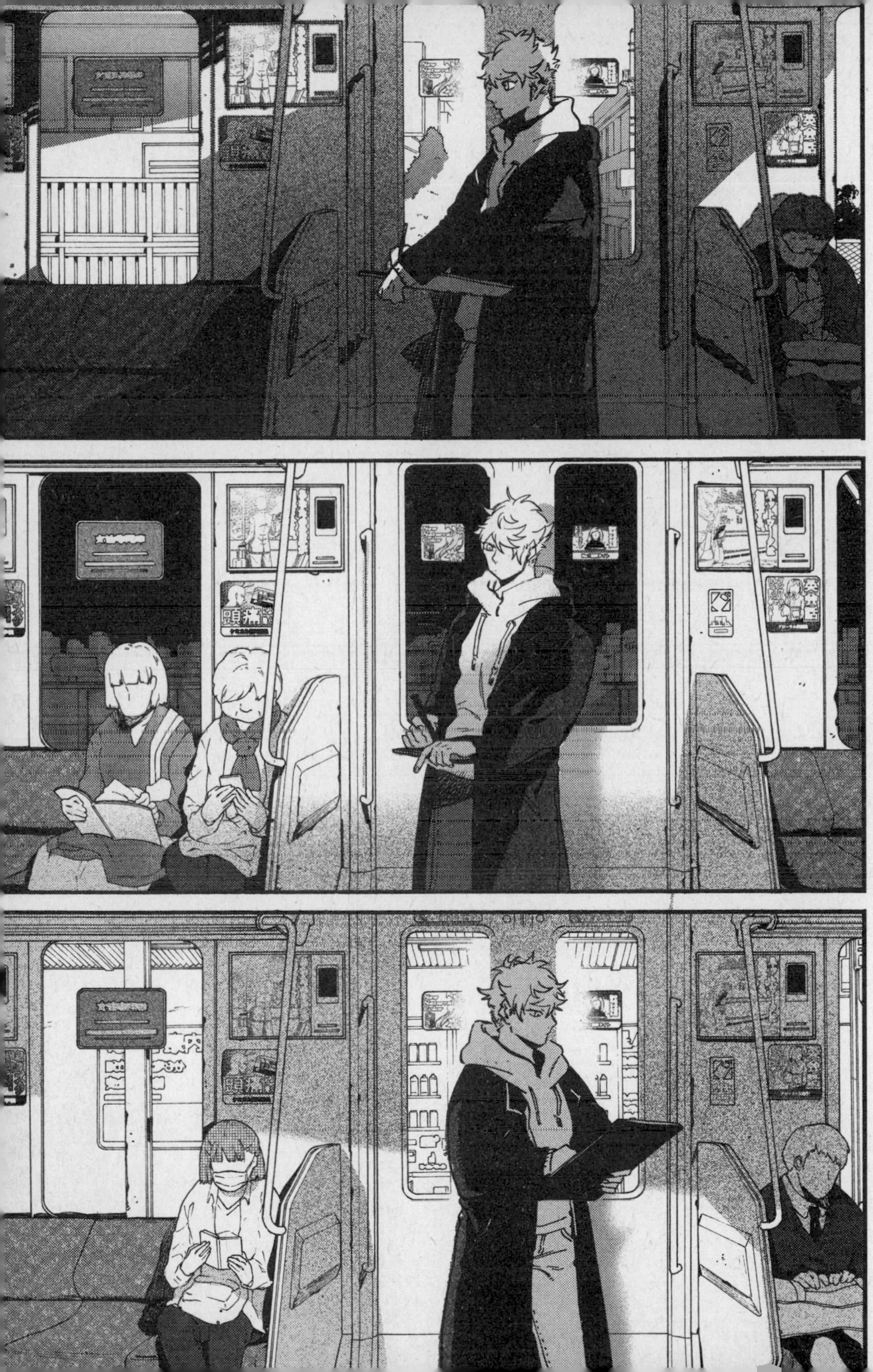

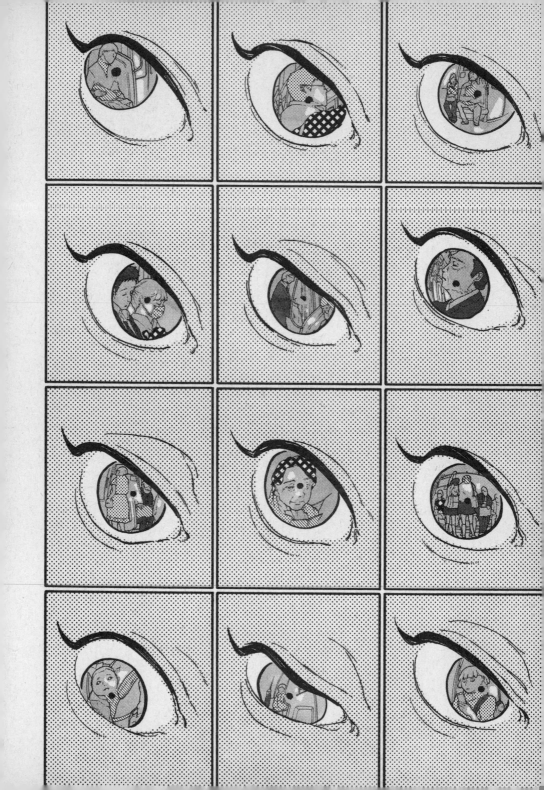

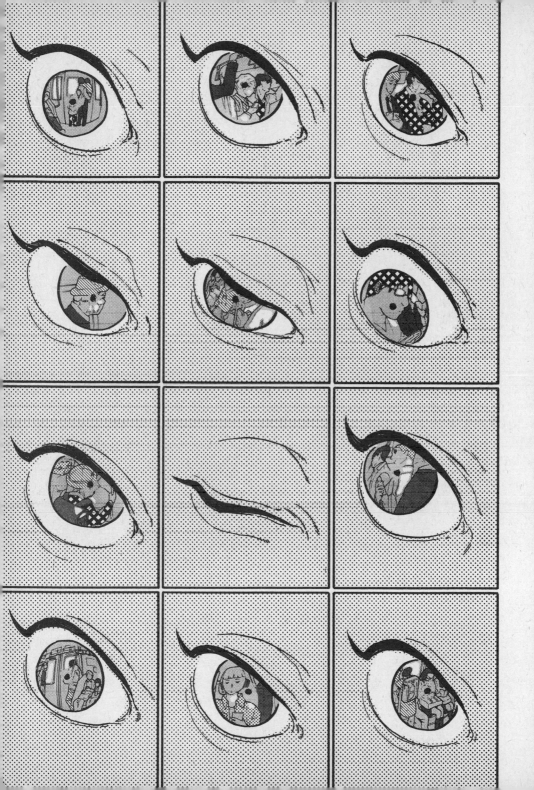

ART: TAMANA MOTEKI

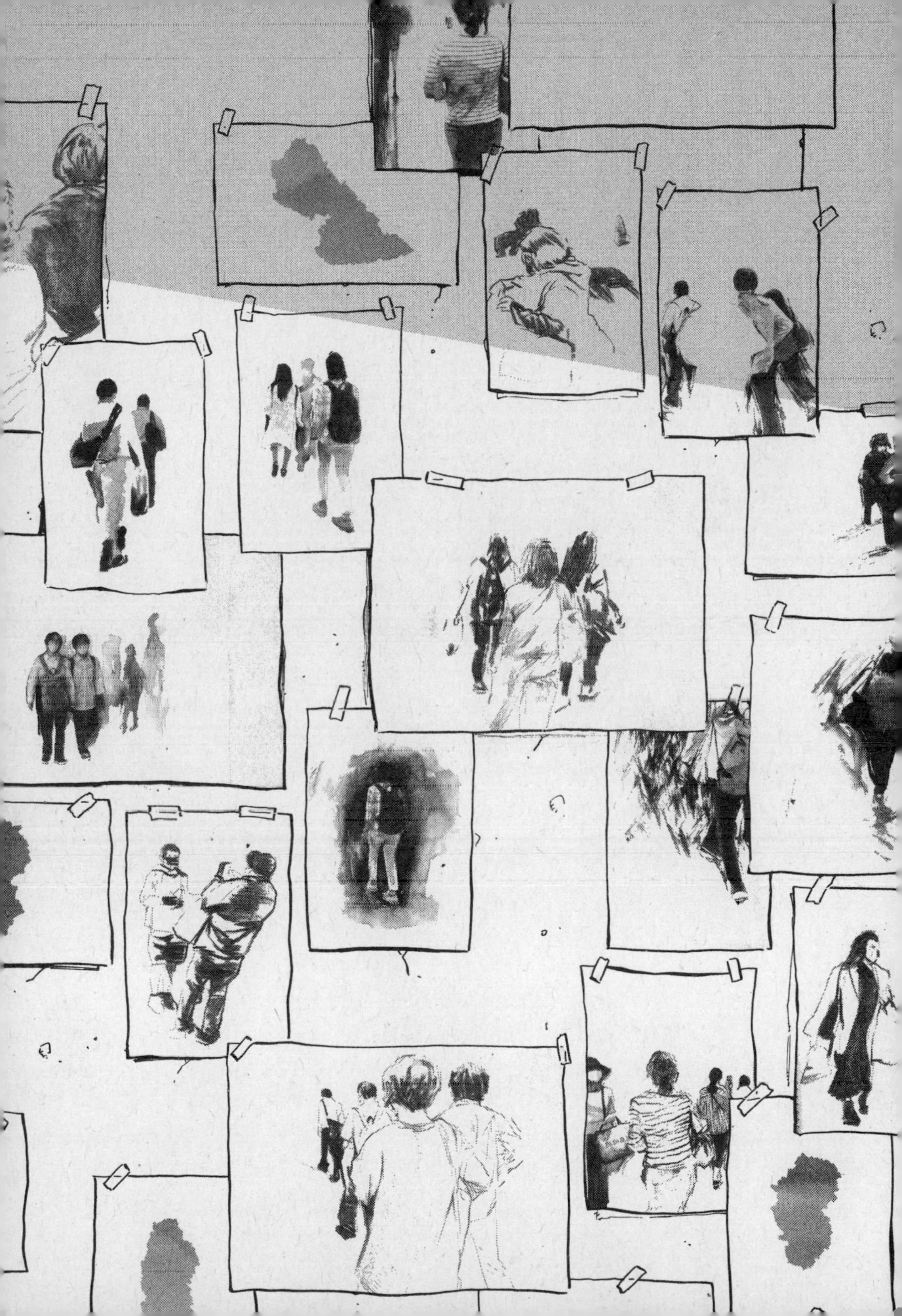

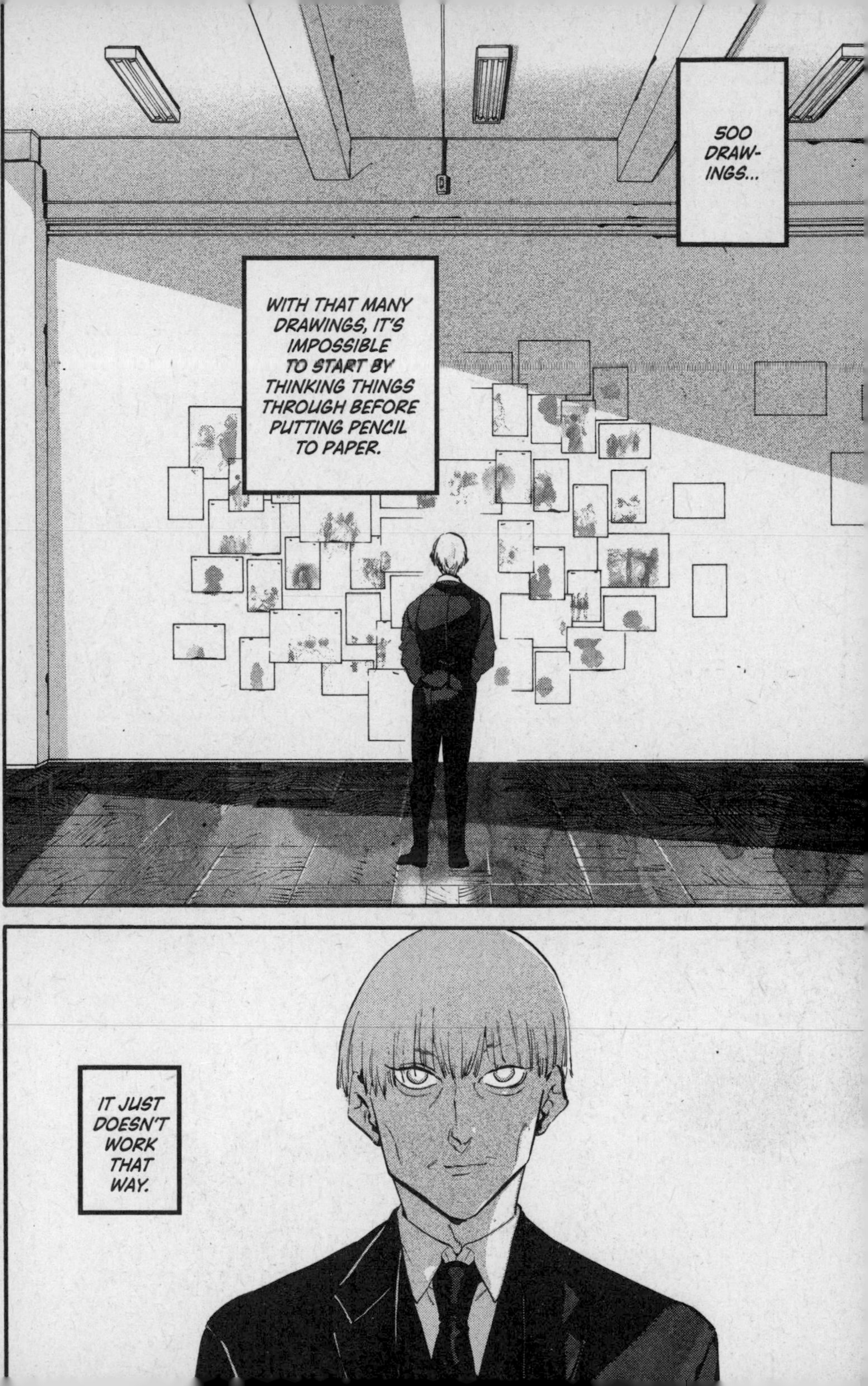
500 DRAW-INGS...
WITH THAT MANY DRAWINGS, IT'S IMPOSSIBLE TO START BY THINKING THINGS THROUGH BEFORE PUTTING PENCIL TO PAPER.
IT JUST DOESN'T WORK THAT WAY.

STROKE 49 END

STROKE 50

ONE OF THOSE SITUATIONS WHERE I TOOK THE HEAT AND KEPT MY COOL

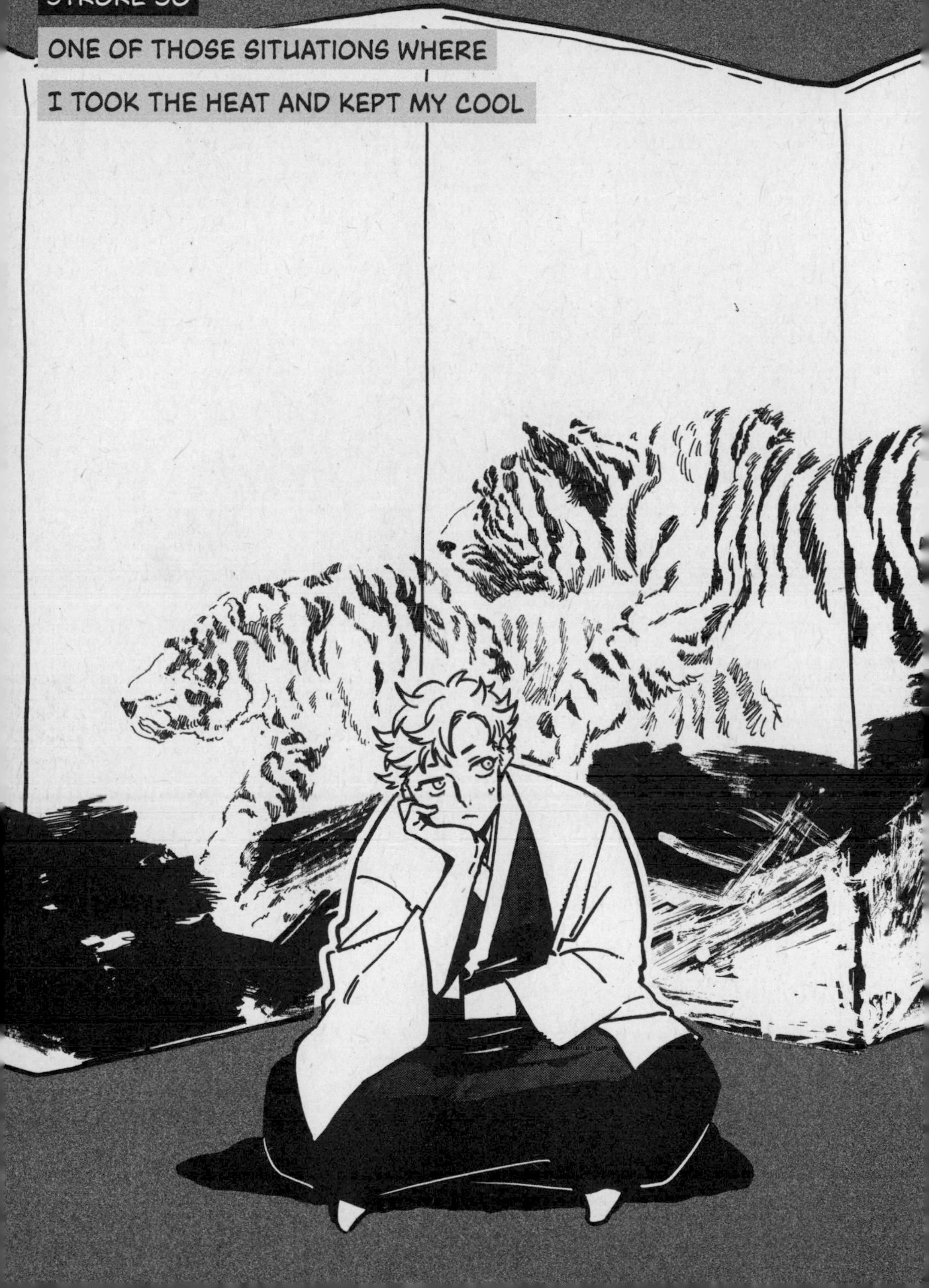

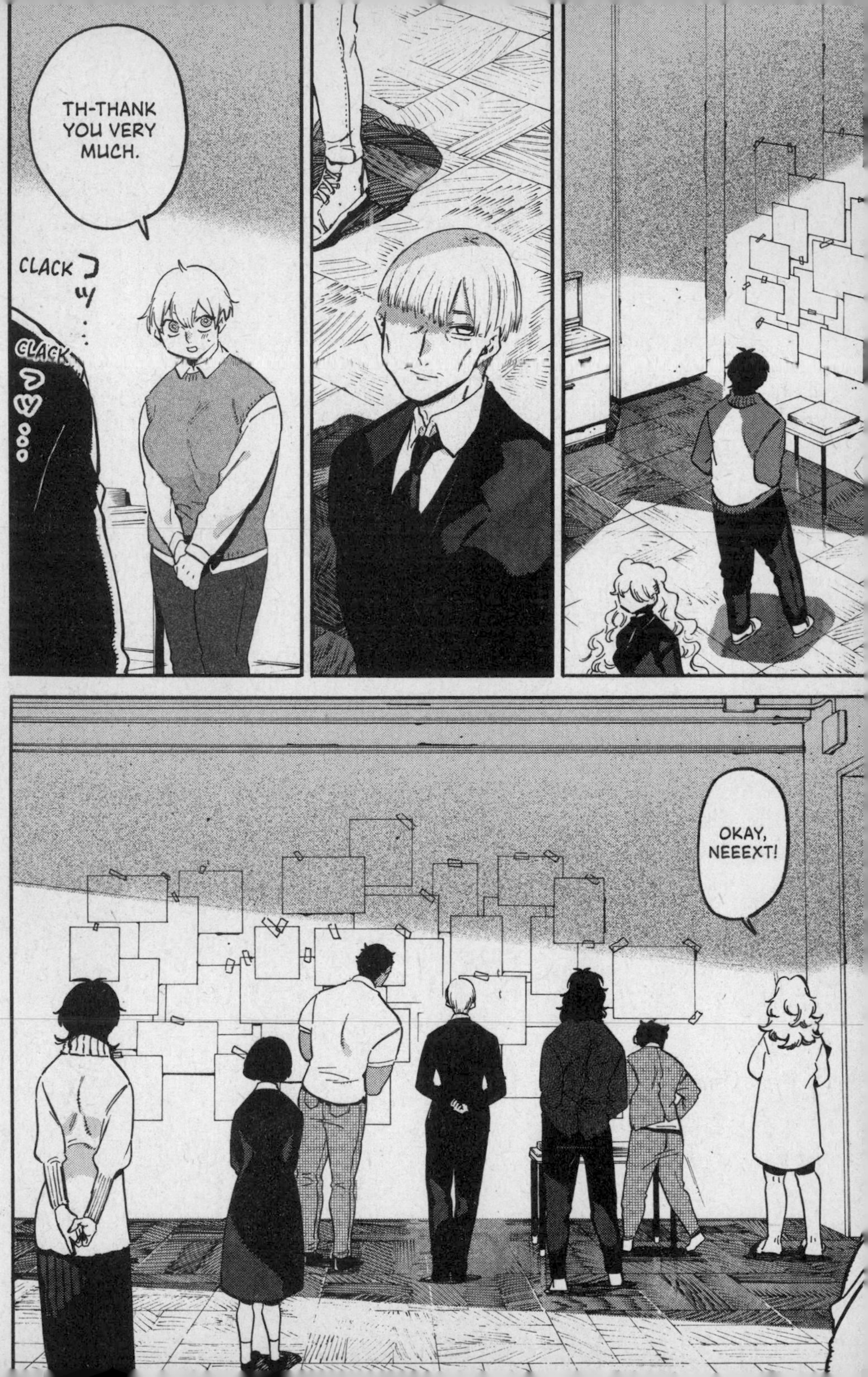
TH-THANK YOU VERY MUCH.
CLACK
CLACK
OKAY, NEEEXT!

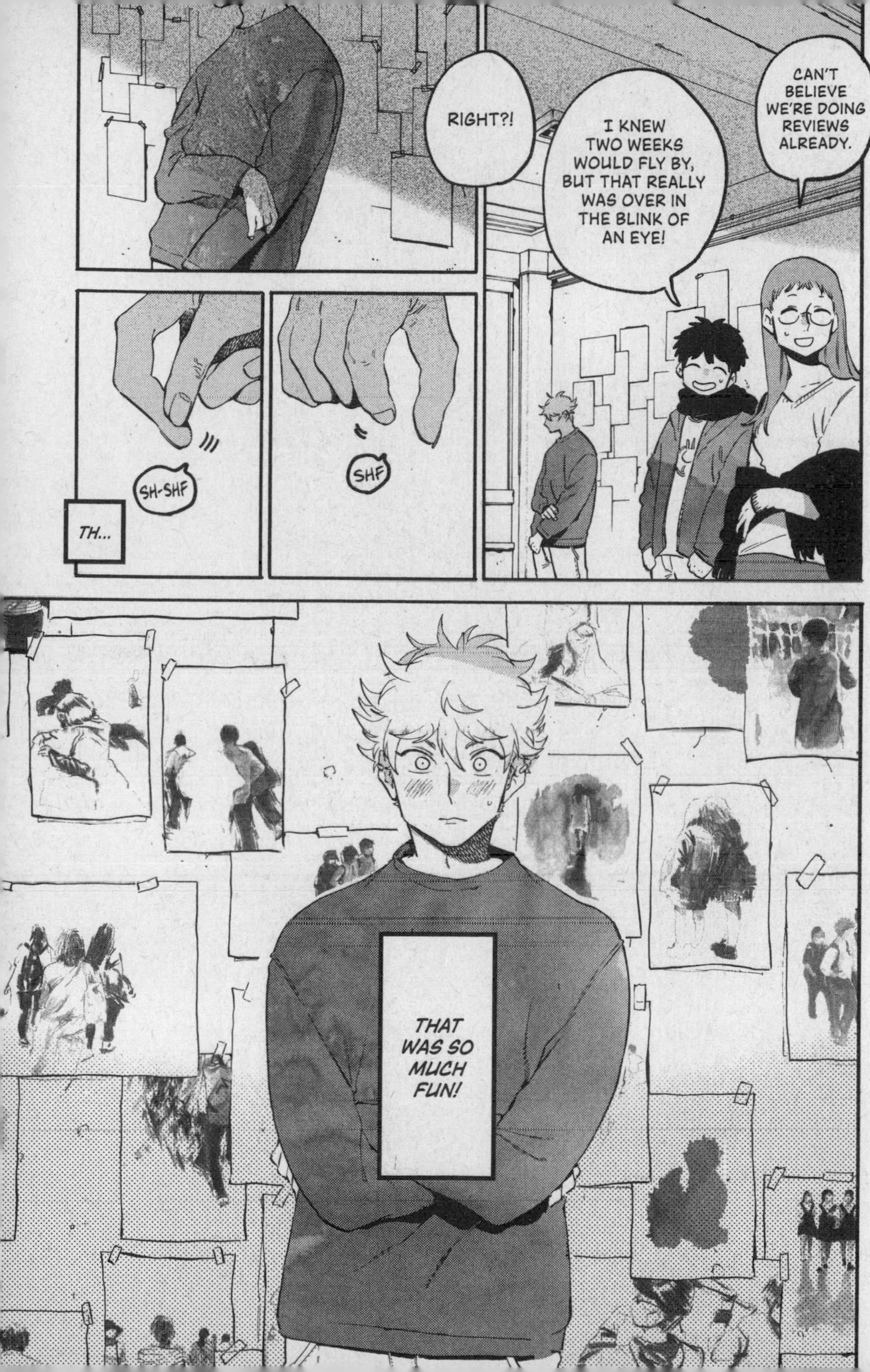
CAN'T BELIEVE WE'RE DOING REVIEWS ALREADY.
I KNEW TWO WEEKS WOULD FLY BY, BUT THAT REALLY WAS OVER IN THE BLINK OF AN EYE!
RIGHT?!
SHF
SH-SHF
TH...
THAT WAS SO MUCH FUN!

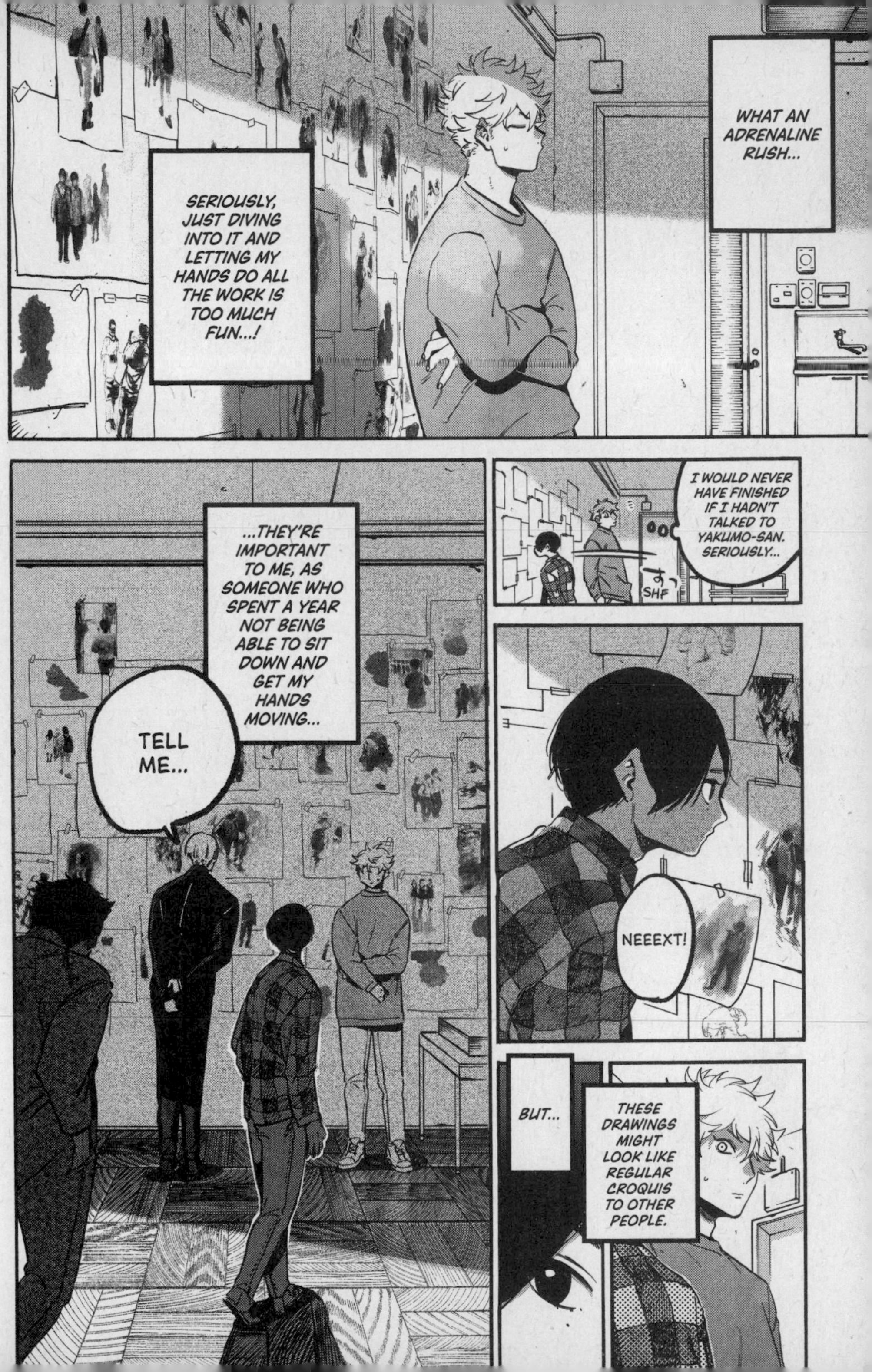
WHAT AN ADRENALINE RUSH...
SERIOUSLY, JUST DIVING INTO IT AND LETTING MY HANDS DO ALL THE WORK IS TOO MUCH FUN...!
I WOULD NEVER HAVE FINISHED IF I HADN'T TALKED TO YAKUMO-SAN. SERIOUSLY...
すっ SHF
NEEEXT!
THESE DRAWINGS MIGHT LOOK LIKE REGULAR CROQUIS TO OTHER PEOPLE.
BUT...
...THEY'RE IMPORTANT TO ME, AS SOMEONE WHO SPENT A YEAR NOT BEING ABLE TO SIT DOWN AND GET MY HANDS MOVING...
TELL ME...

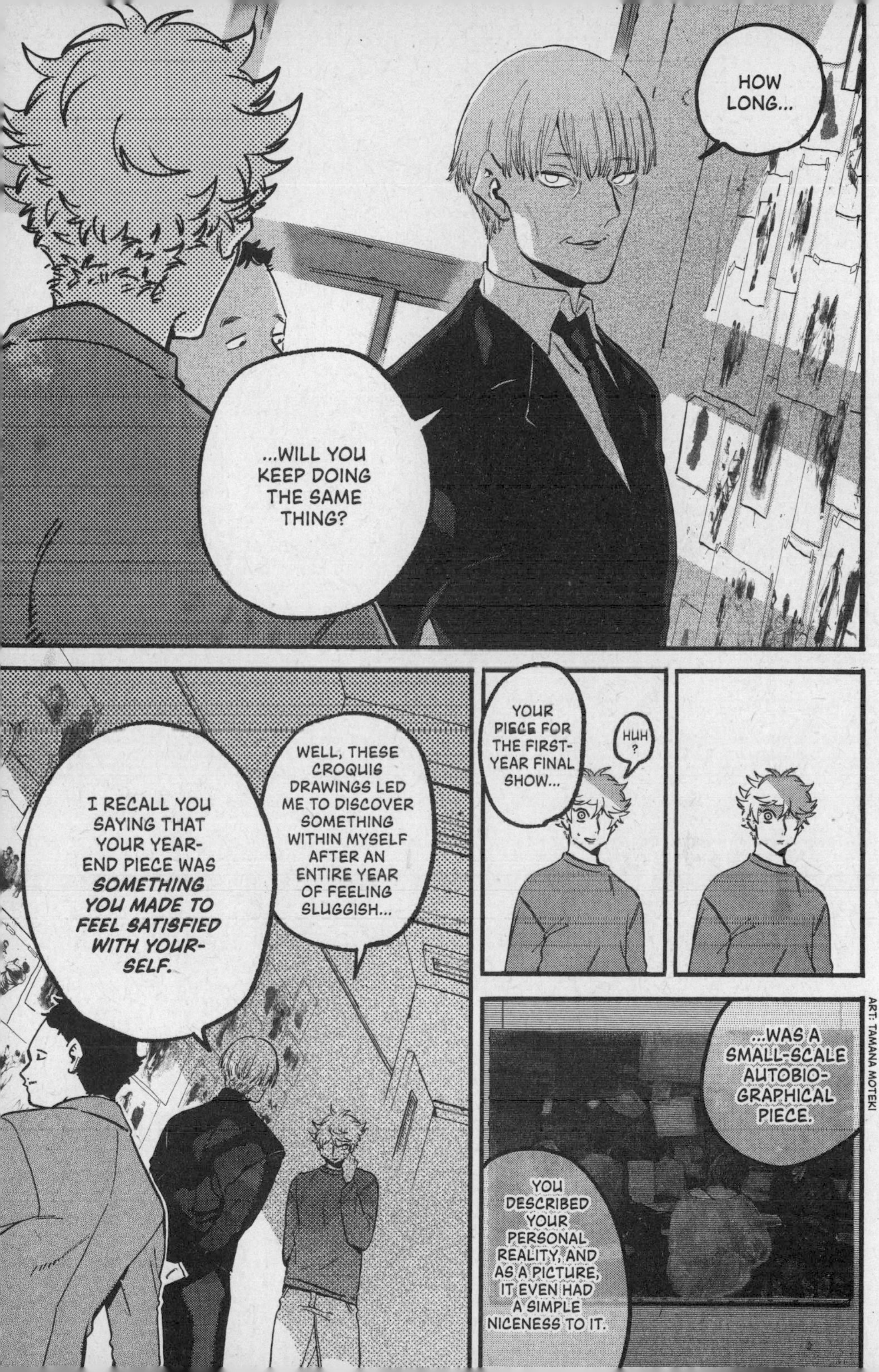
HOW LONG...
...WILL YOU KEEP DOING THE SAME THING?
HUH?
YOUR PIECE FOR THE FIRST-YEAR FINAL SHOW...
...WAS A SMALL-SCALE AUTOBIO-GRAPHICAL PIECE.
YOU DESCRIBED YOUR PERSONAL REALITY, AND AS A PICTURE, IT EVEN HAD A SIMPLE NICENESS TO IT.
WELL, THESE CROQUIS DRAWINGS LED ME TO DISCOVER SOMETHING WITHIN MYSELF AFTER AN ENTIRE YEAR OF FEELING SLUGGISH...
I RECALL YOU SAYING THAT YOUR YEAR-END PIECE WAS *SOMETHING YOU MADE TO FEEL SATISFIED WITH YOUR-SELF.*

ART: TAMANA MOTEKI

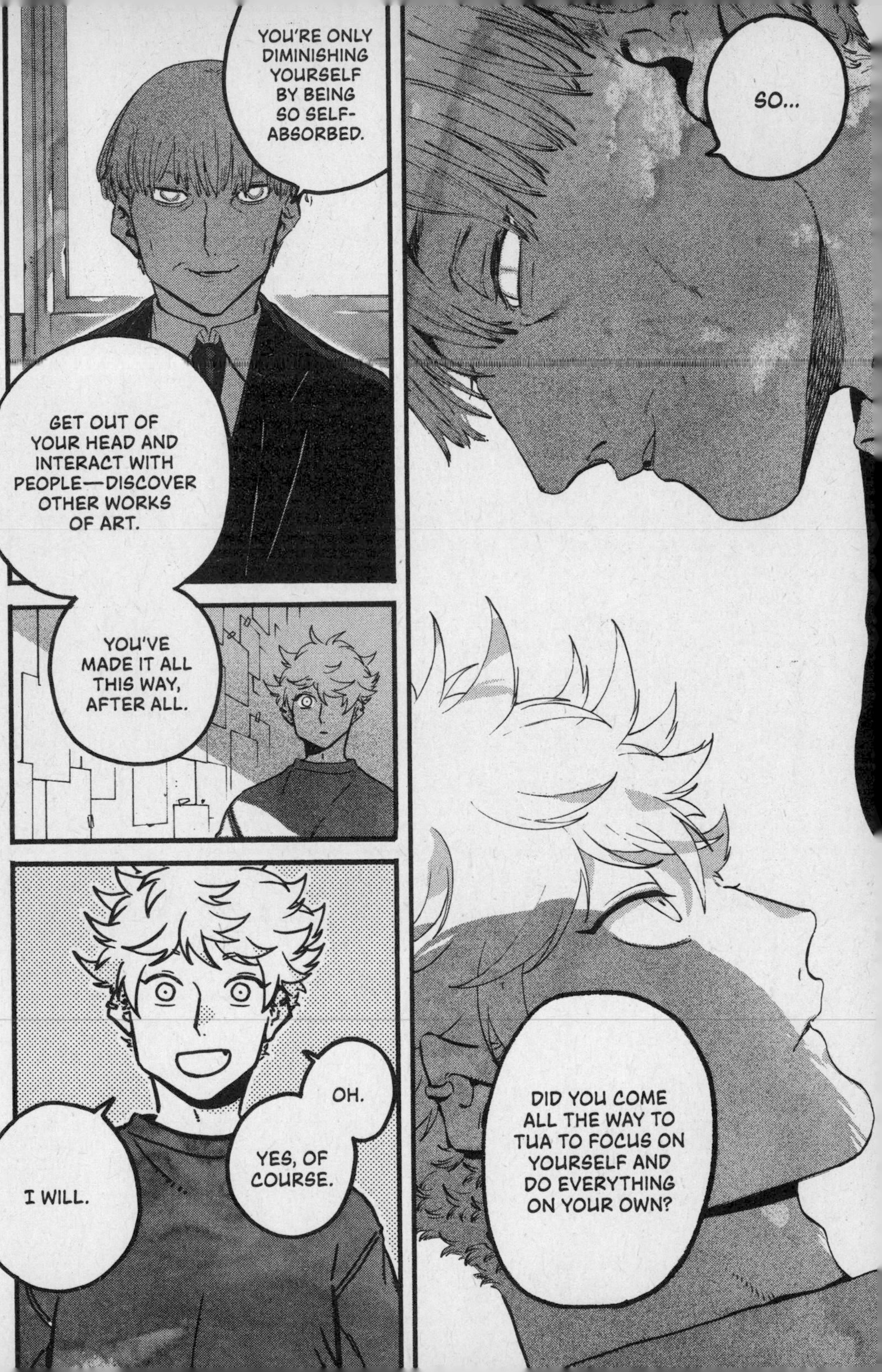
SO...
DID YOU COME ALL THE WAY TO TUA TO FOCUS ON YOURSELF AND DO EVERYTHING ON YOUR OWN?
YOU'RE ONLY DIMINISHING YOURSELF BY BEING SO SELF-ABSORBED.
GET OUT OF YOUR HEAD AND INTERACT WITH PEOPLE—DISCOVER OTHER WORKS OF ART.
YOU'VE MADE IT ALL THIS WAY, AFTER ALL.
OH.
YES, OF COURSE.
I WILL.

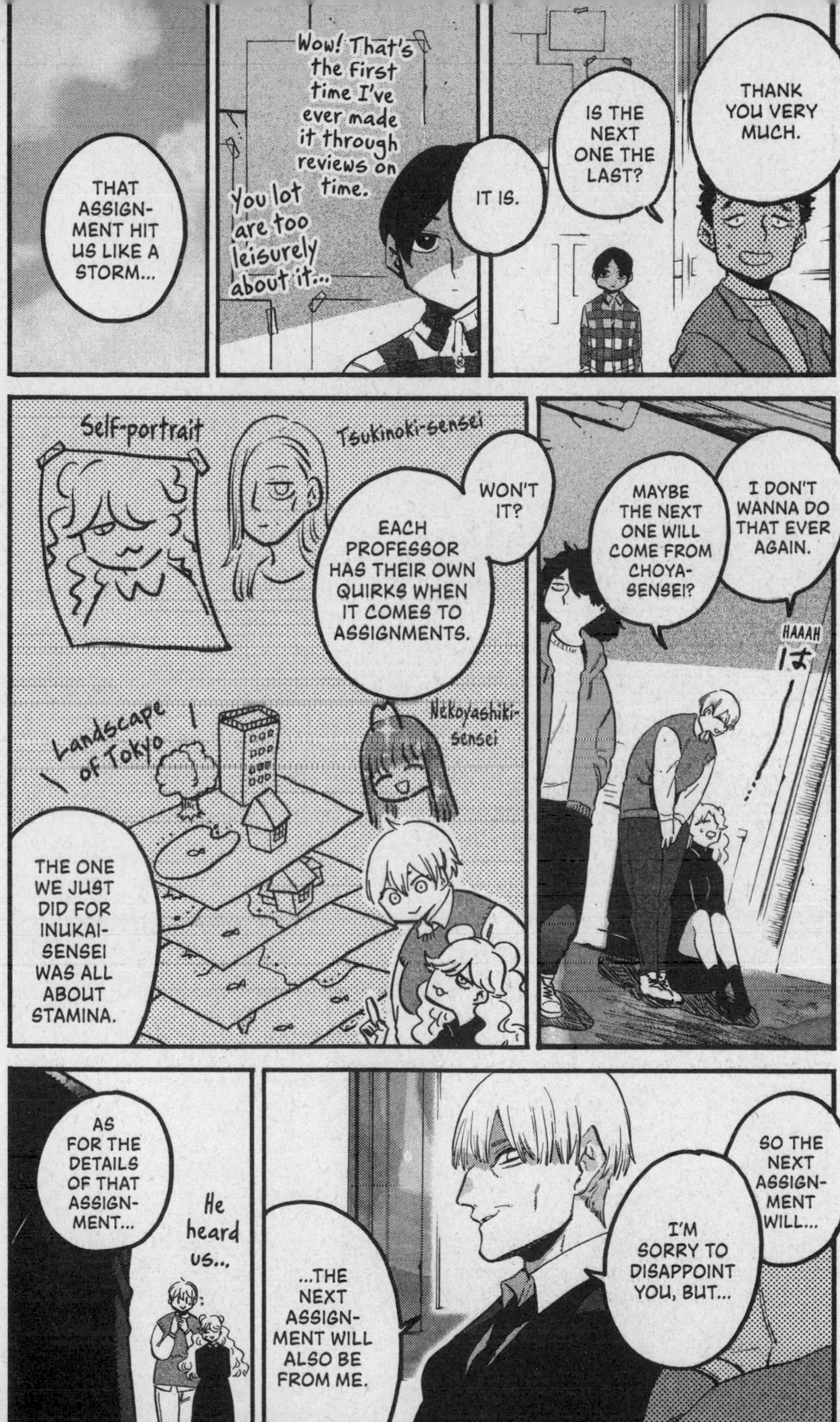
THANK YOU VERY MUCH.
IS THE NEXT ONE THE LAST?
IT IS.
Wow! That's the first time I've ever made it through reviews on time.
You lot are too leisurely about it...
THAT ASSIGNMENT HIT US LIKE A STORM...
I DON'T WANNA DO THAT EVER AGAIN.
MAYBE THE NEXT ONE WILL COME FROM CHOYA-SENSEI?
HAAAH
は
WON'T IT?
EACH PROFESSOR HAS THEIR OWN QUIRKS WHEN IT COMES TO ASSIGNMENTS.
Tsukinoki-sensei
Self-portrait
Nekoyashiki-sensei
Landscape of Tokyo
THE ONE WE JUST DID FOR INUKAI-SENSEI WAS ALL ABOUT STAMINA.
SO THE NEXT ASSIGNMENT WILL...
I'M SORRY TO DISAPPOINT YOU, BUT...
...THE NEXT ASSIGNMENT WILL ALSO BE FROM ME.
AS FOR THE DETAILS OF THAT ASSIGNMENT...
He heard us...

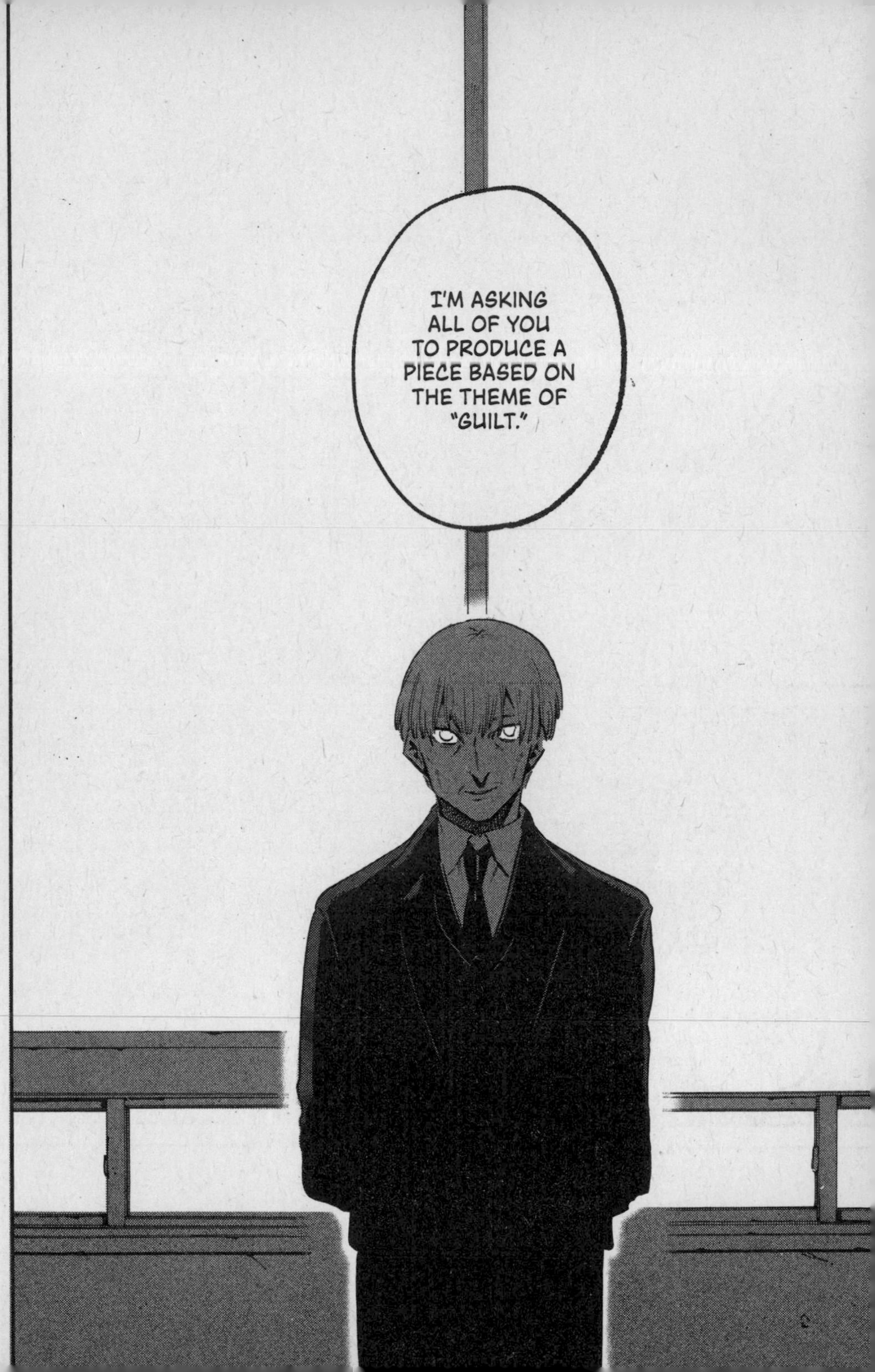
I'M ASKING ALL OF YOU TO PRODUCE A PIECE BASED ON THE THEME OF "GUILT."

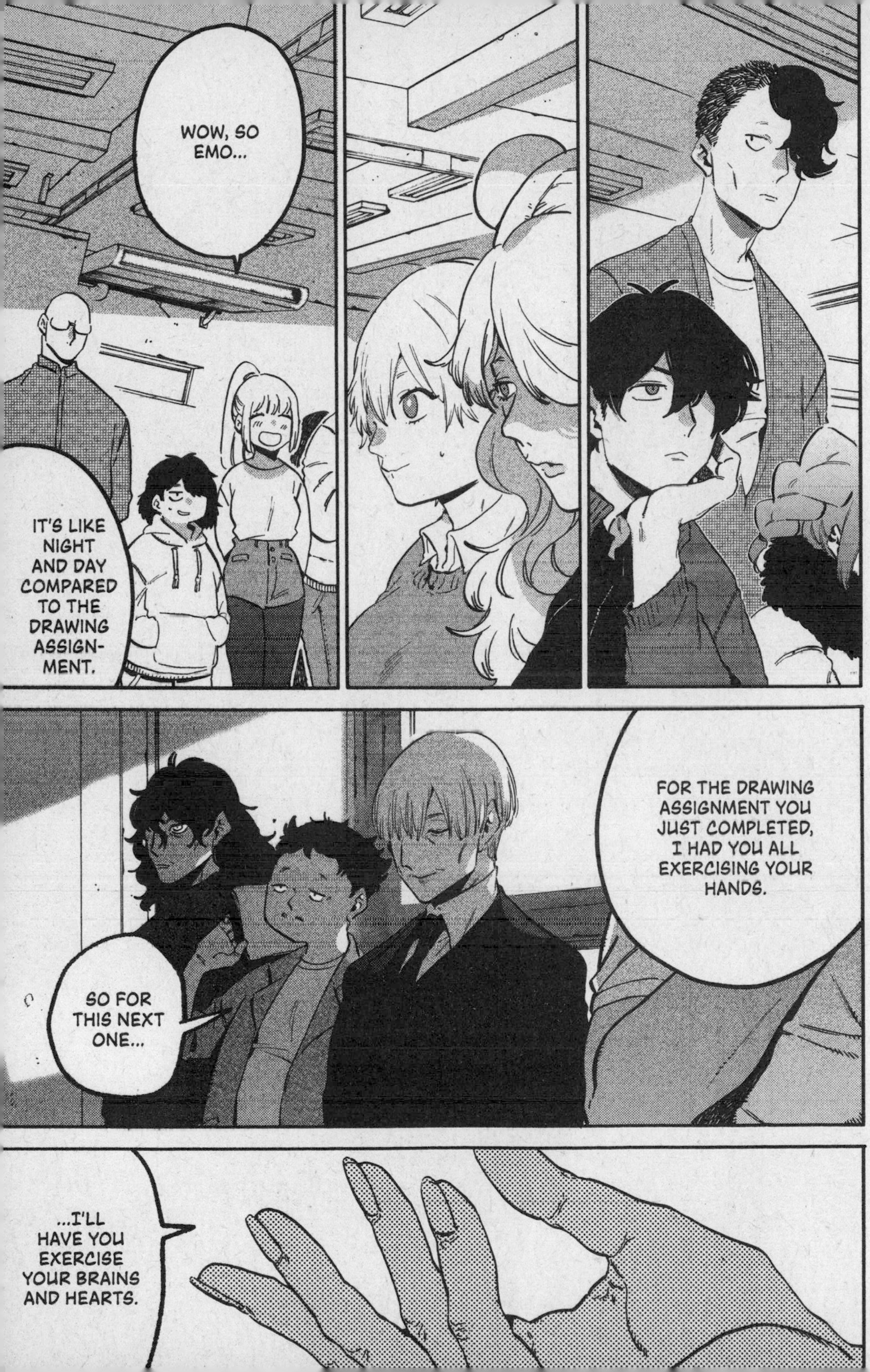
WOW, SO EMO...
IT'S LIKE NIGHT AND DAY COMPARED TO THE DRAWING ASSIGN-MENT.
FOR THE DRAWING ASSIGNMENT YOU JUST COMPLETED, I HAD YOU ALL EXERCISING YOUR HANDS.
SO FOR THIS NEXT ONE...
...I'LL HAVE YOU EXERCISE YOUR BRAINS AND HEARTS.

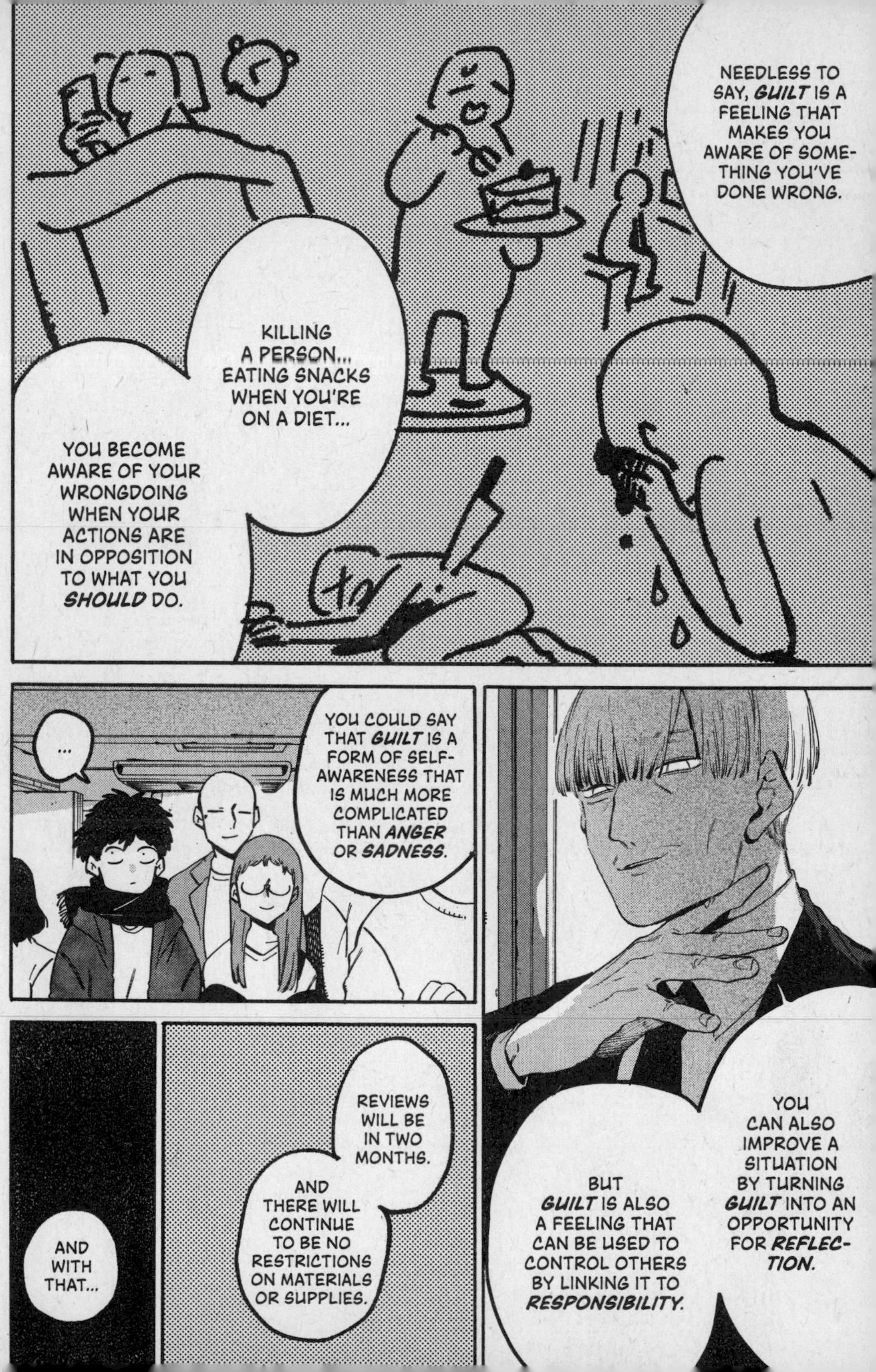
NEEDLESS TO SAY, GUILT IS A FEELING THAT MAKES YOU AWARE OF SOMETHING YOU'VE DONE WRONG.
KILLING A PERSON... EATING SNACKS WHEN YOU'RE ON A DIET...
YOU BECOME AWARE OF YOUR WRONGDOING WHEN YOUR ACTIONS ARE IN OPPOSITION TO WHAT YOU SHOULD DO.
YOU CAN ALSO IMPROVE A SITUATION BY TURNING GUILT INTO AN OPPORTUNITY FOR REFLECTION.
BUT GUILT IS ALSO A FEELING THAT CAN BE USED TO CONTROL OTHERS BY LINKING IT TO RESPONSIBILITY.
YOU COULD SAY THAT GUILT IS A FORM OF SELF-AWARENESS THAT IS MUCH MORE COMPLICATED THAN ANGER OR SADNESS.
...
REVIEWS WILL BE IN TWO MONTHS.
AND THERE WILL CONTINUE TO BE NO RESTRICTIONS ON MATERIALS OR SUPPLIES.
AND WITH THAT...

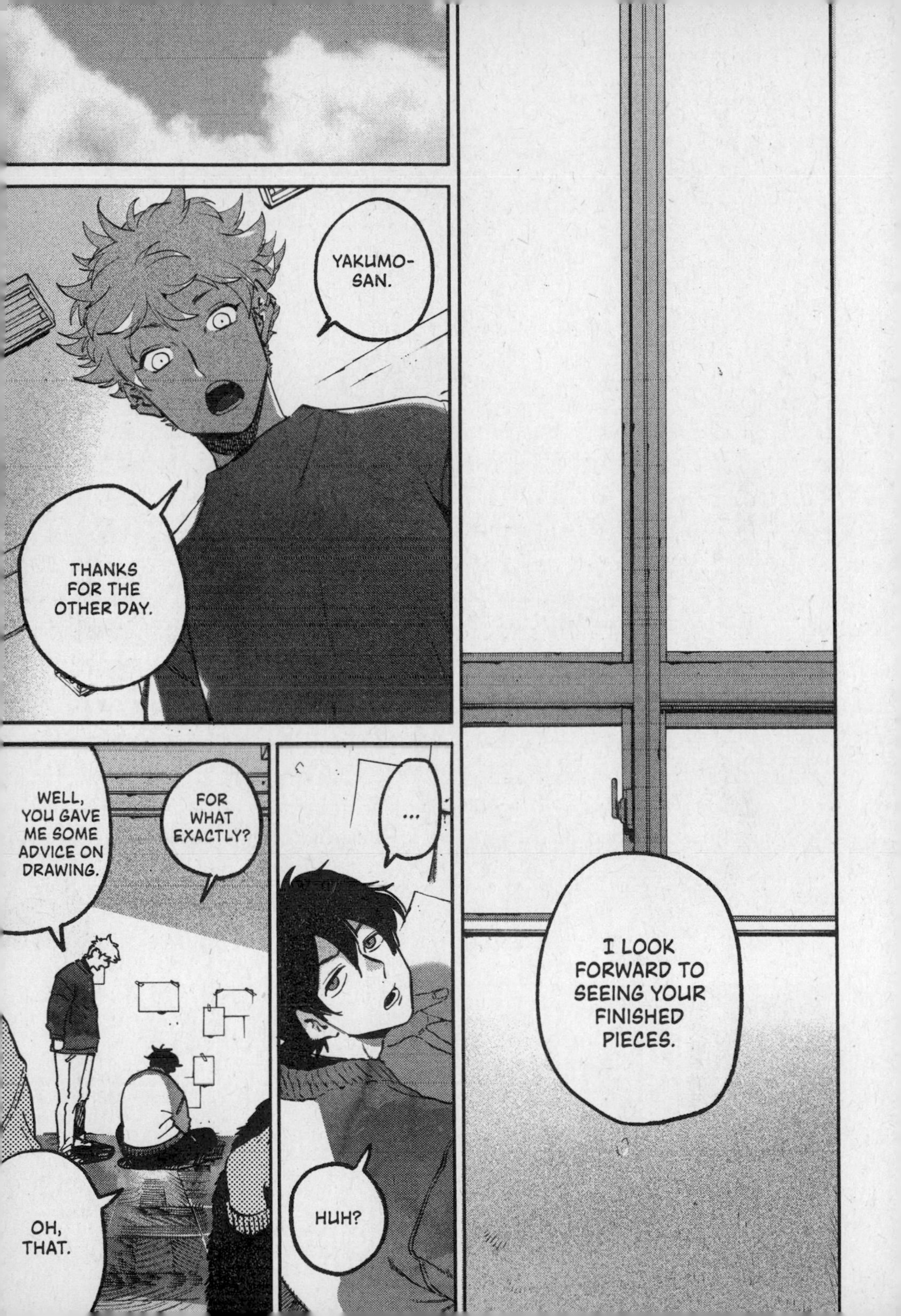
I LOOK FORWARD TO SEEING YOUR FINISHED PIECES.
YAKUMO-SAN.
THANKS FOR THE OTHER DAY.
...
HUH?
FOR WHAT EXACTLY?
WELL, YOU GAVE ME SOME ADVICE ON DRAWING.
OH, THAT.

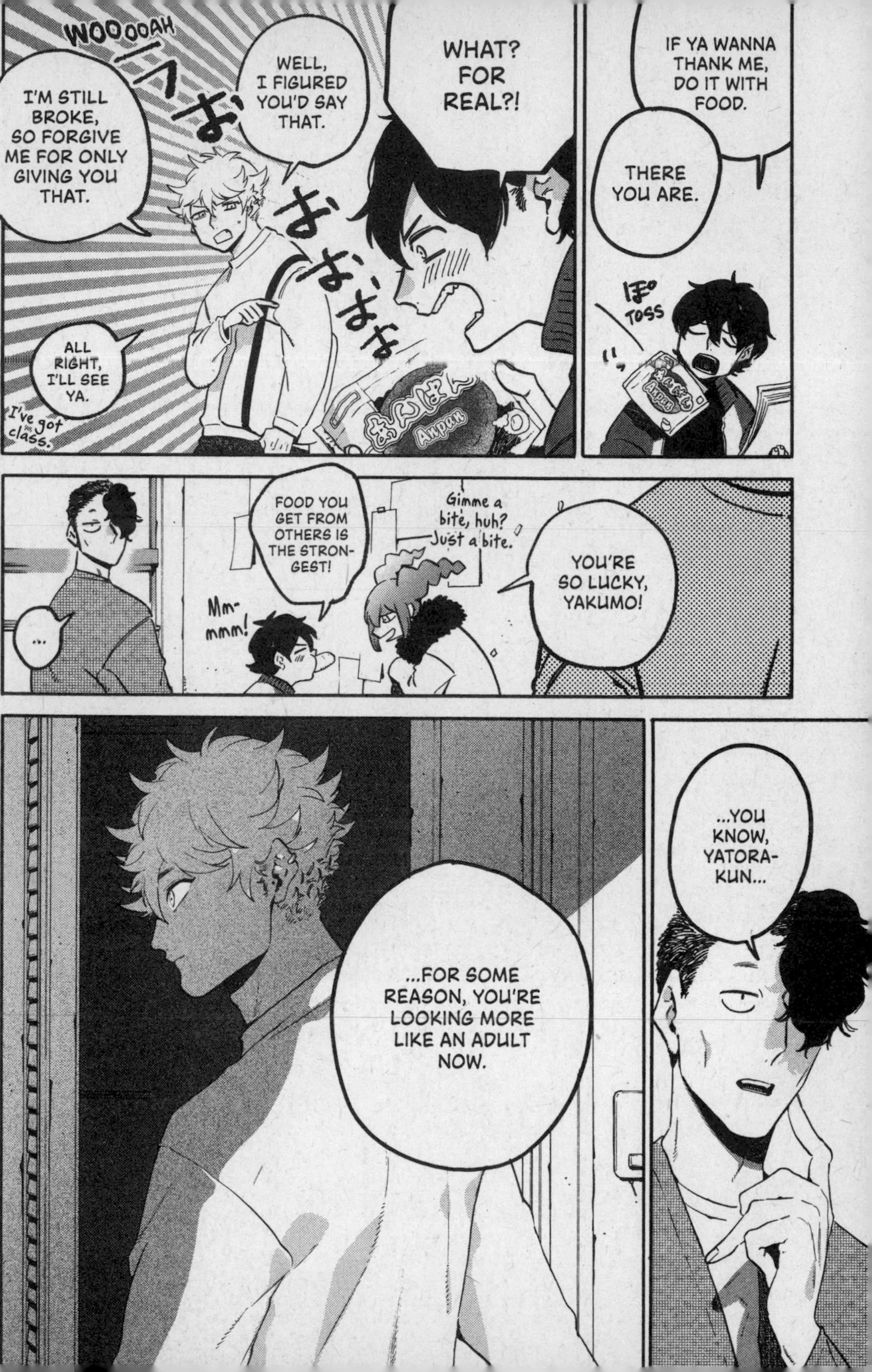
IF YA WANNA THANK ME, DO IT WITH FOOD.
THERE YOU ARE.
TOSS
Anpan
WHAT? FOR REAL?!
WELL, I FIGURED YOU'D SAY THAT.
WOOOOAH
I'M STILL BROKE, SO FORGIVE ME FOR ONLY GIVING YOU THAT.
Anpan
ALL RIGHT, I'LL SEE YA.
I've got class.
YOU'RE SO LUCKY, YAKUMO!
Gimme a bite, huh? Just a bite.
FOOD YOU GET FROM OTHERS IS THE STRON-GEST!
Mm-mmm!
...
...YOU KNOW, YATORA-KUN...
...FOR SOME REASON, YOU'RE LOOKING MORE LIKE AN ADULT NOW.

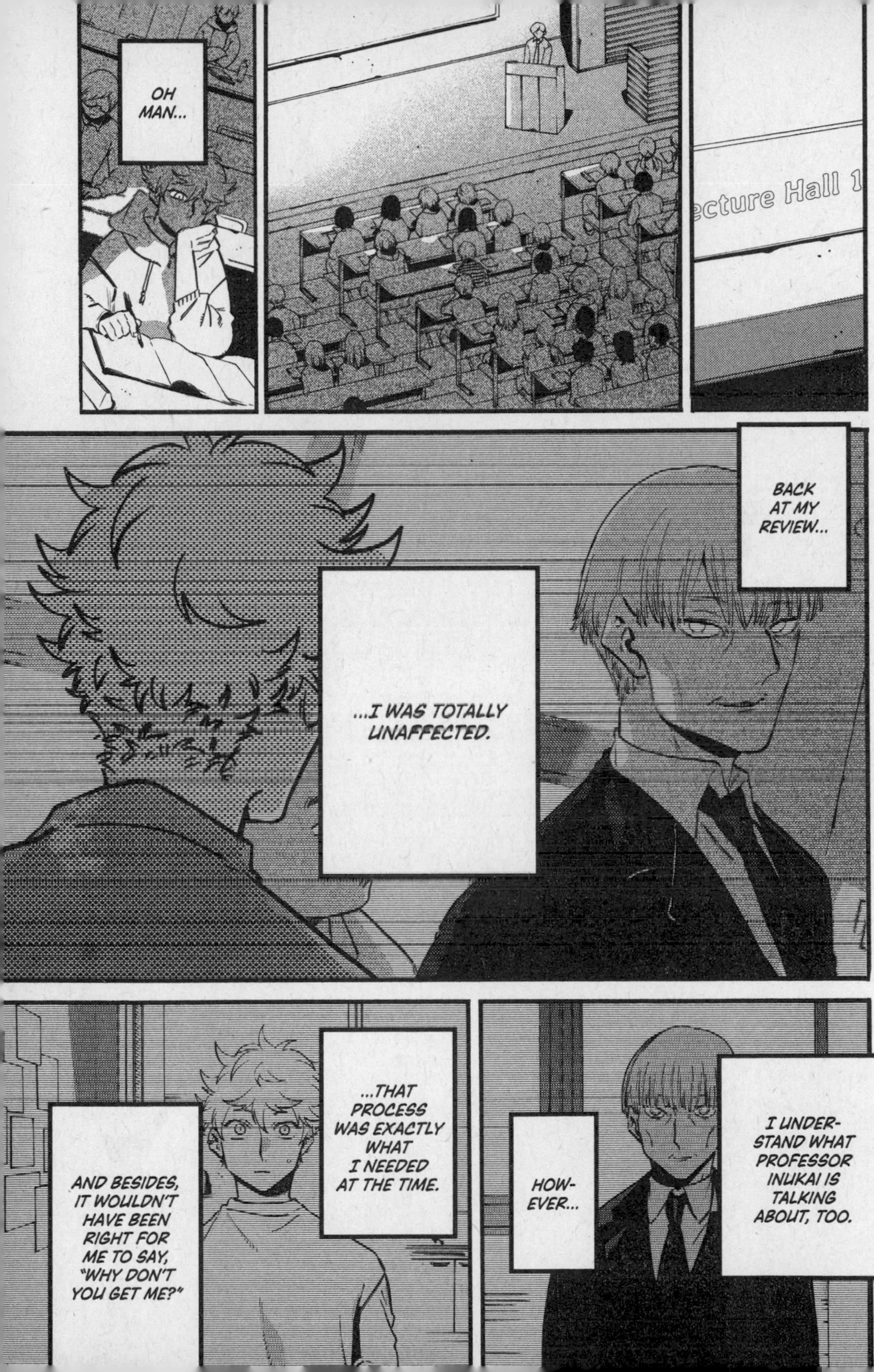
ecture Hall 1
OH MAN...
BACK AT MY REVIEW...
...I WAS TOTALLY UNAFFECTED.
I UNDER-STAND WHAT PROFESSOR INUKAI IS TALKING ABOUT, TOO.
HOW-EVER...
...THAT PROCESS WAS EXACTLY WHAT I NEEDED AT THE TIME.
AND BESIDES, IT WOULDN'T HAVE BEEN RIGHT FOR ME TO SAY, "WHY DON'T YOU GET ME?"

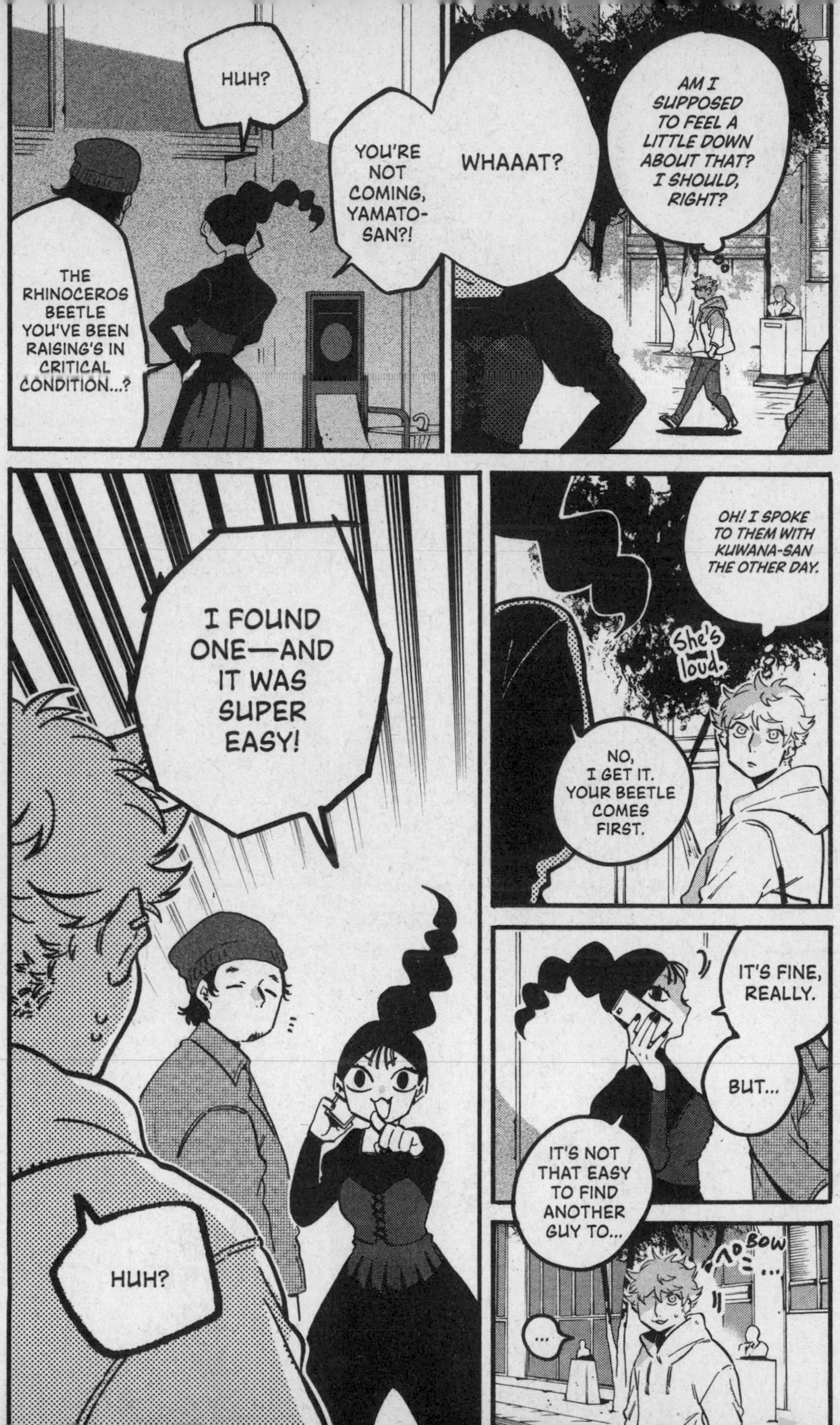
AM I SUPPOSED TO FEEL A LITTLE DOWN ABOUT THAT? I SHOULD, RIGHT?
WHAAAT?
YOU'RE NOT COMING, YAMATO-SAN?!
HUH?
THE RHINOCEROS BEETLE YOU'VE BEEN RAISING'S IN CRITICAL CONDITION...?
OH! I SPOKE TO THEM WITH KUWANA-SAN THE OTHER DAY.
She's loud.
NO, I GET IT. YOUR BEETLE COMES FIRST.
IT'S FINE, REALLY.
BUT...
IT'S NOT THAT EASY TO FIND ANOTHER GUY TO...
BOW
...
...
I FOUND ONE—AND IT WAS SUPER EASY!
HUH?

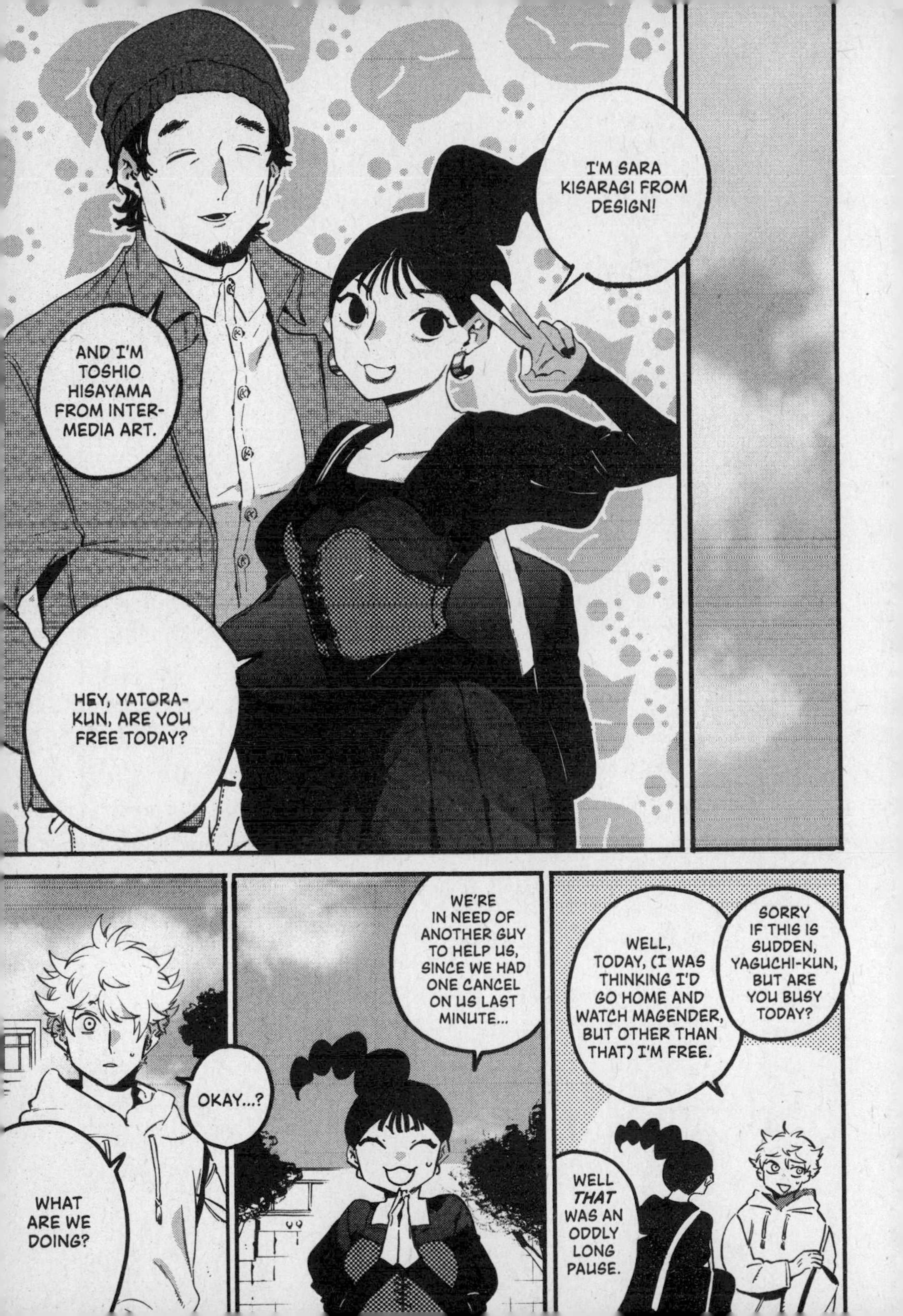
I'M SARA KISARAGI FROM DESIGN!
AND I'M TOSHIO HISAYAMA FROM INTER-MEDIA ART.
HEY, YATORA-KUN, ARE YOU FREE TODAY?
SORRY IF THIS IS SUDDEN, YAGUCHI-KUN, BUT ARE YOU BUSY TODAY?
WELL, TODAY, (I WAS THINKING I'D GO HOME AND WATCH MAGENDER, BUT OTHER THAN THAT) I'M FREE.
WELL *THAT* WAS AN ODDLY LONG PAUSE.
WE'RE IN NEED OF ANOTHER GUY TO HELP US, SINCE WE HAD ONE CANCEL ON US LAST MINUTE...
OKAY...?
WHAT ARE WE DOING?

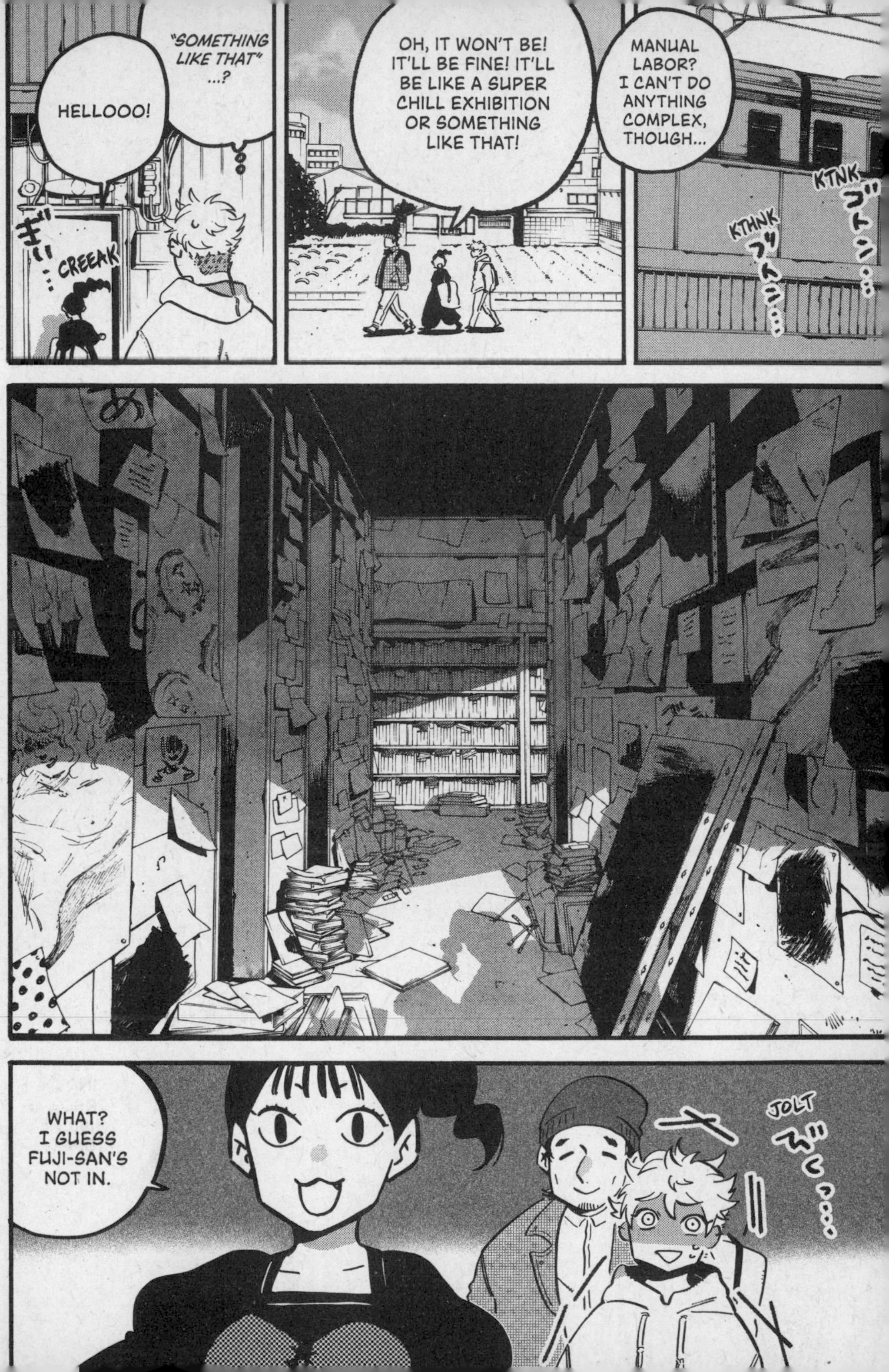
MANUAL LABOR? I CAN'T DO ANYTHING COMPLEX, THOUGH...
KTNK
KTHNK
OH, IT WON'T BE! IT'LL BE FINE! IT'LL BE LIKE A SUPER CHILL EXHIBITION OR SOMETHING LIKE THAT!
"SOMETHING LIKE THAT" ...?
HELLOOO!
CREEAK
JOLT
WHAT? I GUESS FUJI-SAN'S NOT IN.

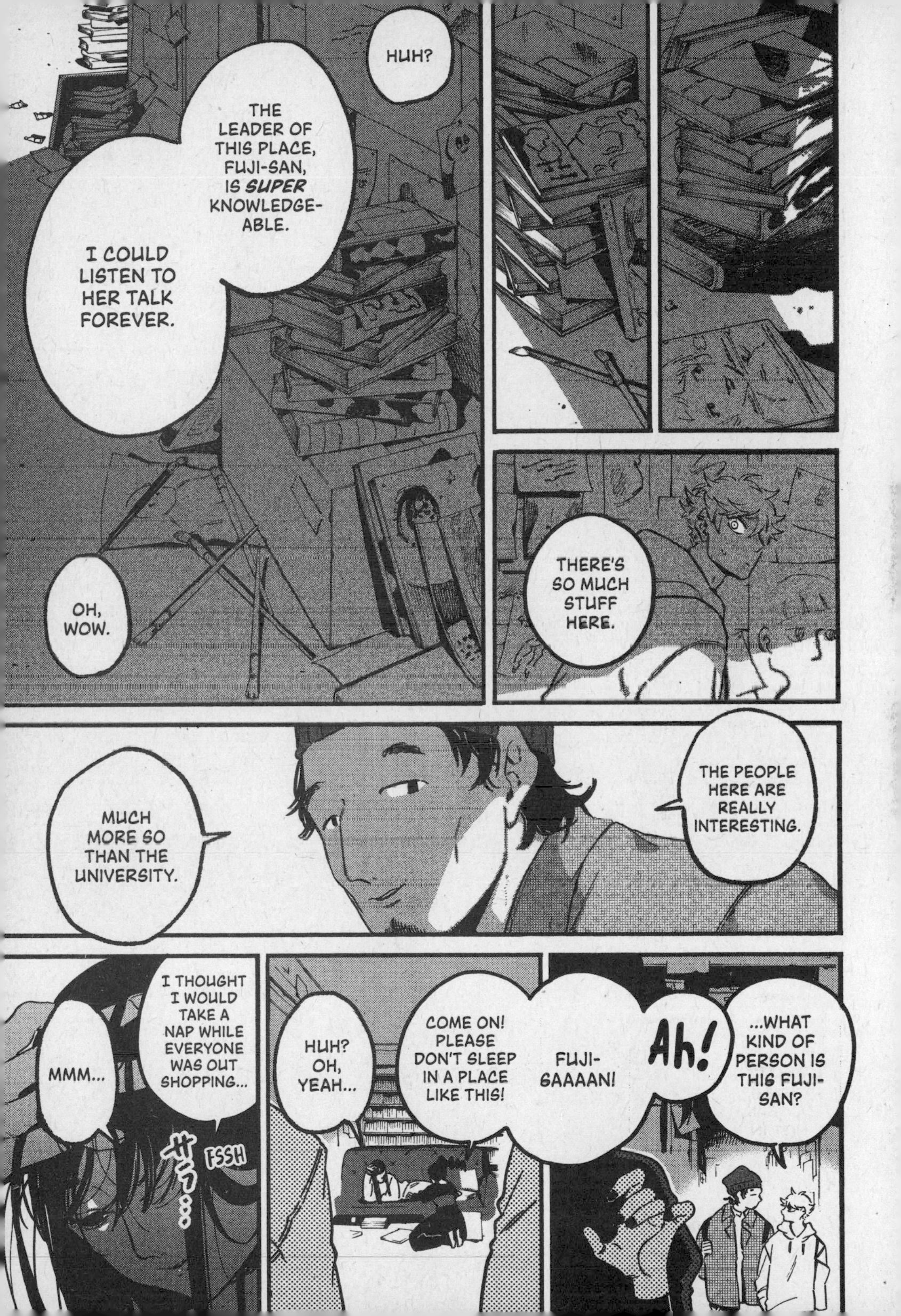
THERE'S SO MUCH STUFF HERE.
HUH?
THE LEADER OF THIS PLACE, FUJI-SAN, IS *SUPER* KNOWLEDGE-ABLE.
I COULD LISTEN TO HER TALK FOREVER.
OH, WOW.
THE PEOPLE HERE ARE REALLY INTERESTING.
MUCH MORE SO THAN THE UNIVERSITY.
...WHAT KIND OF PERSON IS THIS FUJI-SAN?
Ah!
FUJI-GAAAAN!
COME ON! PLEASE DON'T SLEEP IN A PLACE LIKE THIS!
HUH? OH, YEAH...
I THOUGHT I WOULD TAKE A NAP WHILE EVERYONE WAS OUT SHOPPING...
MMM...
FSSH

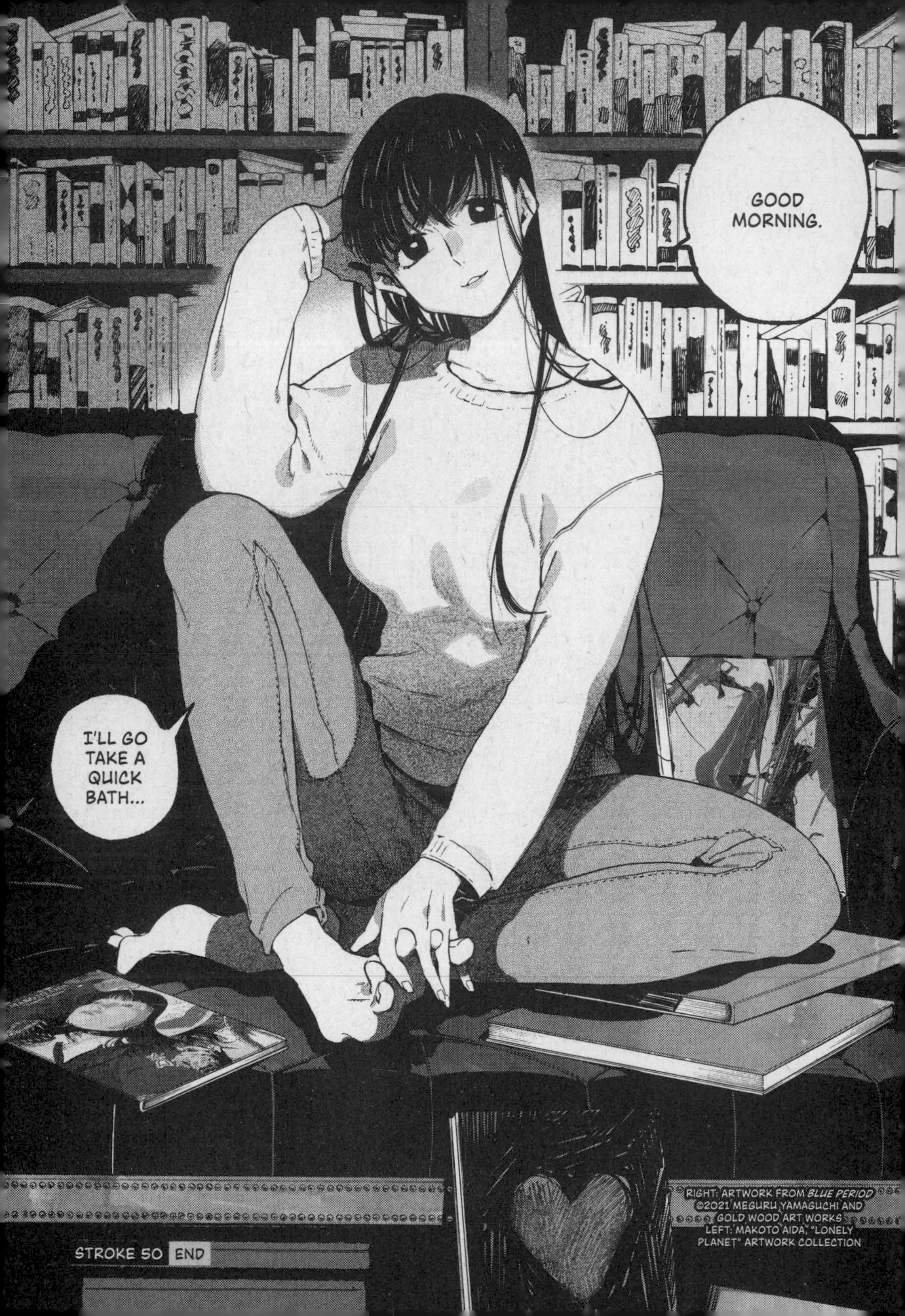
GOOD MORNING.
I'LL GO TAKE A QUICK BATH...
STROKE 50 END
RIGHT: ARTWORK FROM BLUE PERIOD ©2021 MEGURU YAMAGUCHI AND GOLD WOOD ART WORKS
LEFT: MAKOTO AIDA, "LONELY PLANET" ARTWORK COLLECTION

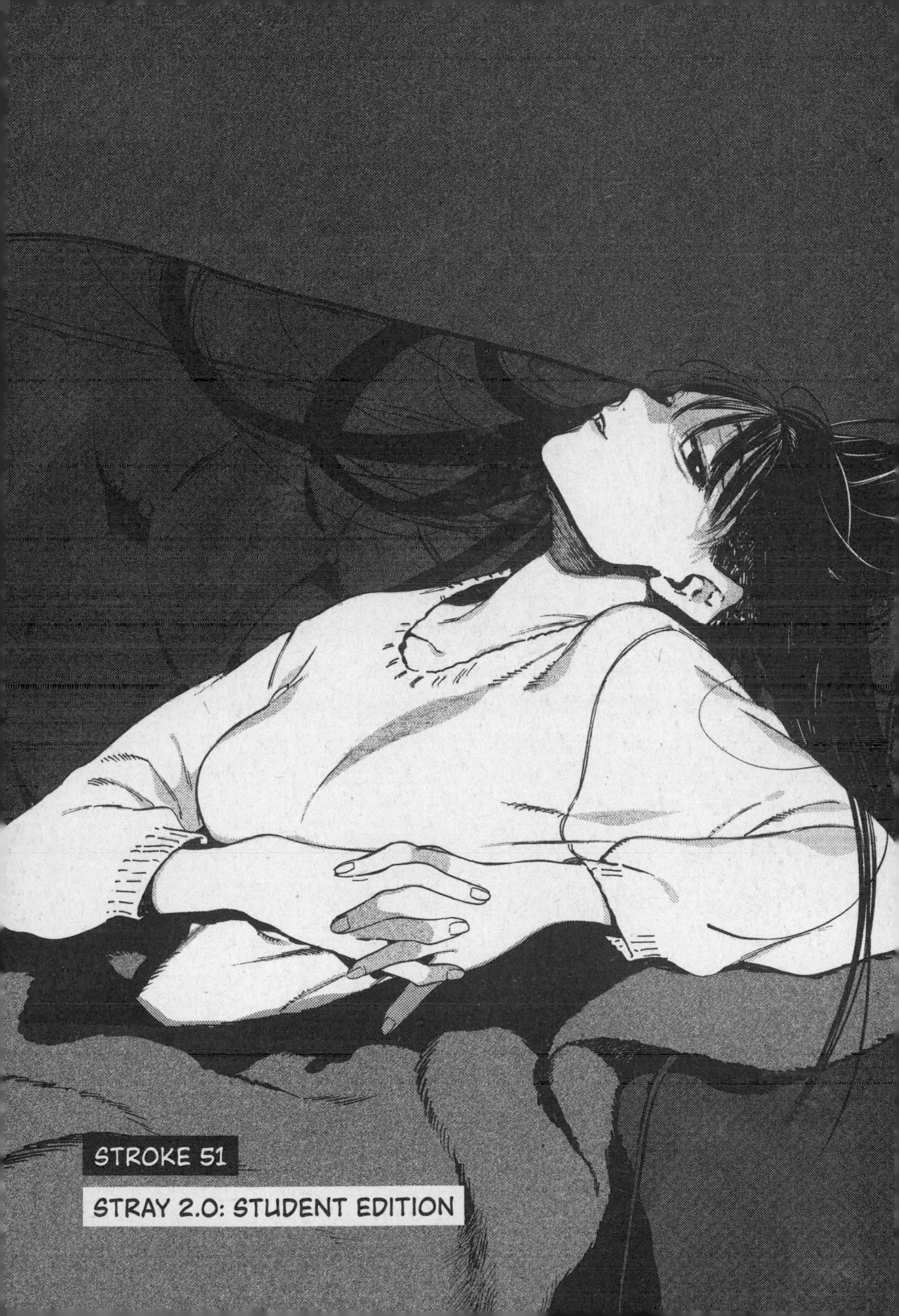
STROKE 51
STRAY 2.0: STUDENT EDITION

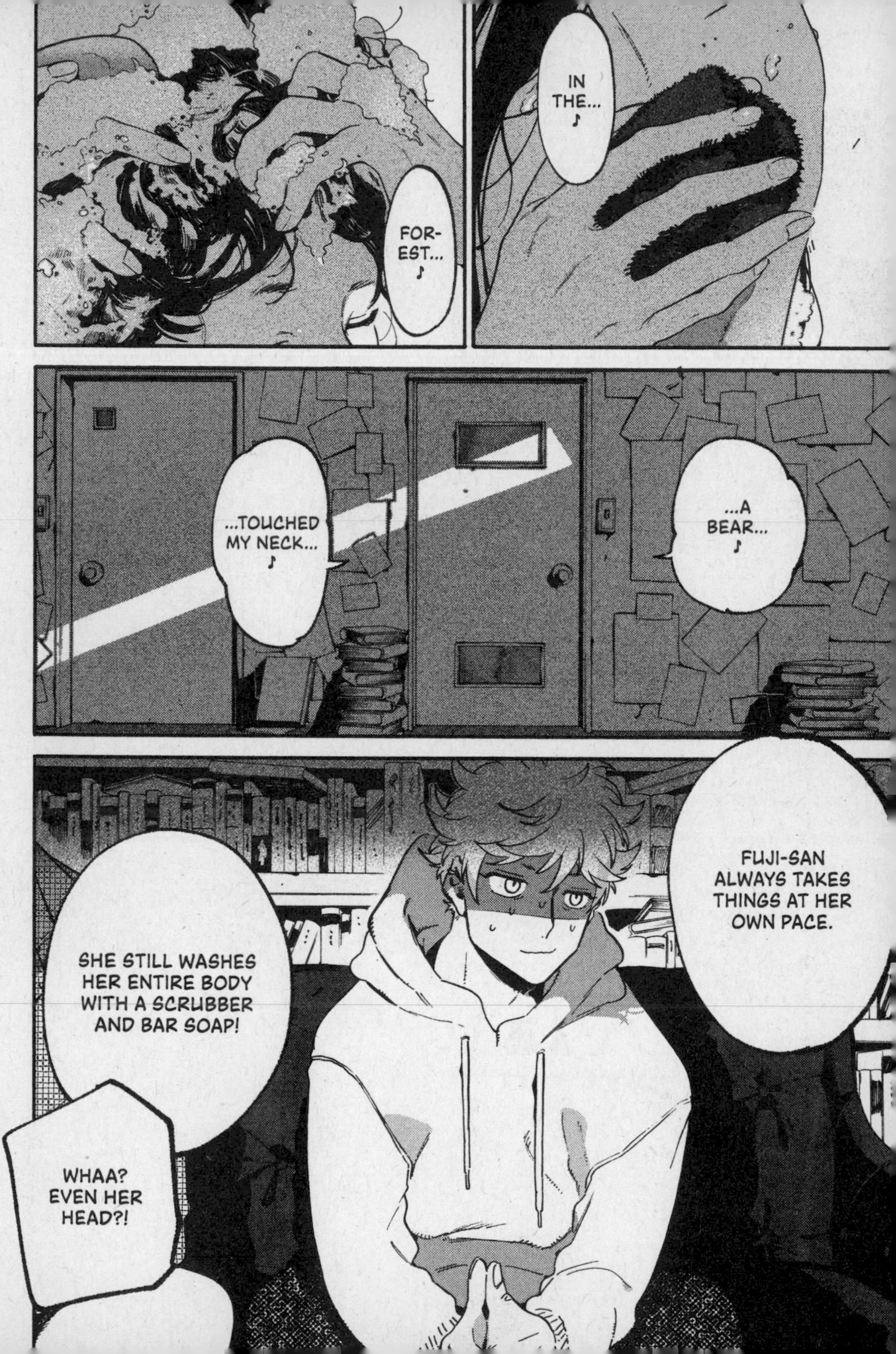
IN THE... ♪
FOR-EST... ♪
...A BEAR... ♪
...TOUCHED MY NECK... ♪
FUJI-SAN ALWAYS TAKES THINGS AT HER OWN PACE.
SHE STILL WASHES HER ENTIRE BODY WITH A SCRUBBER AND BAR SOAP!
WHAA? EVEN HER HEAD?!

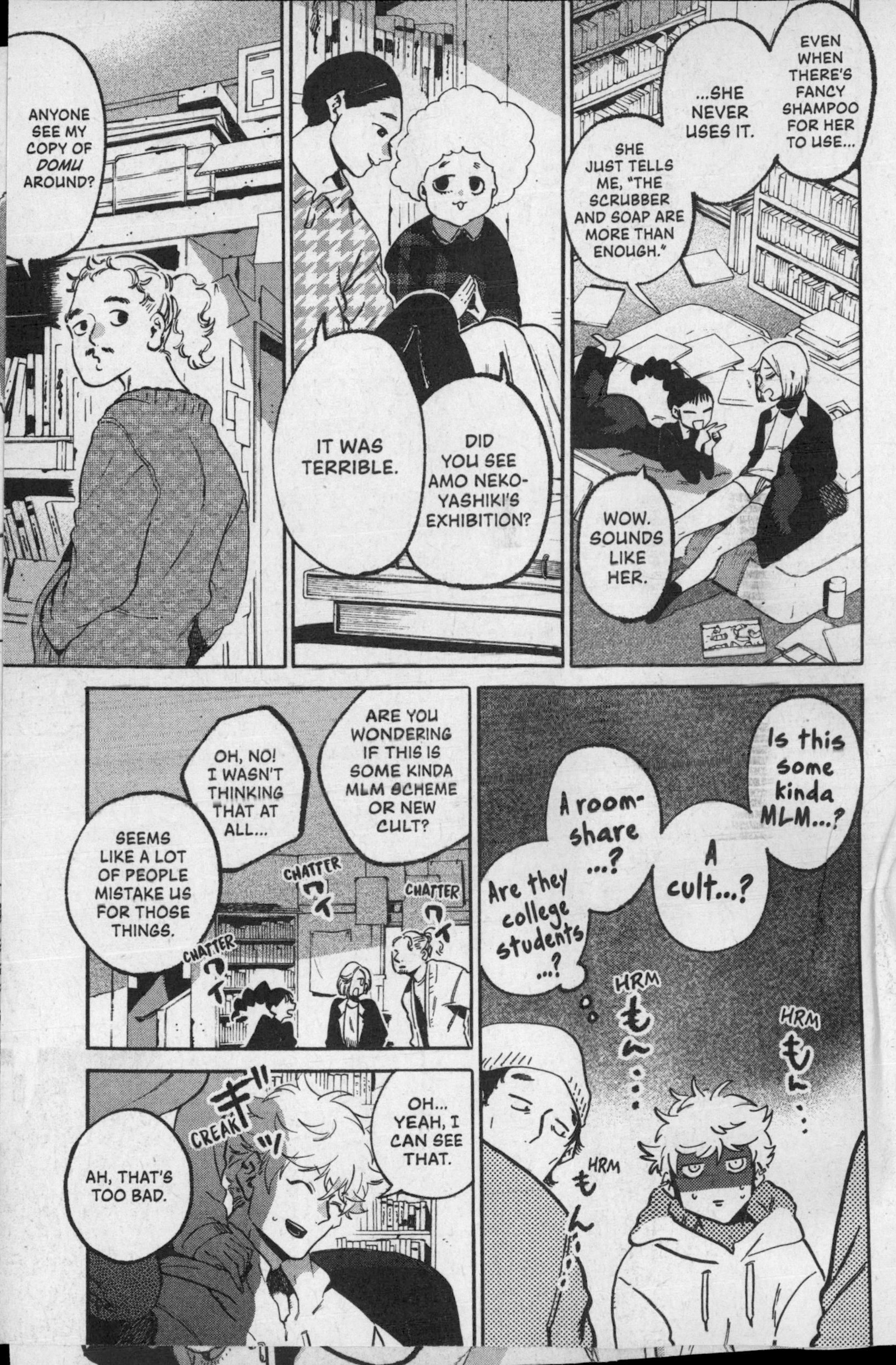
EVEN WHEN THERE'S FANCY SHAMPOO FOR HER TO USE...
...SHE NEVER USES IT.
SHE JUST TELLS ME, "THE SCRUBBER AND SOAP ARE MORE THAN ENOUGH."
WOW. SOUNDS LIKE HER.
DID YOU SEE AMO NEKO-YASHIKI'S EXHIBITION?
IT WAS TERRIBLE.
ANYONE SEE MY COPY OF *DOMU* AROUND?
Is this some kinda MLM...?
A cult...?
A room-share...?
Are they college students...?
HRM
もん...
HRM
もん...
HRM
もん...
ARE YOU WONDERING IF THIS IS SOME KINDA MLM SCHEME OR NEW CULT?
OH, NO! I WASN'T THINKING THAT AT ALL...
SEEMS LIKE A LOT OF PEOPLE MISTAKE US FOR THOSE THINGS.
CHATTER
ワイ
CHATTER
ワイ
CHATTER
ワイ
OH... YEAH, I CAN SEE THAT.
CREAK
ギッ
AH, THAT'S TOO BAD.

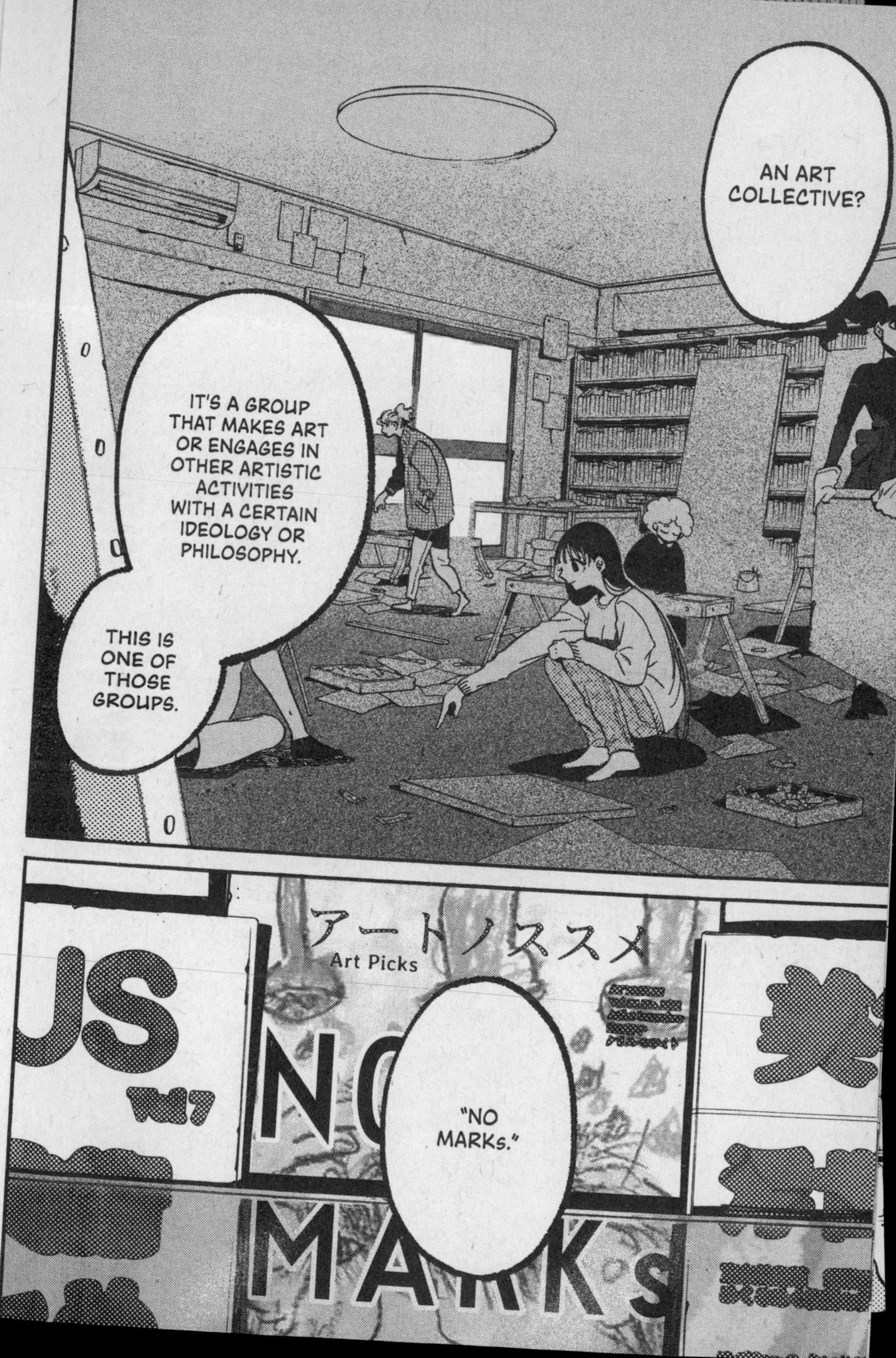
AN ART COLLECTIVE?
IT'S A GROUP THAT MAKES ART OR ENGAGES IN OTHER ARTISTIC ACTIVITIES WITH A CERTAIN IDEOLOGY OR PHILOSOPHY.
THIS IS ONE OF THOSE GROUPS.
アートノススメ
Art Picks
"NO MARKs."

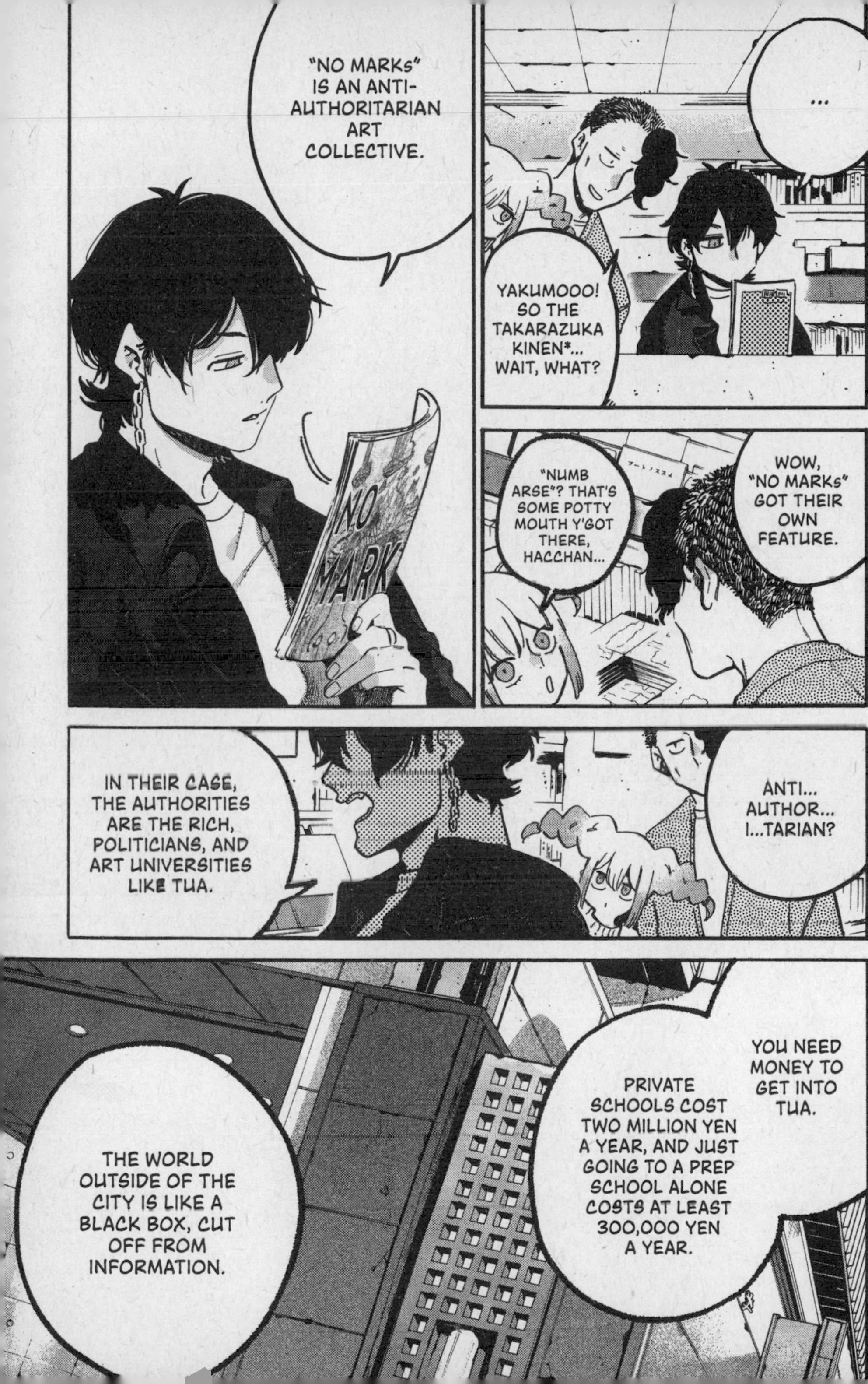
...
YAKUMOOO! SO THE TAKARAZUKA KINEN*... WAIT, WHAT?
WOW, "NO MARKs" GOT THEIR OWN FEATURE.
"NUMB ARSE"? THAT'S SOME POTTY MOUTH Y'GOT THERE, HACCHAN...
"NO MARKs" IS AN ANTI-AUTHORITARIAN ART COLLECTIVE.
NO MARK
ANTI... AUTHOR... I...TARIAN?
IN THEIR CASE, THE AUTHORITIES ARE THE RICH, POLITICIANS, AND ART UNIVERSITIES LIKE TUA.
YOU NEED MONEY TO GET INTO TUA.
PRIVATE SCHOOLS COST TWO MILLION YEN A YEAR, AND JUST GOING TO A PREP SCHOOL ALONE COSTS AT LEAST 300,000 YEN A YEAR.
THE WORLD OUTSIDE OF THE CITY IS LIKE A BLACK BOX, CUT OFF FROM INFORMATION.

*A FAMOUS HORSE RACE HELD IN THE CITY OF TAKARAZUKA IN HYOGO PREFECTURE, JAPAN.

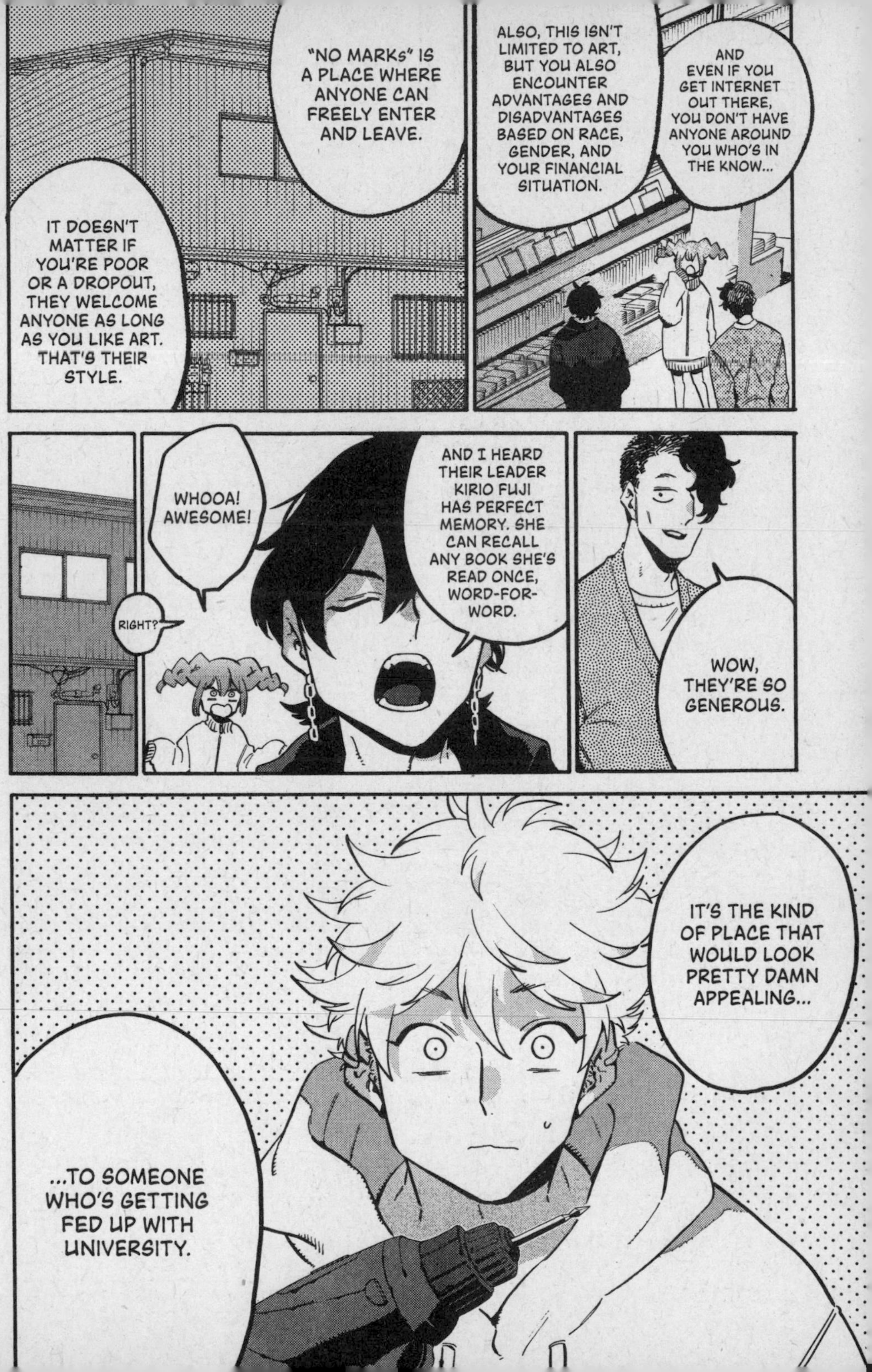
ALSO, THIS ISN'T LIMITED TO ART, BUT YOU ALSO ENCOUNTER ADVANTAGES AND DISADVANTAGES BASED ON RACE, GENDER, AND YOUR FINANCIAL SITUATION.
AND EVEN IF YOU GET INTERNET OUT THERE, YOU DON'T HAVE ANYONE AROUND YOU WHO'S IN THE KNOW...
"NO MARKs" IS A PLACE WHERE ANYONE CAN FREELY ENTER AND LEAVE.
IT DOESN'T MATTER IF YOU'RE POOR OR A DROPOUT, THEY WELCOME ANYONE AS LONG AS YOU LIKE ART. THAT'S THEIR STYLE.
WOW, THEY'RE SO GENEROUS.
AND I HEARD THEIR LEADER KIRIO FUJI HAS PERFECT MEMORY. SHE CAN RECALL ANY BOOK SHE'S READ ONCE, WORD-FOR-WORD.
WHOOA! AWESOME!
RIGHT?
IT'S THE KIND OF PLACE THAT WOULD LOOK PRETTY DAMN APPEALING...
...TO SOMEONE WHO'S GETTING FED UP WITH UNIVERSITY.

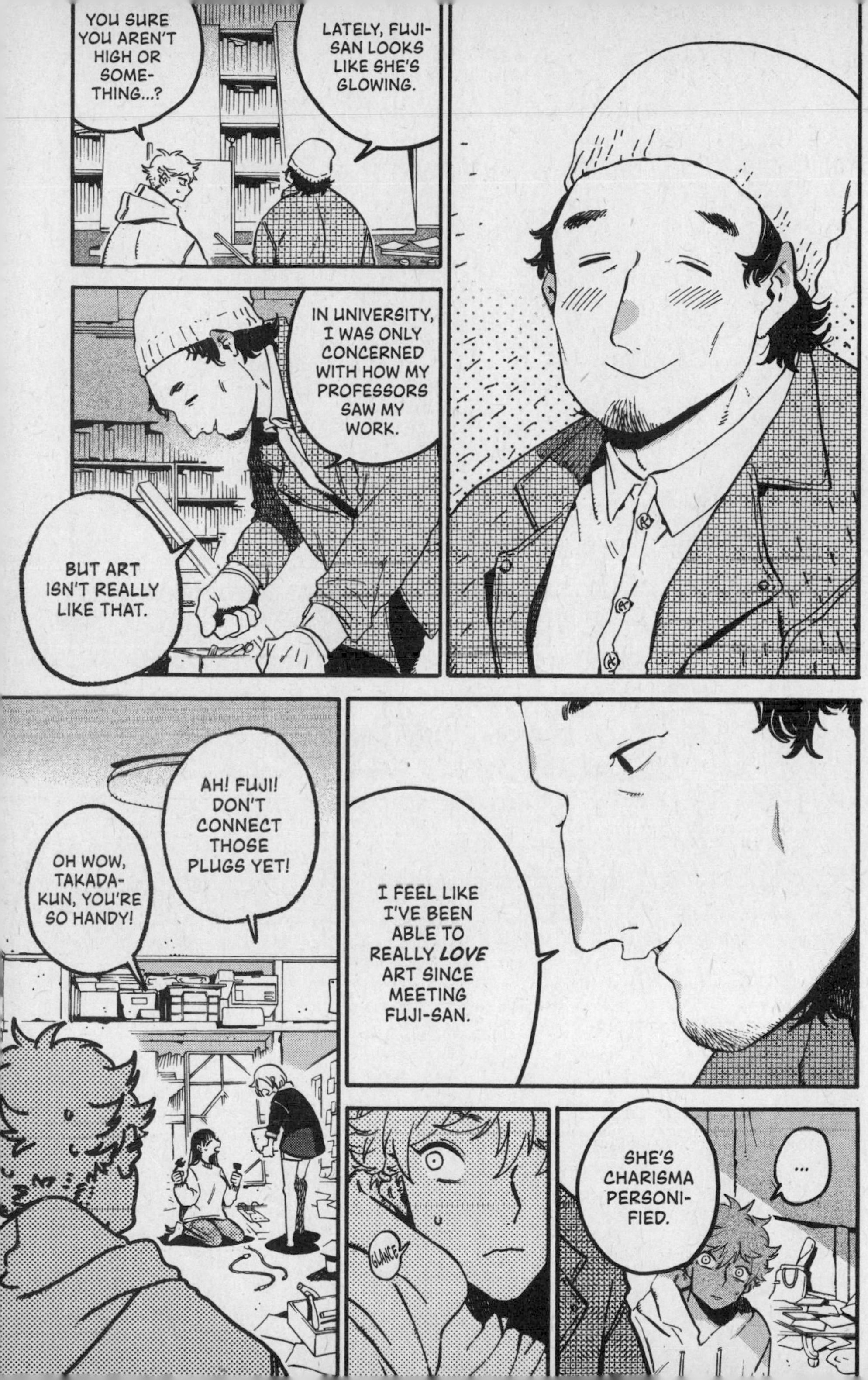
LATELY, FUJI-SAN LOOKS LIKE SHE'S GLOWING.
YOU SURE YOU AREN'T HIGH OR SOMETHING...?
IN UNIVERSITY, I WAS ONLY CONCERNED WITH HOW MY PROFESSORS SAW MY WORK.
BUT ART ISN'T REALLY LIKE THAT.
I FEEL LIKE I'VE BEEN ABLE TO REALLY *LOVE* ART SINCE MEETING FUJI-SAN.
AH! FUJI! DON'T CONNECT THOSE PLUGS YET!
OH WOW, TAKADA-KUN, YOU'RE SO HANDY!
...
SHE'S CHARISMA PERSONIFIED.
GLANCE

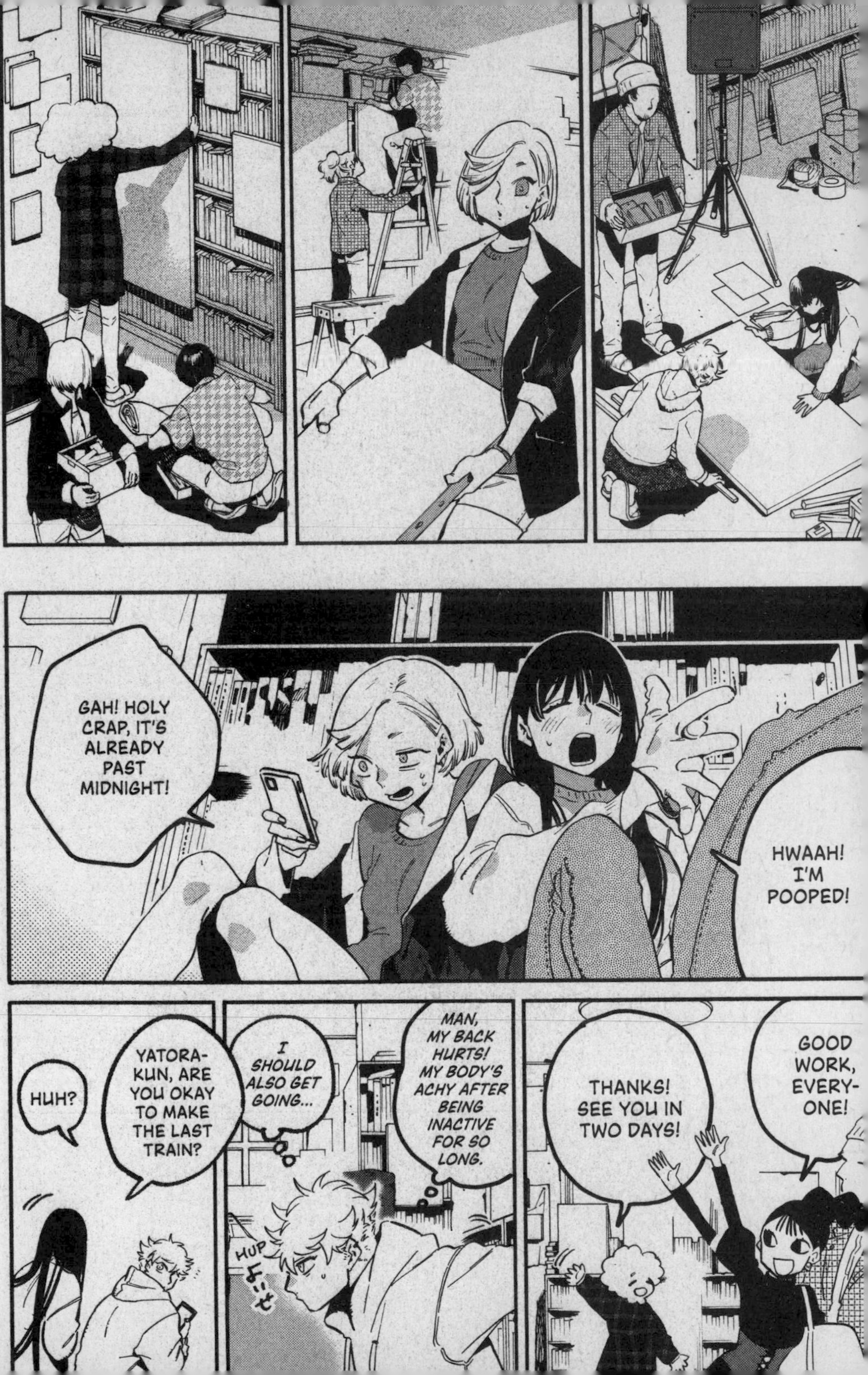
HWAAH! I'M POOPED!
GAH! HOLY CRAP, IT'S ALREADY PAST MIDNIGHT!
GOOD WORK, EVERY-ONE!
THANKS! SEE YOU IN TWO DAYS!
MAN, MY BACK HURTS! MY BODY'S ACHY AFTER BEING INACTIVE FOR SO LONG.
I SHOULD ALSO GET GOING...
HUP
よいせ
YATORA-KUN, ARE YOU OKAY TO MAKE THE LAST TRAIN?
HUH?

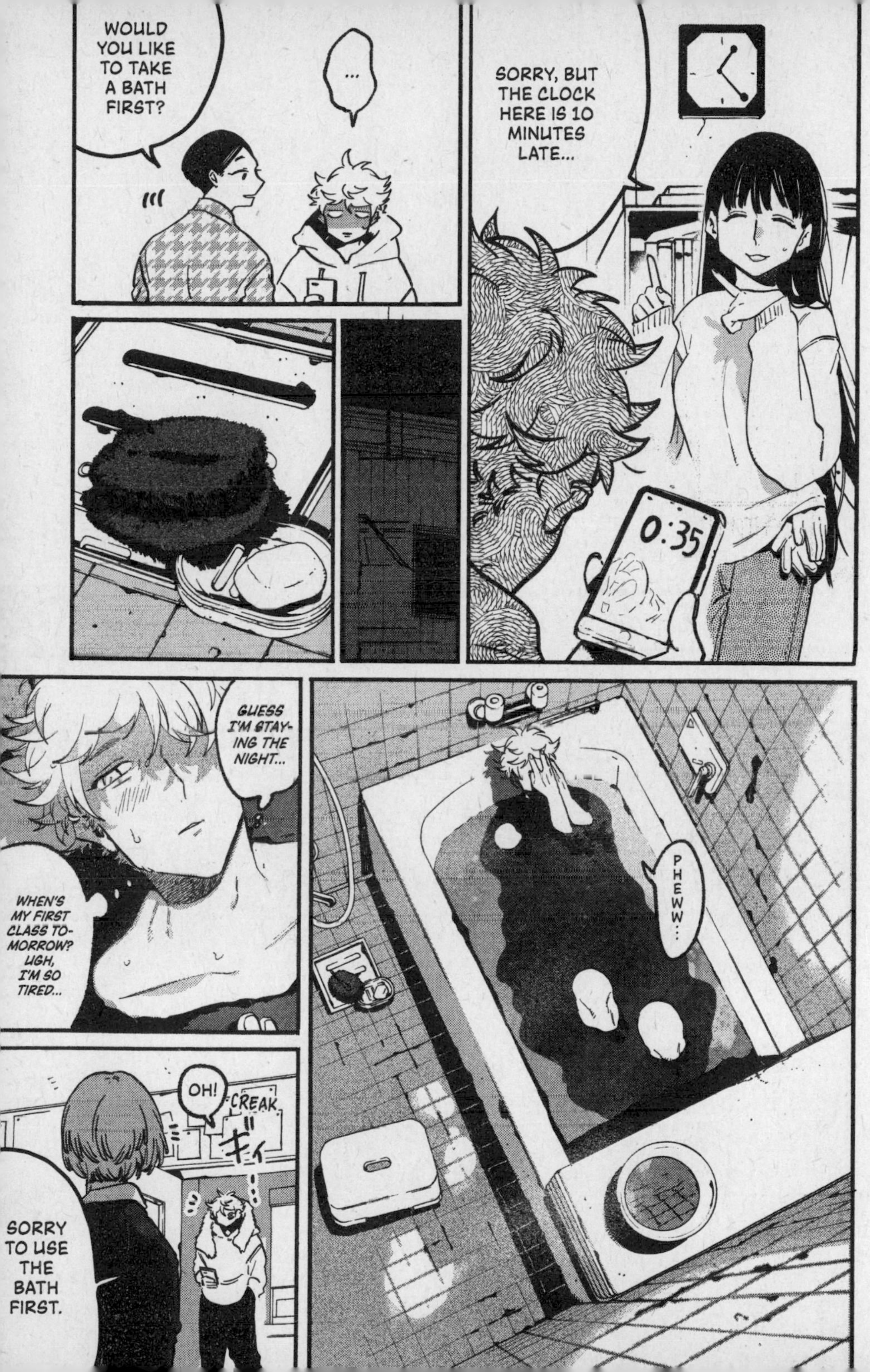
SORRY, BUT THE CLOCK HERE IS 10 MINUTES LATE...
0:35
WOULD YOU LIKE TO TAKE A BATH FIRST?
...
PHEWW...
GUESS I'M STAYING THE NIGHT...
WHEN'S MY FIRST CLASS TOMORROW? UGH, I'M SO TIRED...
OH!
CREAK
ギイ
SORRY TO USE THE BATH FIRST.

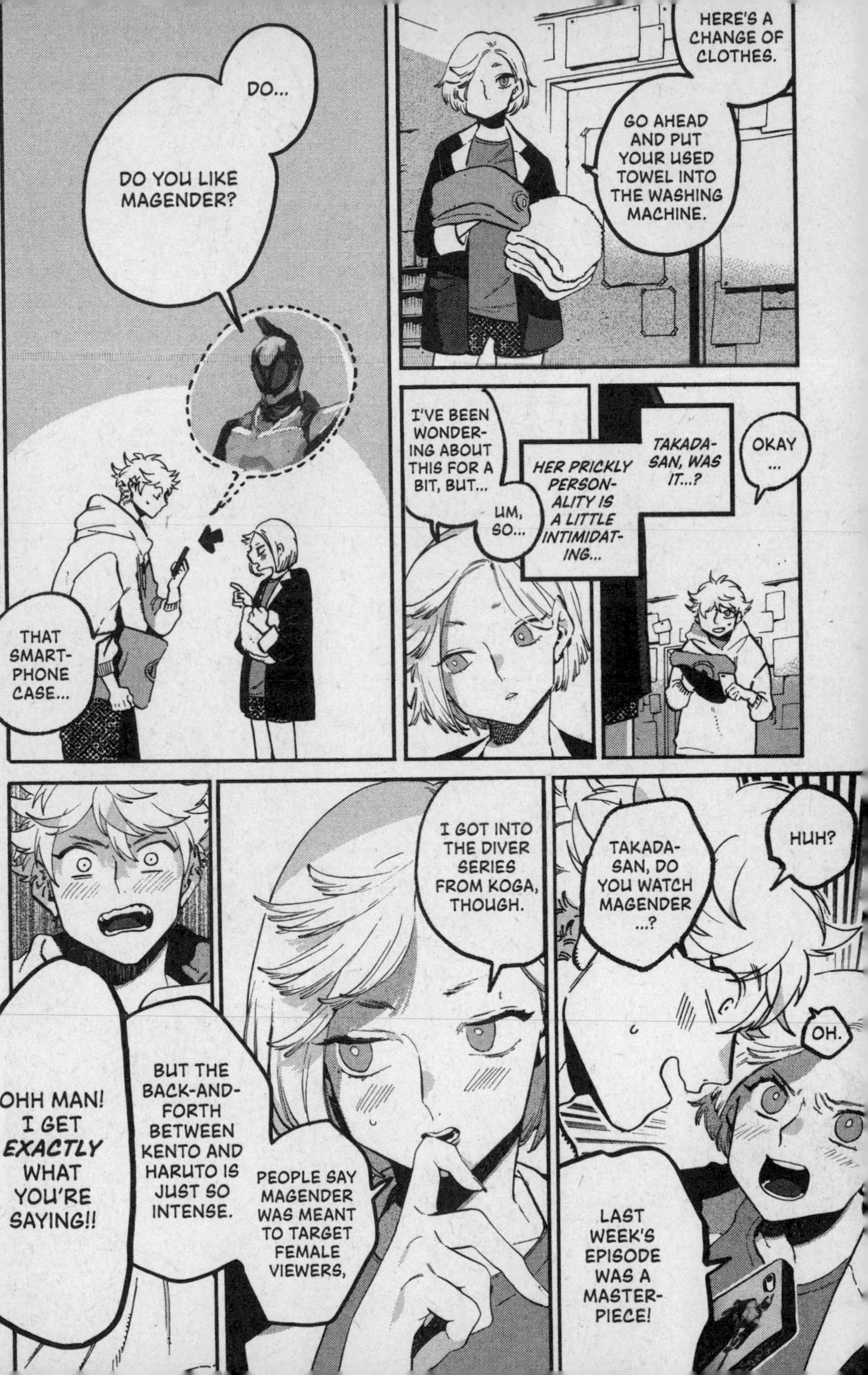
HERE'S A CHANGE OF CLOTHES.
GO AHEAD AND PUT YOUR USED TOWEL INTO THE WASHING MACHINE.
OKAY ...
TAKADA-SAN, WAS IT...?
HER PRICKLY PERSONALITY IS A LITTLE INTIMIDATING...
I'VE BEEN WONDERING ABOUT THIS FOR A BIT, BUT...
UM, SO...
DO...
DO YOU LIKE MAGENDER?
THAT SMARTPHONE CASE...
MAGENDER/WO-SAKANA
HUH?
TAKADA-SAN, DO YOU WATCH MAGENDER ...?
OH.
LAST WEEK'S EPISODE WAS A MASTERPIECE!
I GOT INTO THE DIVER SERIES FROM KOGA, THOUGH.
PEOPLE SAY MAGENDER WAS MEANT TO TARGET FEMALE VIEWERS,
BUT THE BACK-AND-FORTH BETWEEN KENTO AND HARUTO IS JUST SO INTENSE.
OHH MAN! I GET *EXACTLY* WHAT YOU'RE SAYING!!

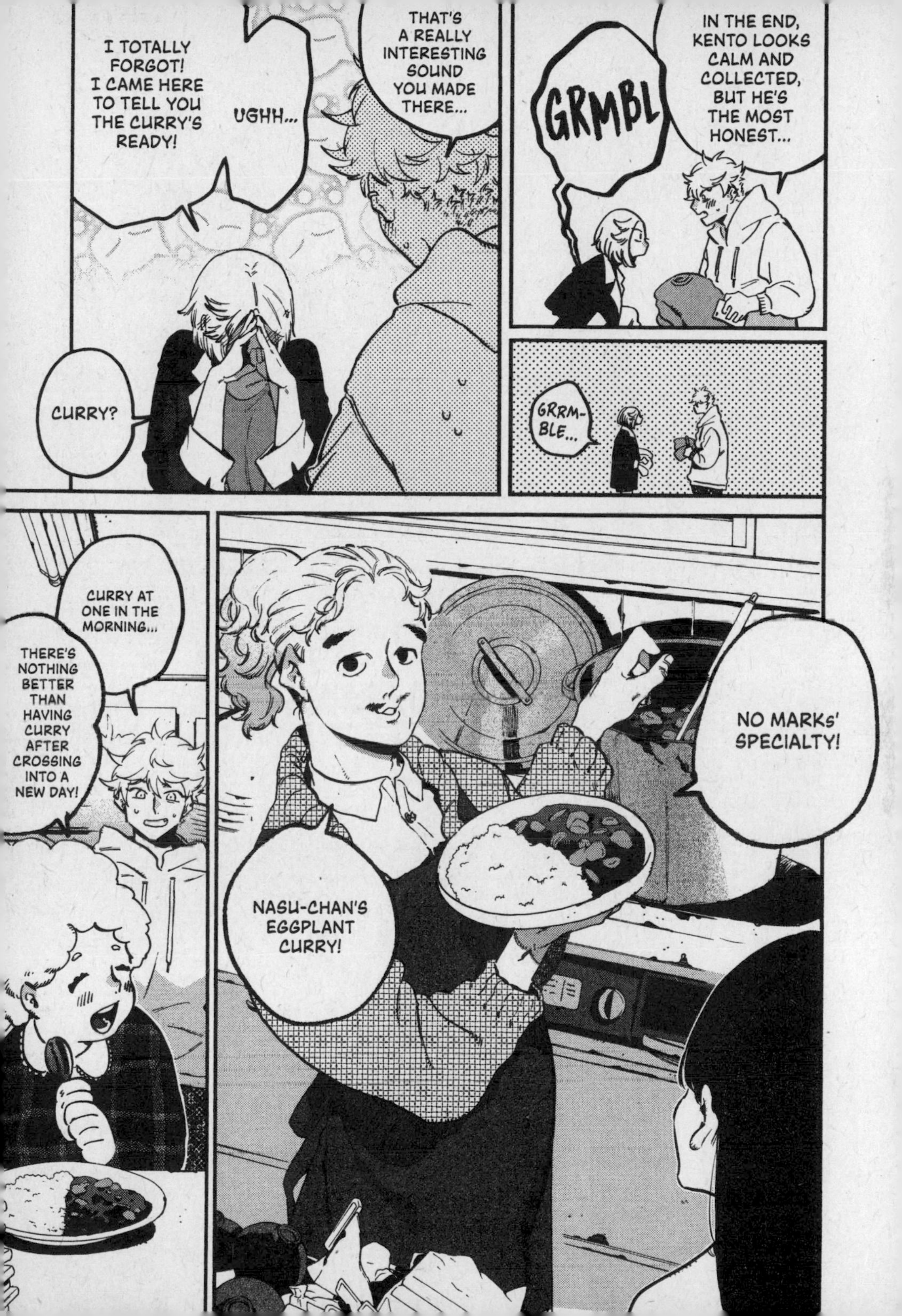
IN THE END, KENTO LOOKS CALM AND COLLECTED, BUT HE'S THE MOST HONEST...
GRMBL
GRRM-BLE...
THAT'S A REALLY INTERESTING SOUND YOU MADE THERE...
UGHH...
I TOTALLY FORGOT! I CAME HERE TO TELL YOU THE CURRY'S READY!
CURRY?
NO MARKs' SPECIALTY!
NASU-CHAN'S EGGPLANT CURRY!
CURRY AT ONE IN THE MORNING...
THERE'S NOTHING BETTER THAN HAVING CURRY AFTER CROSSING INTO A NEW DAY!

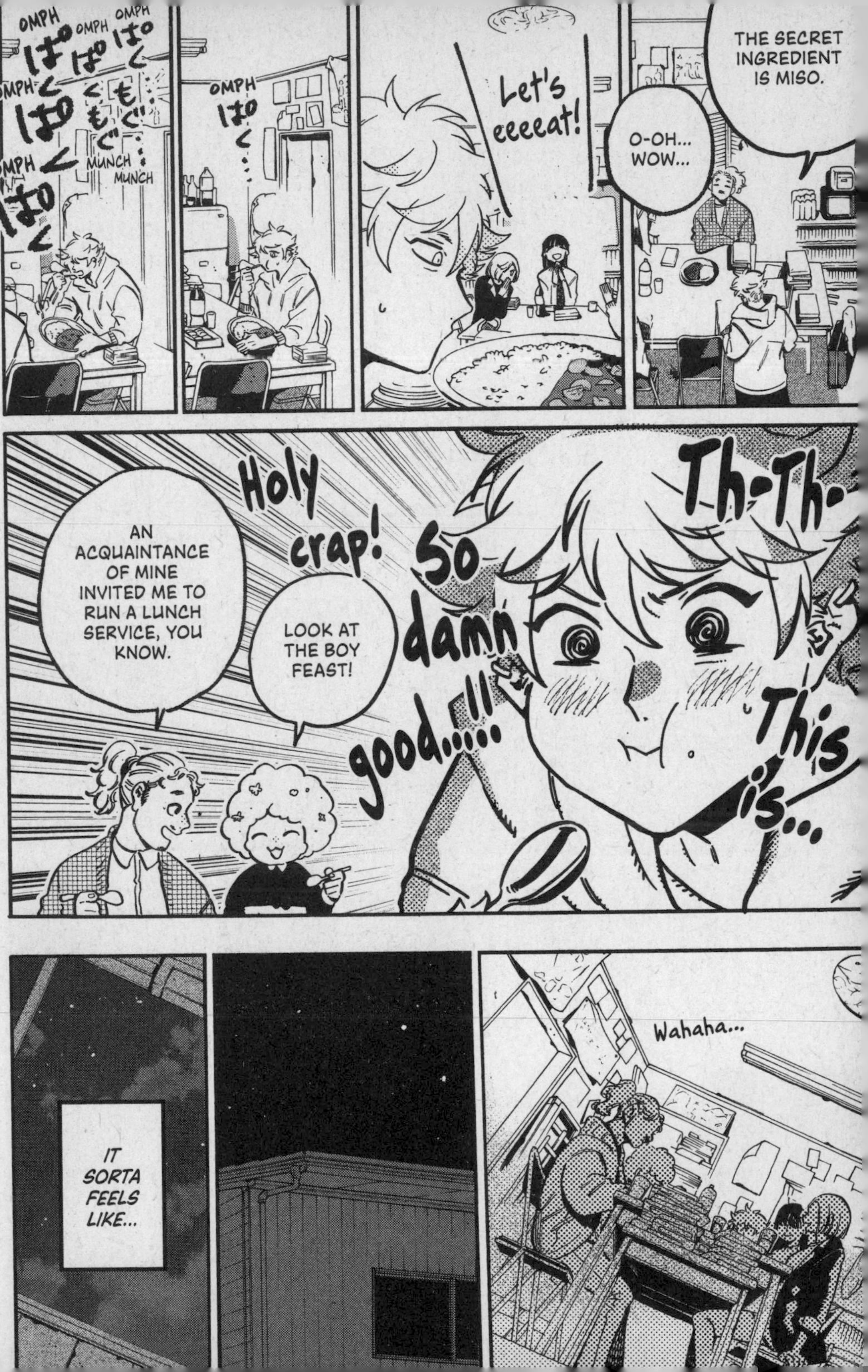
THE SECRET INGREDIENT IS MISO.
O-OH... WOW...
Let's eeeeat!
OMPH
ぱく
OMPH
ぱく
OMPH
ぱく
OMPH
ぱく
OMPH
ぱく
もぐもぐ
MUNCH MUNCH
Th-Th-This is...
So damn good...!!
Holy crap!
LOOK AT THE BOY FEAST!
AN ACQUAINTANCE OF MINE INVITED ME TO RUN A LUNCH SERVICE, YOU KNOW.
Wahaha...
IT SORTA FEELS LIKE...

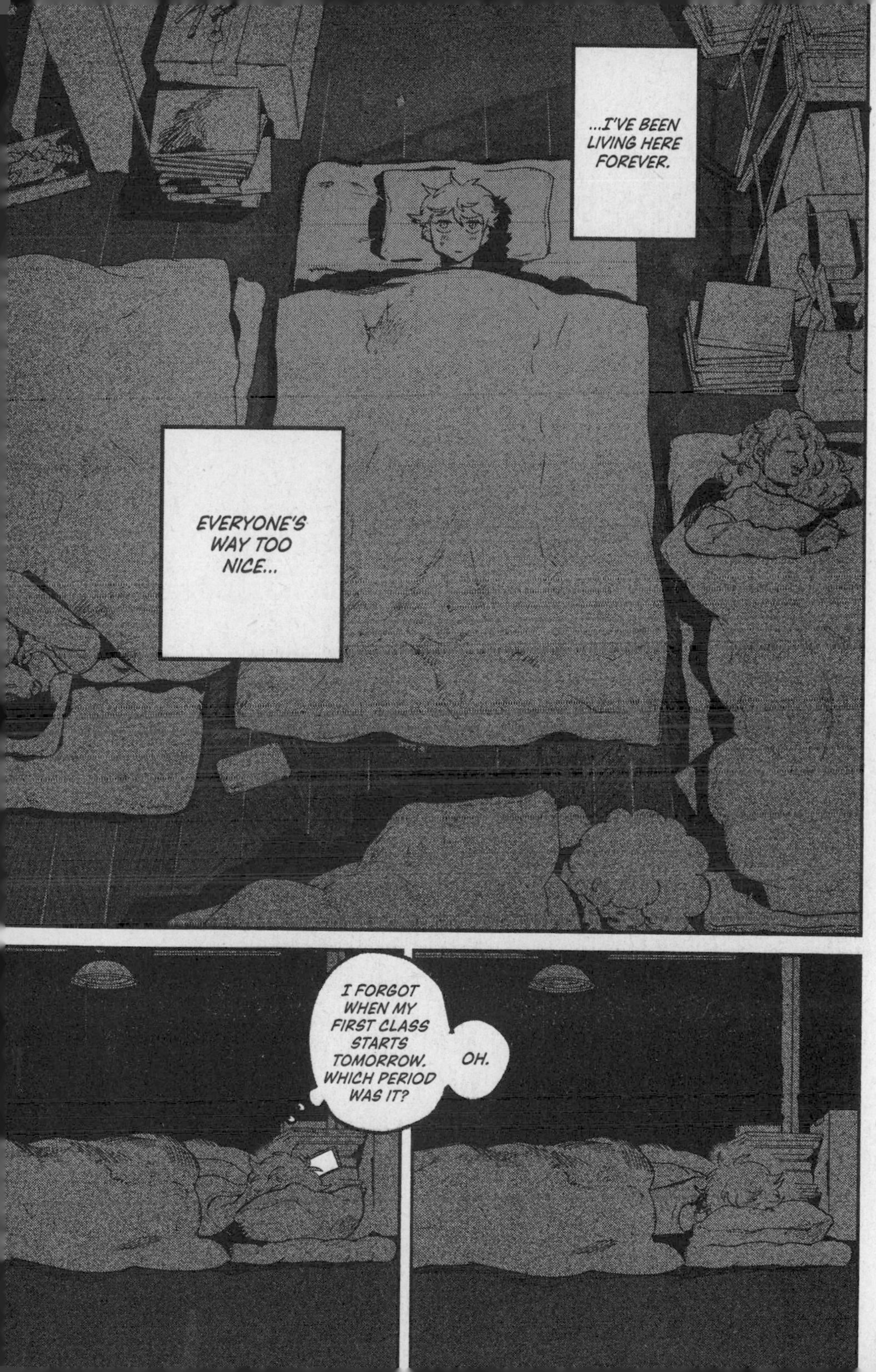
...I'VE BEEN LIVING HERE FOREVER.
EVERYONE'S WAY TOO NICE...
OH.
I FORGOT WHEN MY FIRST CLASS STARTS TOMORROW. WHICH PERIOD WAS IT?

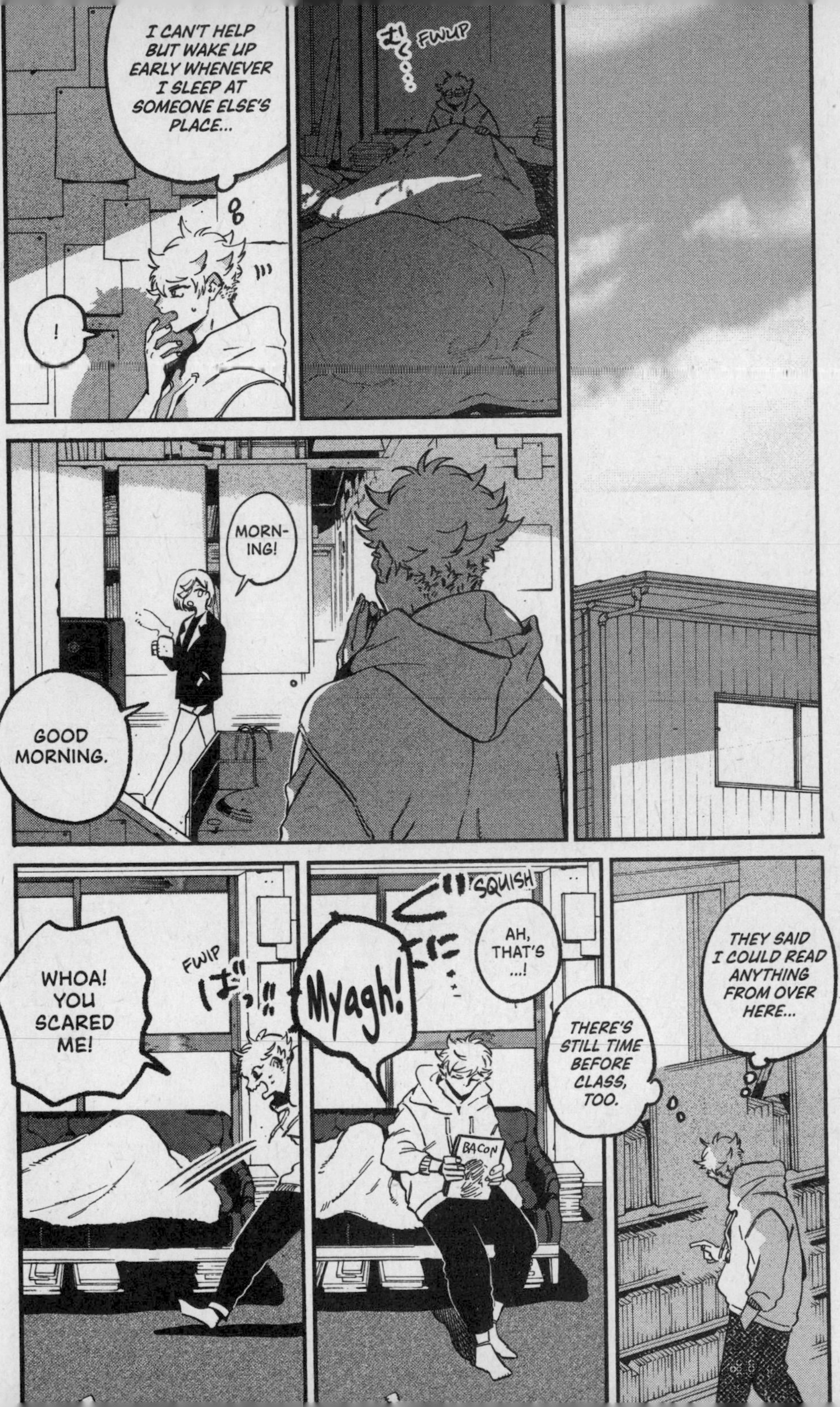
FWUP
I CAN'T HELP BUT WAKE UP EARLY WHENEVER I SLEEP AT SOMEONE ELSE'S PLACE...
!
MORN-ING!
GOOD MORNING.
THEY SAID I COULD READ ANYTHING FROM OVER HERE...
SQUISH
AH, THAT'S ...!
THERE'S STILL TIME BEFORE CLASS, TOO.
Myagh!
FWIP
WHOA! YOU SCARED ME!

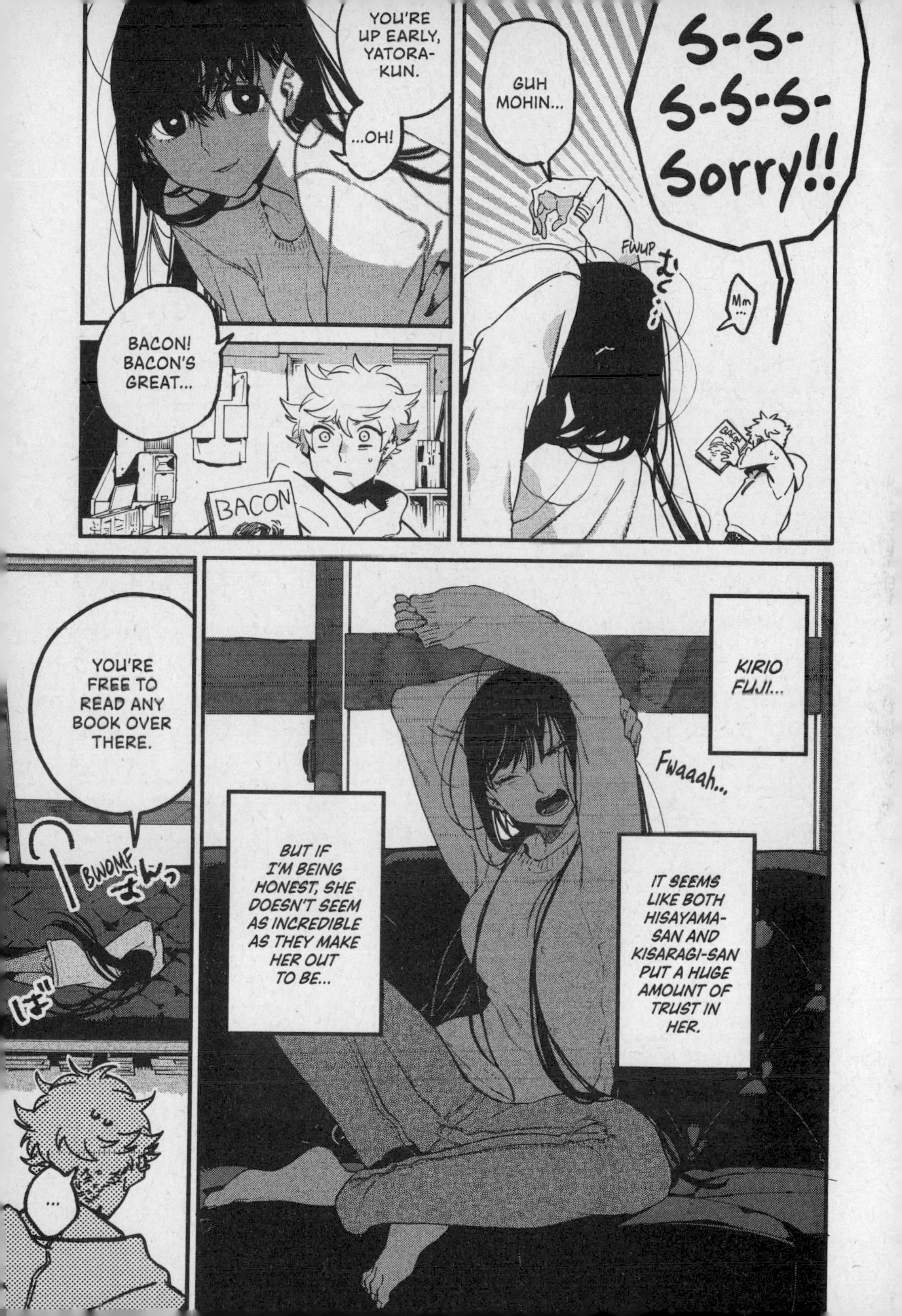
S-S-S-S-S-Sorry!!
GUH MOHIN...
FWUP
Mm ...
YOU'RE UP EARLY, YATORA-KUN.
...OH!
BACON! BACON'S GREAT...
BACON
KIRIO FUJI...
Fwaaah...
IT SEEMS LIKE BOTH HISAYAMA-SAN AND KISARAGI-SAN PUT A HUGE AMOUNT OF TRUST IN HER.
BUT IF I'M BEING HONEST, SHE DOESN'T SEEM AS INCREDIBLE AS THEY MAKE HER OUT TO BE...
YOU'RE FREE TO READ ANY BOOK OVER THERE.
BWOMF
...

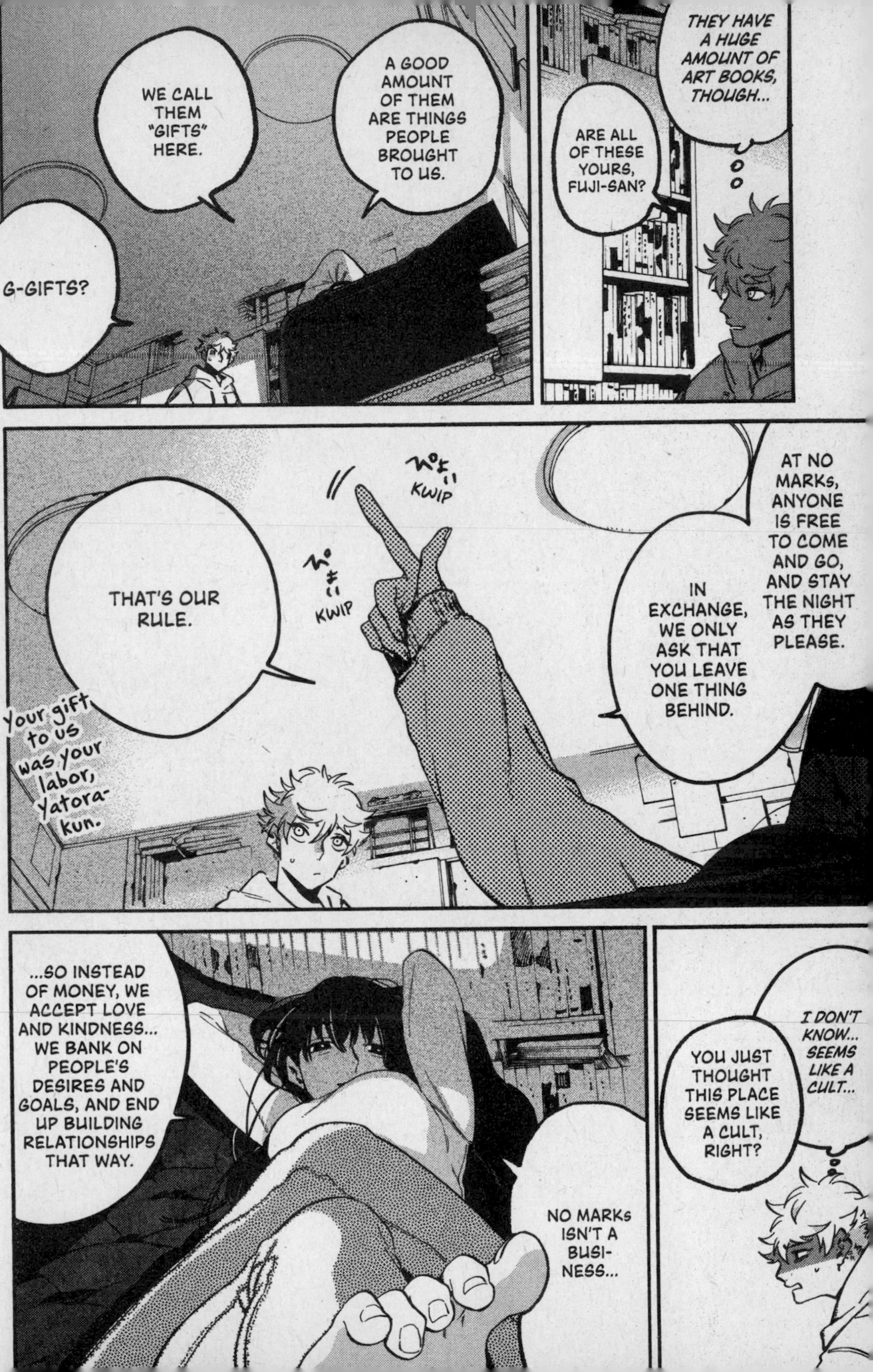
THEY HAVE A HUGE AMOUNT OF ART BOOKS, THOUGH...
ARE ALL OF THESE YOURS, FUJI-SAN?
A GOOD AMOUNT OF THEM ARE THINGS PEOPLE BROUGHT TO US.
WE CALL THEM "GIFTS" HERE.
G-GIFTS?
AT NO MARKS, ANYONE IS FREE TO COME AND GO, AND STAY THE NIGHT AS THEY PLEASE.
IN EXCHANGE, WE ONLY ASK THAT YOU LEAVE ONE THING BEHIND.
KWIP
KWIP
THAT'S OUR RULE.
Your gift to us was your labor, Yatora-kun.
I DON'T KNOW... SEEMS LIKE A CULT...
YOU JUST THOUGHT THIS PLACE SEEMS LIKE A CULT, RIGHT?
NO MARKS ISN'T A BUSI-NESS...
...SO INSTEAD OF MONEY, WE ACCEPT LOVE AND KINDNESS... WE BANK ON PEOPLE'S DESIRES AND GOALS, AND END UP BUILDING RELATIONSHIPS THAT WAY.

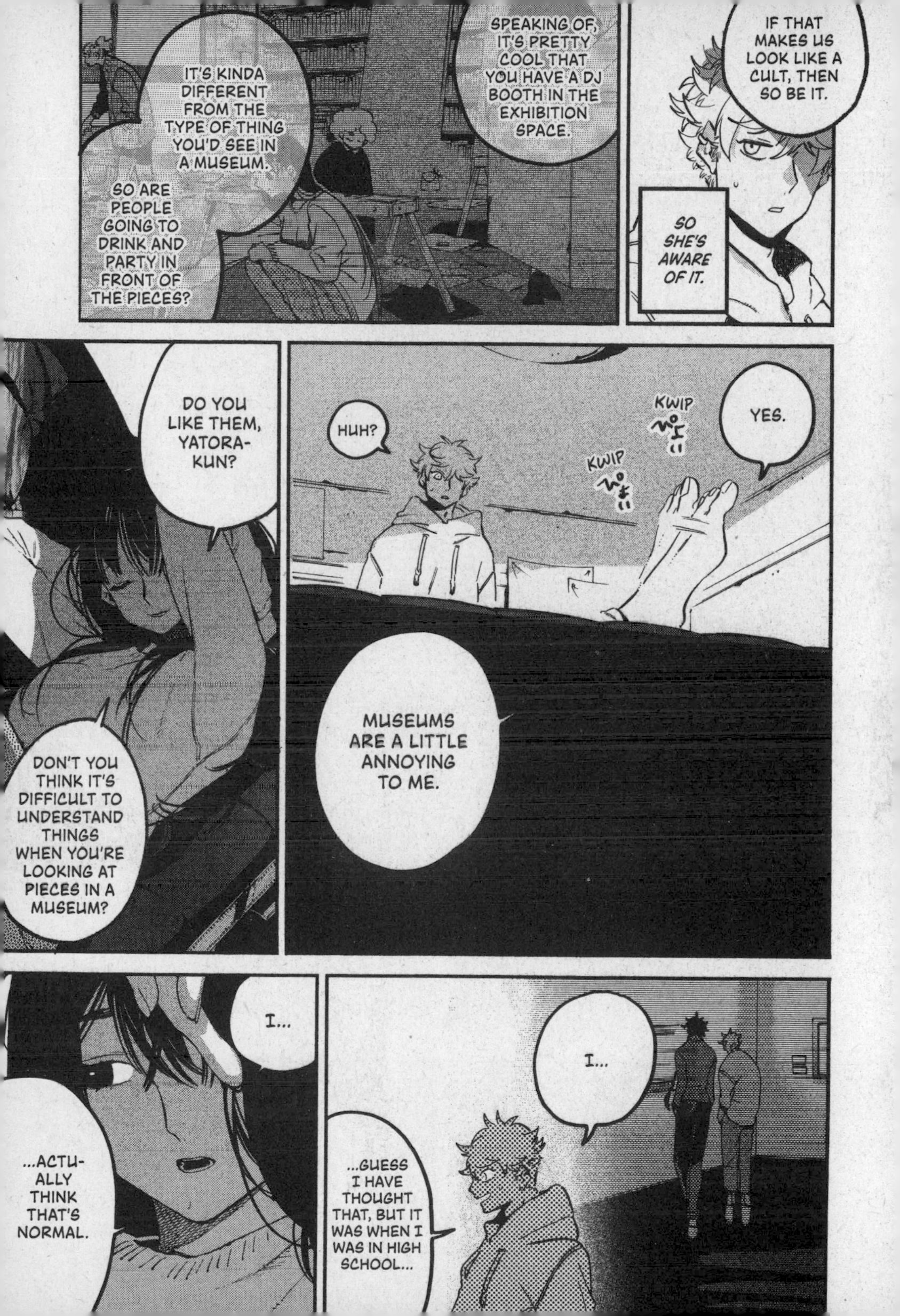
IF THAT MAKES US LOOK LIKE A CULT, THEN SO BE IT.
SO SHE'S AWARE OF IT.
SPEAKING OF, IT'S PRETTY COOL THAT YOU HAVE A DJ BOOTH IN THE EXHIBITION SPACE.
IT'S KINDA DIFFERENT FROM THE TYPE OF THING YOU'D SEE IN A MUSEUM.
SO ARE PEOPLE GOING TO DRINK AND PARTY IN FRONT OF THE PIECES?
YES.
KWIP
KWIP
HUH?
MUSEUMS ARE A LITTLE ANNOYING TO ME.
DO YOU LIKE THEM, YATORA-KUN?
DON'T YOU THINK IT'S DIFFICULT TO UNDERSTAND THINGS WHEN YOU'RE LOOKING AT PIECES IN A MUSEUM?
I...
...GUESS I HAVE THOUGHT THAT, BUT IT WAS WHEN I WAS IN HIGH SCHOOL...
I...
...ACTU-ALLY THINK THAT'S NORMAL.

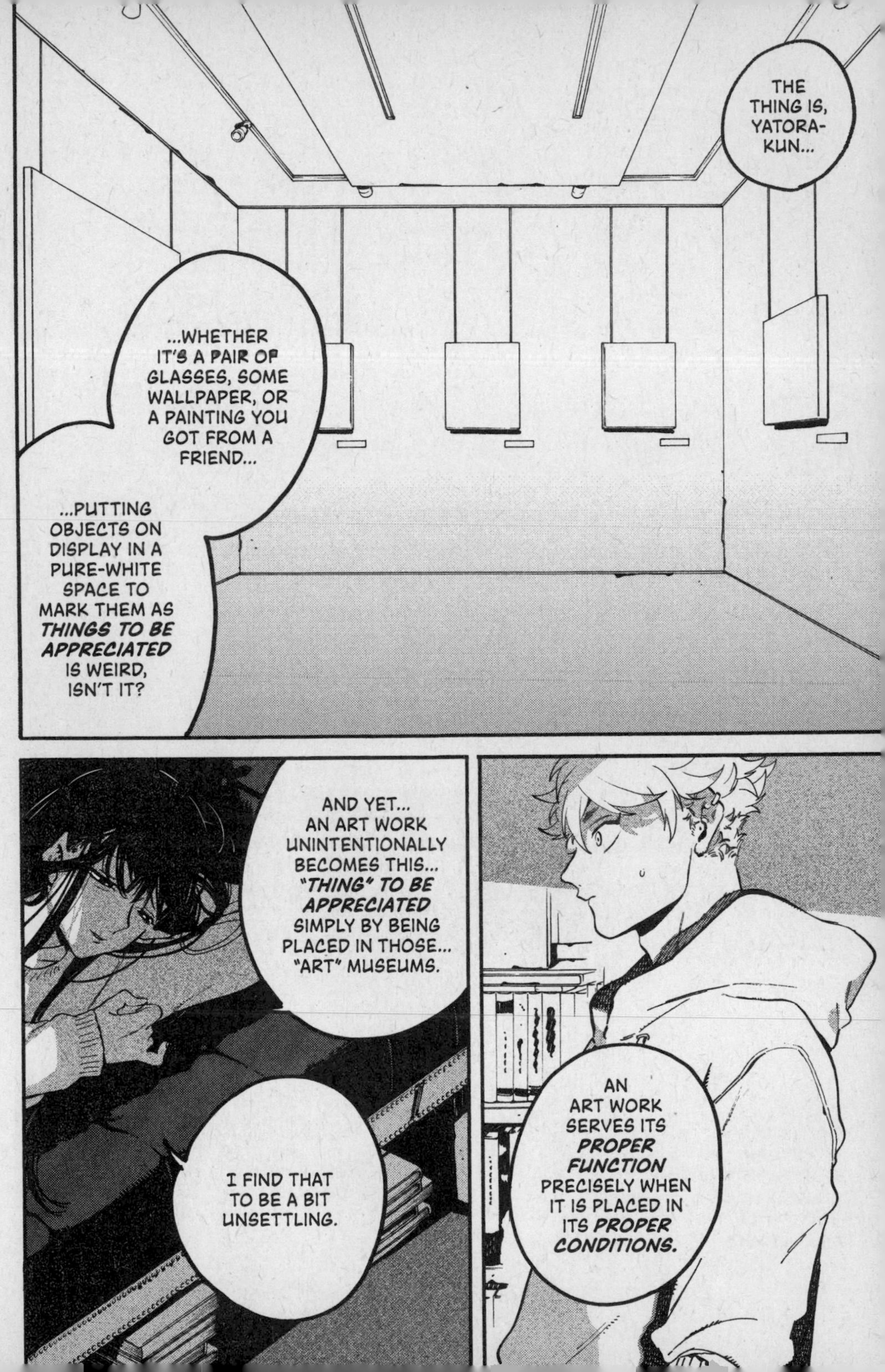
THE THING IS, YATORA-KUN...
...WHETHER IT'S A PAIR OF GLASSES, SOME WALLPAPER, OR A PAINTING YOU GOT FROM A FRIEND...
...PUTTING OBJECTS ON DISPLAY IN A PURE-WHITE SPACE TO MARK THEM AS ***THINGS TO BE APPRECIATED*** IS WEIRD, ISN'T IT?
AN ART WORK SERVES ITS ***PROPER FUNCTION*** PRECISELY WHEN IT IS PLACED IN ITS ***PROPER CONDITIONS.***
AND YET... AN ART WORK UNINTENTIONALLY BECOMES THIS... ***"THING" TO BE APPRECIATED*** SIMPLY BY BEING PLACED IN THOSE... "ART" MUSEUMS.
I FIND THAT TO BE A BIT UNSETTLING.

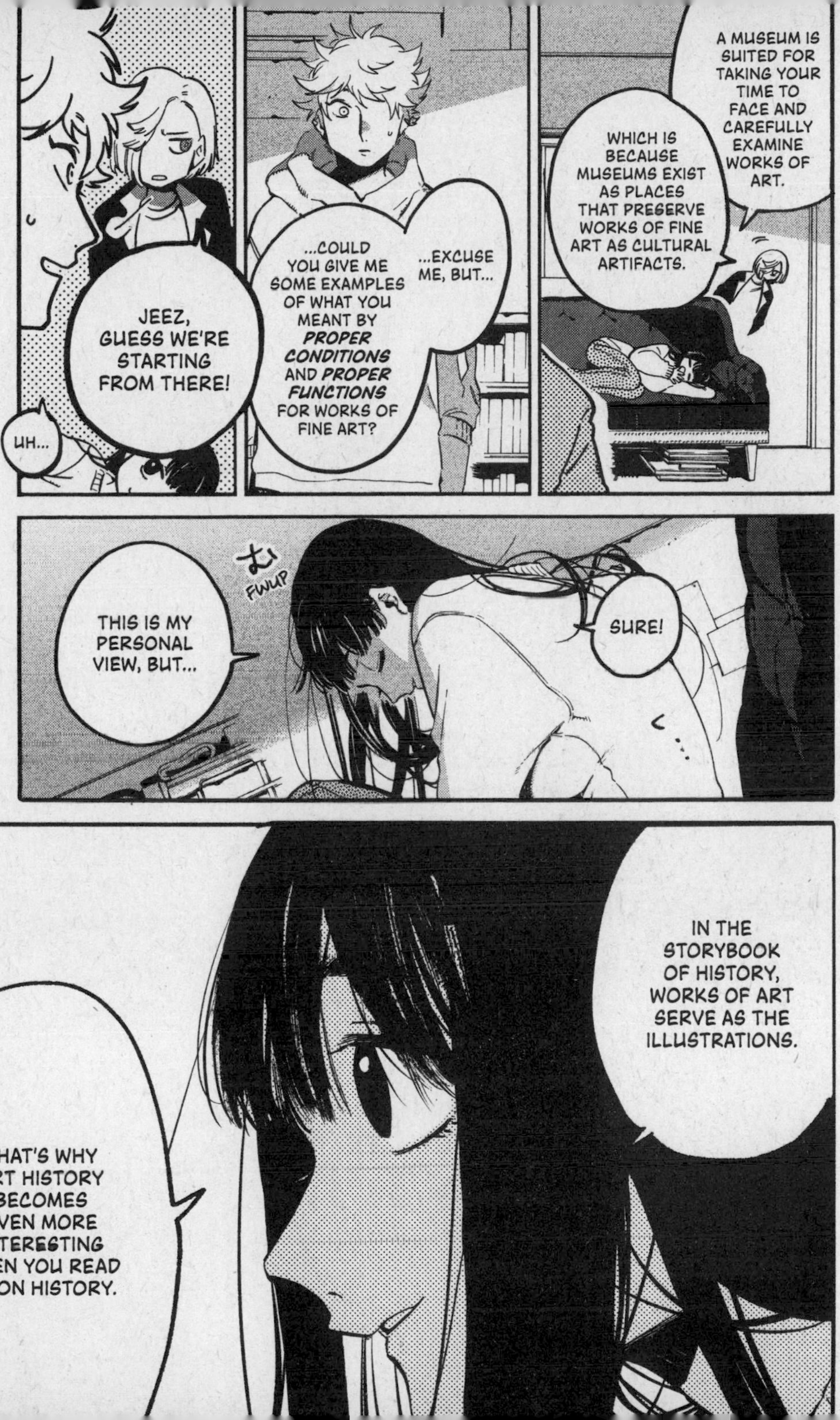
A MUSEUM IS SUITED FOR TAKING YOUR TIME TO FACE AND CAREFULLY EXAMINE WORKS OF ART.
WHICH IS BECAUSE MUSEUMS EXIST AS PLACES THAT PRESERVE WORKS OF FINE ART AS CULTURAL ARTIFACTS.
...EXCUSE ME, BUT...
...COULD YOU GIVE ME SOME EXAMPLES OF WHAT YOU MEANT BY *PROPER CONDITIONS* AND *PROPER FUNCTIONS* FOR WORKS OF FINE ART?
JEEZ, GUESS WE'RE STARTING FROM THERE!
UH...
SURE!
FWUP
THIS IS MY PERSONAL VIEW, BUT...
IN THE STORYBOOK OF HISTORY, WORKS OF ART SERVE AS THE ILLUSTRATIONS.
THAT'S WHY ART HISTORY BECOMES EVEN MORE INTERESTING WHEN YOU READ UP ON HISTORY.

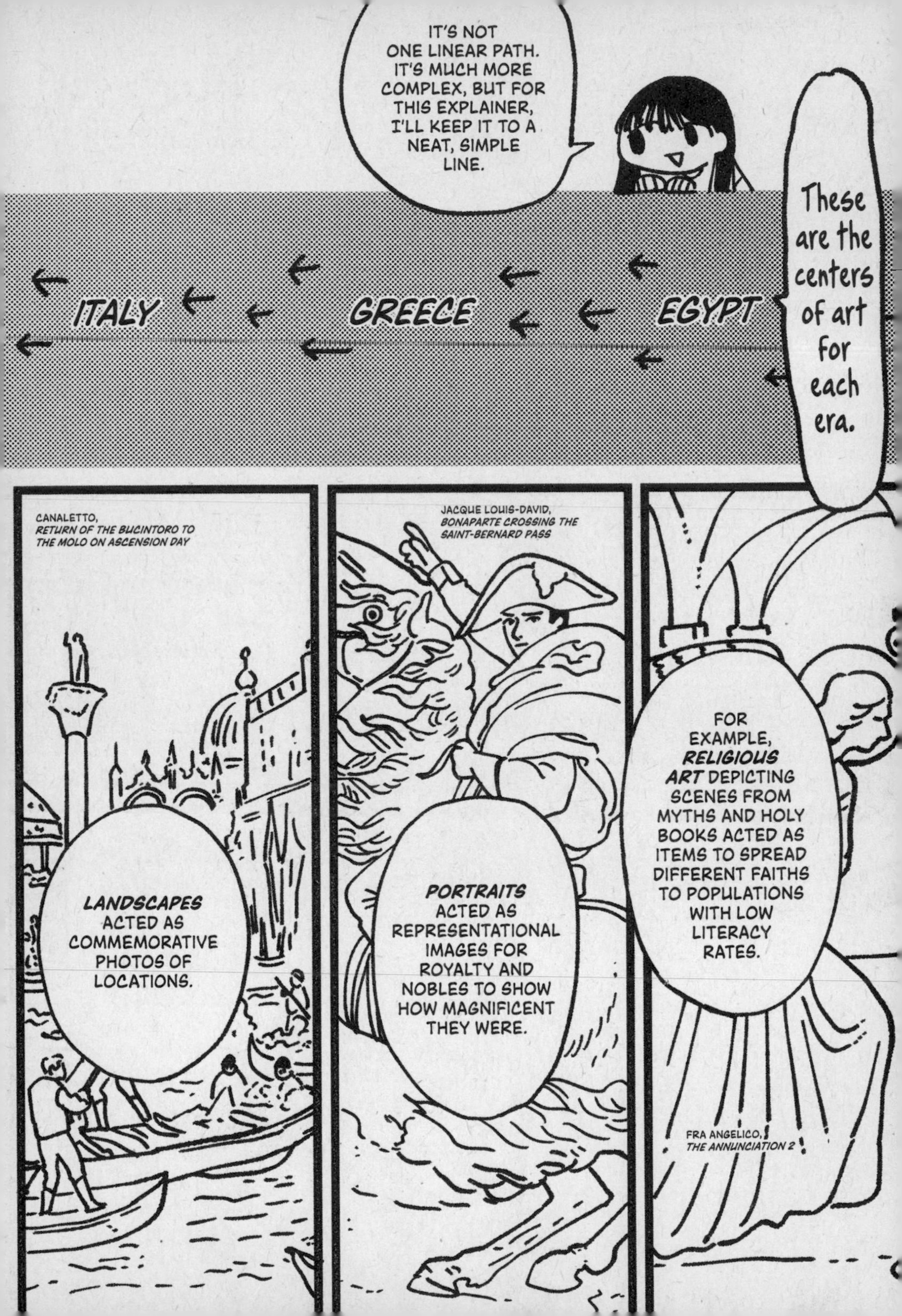
IT'S NOT ONE LINEAR PATH. IT'S MUCH MORE COMPLEX, BUT FOR THIS EXPLAINER, I'LL KEEP IT TO A NEAT, SIMPLE LINE.
These are the centers of art for each era.
EGYPT
GREECE
ITALY
FOR EXAMPLE, ***RELIGIOUS ART*** DEPICTING SCENES FROM MYTHS AND HOLY BOOKS ACTED AS ITEMS TO SPREAD DIFFERENT FAITHS TO POPULATIONS WITH LOW LITERACY RATES.
FRA ANGELICO, *THE ANNUNCIATION 2*
JACQUE LOUIS-DAVID, *BONAPARTE CROSSING THE SAINT-BERNARD PASS*
PORTRAITS ACTED AS REPRESENTATIONAL IMAGES FOR ROYALTY AND NOBLES TO SHOW HOW MAGNIFICENT THEY WERE.
CANALETTO, *RETURN OF THE BUCINTORO TO THE MOLO ON ASCENSION DAY*
LANDSCAPES ACTED AS COMMEMORATIVE PHOTOS OF LOCATIONS.

A super abbreviated version!

Western Art History

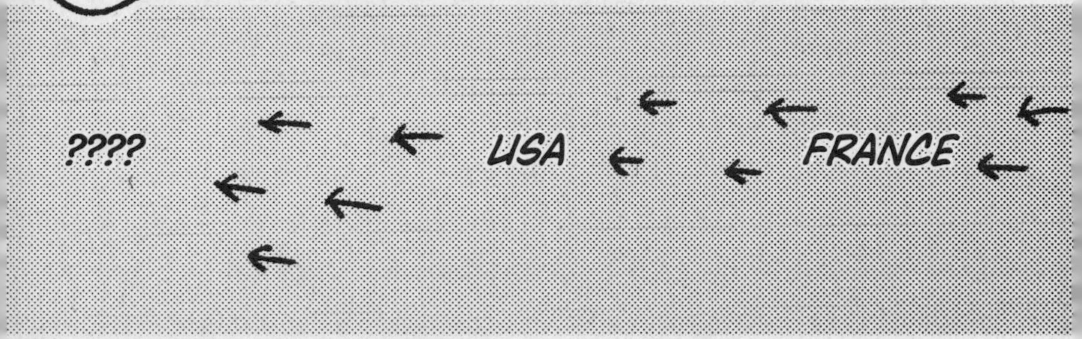
FRANCE
USA
????

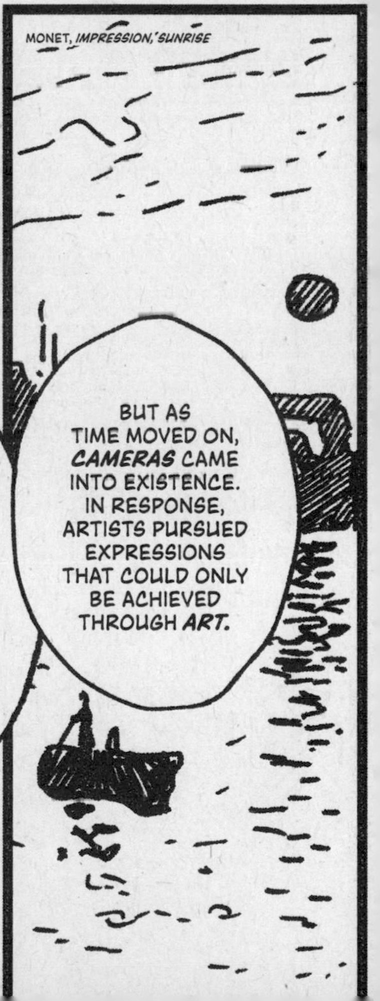
MONET, *IMPRESSION, SUNRISE*
BUT AS TIME MOVED ON, ***CAMERAS*** CAME INTO EXISTENCE. IN RESPONSE, ARTISTS PURSUED EXPRESSIONS THAT COULD ONLY BE ACHIEVED THROUGH ***ART.***

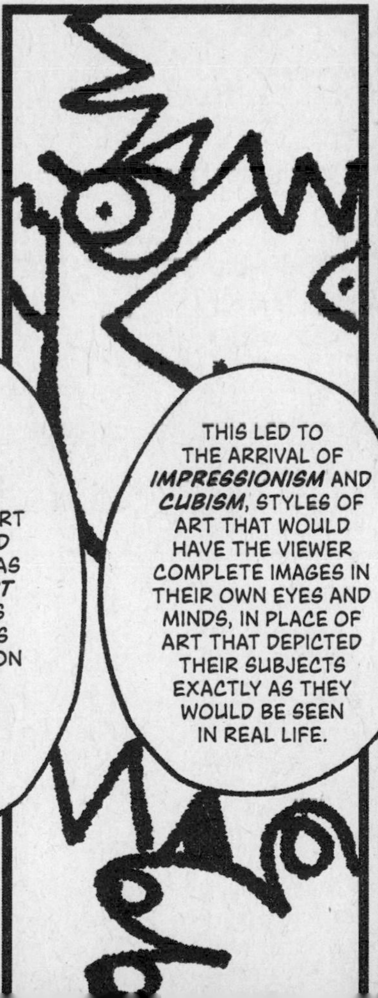
THIS LED TO THE ARRIVAL OF ***IMPRESSIONISM*** AND ***CUBISM***, STYLES OF ART THAT WOULD HAVE THE VIEWER COMPLETE IMAGES IN THEIR OWN EYES AND MINDS, IN PLACE OF ART THAT DEPICTED THEIR SUBJECTS EXACTLY AS THEY WOULD BE SEEN IN REAL LIFE.

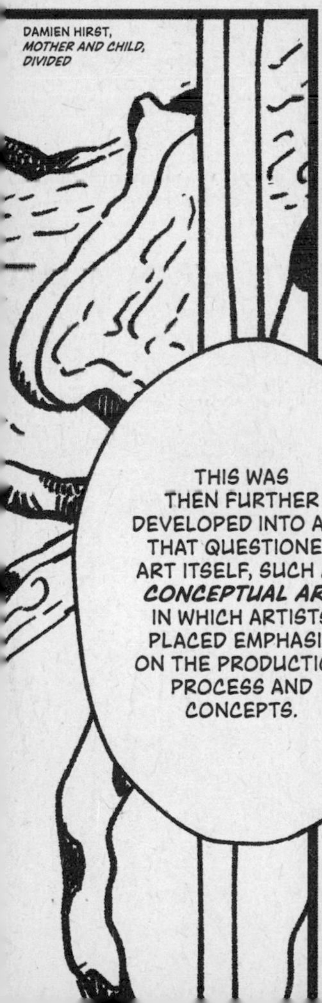
DAMIEN HIRST, *MOTHER AND CHILD, DIVIDED*
THIS WAS THEN FURTHER DEVELOPED INTO ART THAT QUESTIONED ART ITSELF, SUCH AS ***CONCEPTUAL ART*** IN WHICH ARTISTS PLACED EMPHASIS ON THE PRODUCTION PROCESS AND CONCEPTS.

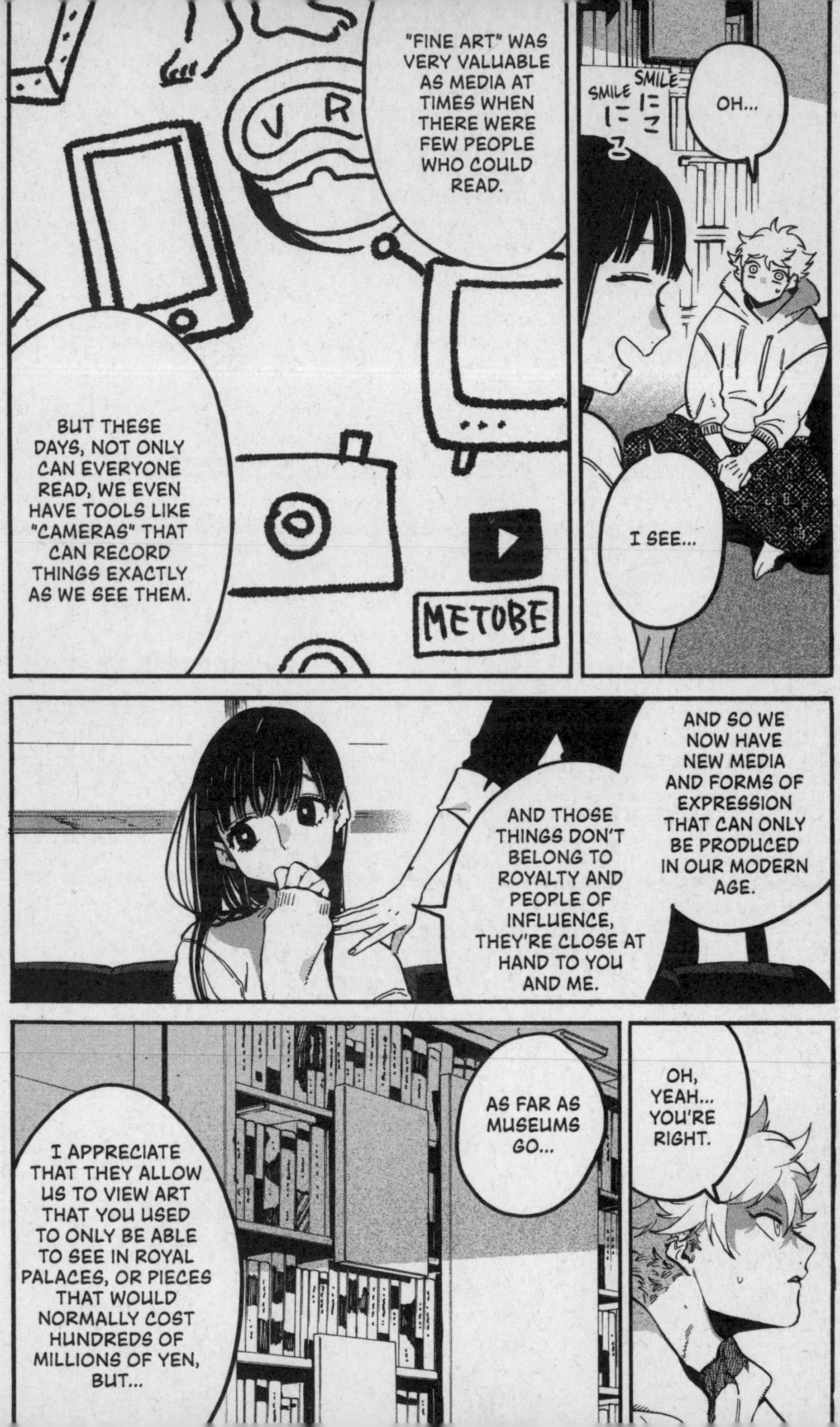
SMILE
SMILE
OH...
I SEE...
"FINE ART" WAS VERY VALUABLE AS MEDIA AT TIMES WHEN THERE WERE FEW PEOPLE WHO COULD READ.
VR
BUT THESE DAYS, NOT ONLY CAN EVERYONE READ, WE EVEN HAVE TOOLS LIKE "CAMERAS" THAT CAN RECORD THINGS EXACTLY AS WE SEE THEM.
METOBE
AND SO WE NOW HAVE NEW MEDIA AND FORMS OF EXPRESSION THAT CAN ONLY BE PRODUCED IN OUR MODERN AGE.
AND THOSE THINGS DON'T BELONG TO ROYALTY AND PEOPLE OF INFLUENCE, THEY'RE CLOSE AT HAND TO YOU AND ME.
OH, YEAH... YOU'RE RIGHT.
AS FAR AS MUSEUMS GO...
I APPRECIATE THAT THEY ALLOW US TO VIEW ART THAT YOU USED TO ONLY BE ABLE TO SEE IN ROYAL PALACES, OR PIECES THAT WOULD NORMALLY COST HUNDREDS OF MILLIONS OF YEN, BUT...

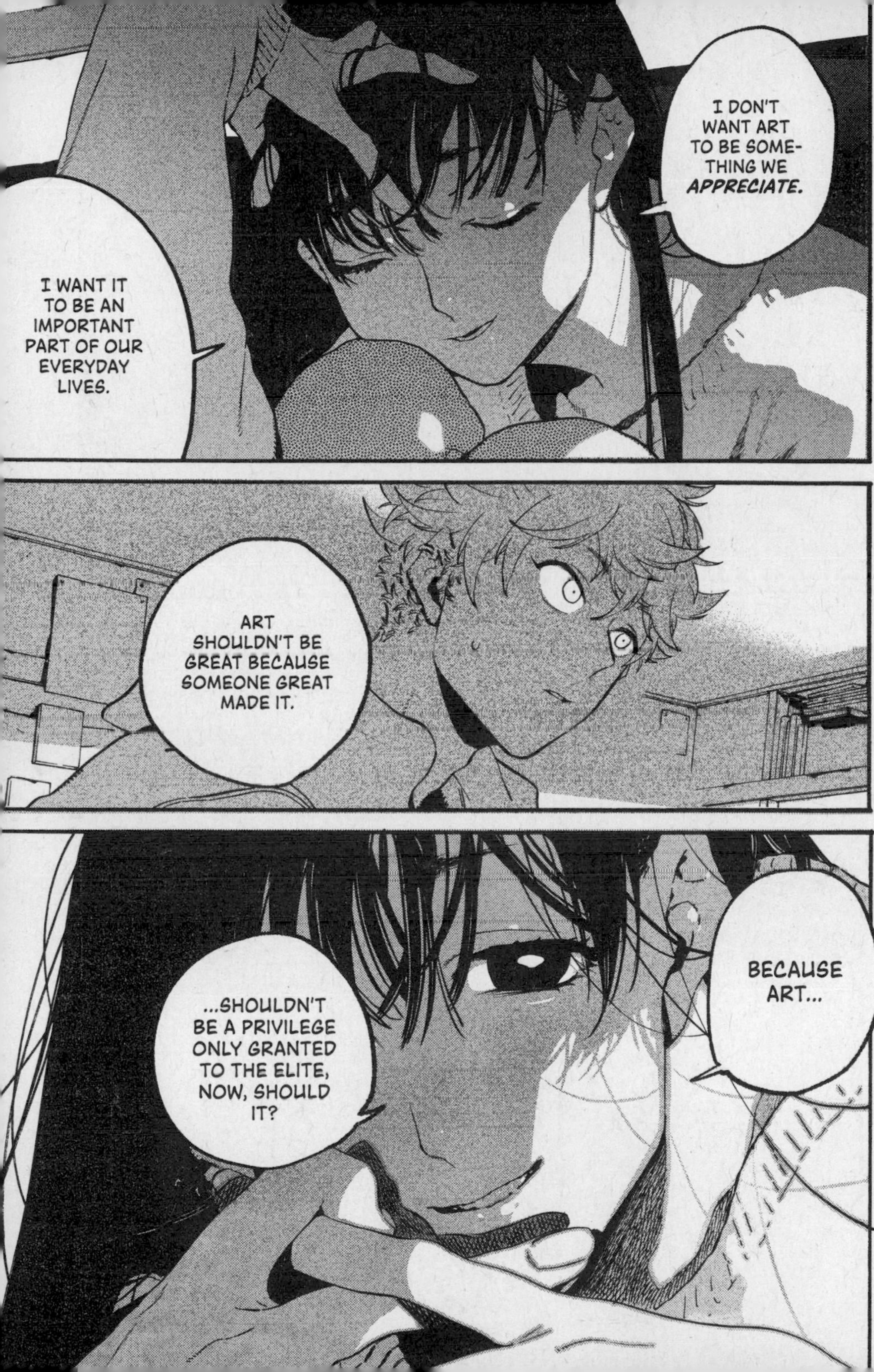
I DON'T WANT ART TO BE SOME-THING WE *APPRECIATE.*
I WANT IT TO BE AN IMPORTANT PART OF OUR EVERYDAY LIVES.
ART SHOULDN'T BE GREAT BECAUSE SOMEONE GREAT MADE IT.
BECAUSE ART...
...SHOULDN'T BE A PRIVILEGE ONLY GRANTED TO THE ELITE, NOW, SHOULD IT?

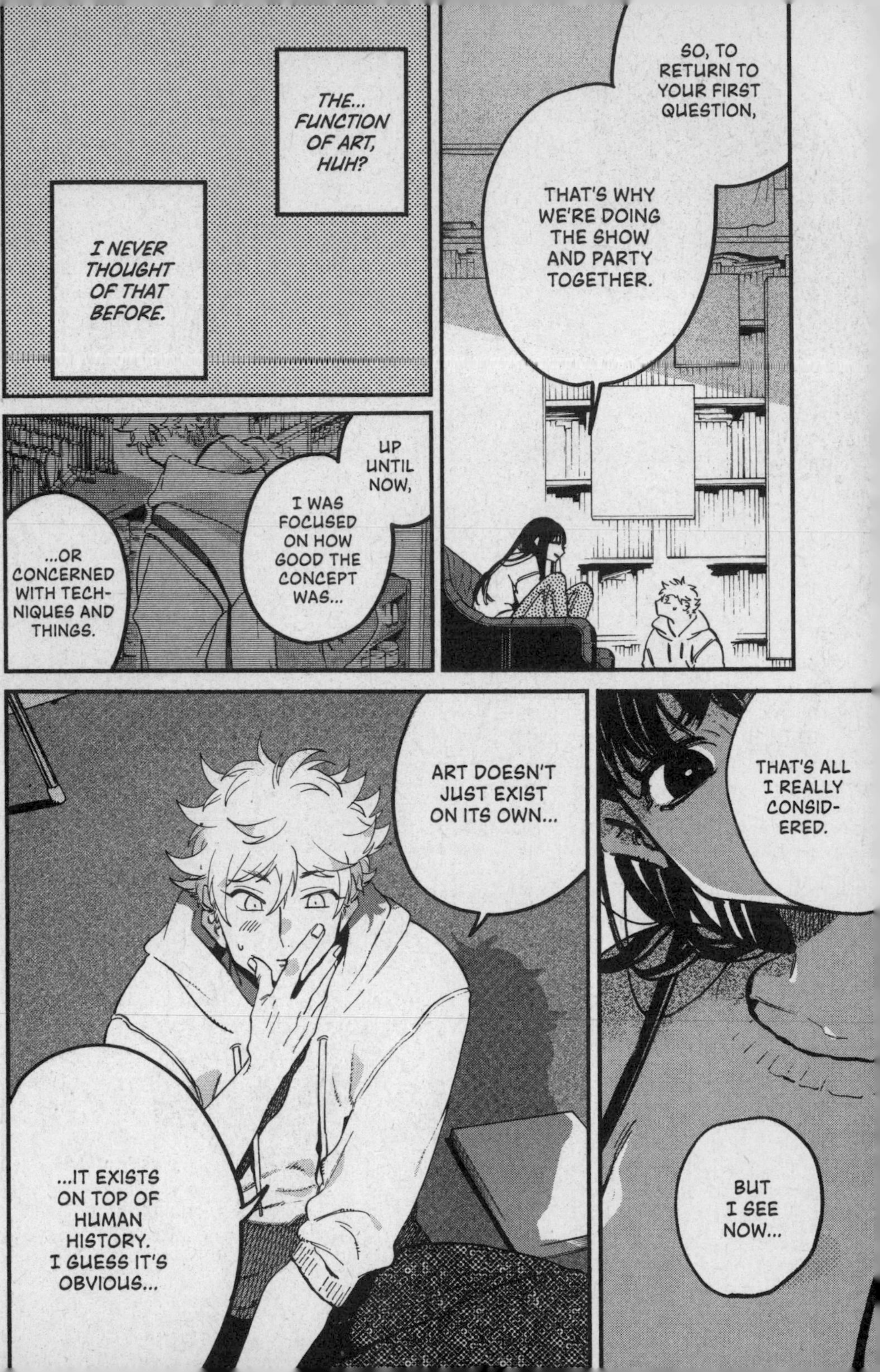
SO, TO RETURN TO YOUR FIRST QUESTION,
THAT'S WHY WE'RE DOING THE SHOW AND PARTY TOGETHER.
THE... FUNCTION OF ART, HUH?
I NEVER THOUGHT OF THAT BEFORE.
UP UNTIL NOW,
I WAS FOCUSED ON HOW GOOD THE CONCEPT WAS...
...OR CONCERNED WITH TECH-NIQUES AND THINGS.
THAT'S ALL I REALLY CONSID-ERED.
BUT I SEE NOW...
ART DOESN'T JUST EXIST ON ITS OWN...
...IT EXISTS ON TOP OF HUMAN HISTORY. I GUESS IT'S OBVIOUS...

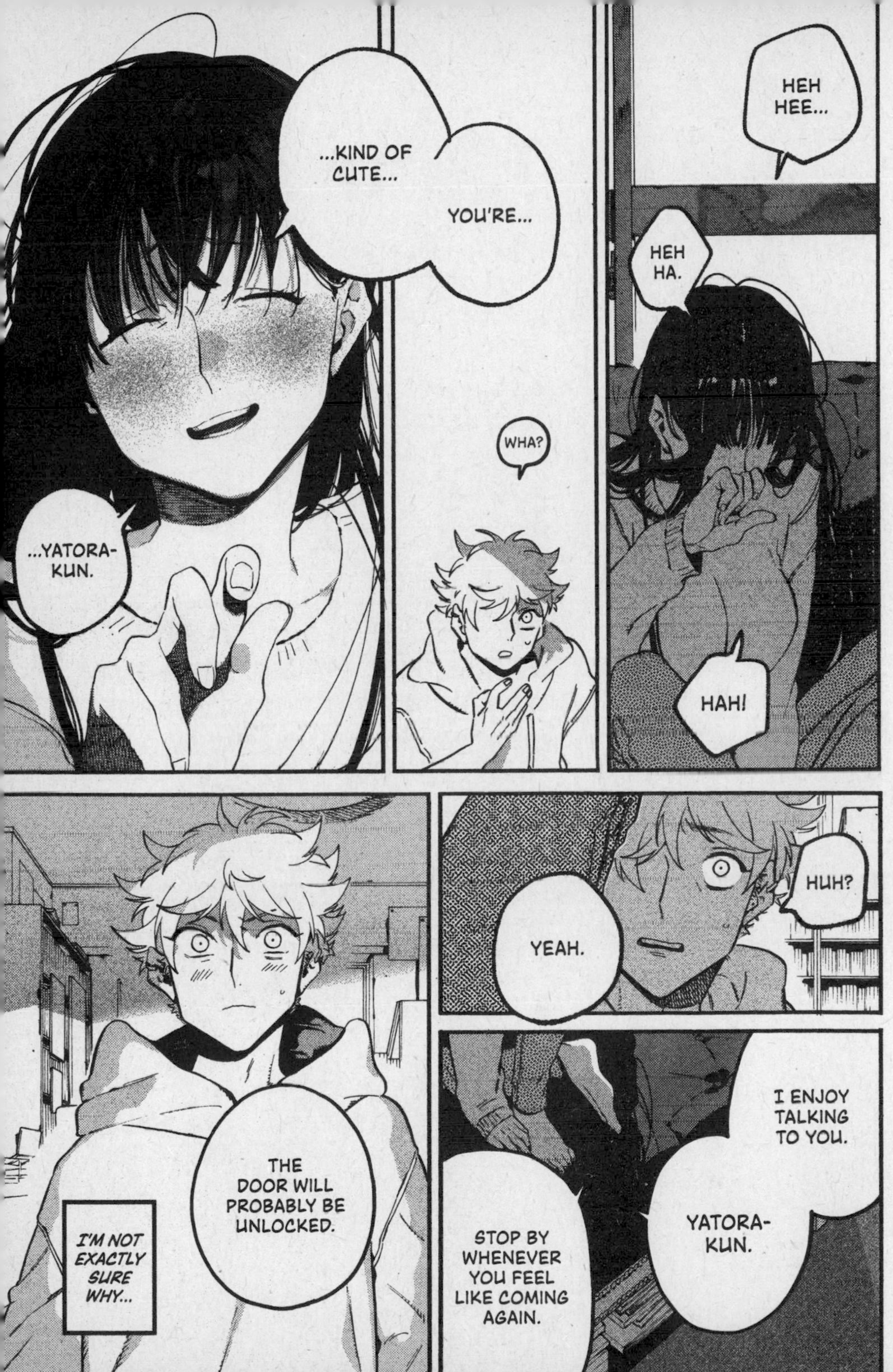
HEH HEE...
HEH HA.
HAH!
WHA?
YOU'RE...
...KIND OF CUTE...
...YATORA-KUN.
HUH?
YEAH.
I ENJOY TALKING TO YOU.
YATORA-KUN.
STOP BY WHENEVER YOU FEEL LIKE COMING AGAIN.
THE DOOR WILL PROBABLY BE UNLOCKED.
I'M NOT EXACTLY SURE WHY...

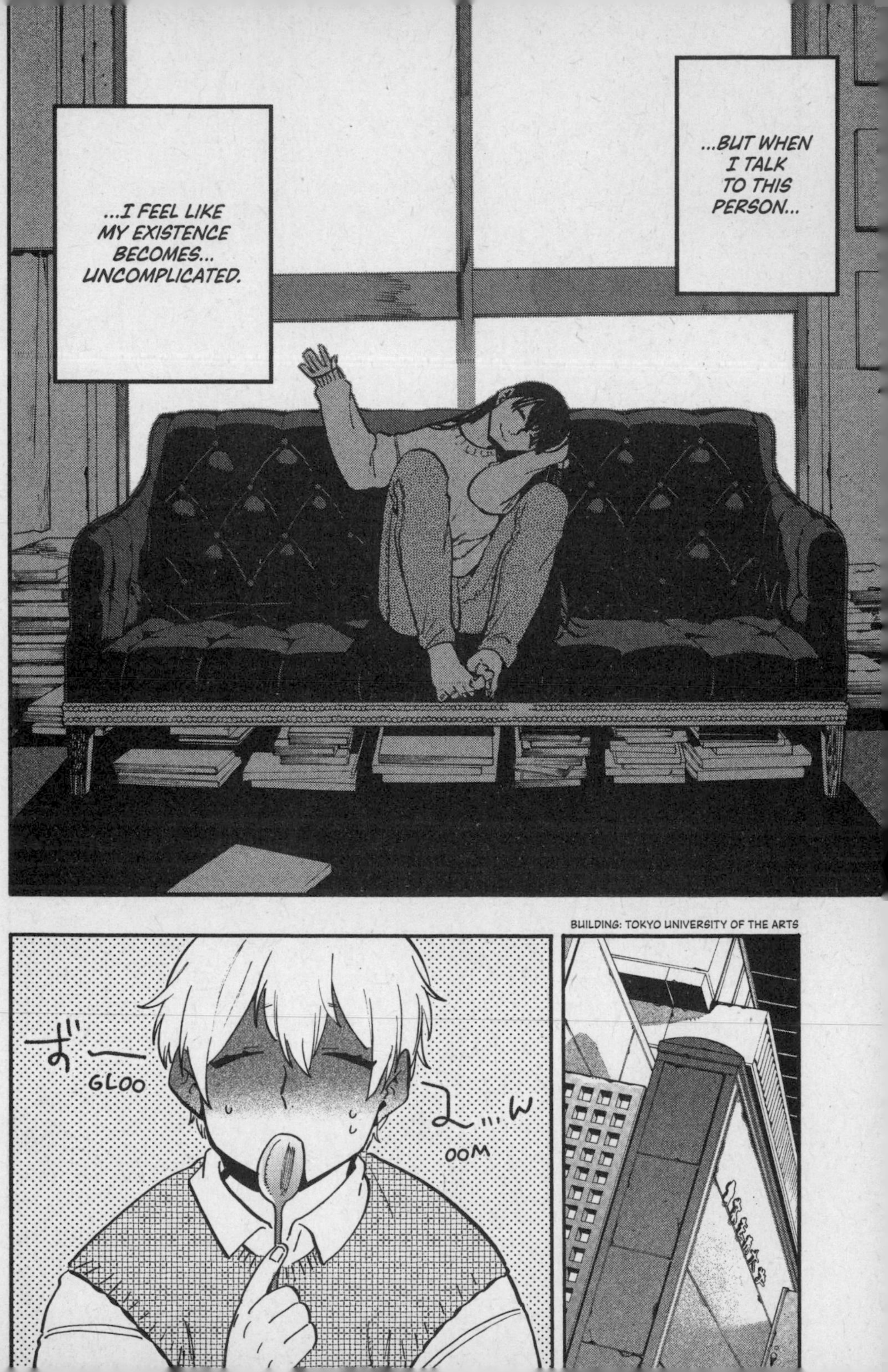
...BUT WHEN I TALK TO THIS PERSON...
...I FEEL LIKE MY EXISTENCE BECOMES... UNCOMPLICATED.
BUILDING: TOKYO UNIVERSITY OF THE ARTS
ずー
GLOO
OOM

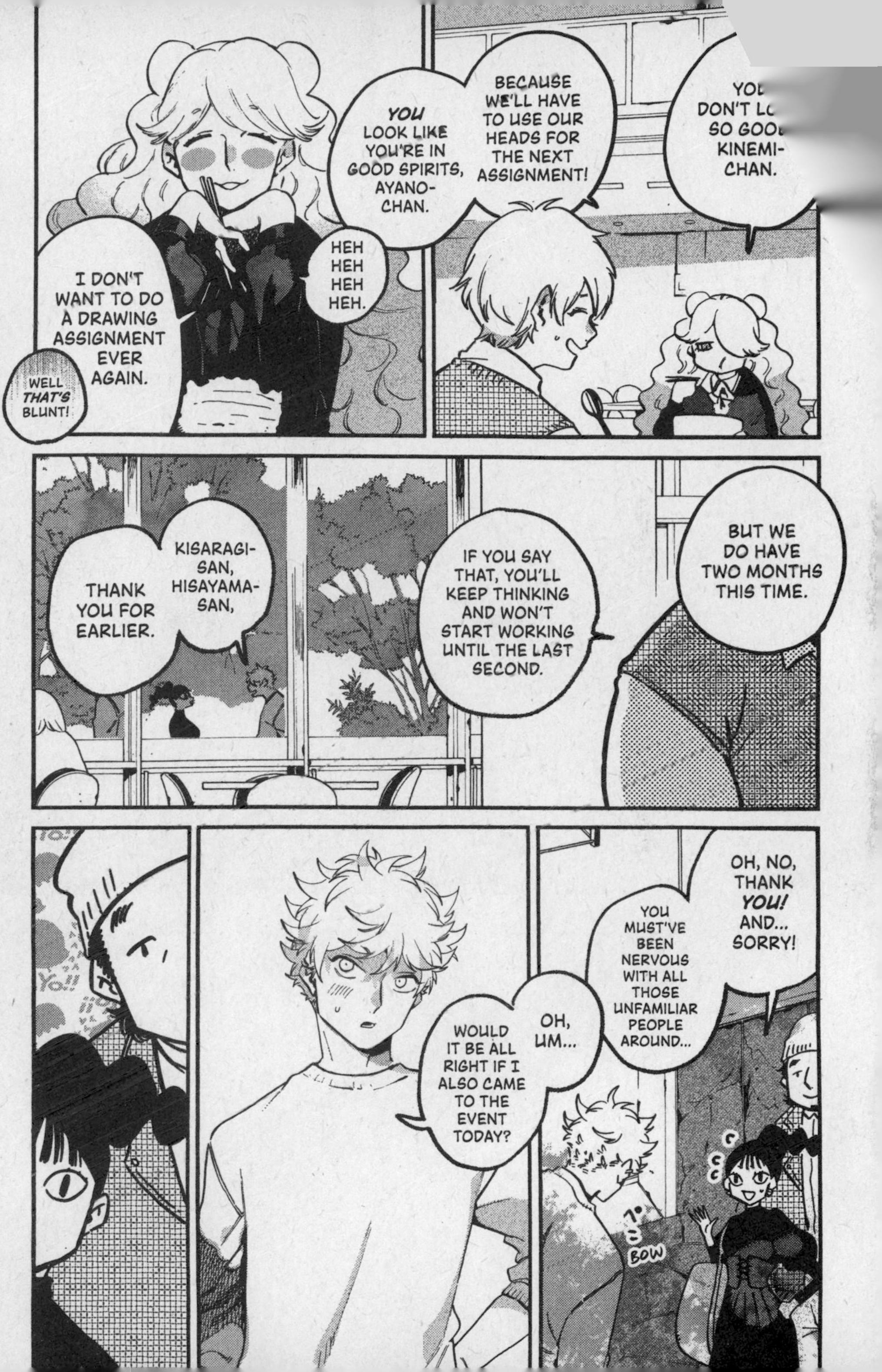
YO DON'T LO SO GOO KINEMI-CHAN.
BECAUSE WE'LL HAVE TO USE OUR HEADS FOR THE NEXT ASSIGNMENT!
YOU LOOK LIKE YOU'RE IN GOOD SPIRITS, AYANO-CHAN.
HEH HEH HEH HEH.
I DON'T WANT TO DO A DRAWING ASSIGNMENT EVER AGAIN.
WELL THAT'S BLUNT!
BUT WE DO HAVE TWO MONTHS THIS TIME.
IF YOU SAY THAT, YOU'LL KEEP THINKING AND WON'T START WORKING UNTIL THE LAST SECOND.
KISARAGI-SAN, HISAYAMA-SAN,
THANK YOU FOR EARLIER.
OH, NO, THANK YOU! AND... SORRY!
YOU MUST'VE BEEN NERVOUS WITH ALL THOSE UNFAMILIAR PEOPLE AROUND...
BOW
OH, UM...
WOULD IT BE ALL RIGHT IF I ALSO CAME TO THE EVENT TODAY?

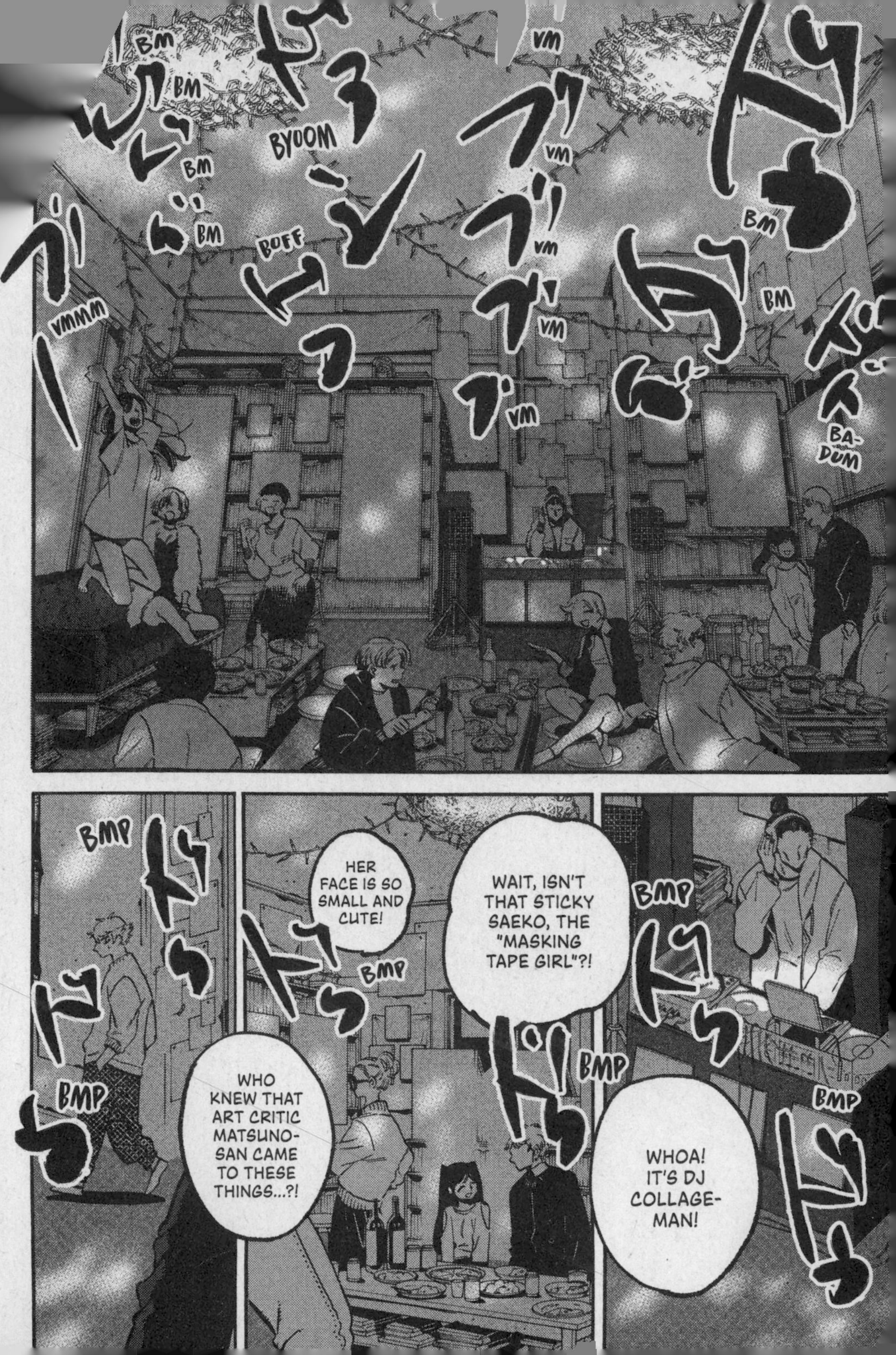
BM
BM
BA-DUM
VM
VM
VM
VM
VM
BYOOM
BM
BM
BM
BM
BOFF
VMMM
BMP
BMP
WHOA! IT'S DJ COLLAGE-MAN!
BMP
WAIT, ISN'T THAT STICKY SAEKO, THE "MASKING TAPE GIRL"?!
HER FACE IS SO SMALL AND CUTE!
BMP
WHO KNEW THAT ART CRITIC MATSUNO-SAN CAME TO THESE THINGS...?!
BMP
BMP

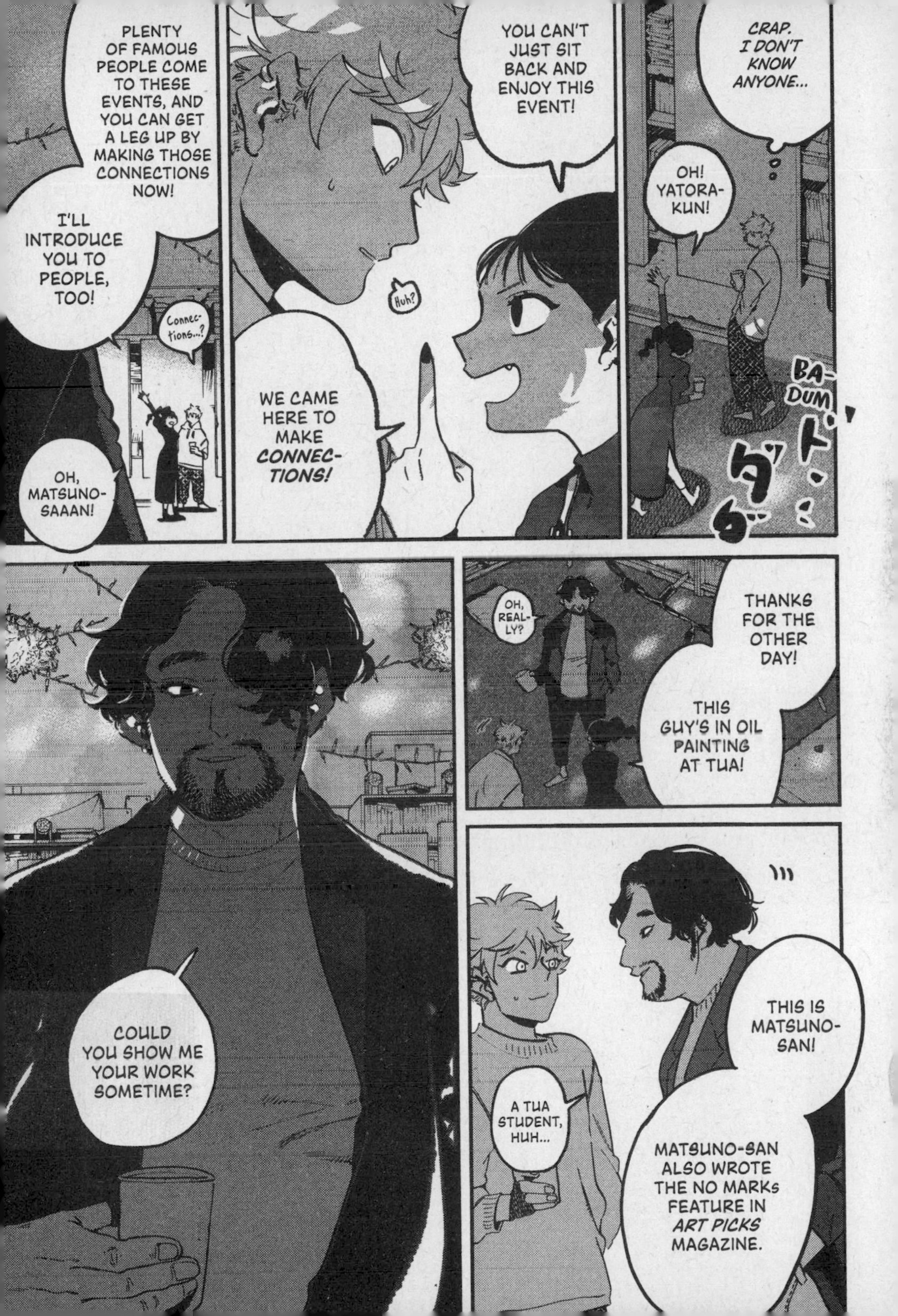
CRAP. I DON'T KNOW ANYONE...
OH! YATORA-KUN!
BA-DUM
YOU CAN'T JUST SIT BACK AND ENJOY THIS EVENT!
Huh?
WE CAME HERE TO MAKE *CONNECTIONS!*
PLENTY OF FAMOUS PEOPLE COME TO THESE EVENTS, AND YOU CAN GET A LEG UP BY MAKING THOSE CONNECTIONS NOW!
I'LL INTRODUCE YOU TO PEOPLE, TOO!
Connections...?
OH, MATSUNO-SAAAN!
THANKS FOR THE OTHER DAY!
THIS GUY'S IN OIL PAINTING AT TUA!
OH, REALLY?
THIS IS MATSUNO-SAN!
MATSUNO-SAN ALSO WROTE THE NO MARKs FEATURE IN *ART PICKS* MAGAZINE.
A TUA STUDENT, HUH...
COULD YOU SHOW ME YOUR WORK SOMETIME?

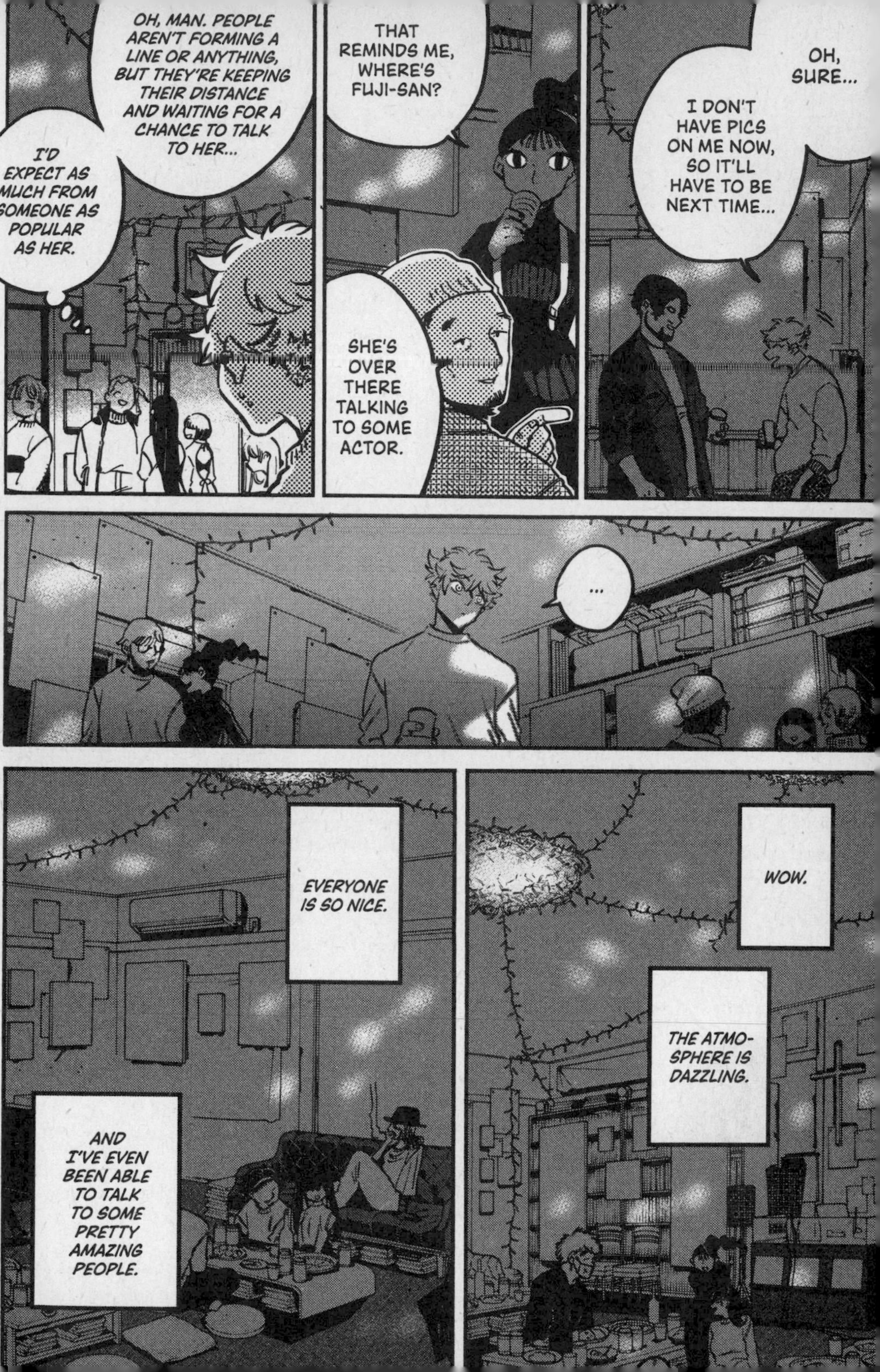
OH, SURE...
I DON'T HAVE PICS ON ME NOW, SO IT'LL HAVE TO BE NEXT TIME...
THAT REMINDS ME, WHERE'S FUJI-SAN?
SHE'S OVER THERE TALKING TO SOME ACTOR.
OH, MAN. PEOPLE AREN'T FORMING A LINE OR ANYTHING, BUT THEY'RE KEEPING THEIR DISTANCE AND WAITING FOR A CHANCE TO TALK TO HER...
I'D EXPECT AS MUCH FROM SOMEONE AS POPULAR AS HER.
...
WOW.
THE ATMOSPHERE IS DAZZLING.
EVERYONE IS SO NICE.
AND I'VE EVEN BEEN ABLE TO TALK TO SOME PRETTY AMAZING PEOPLE.

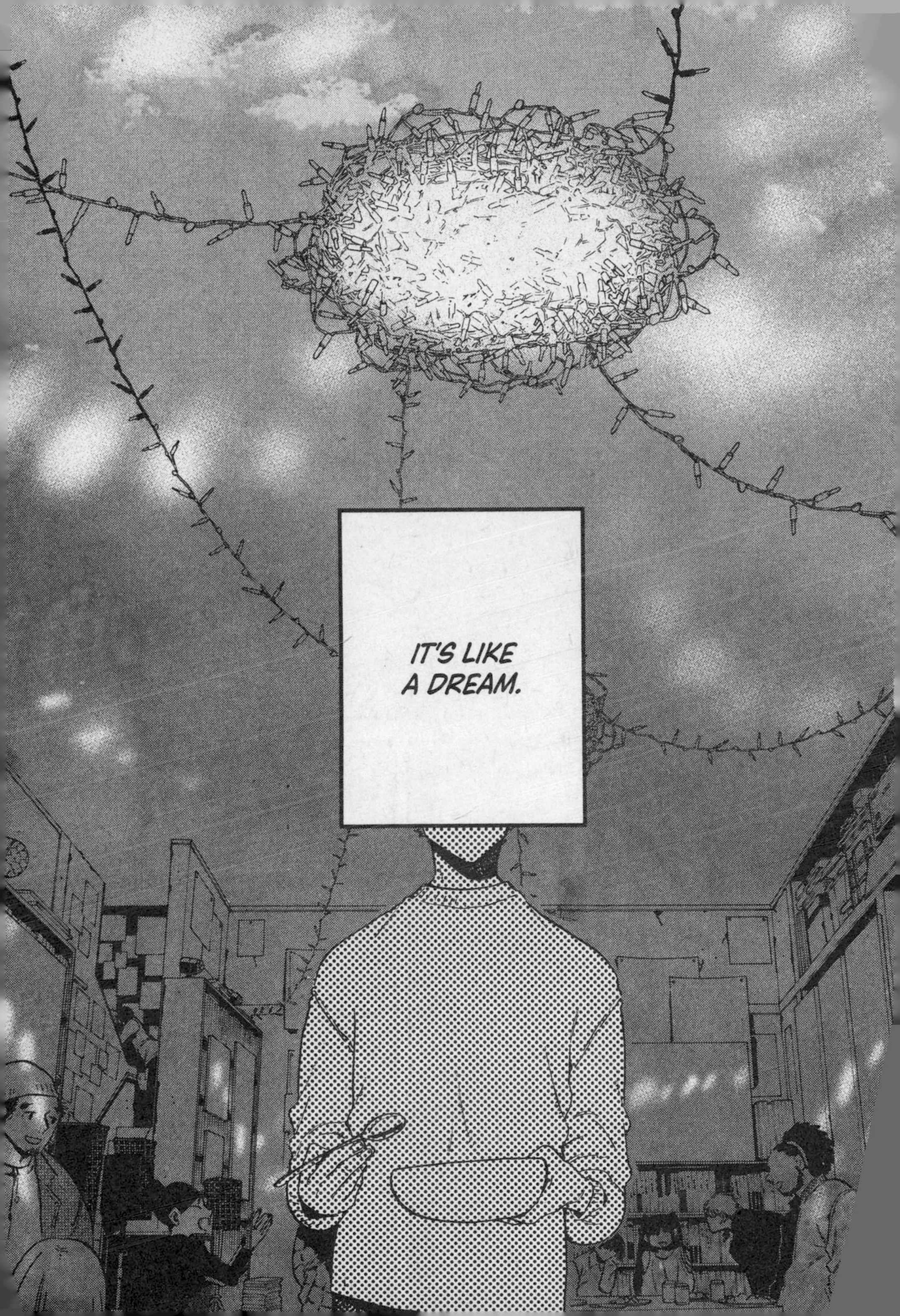
IT'S LIKE A DREAM.

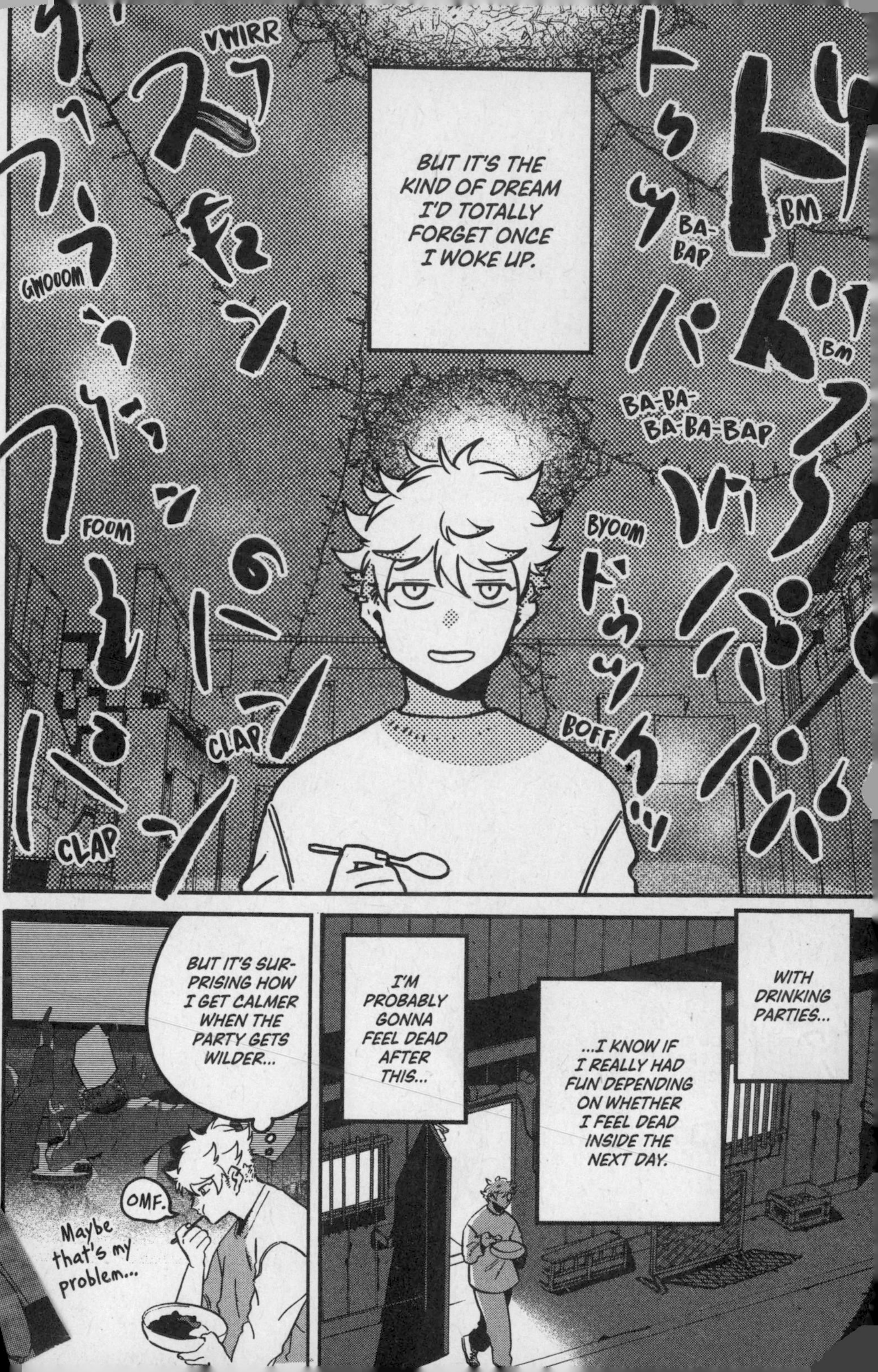
BUT IT'S THE KIND OF DREAM I'D TOTALLY FORGET ONCE I WOKE UP.
BM
BA-BAP
BM
BA-BA-BA-BA-BAP
BYOOM
BOFF
VWIRR
GNOOOM
FOOM
CLAP
CLAP
WITH DRINKING PARTIES...
...I KNOW IF I REALLY HAD FUN DEPENDING ON WHETHER I FEEL DEAD INSIDE THE NEXT DAY.
I'M PROBABLY GONNA FEEL DEAD AFTER THIS...
BUT IT'S SURPRISING HOW I GET CALMER WHEN THE PARTY GETS WILDER...
OMF.
Maybe that's my problem...

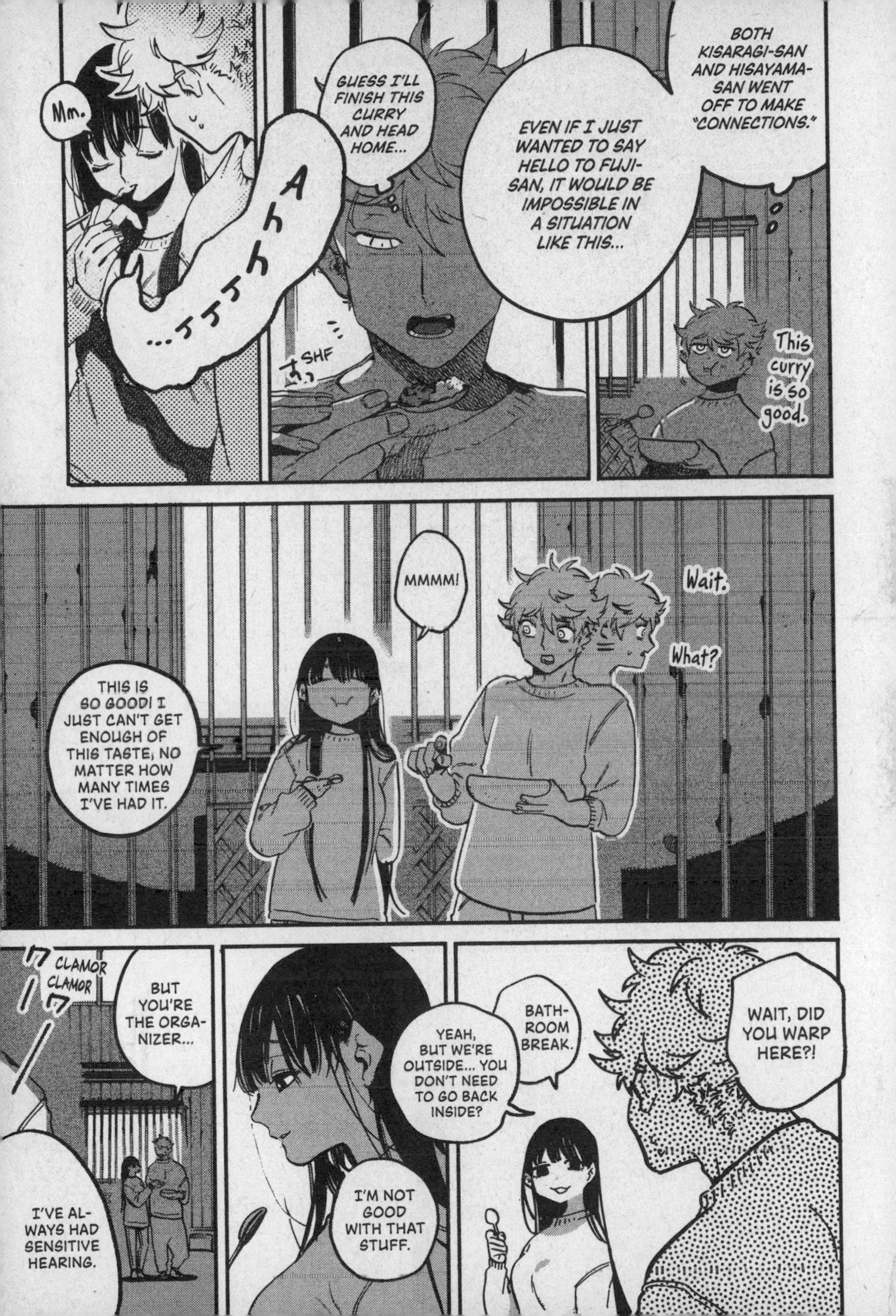

BOTH KISARAGI-SAN AND HISAYAMA-SAN WENT OFF TO MAKE "CONNECTIONS."
This curry is so good.
EVEN IF I JUST WANTED TO SAY HELLO TO FUJI-SAN, IT WOULD BE IMPOSSIBLE IN A SITUATION LIKE THIS...
GUESS I'LL FINISH THIS CURRY AND HEAD HOME...
SHF
Mm.
Wait.
What?
MMMM!
THIS IS SO GOOD! I JUST CAN'T GET ENOUGH OF THIS TASTE, NO MATTER HOW MANY TIMES I'VE HAD IT.
WAIT, DID YOU WARP HERE?!
BATH-ROOM BREAK.
YEAH, BUT WE'RE OUTSIDE... YOU DON'T NEED TO GO BACK INSIDE?
I'M NOT GOOD WITH THAT STUFF.
CLAMOR CLAMOR
BUT YOU'RE THE ORGA-NIZER...
I'VE AL-WAYS HAD SENSITIVE HEARING.

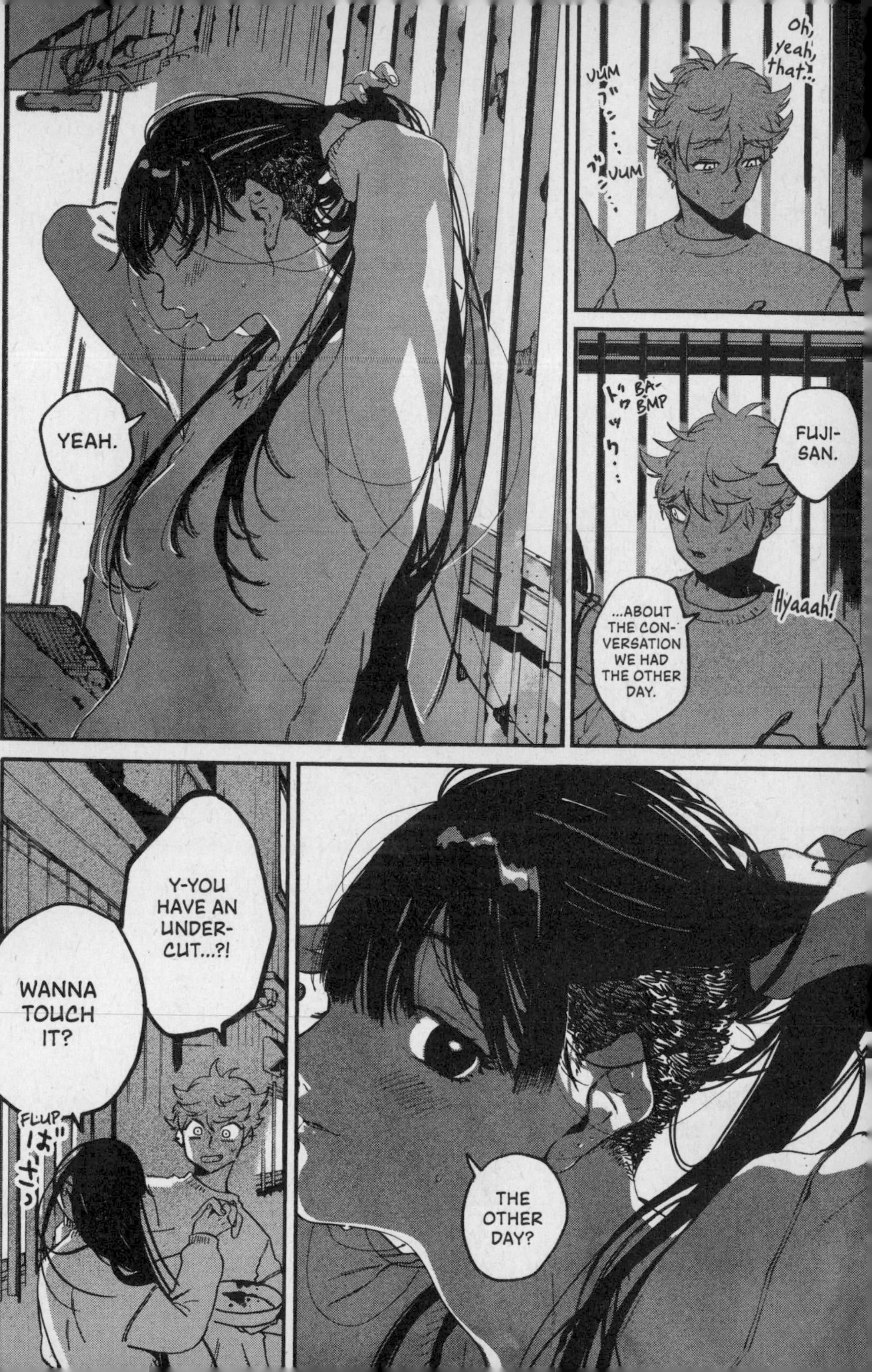

Oh, yeah, that...
VUM
VUM
BA-BMP
FUJI-SAN.
...ABOUT THE CONVERSATION WE HAD THE OTHER DAY.
Hyaaah!
YEAH.
THE OTHER DAY?
Y-YOU HAVE AN UNDERCUT...?!
WANNA TOUCH IT?
FLUP

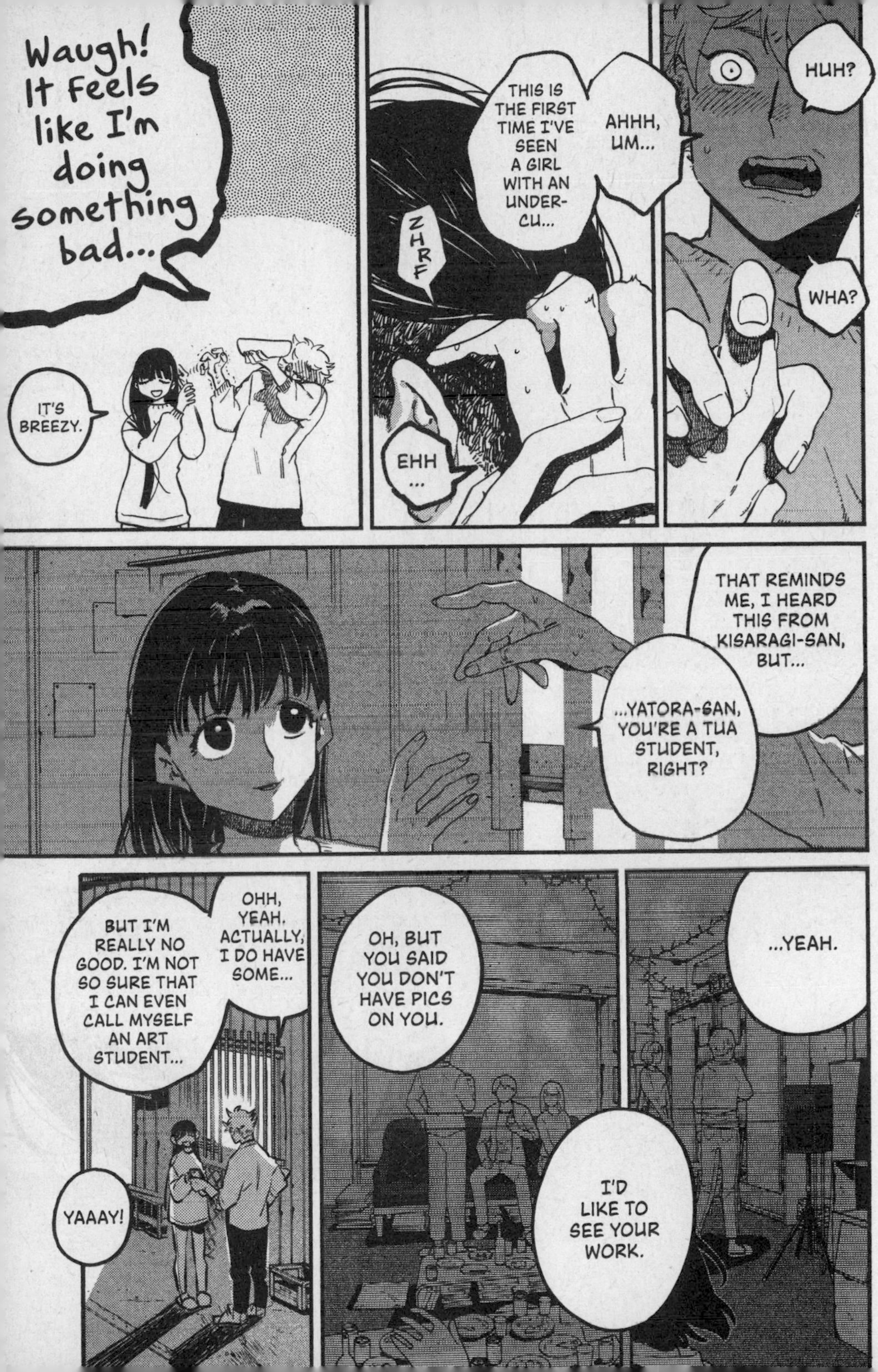
HUH?
WHA?
AHHH, UM...
THIS IS THE FIRST TIME I'VE SEEN A GIRL WITH AN UNDER-CU...
ZHRF
EHH ...
Waugh! It Feels like I'm doing something bad...
IT'S BREEZY.
THAT REMINDS ME, I HEARD THIS FROM KISARAGI-SAN, BUT...
...YATORA-SAN, YOU'RE A TUA STUDENT, RIGHT?
...YEAH.
I'D LIKE TO SEE YOUR WORK.
OH, BUT YOU SAID YOU DON'T HAVE PICS ON YOU.
OHH, YEAH. ACTUALLY, I DO HAVE SOME...
BUT I'M REALLY NO GOOD. I'M NOT SO SURE THAT I CAN EVEN CALL MYSELF AN ART STUDENT...
YAAAY!

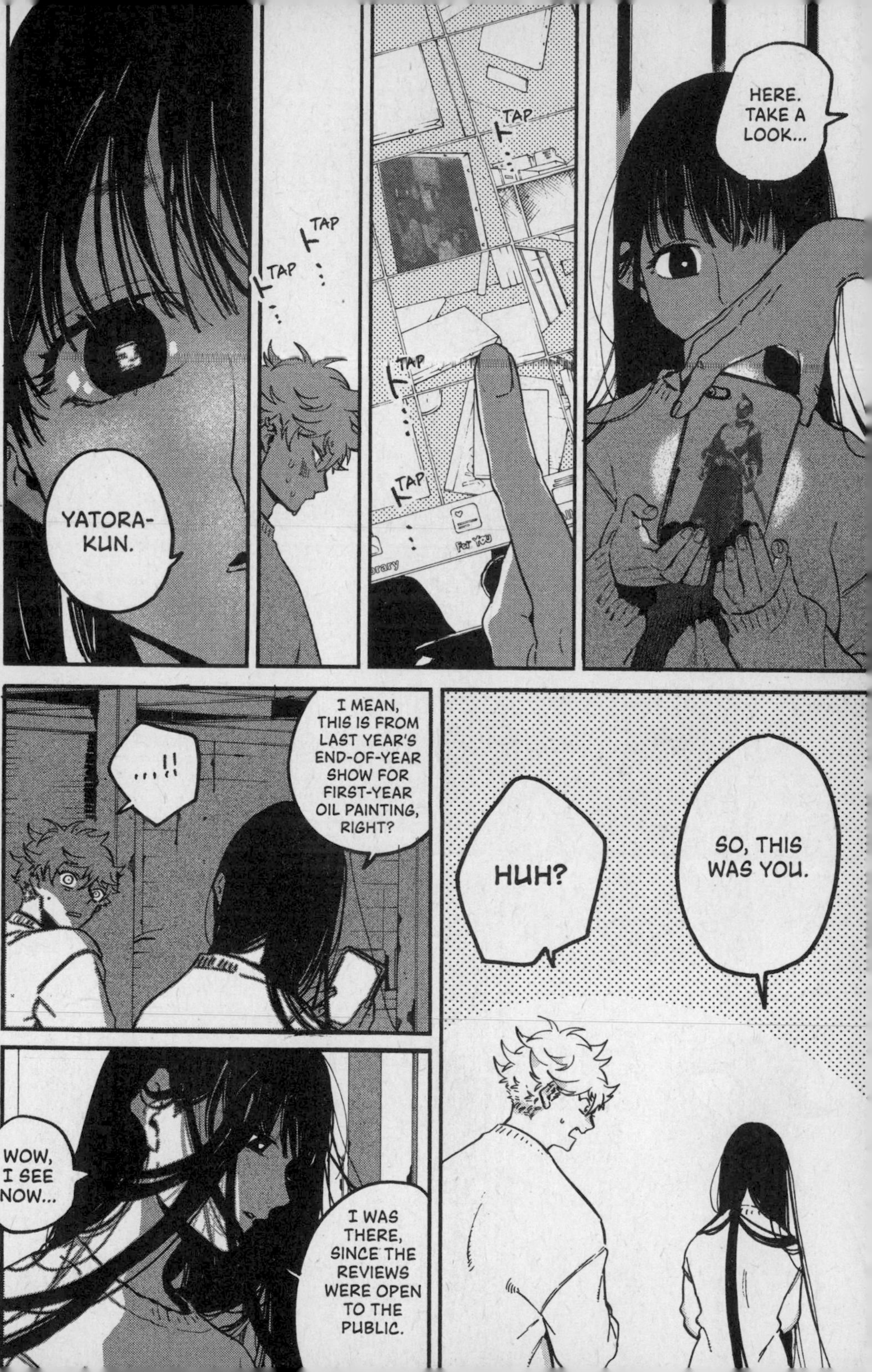
HERE. TAKE A LOOK...
TAP
TAP
TAP
For You
TAP
TAP
YATORA-KUN.
SO, THIS WAS YOU.
HUH?
I MEAN, THIS IS FROM LAST YEAR'S END-OF-YEAR SHOW FOR FIRST-YEAR OIL PAINTING, RIGHT?
...!!
WOW, I SEE NOW...
I WAS THERE, SINCE THE REVIEWS WERE OPEN TO THE PUBLIC.

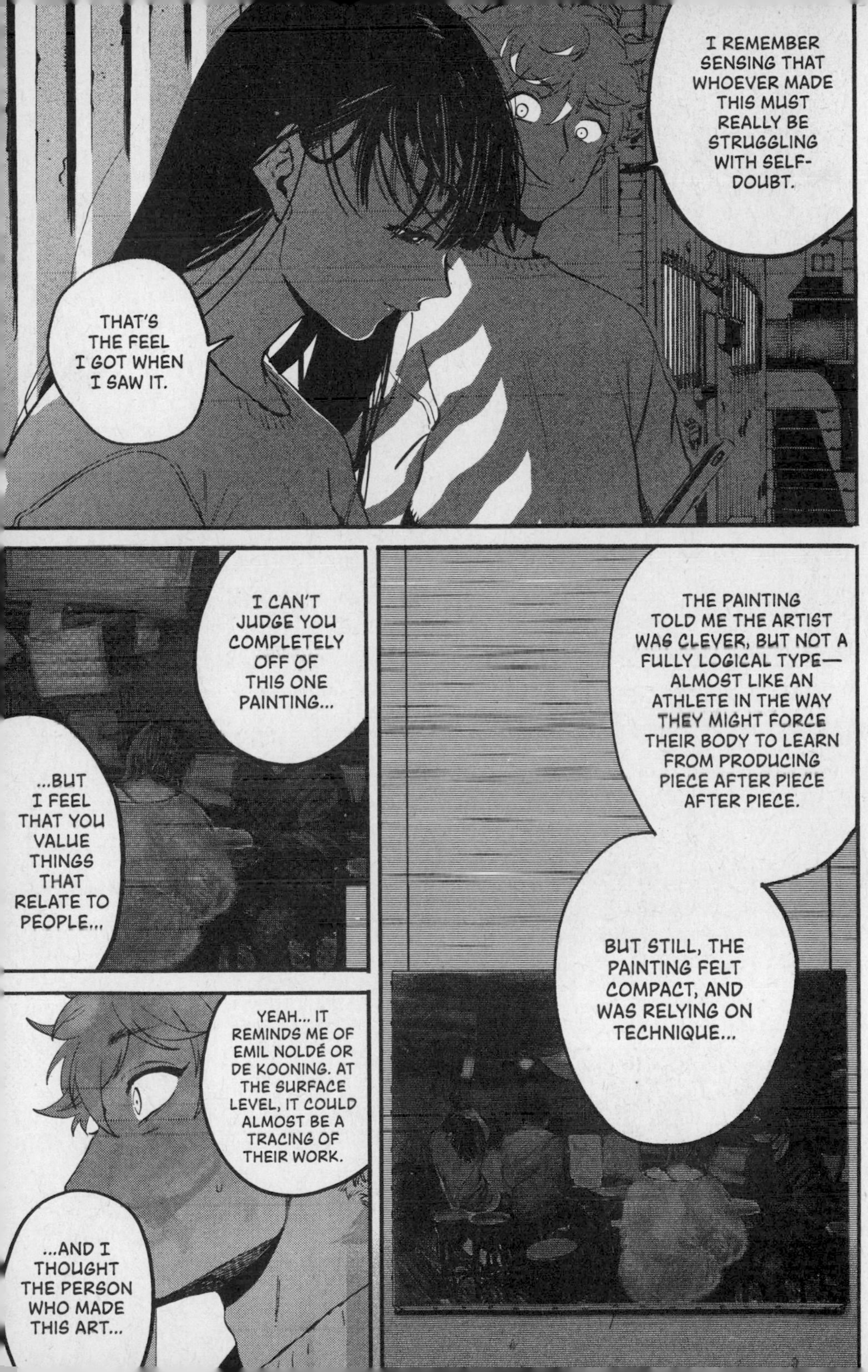
I REMEMBER SENSING THAT WHOEVER MADE THIS MUST REALLY BE STRUGGLING WITH SELF-DOUBT.
THAT'S THE FEEL I GOT WHEN I SAW IT.
THE PAINTING TOLD ME THE ARTIST WAS CLEVER, BUT NOT A FULLY LOGICAL TYPE—ALMOST LIKE AN ATHLETE IN THE WAY THEY MIGHT FORCE THEIR BODY TO LEARN FROM PRODUCING PIECE AFTER PIECE AFTER PIECE.
BUT STILL, THE PAINTING FELT COMPACT, AND WAS RELYING ON TECHNIQUE...
I CAN'T JUDGE YOU COMPLETELY OFF OF THIS ONE PAINTING...
...BUT I FEEL THAT YOU VALUE THINGS THAT RELATE TO PEOPLE...
YEAH... IT REMINDS ME OF EMIL NOLDÉ OR DE KOONING. AT THE SURFACE LEVEL, IT COULD ALMOST BE A TRACING OF THEIR WORK.
...AND I THOUGHT THE PERSON WHO MADE THIS ART...

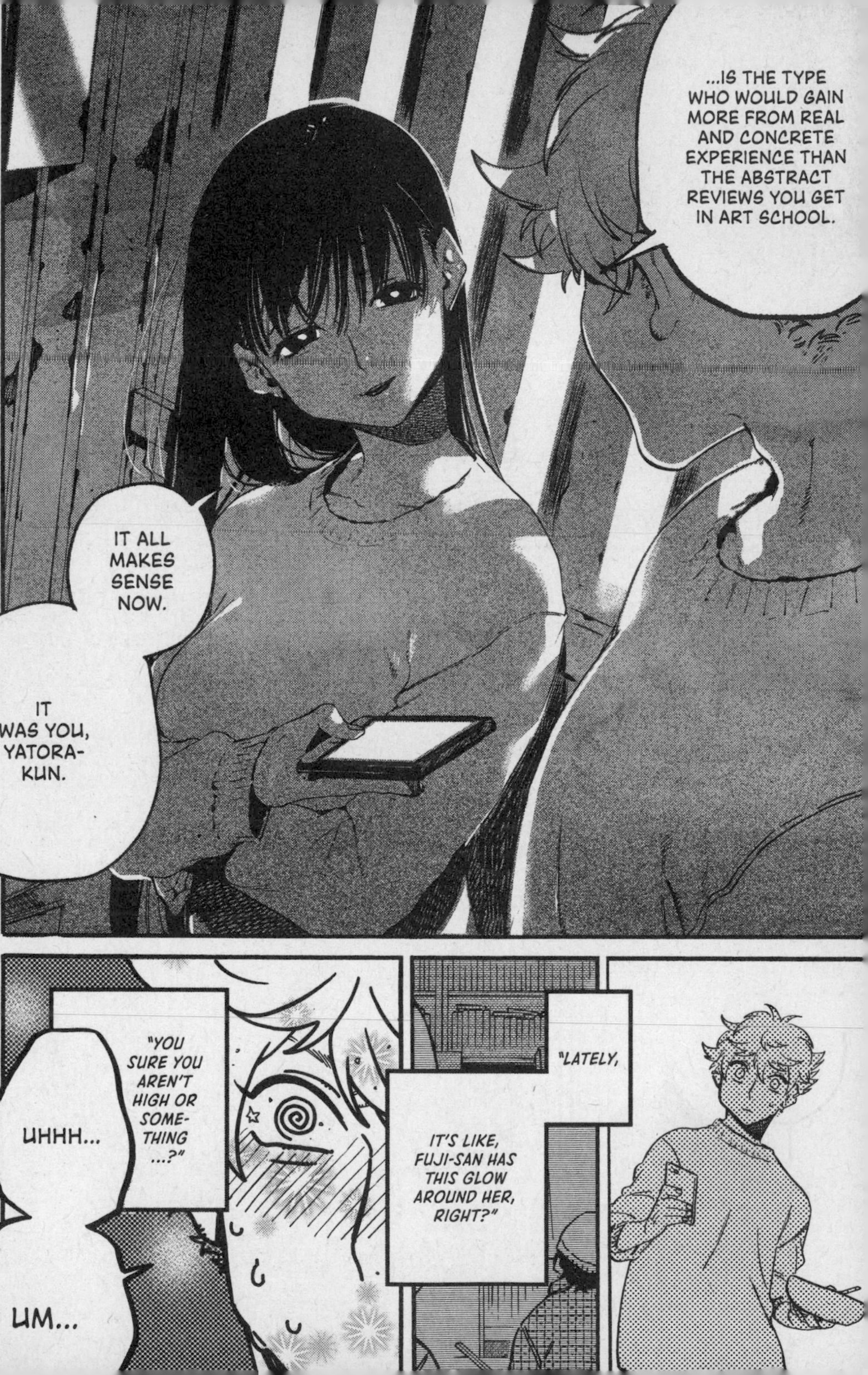
...IS THE TYPE WHO WOULD GAIN MORE FROM REAL AND CONCRETE EXPERIENCE THAN THE ABSTRACT REVIEWS YOU GET IN ART SCHOOL.
IT ALL MAKES SENSE NOW.
IT WAS YOU, YATORA-KUN.
"LATELY,
IT'S LIKE, FUJI-SAN HAS THIS GLOW AROUND HER, RIGHT?"
"YOU SURE YOU AREN'T HIGH OR SOME-THING ...?"
UHHH...
UM...

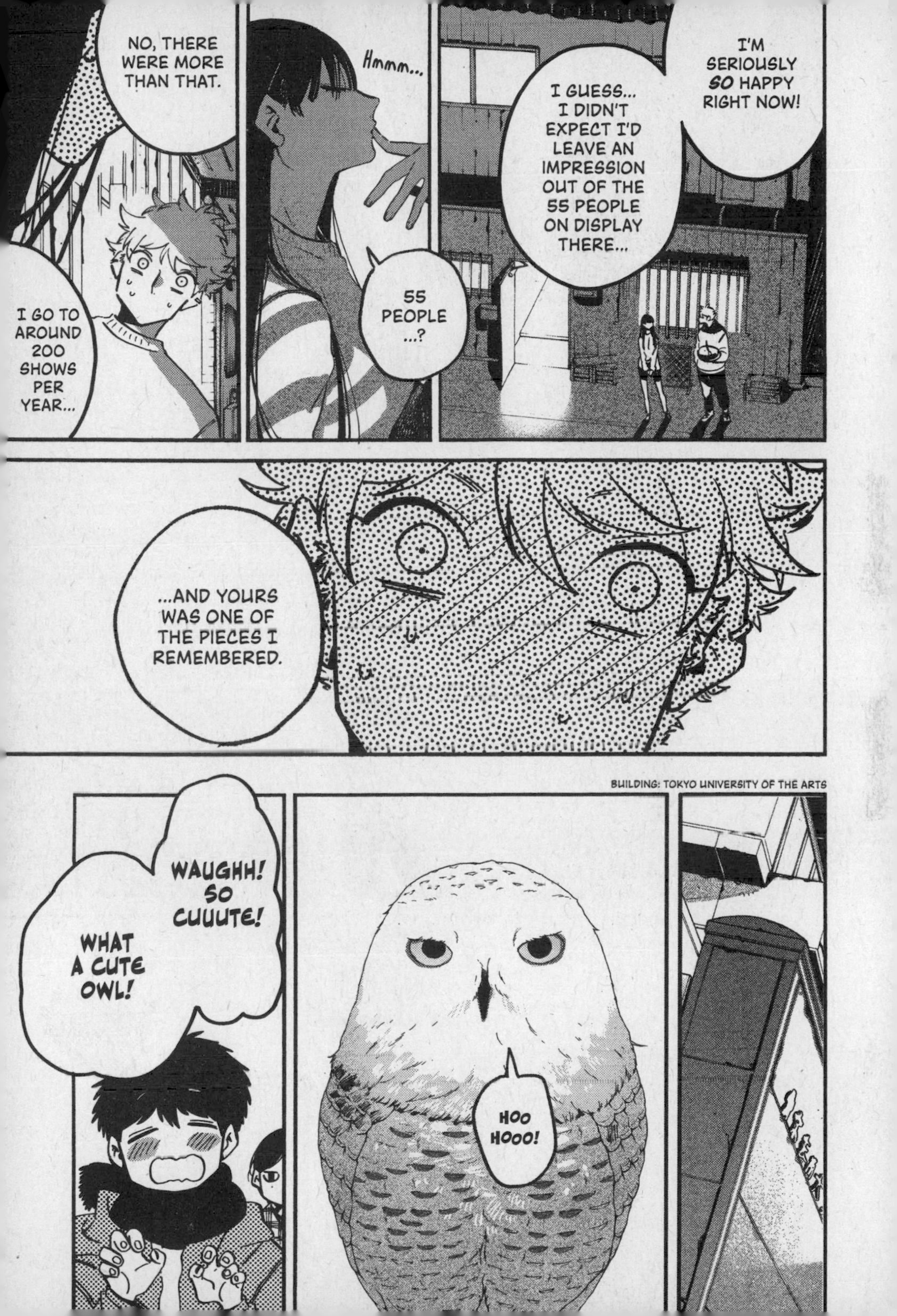
I'M SERIOUSLY SO HAPPY RIGHT NOW!
I GUESS... I DIDN'T EXPECT I'D LEAVE AN IMPRESSION OUT OF THE 55 PEOPLE ON DISPLAY THERE...
55 PEOPLE ...?
Hmmm...
NO, THERE WERE MORE THAN THAT.
I GO TO AROUND 200 SHOWS PER YEAR...
...AND YOURS WAS ONE OF THE PIECES I REMEMBERED.
BUILDING: TOKYO UNIVERSITY OF THE ARTS
HOO HOOO!
WAUGHH! SO CUUUTE!
WHAT A CUTE OWL!

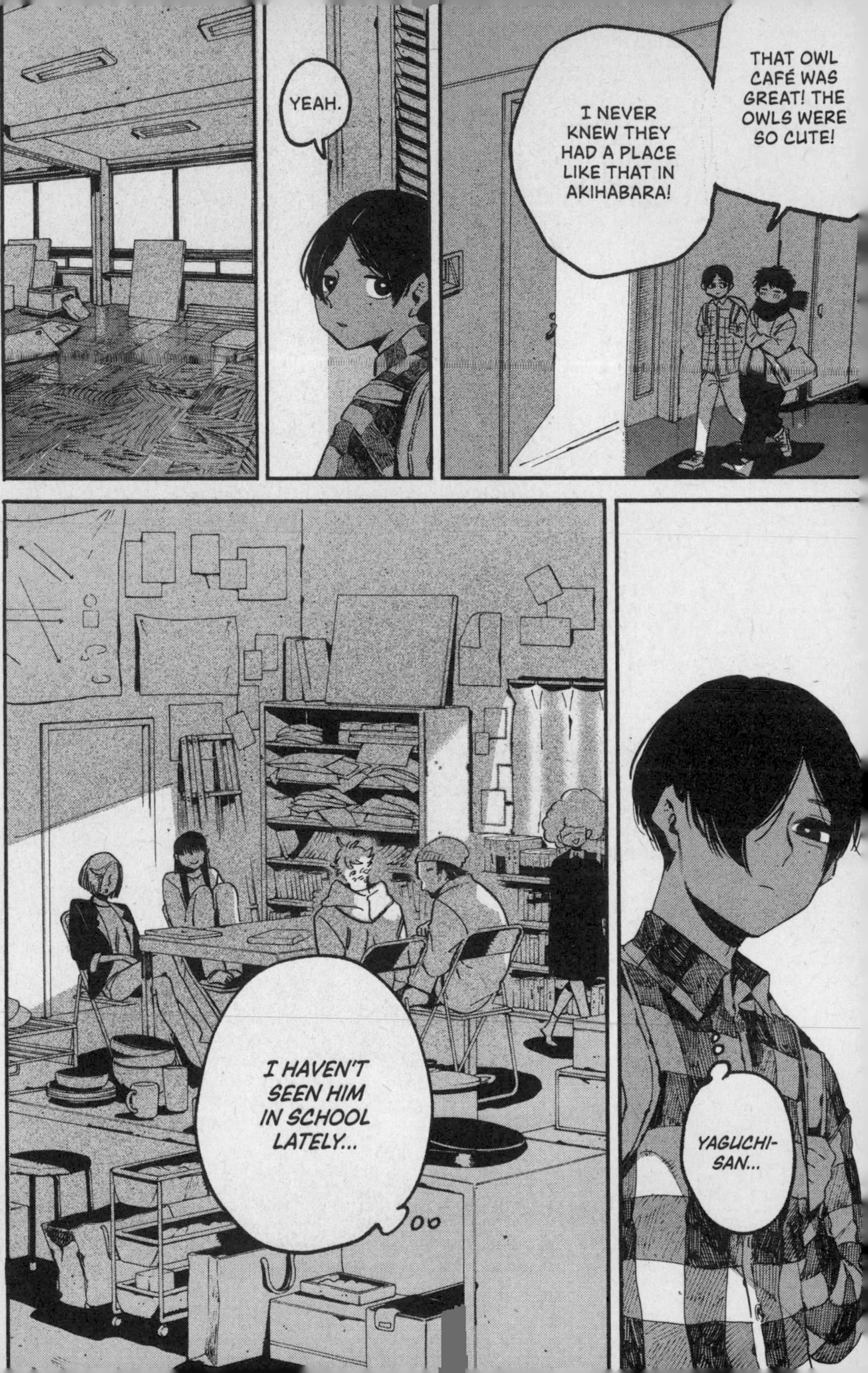
THAT OWL CAFÉ WAS GREAT! THE OWLS WERE SO CUTE!
I NEVER KNEW THEY HAD A PLACE LIKE THAT IN AKIHABARA!
YEAH.
YAGUCHI-SAN...
I HAVEN'T SEEN HIM IN SCHOOL LATELY...

STROKE 51 END

For eggplant curry,
grill the eggplants
and include miso as a
secret ingredient.

BLUE PERIOD

STROKE 52

WHEN THE GROUND SOFTENS, YOU QUICKLY GET STUCK

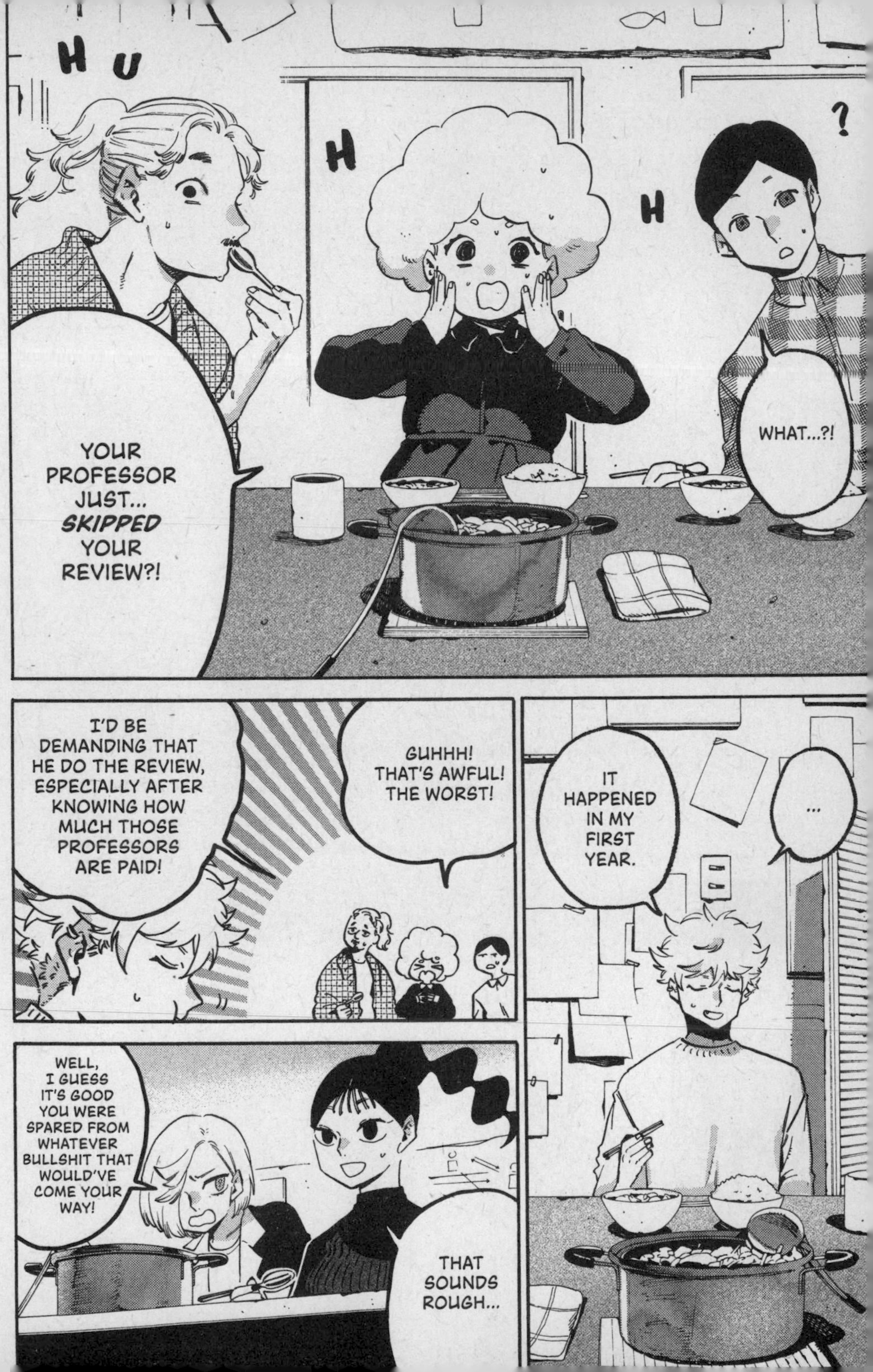
?
HUHH
WHAT...?!
YOUR PROFESSOR JUST... *SKIPPED* YOUR REVIEW?!
...
IT HAPPENED IN MY FIRST YEAR.
GUHHH! THAT'S AWFUL! THE WORST!
I'D BE DEMANDING THAT HE DO THE REVIEW, ESPECIALLY AFTER KNOWING HOW MUCH THOSE PROFESSORS ARE PAID!
THAT SOUNDS ROUGH...
WELL, I GUESS IT'S GOOD YOU WERE SPARED FROM WHATEVER BULLSHIT THAT WOULD'VE COME YOUR WAY!

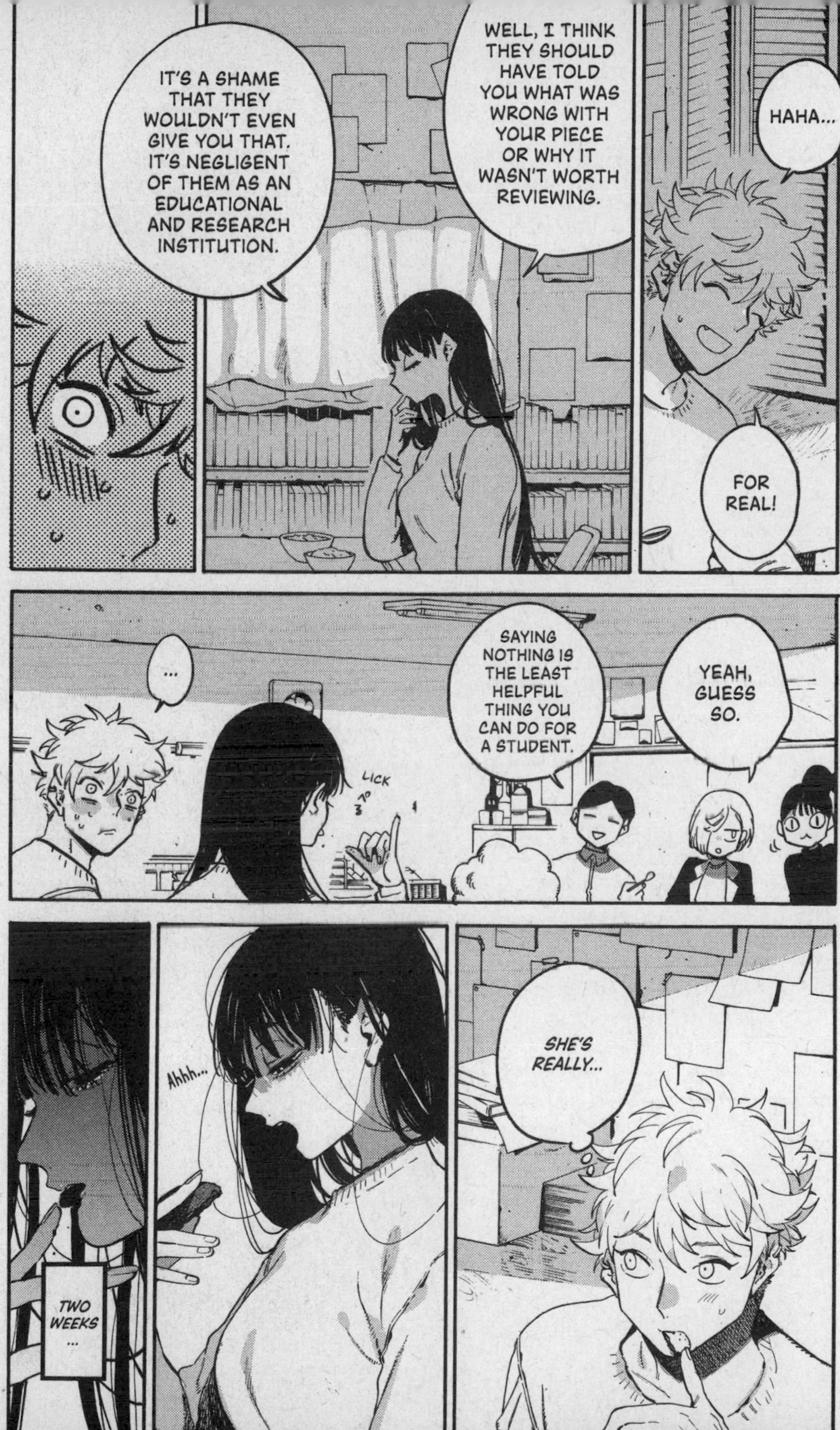
HAHA...
FOR REAL!
WELL, I THINK THEY SHOULD HAVE TOLD YOU WHAT WAS WRONG WITH YOUR PIECE OR WHY IT WASN'T WORTH REVIEWING.
IT'S A SHAME THAT THEY WOULDN'T EVEN GIVE YOU THAT. IT'S NEGLIGENT OF THEM AS AN EDUCATIONAL AND RESEARCH INSTITUTION.
YEAH, GUESS SO.
SAYING NOTHING IS THE LEAST HELPFUL THING YOU CAN DO FOR A STUDENT.
LICK
...
SHE'S REALLY...
Ahhh...
TWO WEEKS ...

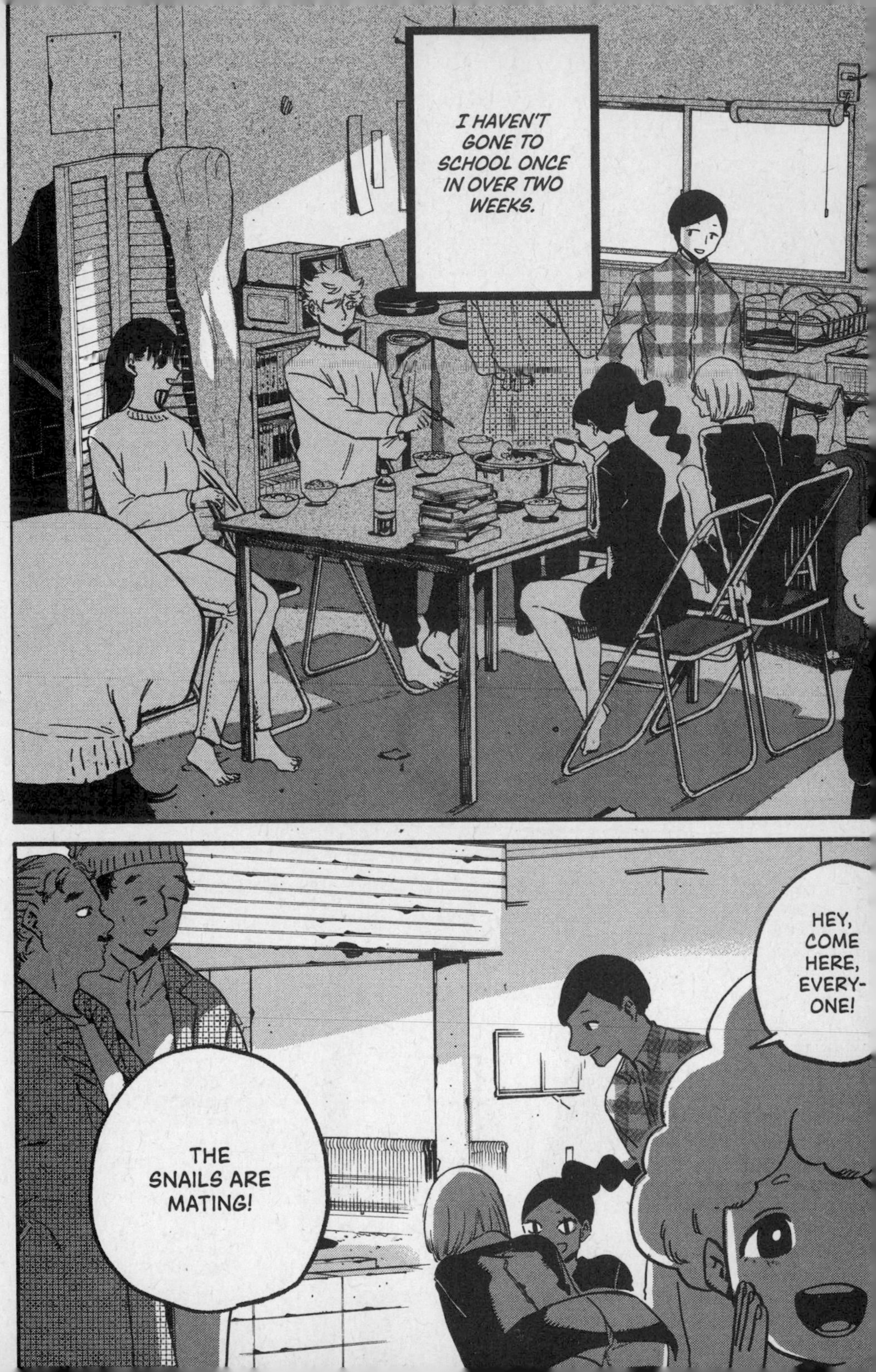
I HAVEN'T GONE TO SCHOOL ONCE IN OVER TWO WEEKS.
HEY, COME HERE, EVERY-ONE!
THE SNAILS ARE MATING!

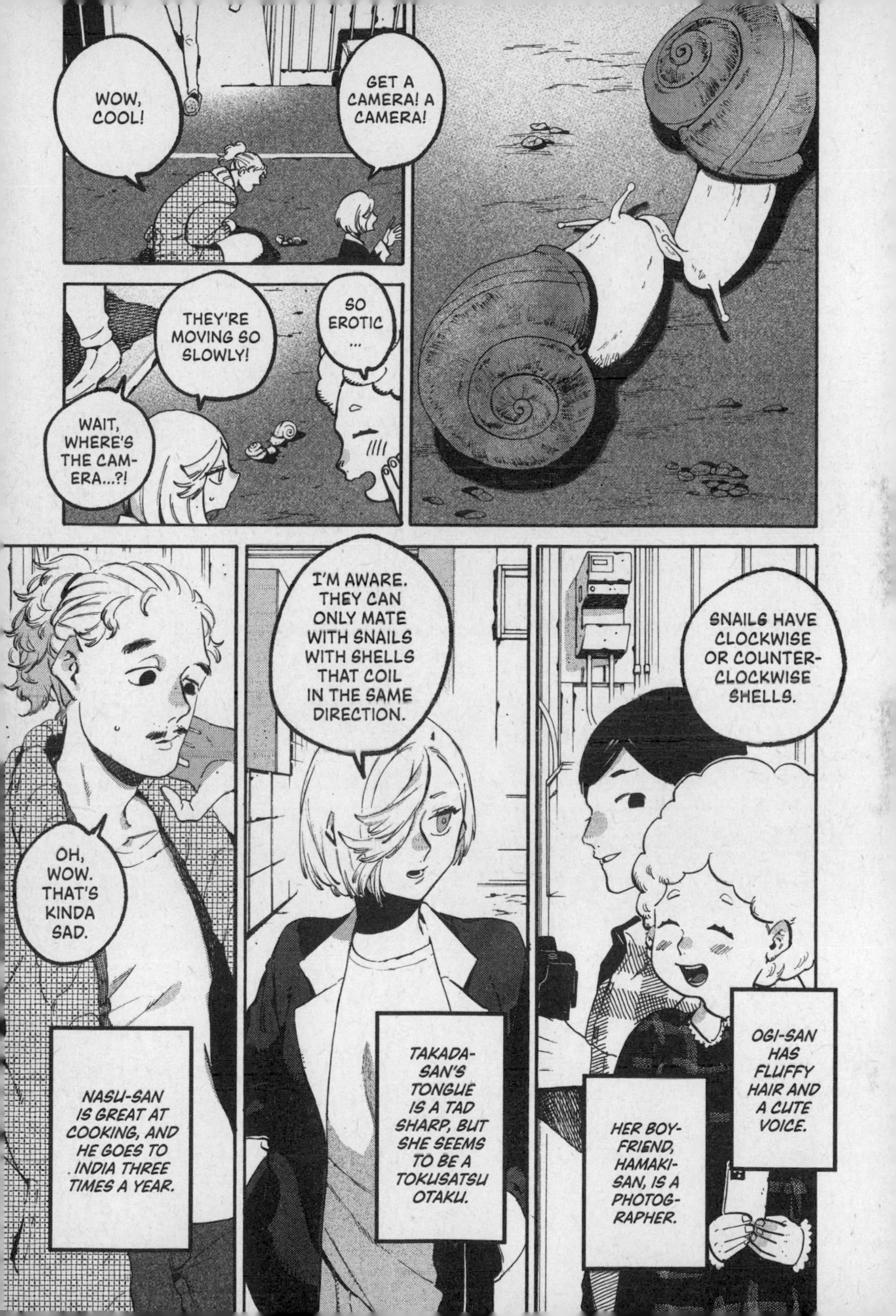
GET A CAMERA! A CAMERA!
WOW, COOL!
SO EROTIC ...
THEY'RE MOVING SO SLOWLY!
WAIT, WHERE'S THE CAM-ERA...?!
SNAILS HAVE CLOCKWISE OR COUNTER-CLOCKWISE SHELLS.
OGI-SAN HAS FLUFFY HAIR AND A CUTE VOICE.
HER BOY-FRIEND, HAMAKI-SAN, IS A PHOTOG-RAPHER.
I'M AWARE. THEY CAN ONLY MATE WITH SNAILS WITH SHELLS THAT COIL IN THE SAME DIRECTION.
TAKADA-SAN'S TONGUE IS A TAD SHARP, BUT SHE SEEMS TO BE A TOKUSATSU OTAKU.
OH, WOW. THAT'S KINDA SAD.
NASU-SAN IS GREAT AT COOKING, AND HE GOES TO INDIA THREE TIMES A YEAR.

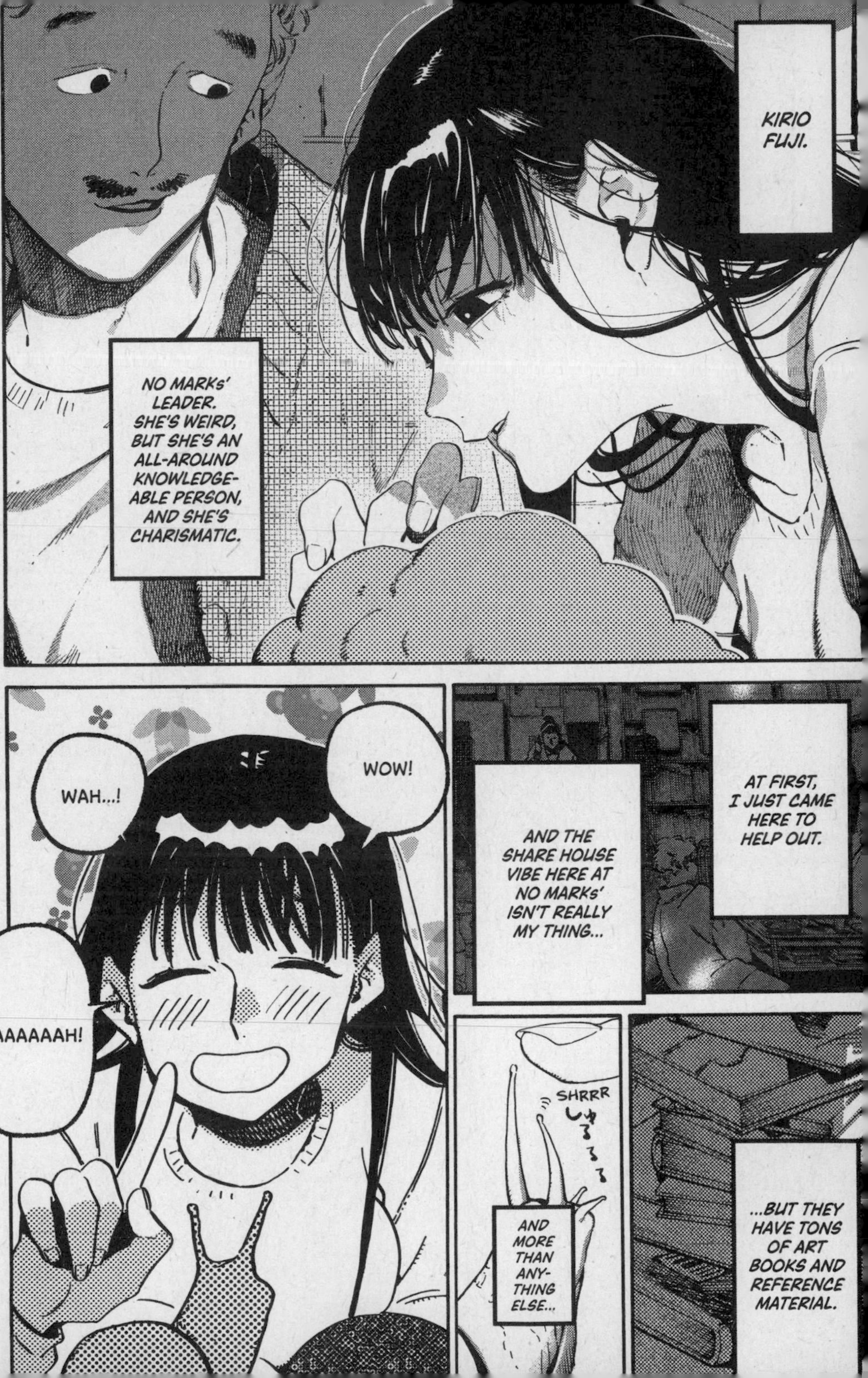
KIRIO FUJI.
NO MARKs' LEADER. SHE'S WEIRD, BUT SHE'S AN ALL-AROUND KNOWLEDGE-ABLE PERSON, AND SHE'S CHARISMATIC.
AT FIRST, I JUST CAME HERE TO HELP OUT.
AND THE SHARE HOUSE VIBE HERE AT NO MARKs' ISN'T REALLY MY THING...
...BUT THEY HAVE TONS OF ART BOOKS AND REFERENCE MATERIAL.
SHRRR
しゅるるる
AND MORE THAN ANY-THING ELSE...
WOW!
WAH...!
WAAAAAAH!

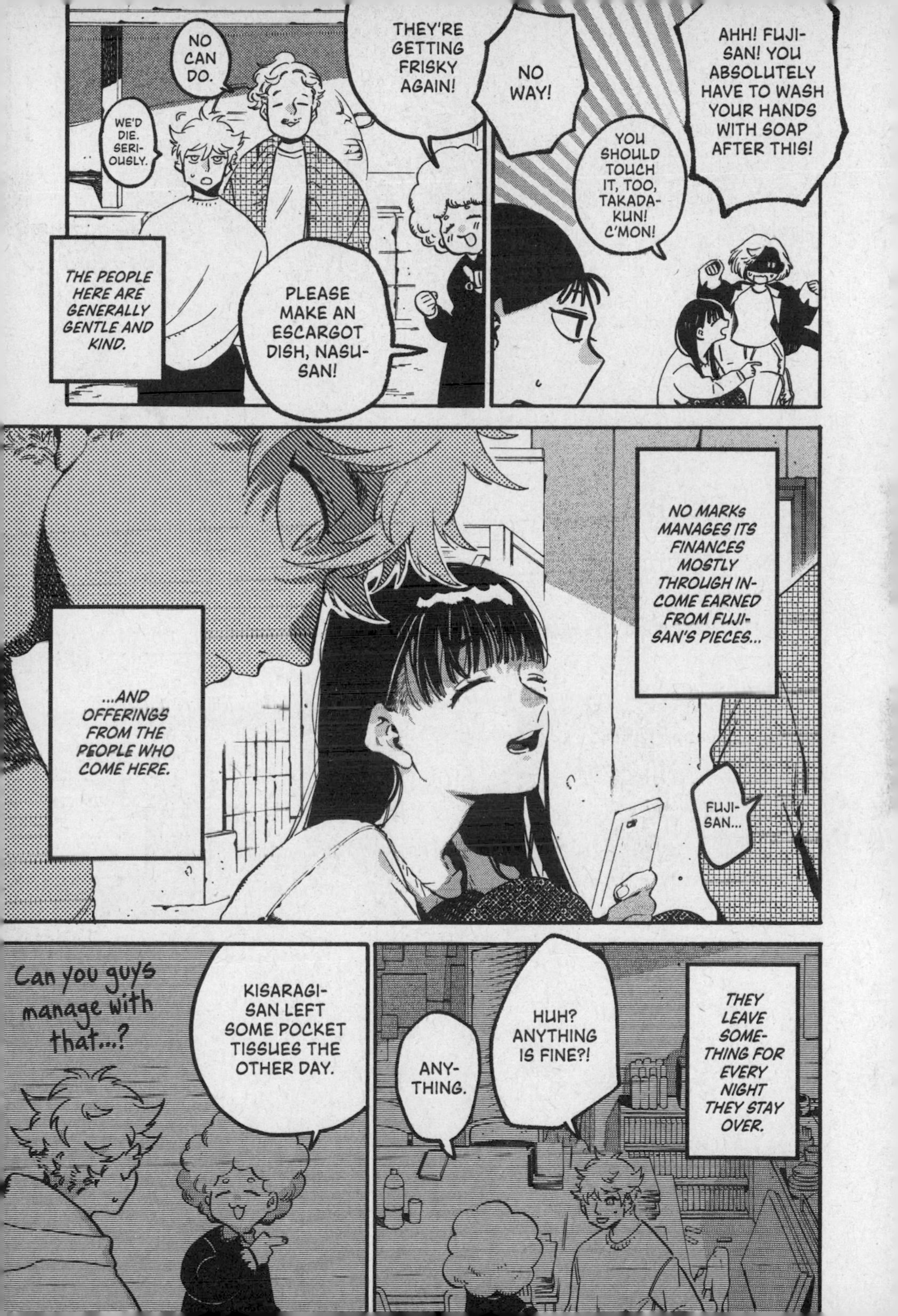
AHH! FUJI-SAN! YOU ABSOLUTELY HAVE TO WASH YOUR HANDS WITH SOAP AFTER THIS!
YOU SHOULD TOUCH IT, TOO, TAKADA-KUN! C'MON!
NO WAY!
THEY'RE GETTING FRISKY AGAIN!
NO CAN DO.
WE'D DIE. SERIOUSLY.
PLEASE MAKE AN ESCARGOT DISH, NASU-SAN!
THE PEOPLE HERE ARE GENERALLY GENTLE AND KIND.
NO MARKs MANAGES ITS FINANCES MOSTLY THROUGH INCOME EARNED FROM FUJI-SAN'S PIECES...
FUJI-SAN...
...AND OFFERINGS FROM THE PEOPLE WHO COME HERE.
THEY LEAVE SOMETHING FOR EVERY NIGHT THEY STAY OVER.
HUH? ANYTHING IS FINE?!
ANYTHING.
KISARAGI-SAN LEFT SOME POCKET TISSUES THE OTHER DAY.
Can you guys manage with that...?

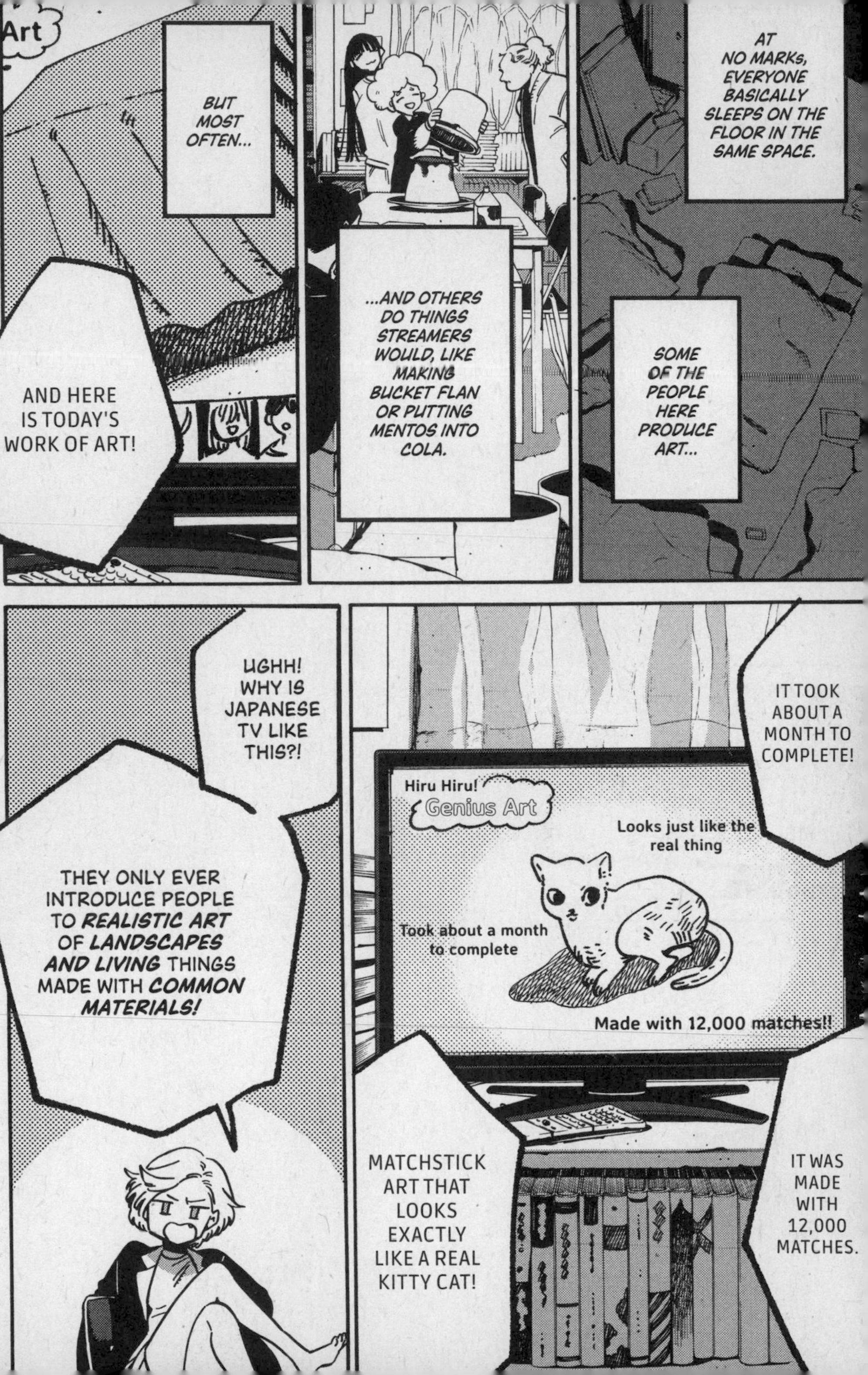

AT NO MARKs, EVERYONE BASICALLY SLEEPS ON THE FLOOR IN THE SAME SPACE.
SOME OF THE PEOPLE HERE PRODUCE ART...
...AND OTHERS DO THINGS STREAMERS WOULD, LIKE MAKING BUCKET FLAN OR PUTTING MENTOS INTO COLA.
BUT MOST OFTEN...
Art
AND HERE IS TODAY'S WORK OF ART!
IT TOOK ABOUT A MONTH TO COMPLETE!
Hiru Hiru!
Genius Art
Looks just like the real thing
Took about a month to complete
Made with 12,000 matches!!
IT WAS MADE WITH 12,000 MATCHES.
MATCHSTICK ART THAT LOOKS EXACTLY LIKE A REAL KITTY CAT!
UGHH! WHY IS JAPANESE TV LIKE THIS?!
THEY ONLY EVER INTRODUCE PEOPLE TO REALISTIC ART OF LANDSCAPES AND LIVING THINGS MADE WITH COMMON MATERIALS!

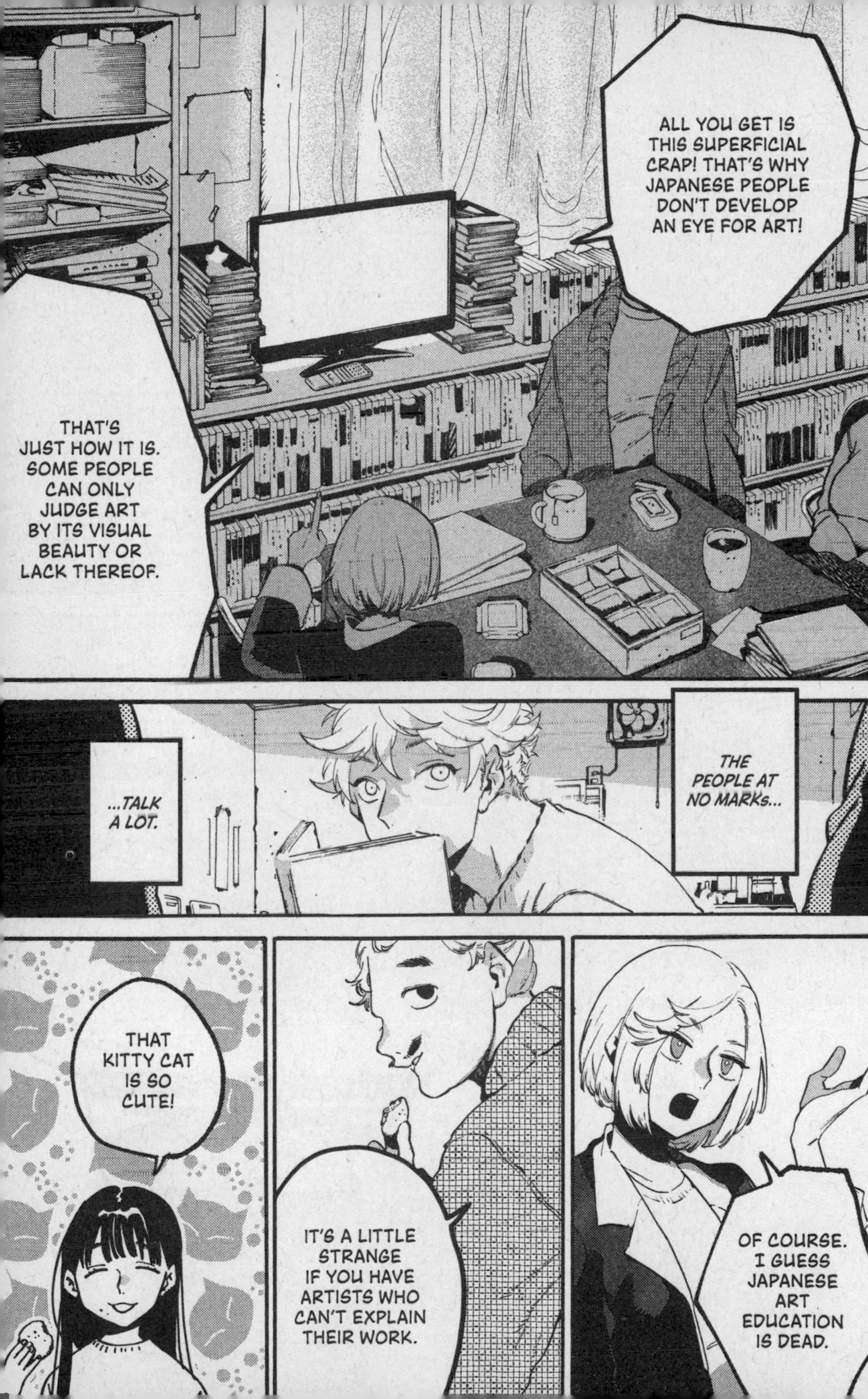
ALL YOU GET IS THIS SUPERFICIAL CRAP! THAT'S WHY JAPANESE PEOPLE DON'T DEVELOP AN EYE FOR ART!
THAT'S JUST HOW IT IS. SOME PEOPLE CAN ONLY JUDGE ART BY ITS VISUAL BEAUTY OR LACK THEREOF.
THE PEOPLE AT NO MARKs...
...TALK A LOT.
OF COURSE. I GUESS JAPANESE ART EDUCATION IS DEAD.
IT'S A LITTLE STRANGE IF YOU HAVE ARTISTS WHO CAN'T EXPLAIN THEIR WORK.
THAT KITTY CAT IS SO CUTE!

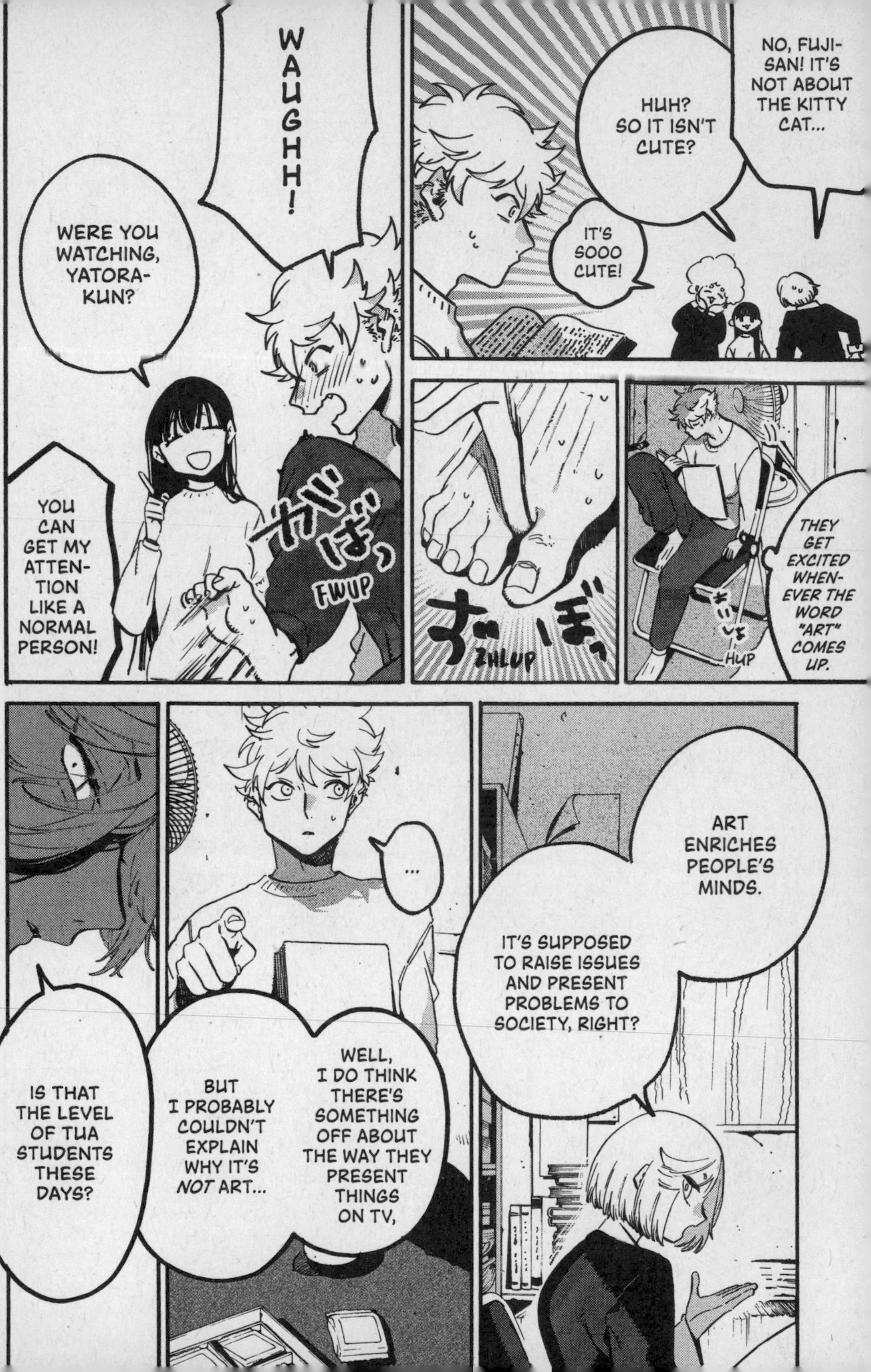
NO, FUJI-SAN! IT'S NOT ABOUT THE KITTY CAT...
HUH? SO IT ISN'T CUTE?
IT'S SOOO CUTE!
THEY GET EXCITED WHENEVER THE WORD "ART" COMES UP.
HUP
ZHLUP
WAUGHH!
WERE YOU WATCHING, YATORA-KUN?
FWUP
YOU CAN GET MY ATTENTION LIKE A NORMAL PERSON!
ART ENRICHES PEOPLE'S MINDS.
IT'S SUPPOSED TO RAISE ISSUES AND PRESENT PROBLEMS TO SOCIETY, RIGHT?
...
WELL, I DO THINK THERE'S SOMETHING OFF ABOUT THE WAY THEY PRESENT THINGS ON TV,
BUT I PROBABLY COULDN'T EXPLAIN WHY IT'S *NOT* ART...
IS THAT THE LEVEL OF TUA STUDENTS THESE DAYS?

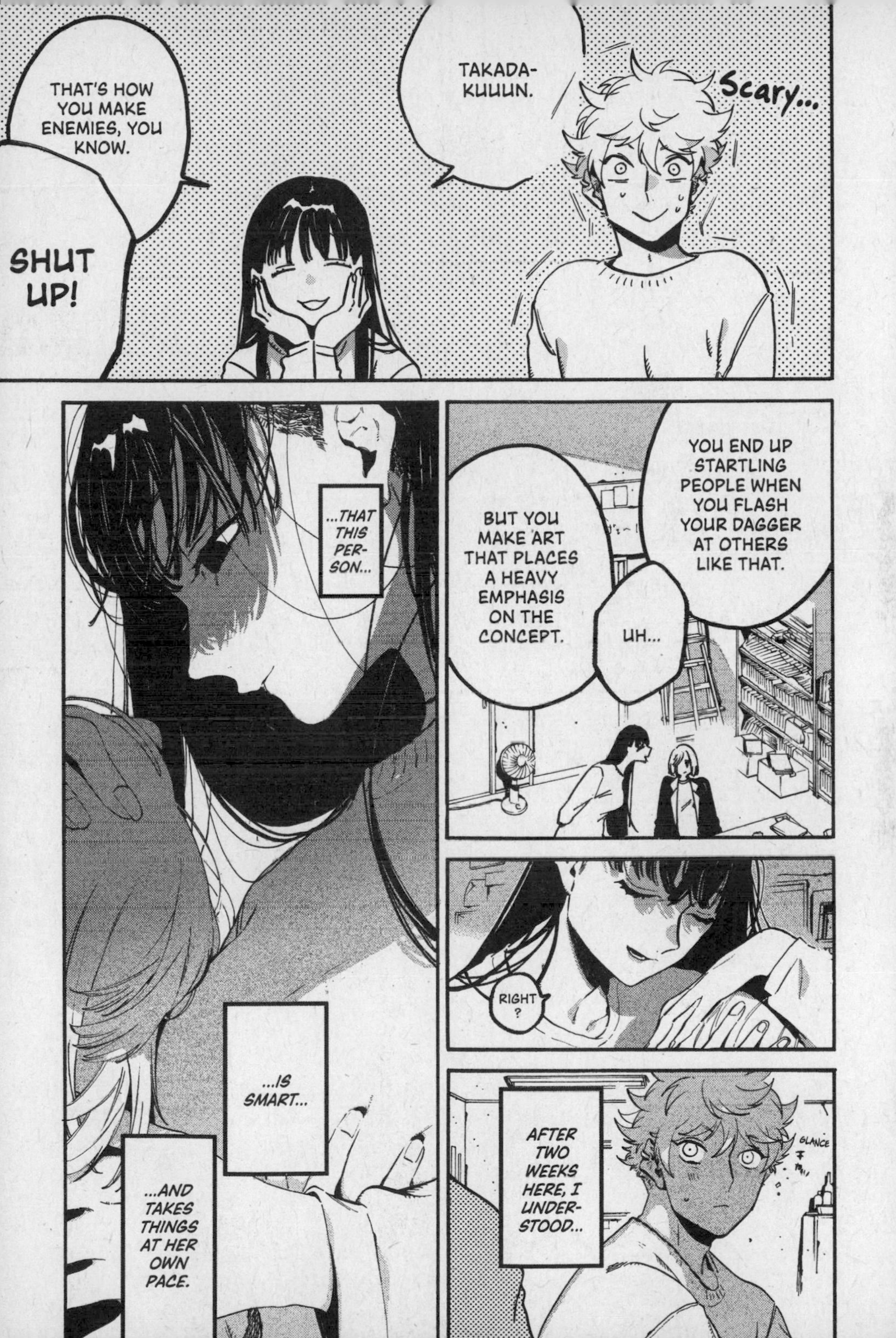
Scary...
TAKADA-KUUUN.
THAT'S HOW YOU MAKE ENEMIES, YOU KNOW.
SHUT UP!
YOU END UP STARTLING PEOPLE WHEN YOU FLASH YOUR DAGGER AT OTHERS LIKE THAT.
UH...
BUT YOU MAKE ART THAT PLACES A HEAVY EMPHASIS ON THE CONCEPT.
RIGHT?
AFTER TWO WEEKS HERE, I UNDERSTOOD...
GLANCE
...THAT THIS PERSON...
...IS SMART...
...AND TAKES THINGS AT HER OWN PACE.

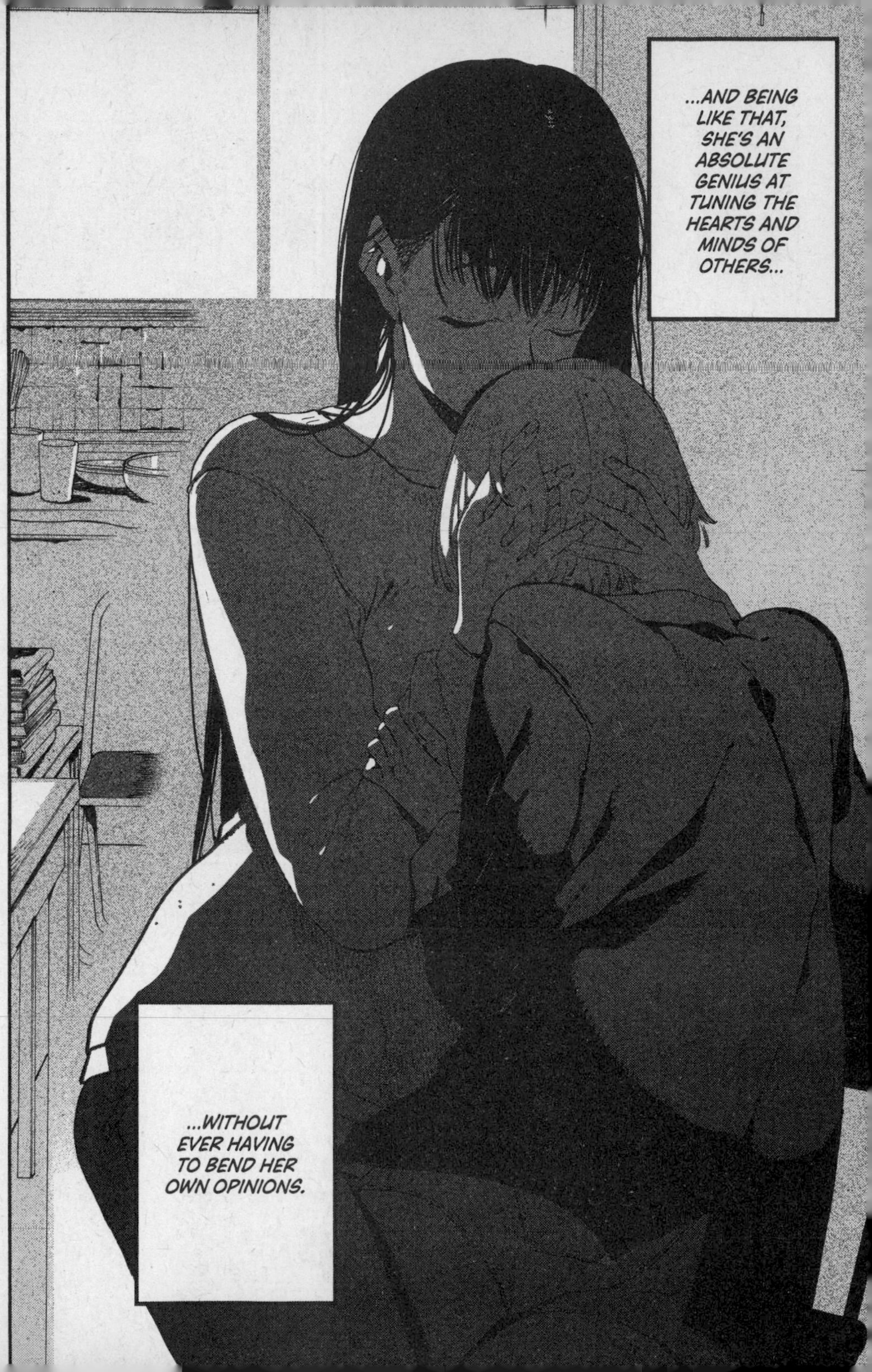
...AND BEING LIKE THAT, SHE'S AN ABSOLUTE GENIUS AT TUNING THE HEARTS AND MINDS OF OTHERS...
...WITHOUT EVER HAVING TO BEND HER OWN OPINIONS.

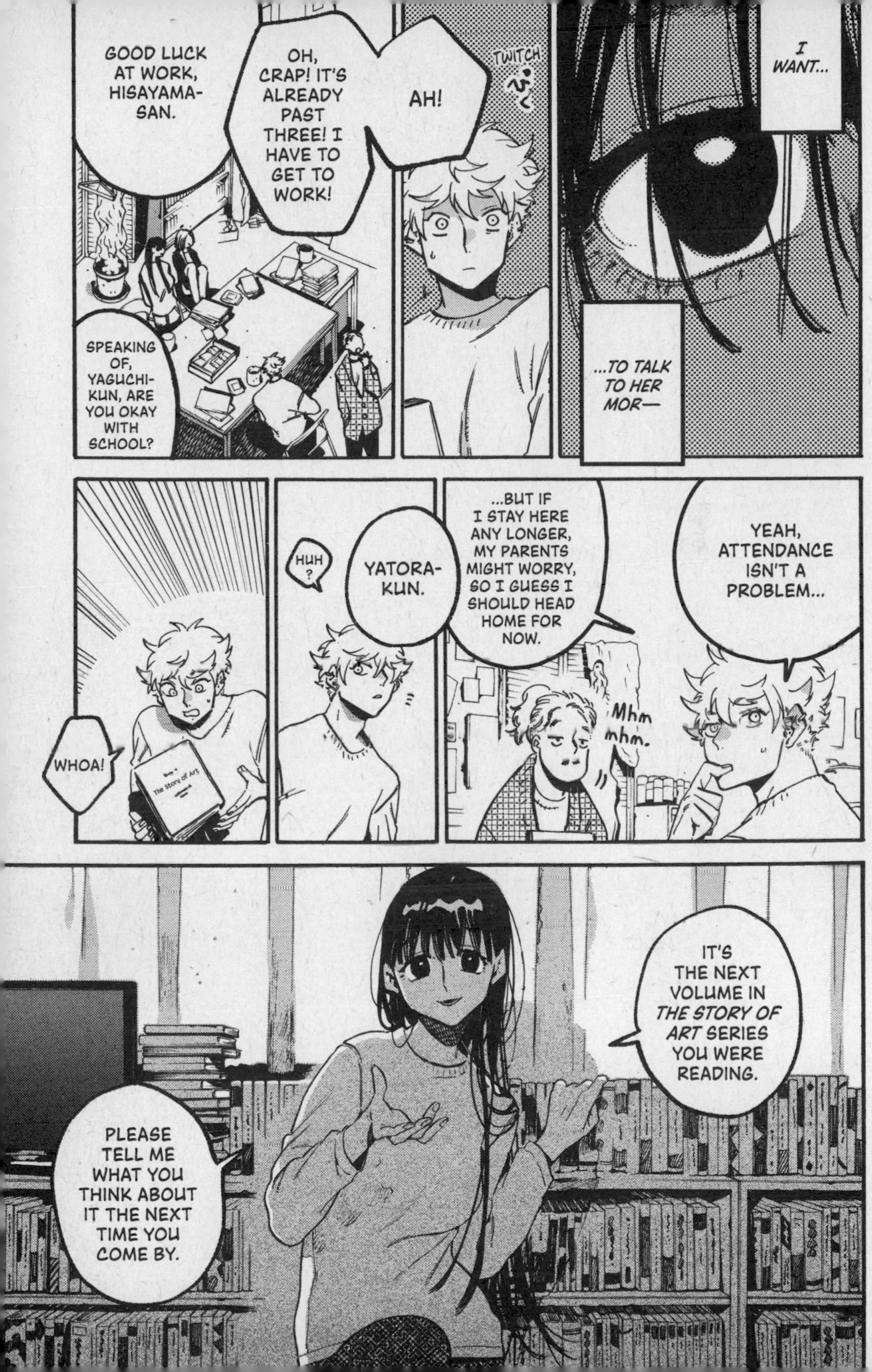

I WANT...
...TO TALK TO HER MOR—
TWITCH
AH!
OH, CRAP! IT'S ALREADY PAST THREE! I HAVE TO GET TO WORK!
GOOD LUCK AT WORK, HISAYAMA-SAN.
SPEAKING OF, YAGUCHI-KUN, ARE YOU OKAY WITH SCHOOL?
YEAH, ATTENDANCE ISN'T A PROBLEM...
...BUT IF I STAY HERE ANY LONGER, MY PARENTS MIGHT WORRY, SO I GUESS I SHOULD HEAD HOME FOR NOW.
Mhm mhm.
YATORA-KUN.
HUH?
WHOA!
The Story of Art
IT'S THE NEXT VOLUME IN *THE STORY OF ART* SERIES YOU WERE READING.
PLEASE TELL ME WHAT YOU THINK ABOUT IT THE NEXT TIME YOU COME BY.

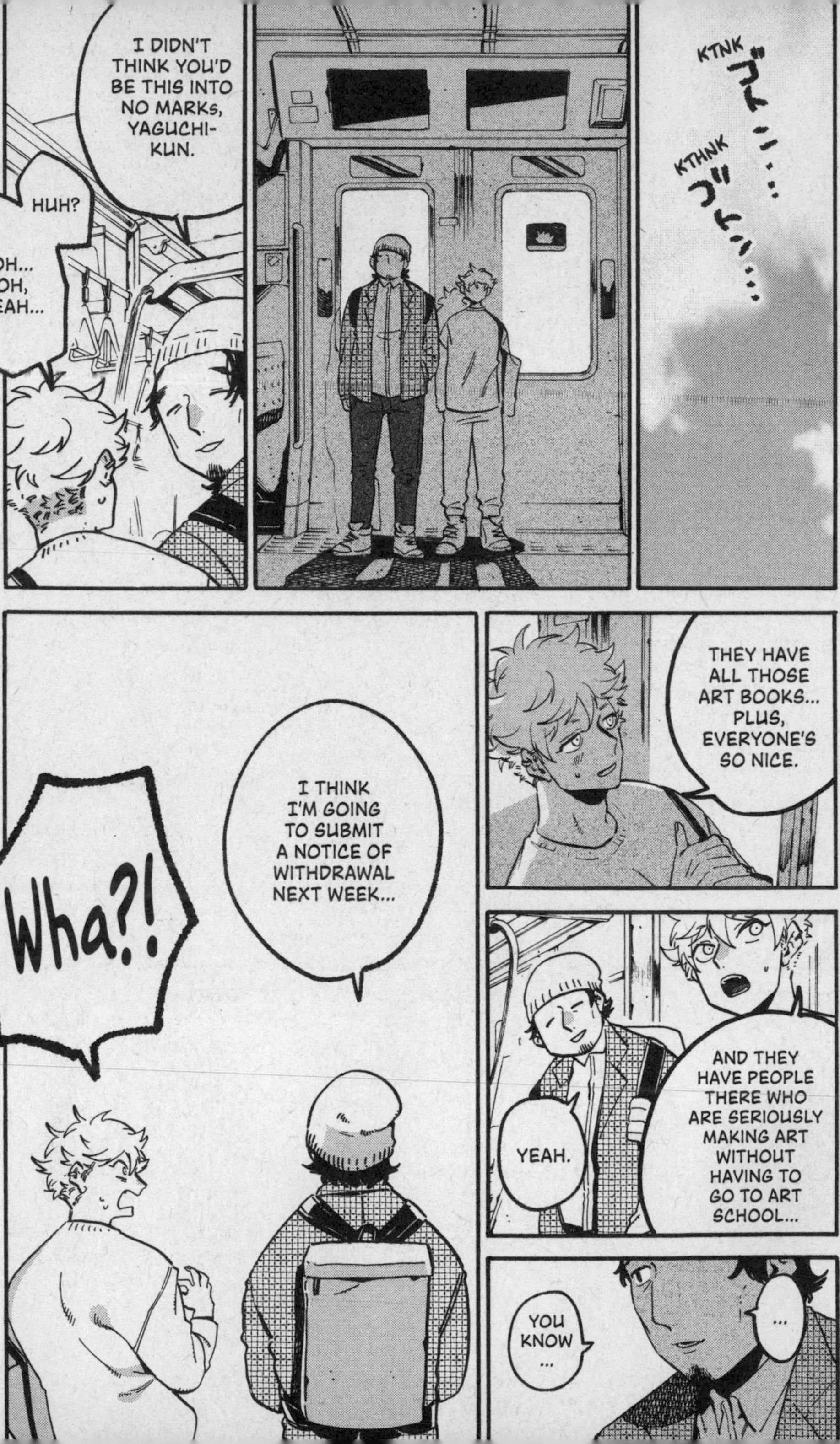
KTNK
ゴトン…
KTHNK
ゴトン…
I DIDN'T THINK YOU'D BE THIS INTO NO MARKS, YAGUCHI-KUN.
HUH?
OH... OH, YEAH...
THEY HAVE ALL THOSE ART BOOKS... PLUS, EVERYONE'S SO NICE.
AND THEY HAVE PEOPLE THERE WHO ARE SERIOUSLY MAKING ART WITHOUT HAVING TO GO TO ART SCHOOL...
YEAH.
...
YOU KNOW ...
I THINK I'M GOING TO SUBMIT A NOTICE OF WITHDRAWAL NEXT WEEK...
Wha?!

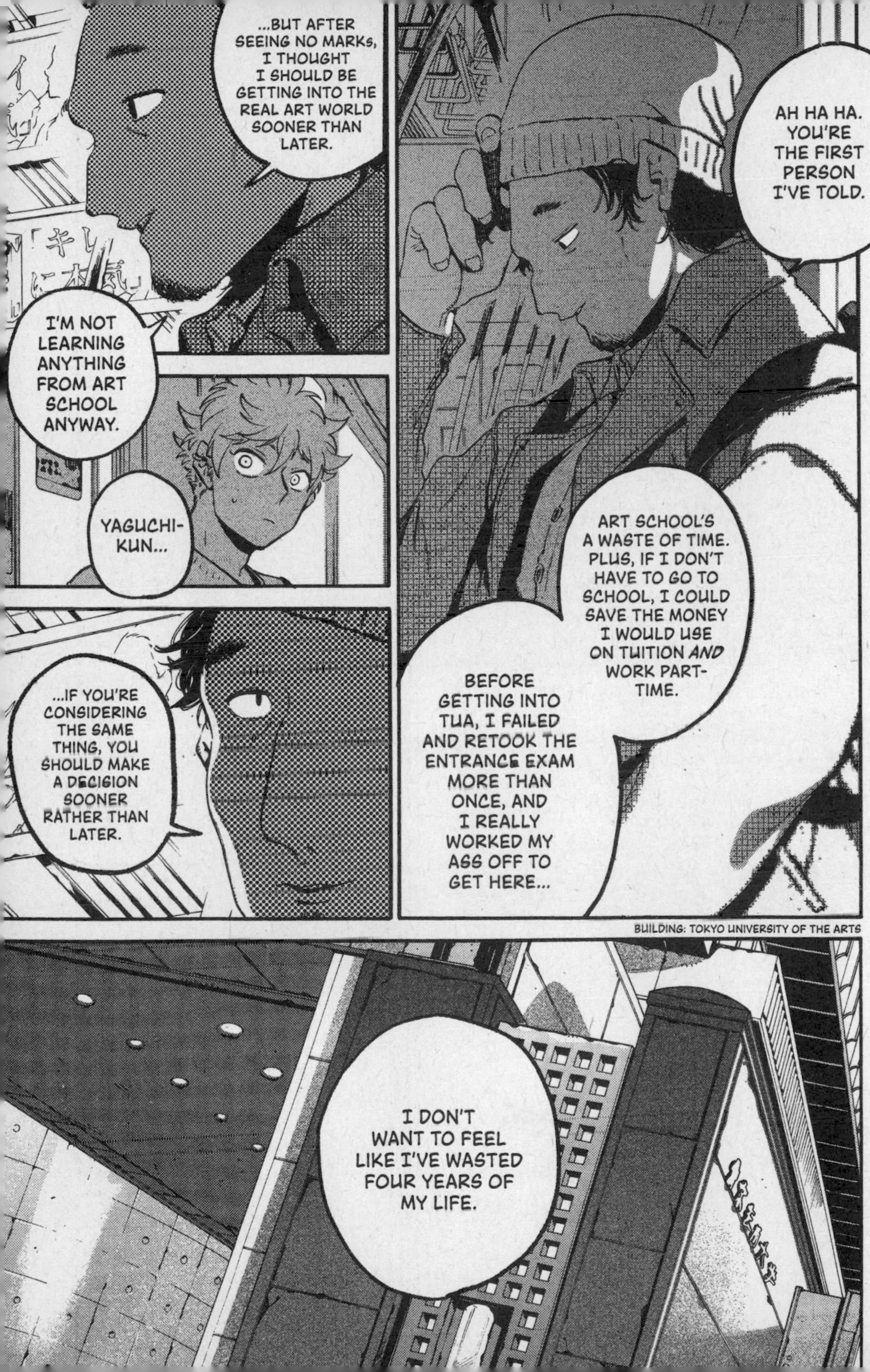
AH HA HA. YOU'RE THE FIRST PERSON I'VE TOLD.
ART SCHOOL'S A WASTE OF TIME. PLUS, IF I DON'T HAVE TO GO TO SCHOOL, I COULD SAVE THE MONEY I WOULD USE ON TUITION *AND* WORK PART-TIME.
BEFORE GETTING INTO TUA, I FAILED AND RETOOK THE ENTRANCE EXAM MORE THAN ONCE, AND I REALLY WORKED MY ASS OFF TO GET HERE...
...BUT AFTER SEEING NO MARKS, I THOUGHT I SHOULD BE GETTING INTO THE REAL ART WORLD SOONER THAN LATER.
I'M NOT LEARNING ANYTHING FROM ART SCHOOL ANYWAY.
YAGUCHI-KUN...
...IF YOU'RE CONSIDERING THE SAME THING, YOU SHOULD MAKE A DECISION SOONER RATHER THAN LATER.
BUILDING: TOKYO UNIVERSITY OF THE ARTS
I DON'T WANT TO FEEL LIKE I'VE WASTED FOUR YEARS OF MY LIFE.

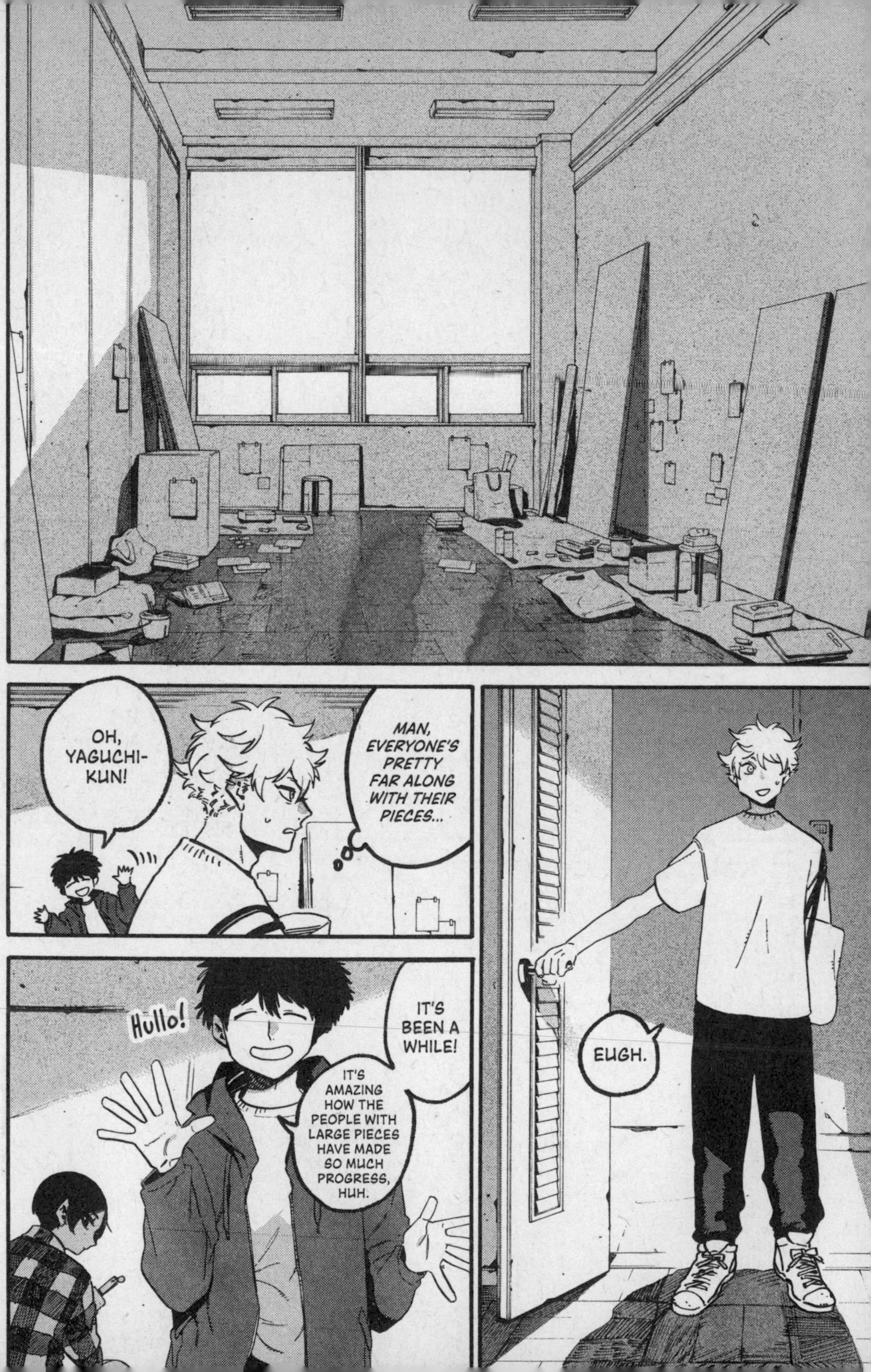
EUGH.
MAN, EVERYONE'S PRETTY FAR ALONG WITH THEIR PIECES...
OH, YAGUCHI-KUN!
IT'S BEEN A WHILE!
IT'S AMAZING HOW THE PEOPLE WITH LARGE PIECES HAVE MADE SO MUCH PROGRESS, HUH.
Hullo!

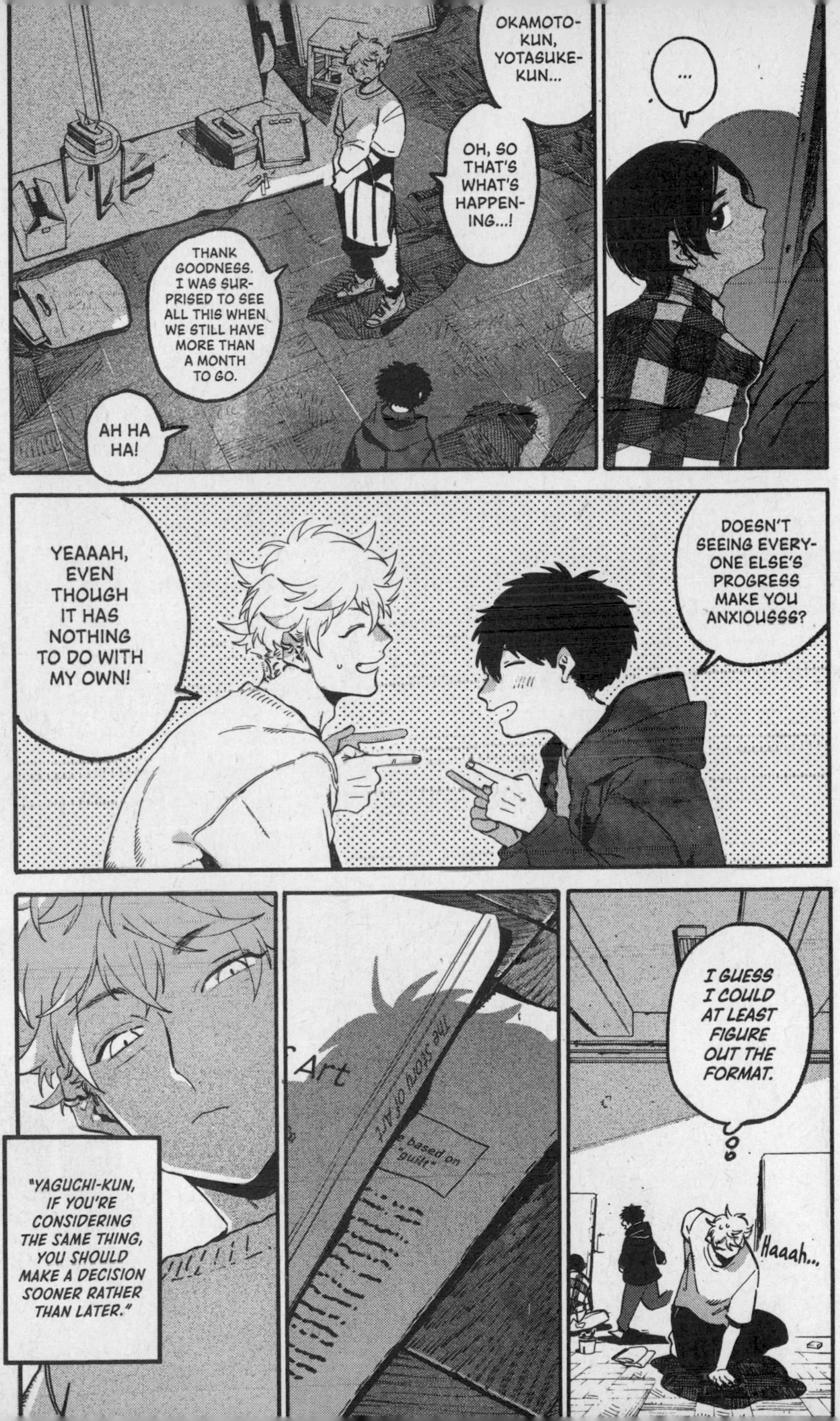
...
OKAMOTO-KUN, YOTASUKE-KUN...
OH, SO THAT'S WHAT'S HAPPENING...!
THANK GOODNESS. I WAS SURPRISED TO SEE ALL THIS WHEN WE STILL HAVE MORE THAN A MONTH TO GO.
AH HA HA!
DOESN'T SEEING EVERYONE ELSE'S PROGRESS MAKE YOU ANXIOUSSS?
YEAAAH, EVEN THOUGH IT HAS NOTHING TO DO WITH MY OWN!
I GUESS I COULD AT LEAST FIGURE OUT THE FORMAT.
Haaah...
The Story of Art
* based on "guilt"
"YAGUCHI-KUN, IF YOU'RE CONSIDERING THE SAME THING, YOU SHOULD MAKE A DECISION SOONER RATHER THAN LATER."

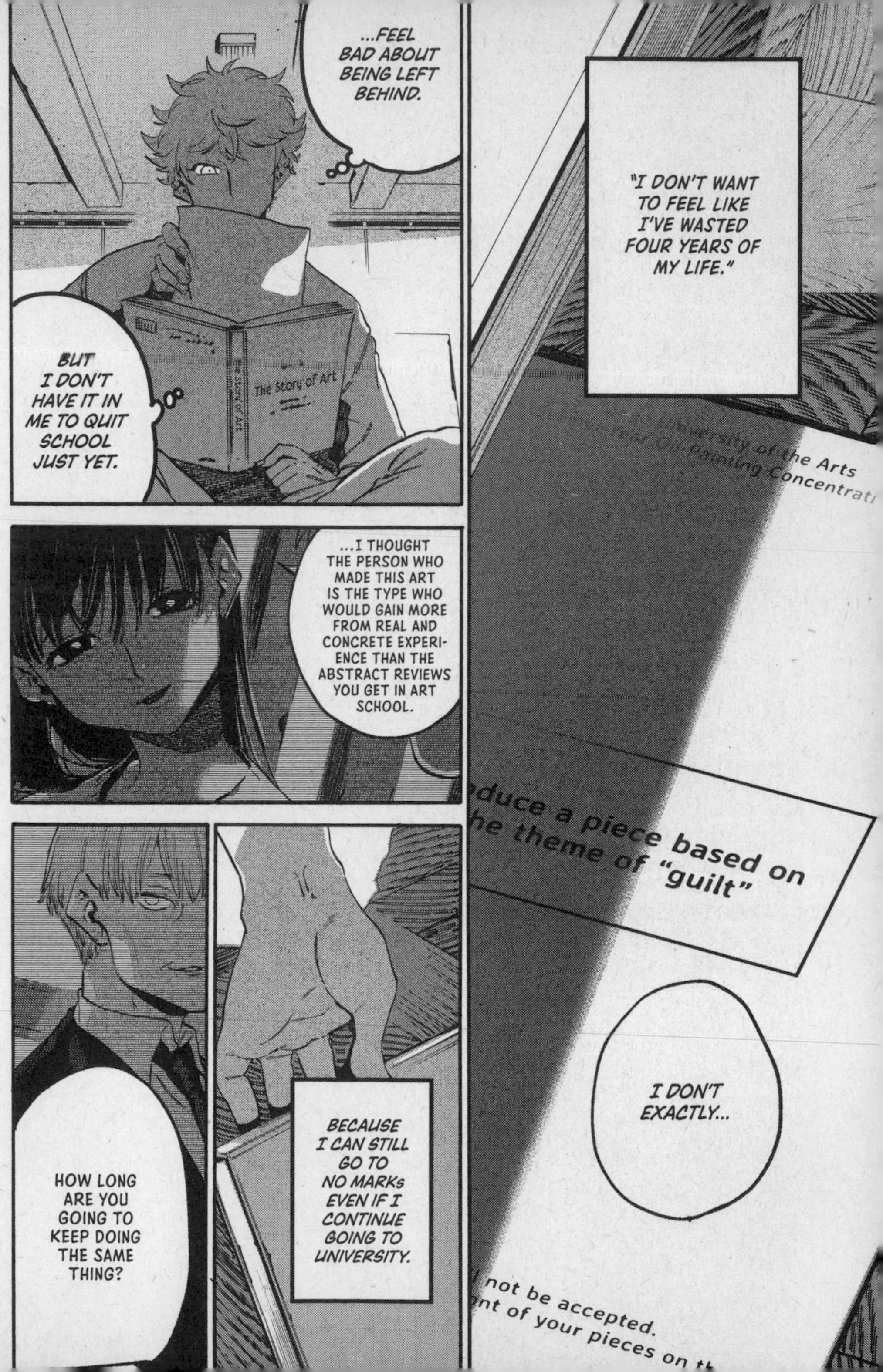
"I DON'T WANT TO FEEL LIKE I'VE WASTED FOUR YEARS OF MY LIFE."
University of the Arts
Oil Painting Concentrati
duce a piece based on
he theme of "guilt"
not be accepted.
nt of your pieces on th
I DON'T EXACTLY...
...FEEL BAD ABOUT BEING LEFT BEHIND.
The Story of Art
BUT I DON'T HAVE IT IN ME TO QUIT SCHOOL JUST YET.
...I THOUGHT THE PERSON WHO MADE THIS ART IS THE TYPE WHO WOULD GAIN MORE FROM REAL AND CONCRETE EXPERIENCE THAN THE ABSTRACT REVIEWS YOU GET IN ART SCHOOL.
BECAUSE I CAN STILL GO TO NO MARKs EVEN IF I CONTINUE GOING TO UNIVERSITY.
HOW LONG ARE YOU GOING TO KEEP DOING THE SAME THING?

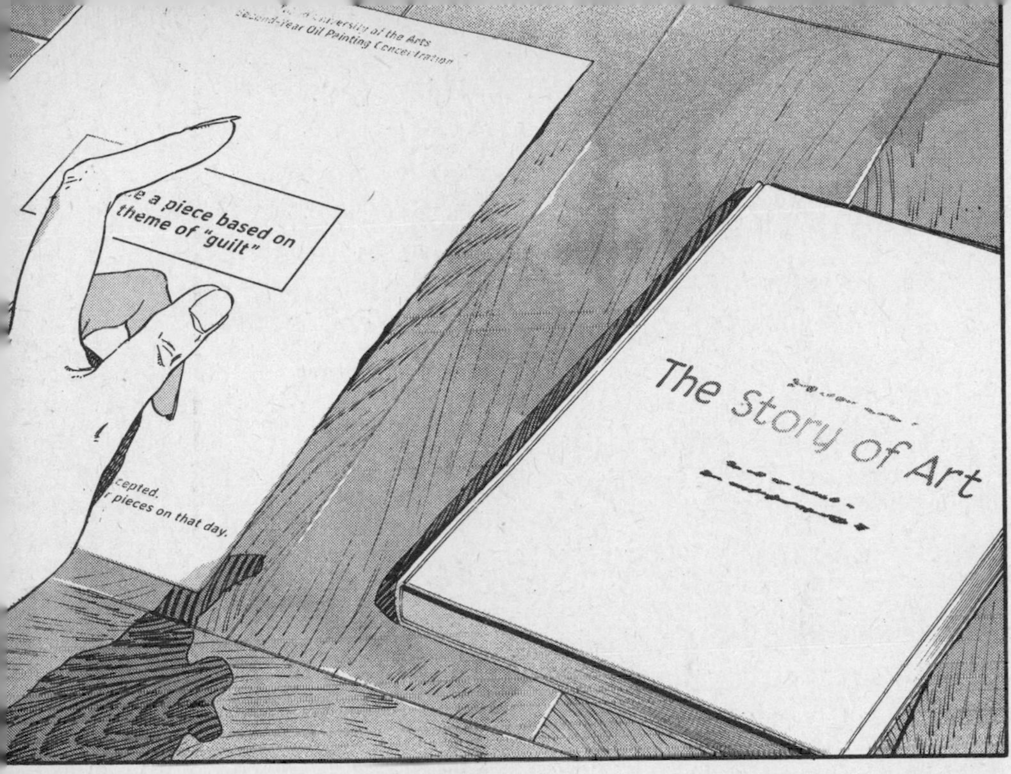
University of the Arts
Second-Year Oil Painting Concentration
theme of "guilt"
pieces on that day.
The Story of Art

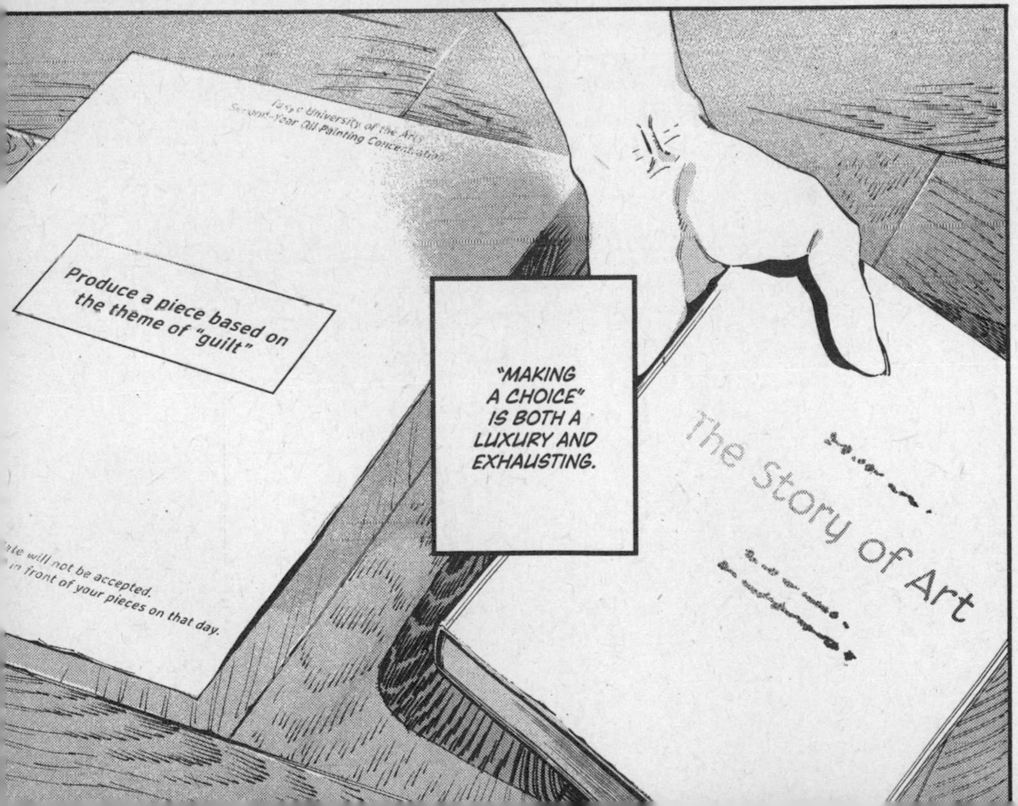
"MAKING A CHOICE" IS BOTH A LUXURY AND EXHAUSTING.
The Story of Art
Produce a piece based on the theme of "guilt"
University of the Arts
will not be accepted.
in front of your pieces on that day.

IF SOMEONE
COULD CHOOSE
MY ENTIRE LIFE
FOR ME...

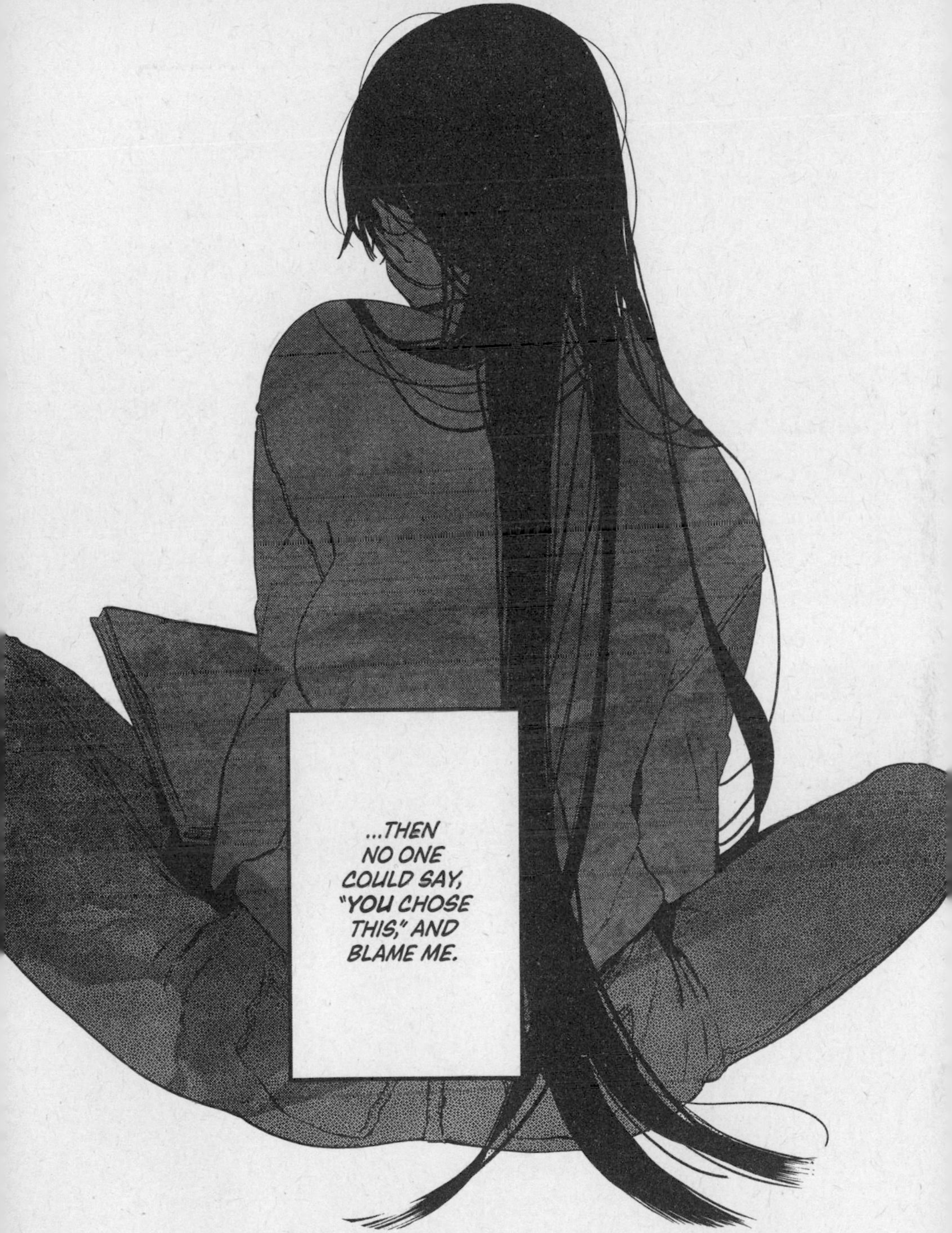
...THEN NO ONE COULD SAY, "YOU CHOSE THIS," AND BLAME ME.

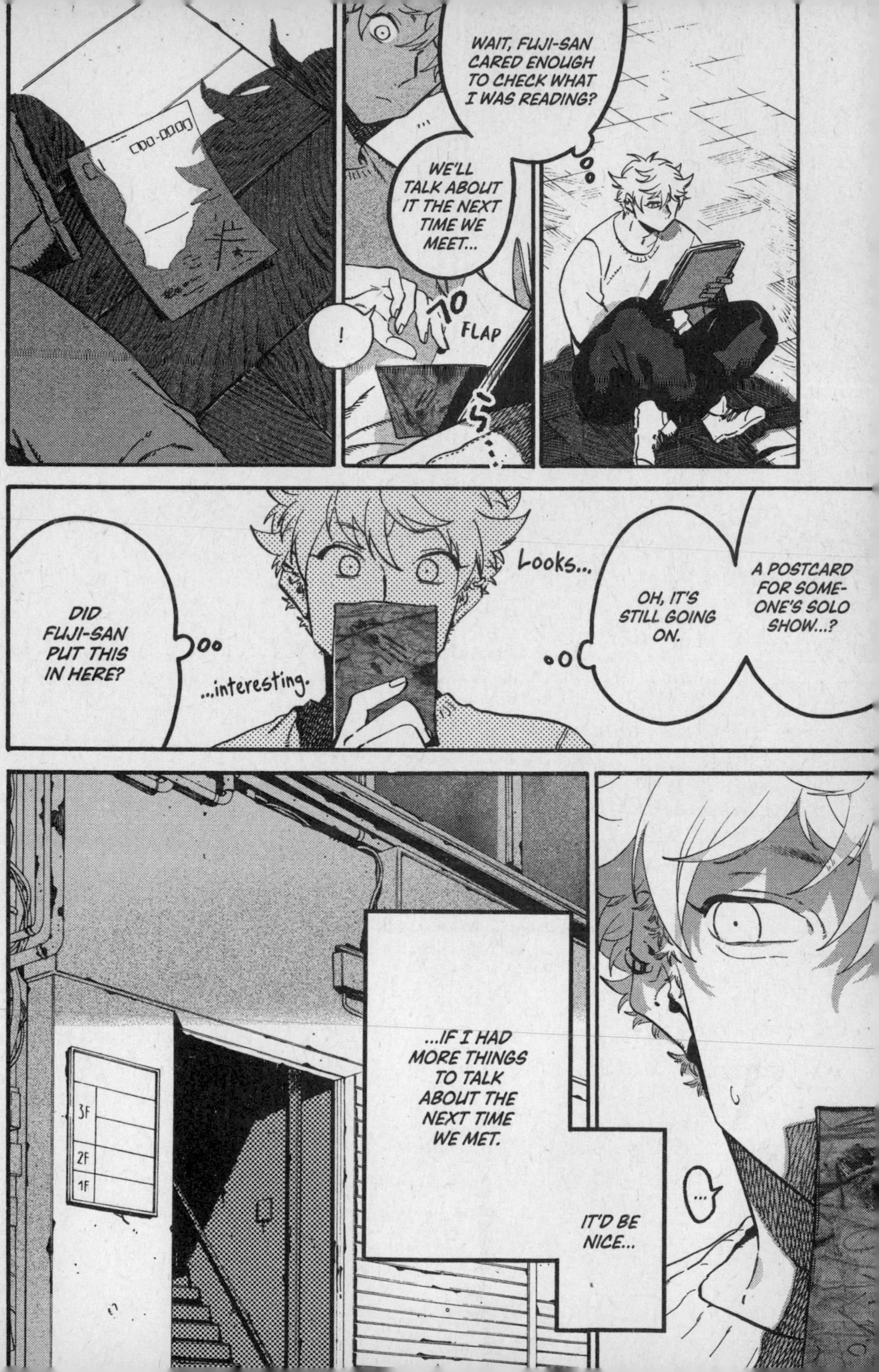
WAIT, FUJI-SAN CARED ENOUGH TO CHECK WHAT I WAS READING?
...
WE'LL TALK ABOUT IT THE NEXT TIME WE MEET...
FLAP
!
A POSTCARD FOR SOME-ONE'S SOLO SHOW...?
OH, IT'S STILL GOING ON.
Looks...
...interesting.
DID FUJI-SAN PUT THIS IN HERE?
...IF I HAD MORE THINGS TO TALK ABOUT THE NEXT TIME WE MET.
IT'D BE NICE...
...
3F
2F
1F

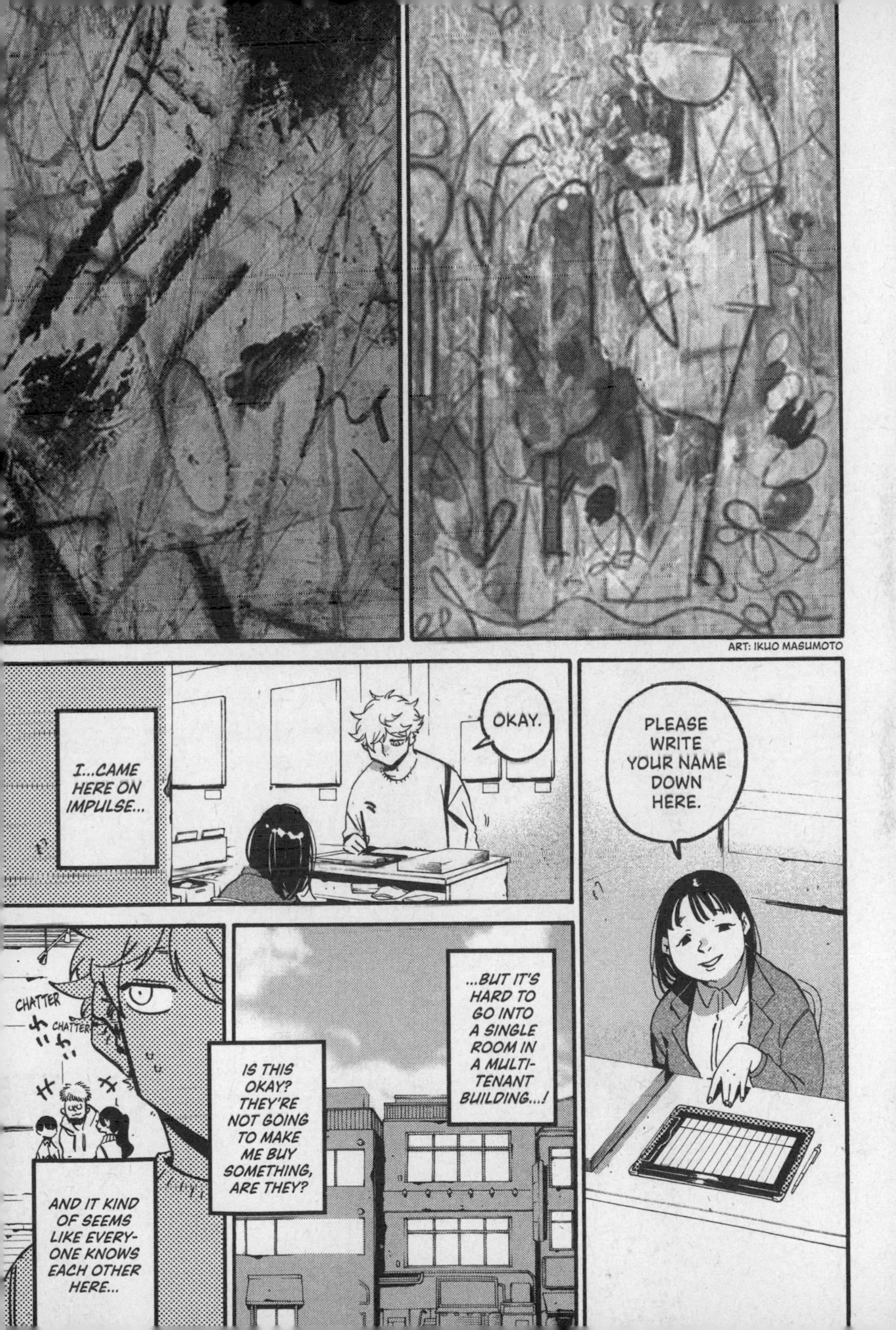
ART: IKUO MASUMOTO
PLEASE WRITE YOUR NAME DOWN HERE.
OKAY.
I...CAME HERE ON IMPULSE...
...BUT IT'S HARD TO GO INTO A SINGLE ROOM IN A MULTI-TENANT BUILDING...!
IS THIS OKAY? THEY'RE NOT GOING TO MAKE ME BUY SOMETHING, ARE THEY?
CHATTER
CHATTER
AND IT KIND OF SEEMS LIKE EVERYONE KNOWS EACH OTHER HERE...

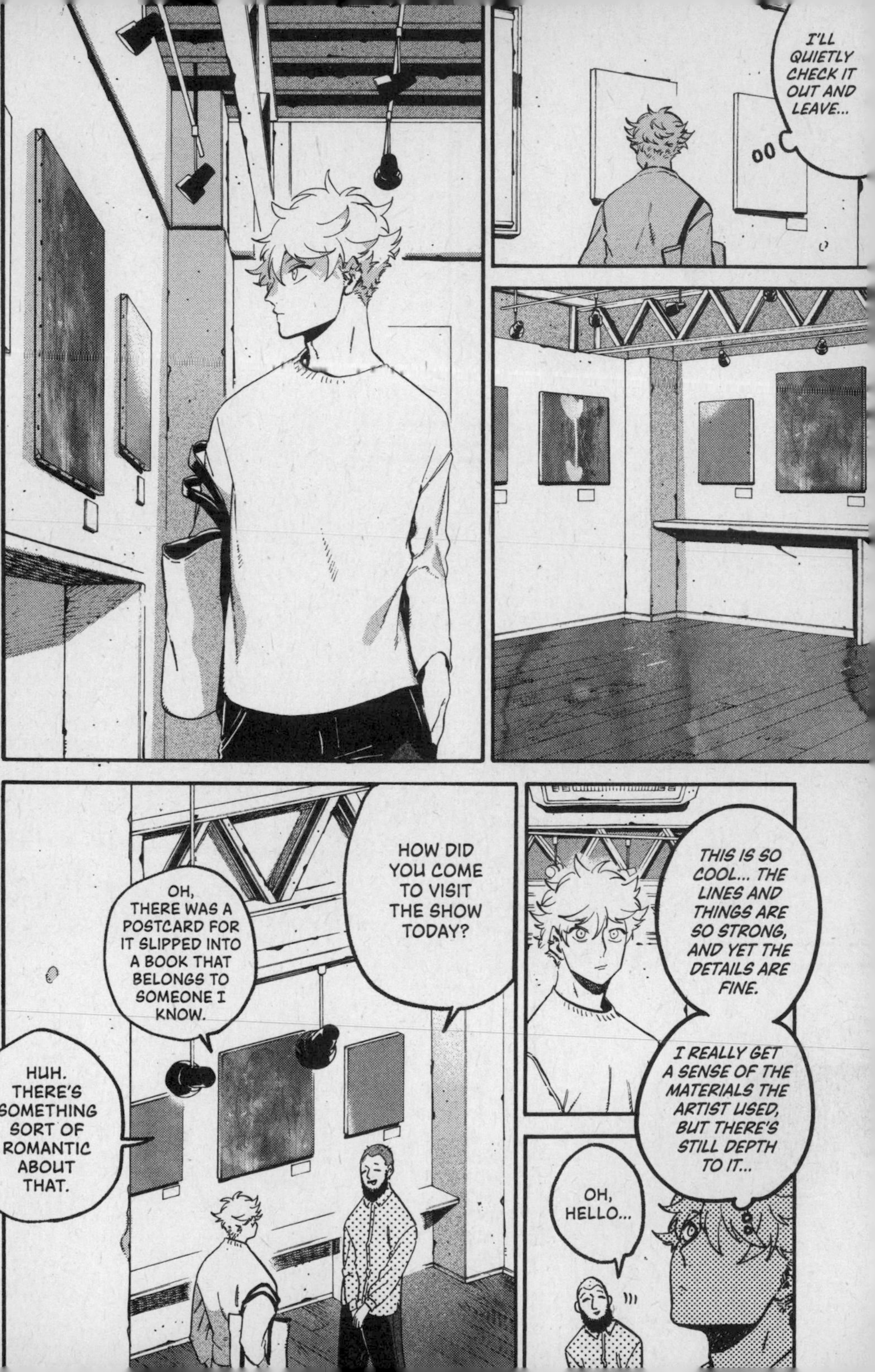
I'LL QUIETLY CHECK IT OUT AND LEAVE...
THIS IS SO COOL... THE LINES AND THINGS ARE SO STRONG, AND YET THE DETAILS ARE FINE.
I REALLY GET A SENSE OF THE MATERIALS THE ARTIST USED, BUT THERE'S STILL DEPTH TO IT...
OH, HELLO...
HOW DID YOU COME TO VISIT THE SHOW TODAY?
OH, THERE WAS A POSTCARD FOR IT SLIPPED INTO A BOOK THAT BELONGS TO SOMEONE I KNOW.
HUH. THERE'S SOMETHING SORT OF ROMANTIC ABOUT THAT.

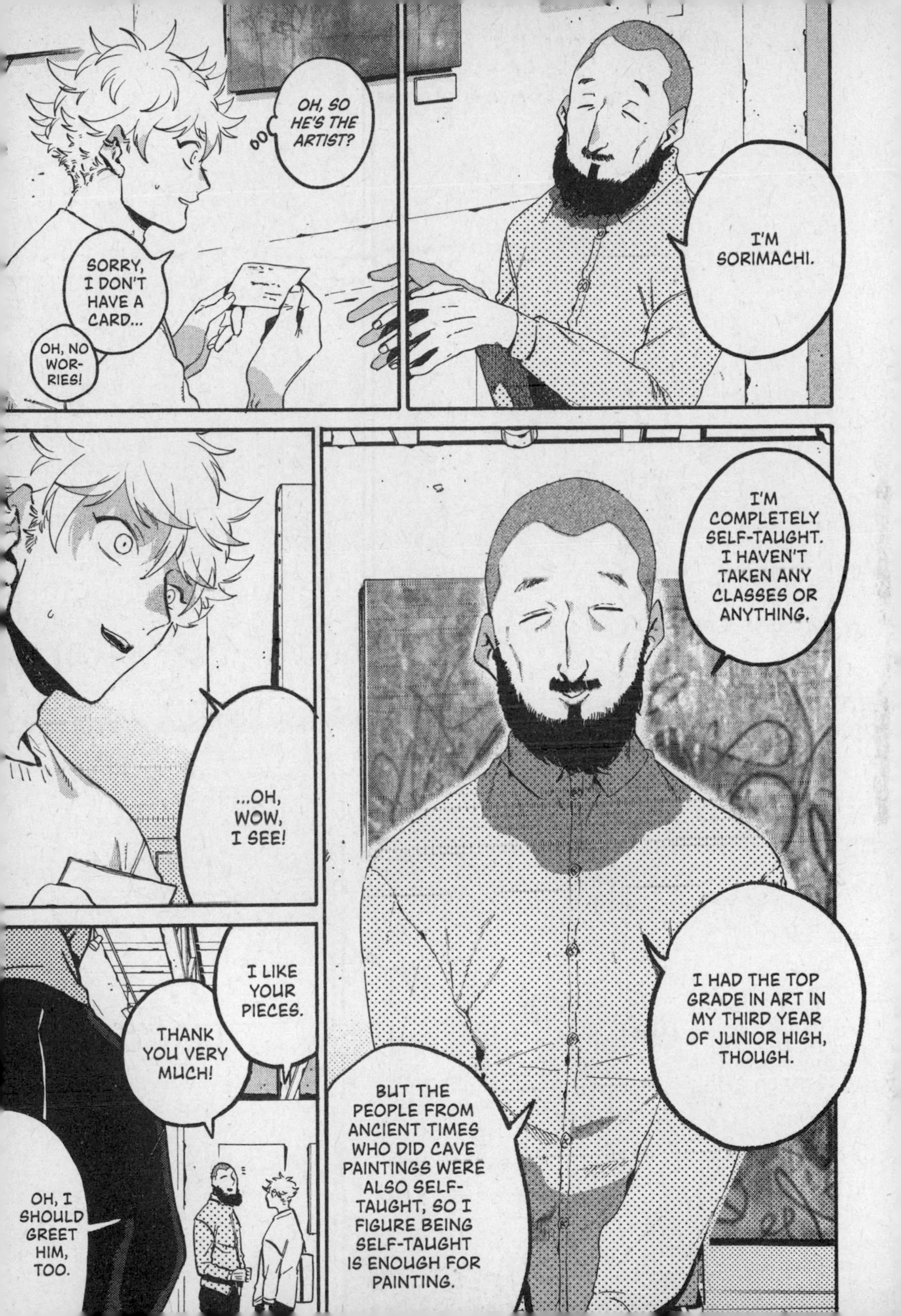

I'M SORIMACHI.
OH, SO HE'S THE ARTIST?
SORRY, I DON'T HAVE A CARD...
OH, NO WORRIES!
I'M COMPLETELY SELF-TAUGHT. I HAVEN'T TAKEN ANY CLASSES OR ANYTHING.
I HAD THE TOP GRADE IN ART IN MY THIRD YEAR OF JUNIOR HIGH, THOUGH.
BUT THE PEOPLE FROM ANCIENT TIMES WHO DID CAVE PAINTINGS WERE ALSO SELF-TAUGHT, SO I FIGURE BEING SELF-TAUGHT IS ENOUGH FOR PAINTING.
...OH, WOW, I SEE!
I LIKE YOUR PIECES.
THANK YOU VERY MUCH!
OH, I SHOULD GREET HIM, TOO.

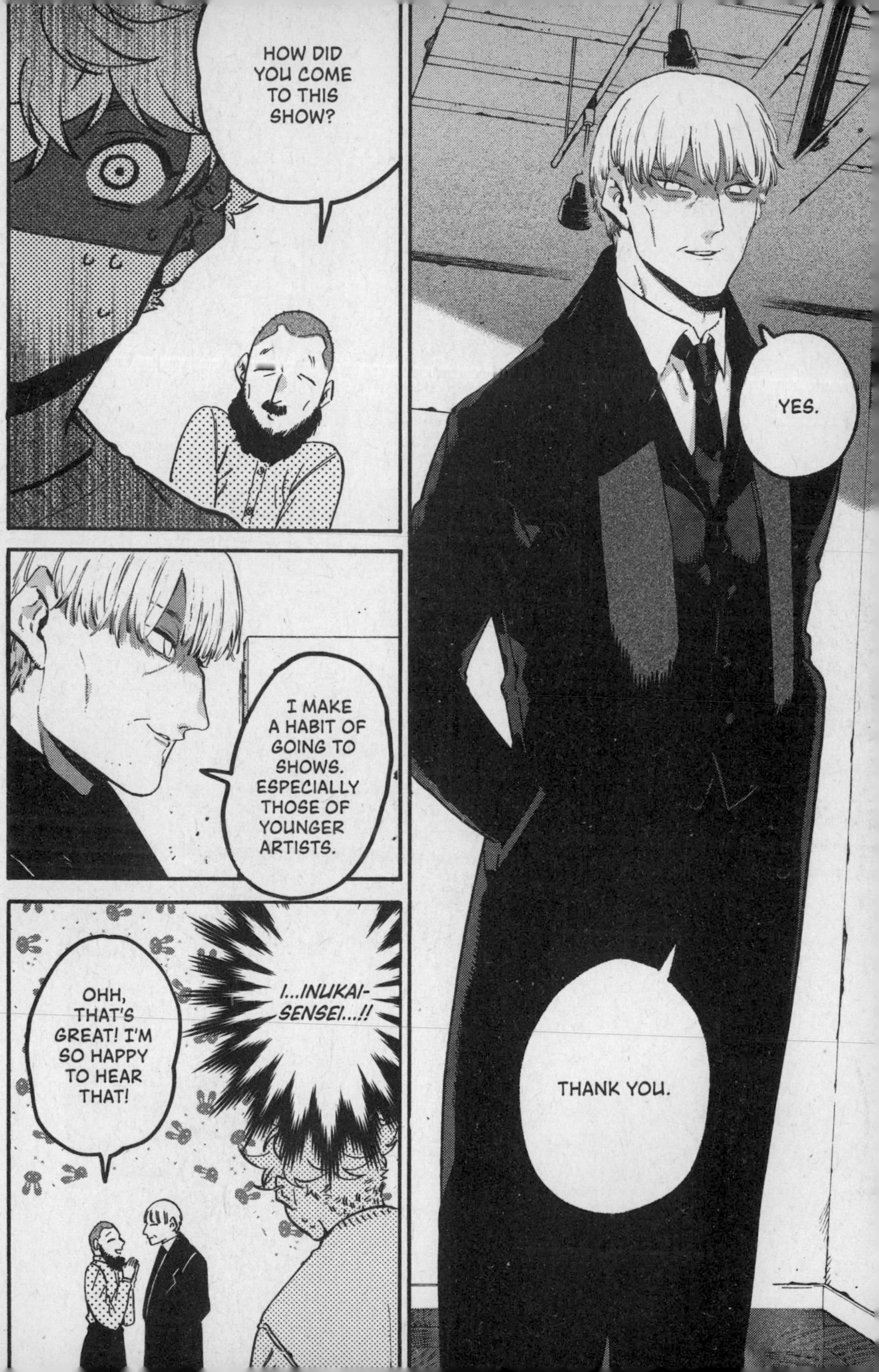
YES.
THANK YOU.
HOW DID YOU COME TO THIS SHOW?
I MAKE A HABIT OF GOING TO SHOWS. ESPECIALLY THOSE OF YOUNGER ARTISTS.
I...INUKAI-SENSEI...!!
OHH, THAT'S GREAT! I'M SO HAPPY TO HEAR THAT!

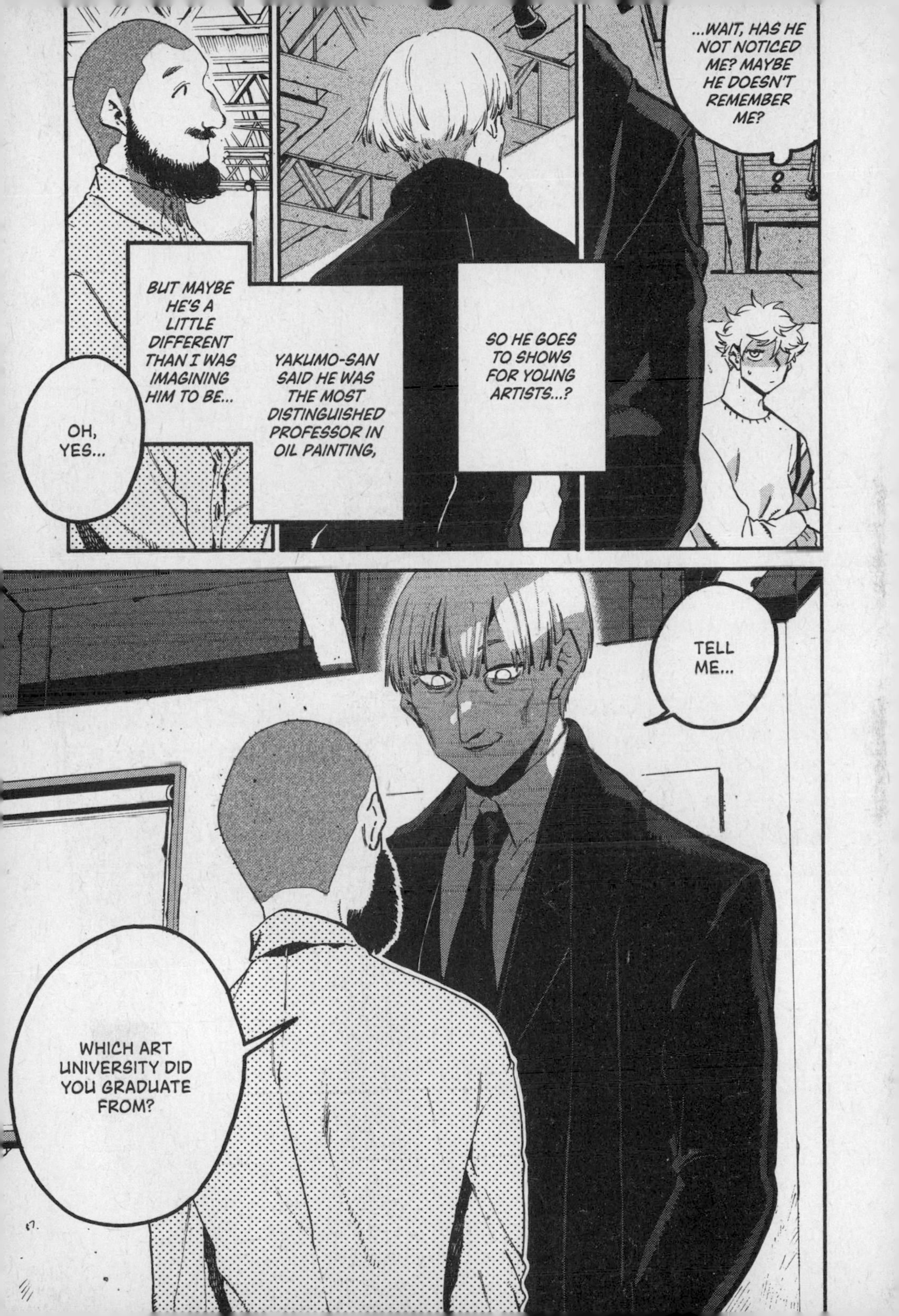
...WAIT, HAS HE NOT NOTICED ME? MAYBE HE DOESN'T REMEMBER ME?
SO HE GOES TO SHOWS FOR YOUNG ARTISTS...?
YAKUMO-SAN SAID HE WAS THE MOST DISTINGUISHED PROFESSOR IN OIL PAINTING,
BUT MAYBE HE'S A LITTLE DIFFERENT THAN I WAS IMAGINING HIM TO BE...
OH, YES...
TELL ME...
WHICH ART UNIVERSITY DID YOU GRADUATE FROM?

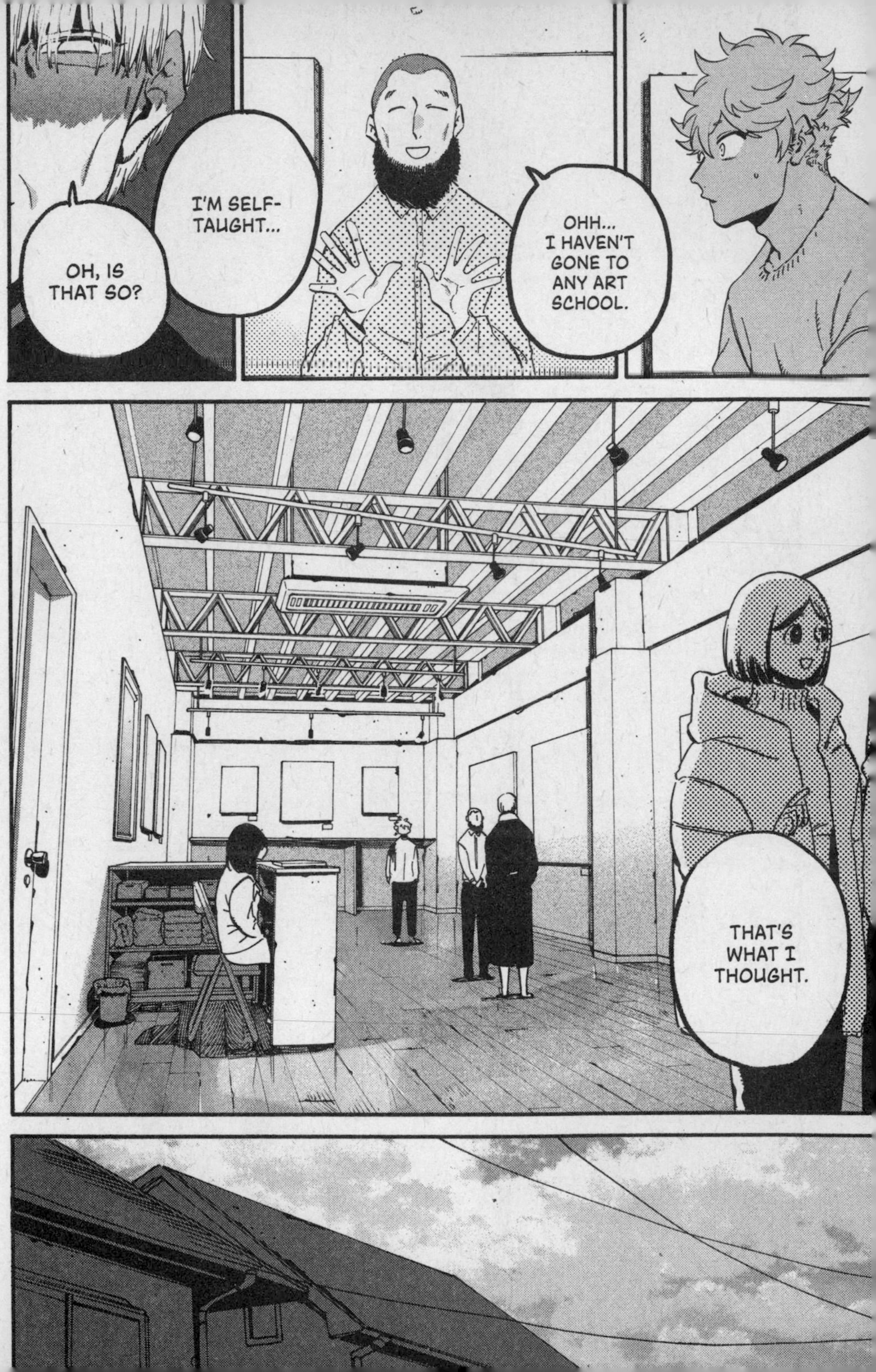
OHH... I HAVEN'T GONE TO ANY ART SCHOOL.
I'M SELF-TAUGHT...
OH, IS THAT SO?
THAT'S WHAT I THOUGHT.

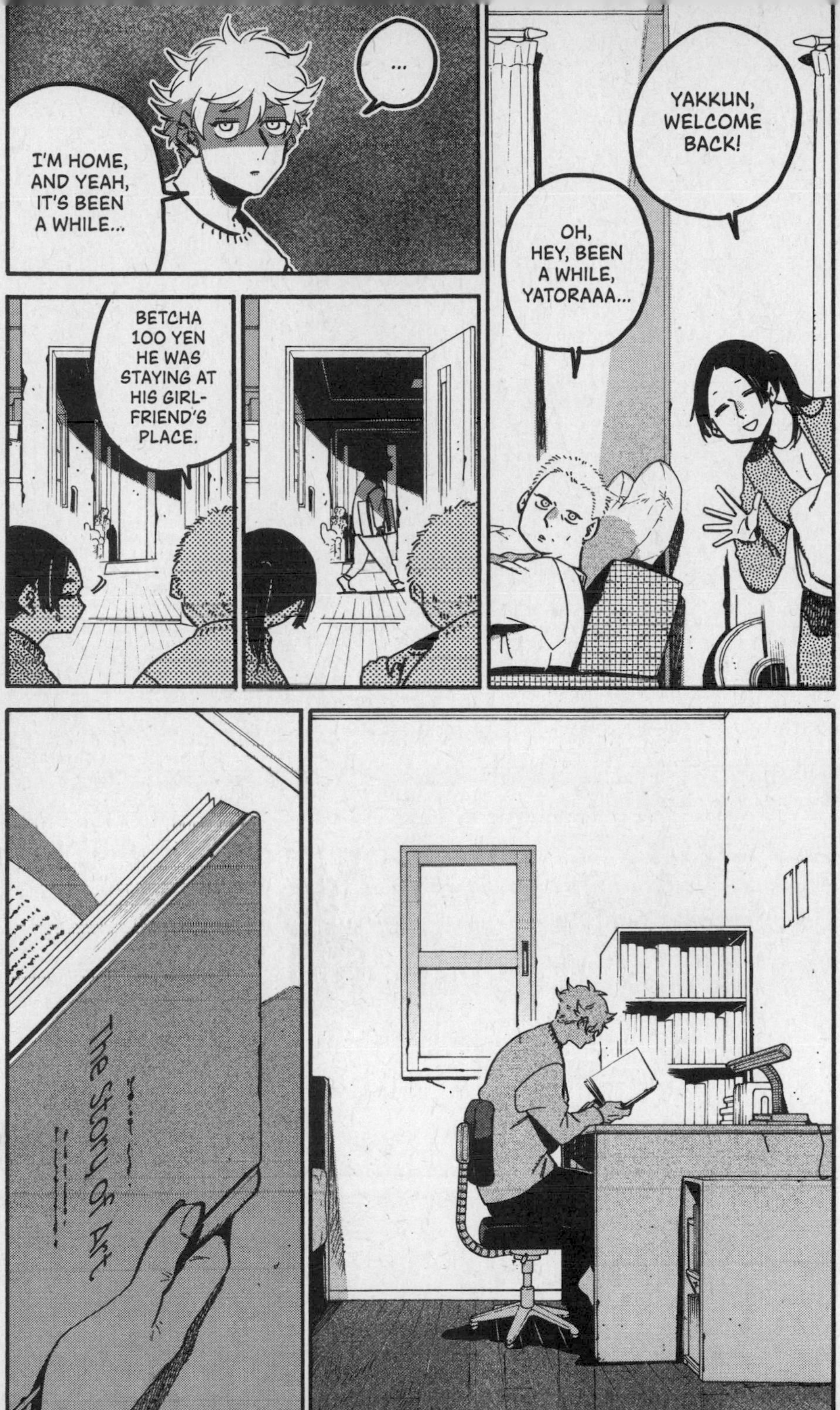
YAKKUN, WELCOME BACK!
OH, HEY, BEEN A WHILE, YATORAAA...
...
I'M HOME, AND YEAH, IT'S BEEN A WHILE...
BETCHA 100 YEN HE WAS STAYING AT HIS GIRL-FRIEND'S PLACE.
The Story of Art

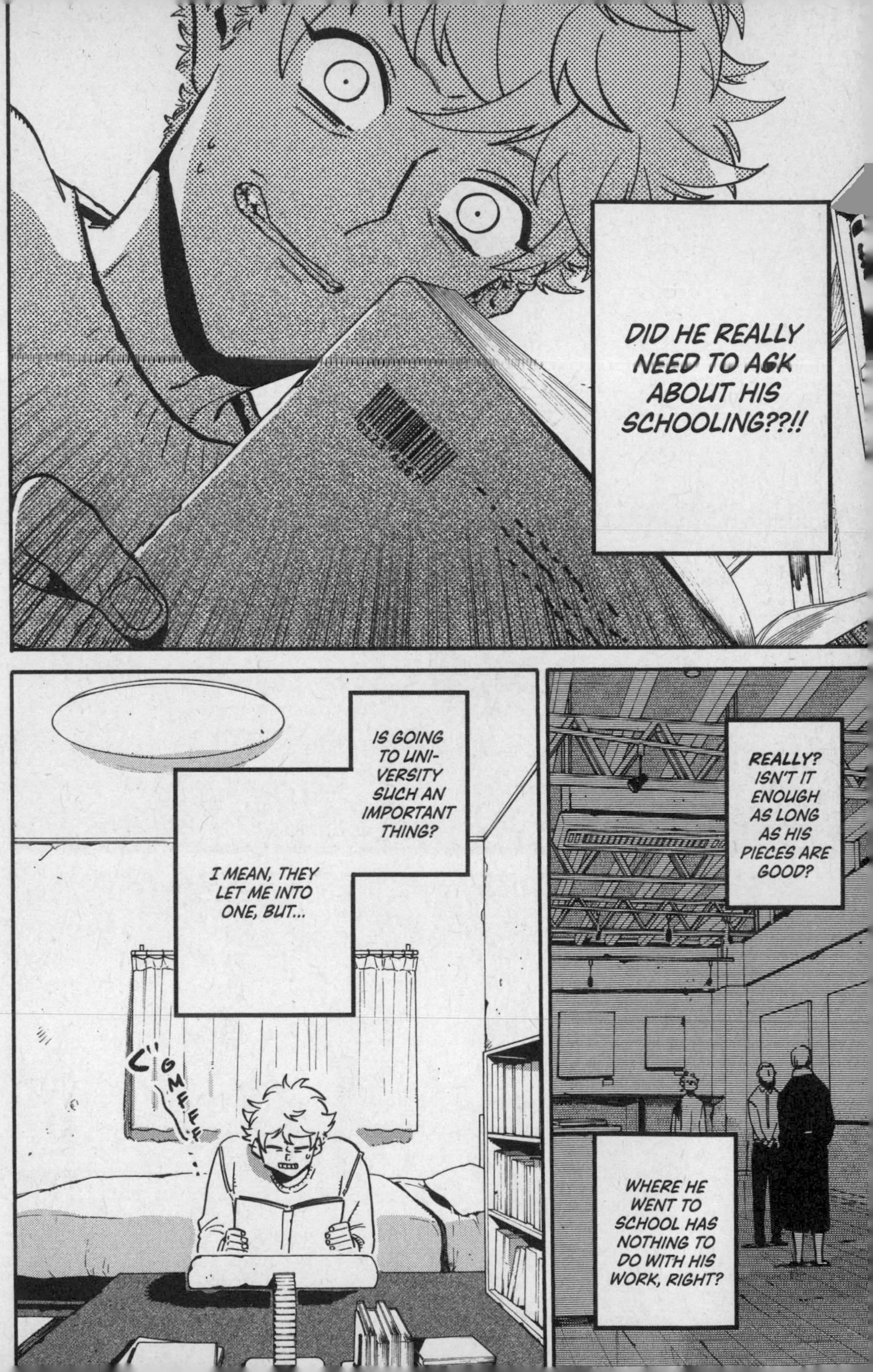
DID HE REALLY NEED TO ASK ABOUT HIS SCHOOLING??!!
REALLY? ISN'T IT ENOUGH AS LONG AS HIS PIECES ARE GOOD?
WHERE HE WENT TO SCHOOL HAS NOTHING TO DO WITH HIS WORK, RIGHT?
IS GOING TO UNI-VERSITY SUCH AN IMPORTANT THING?
I MEAN, THEY LET ME INTO ONE, BUT...

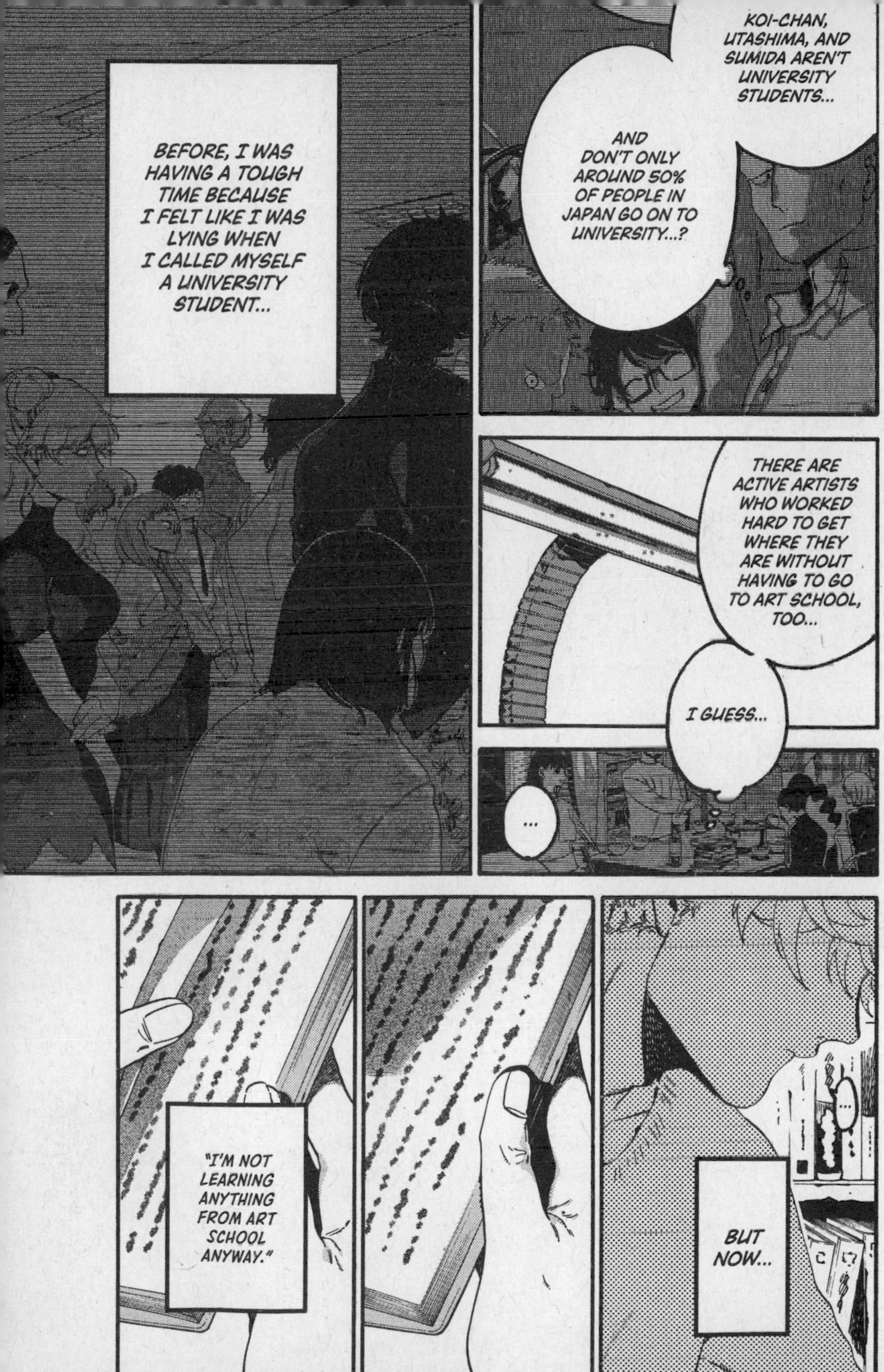
KOI-CHAN, UTASHIMA, AND SUMIDA AREN'T UNIVERSITY STUDENTS...
AND DON'T ONLY AROUND 50% OF PEOPLE IN JAPAN GO ON TO UNIVERSITY...?
THERE ARE ACTIVE ARTISTS WHO WORKED HARD TO GET WHERE THEY ARE WITHOUT HAVING TO GO TO ART SCHOOL, TOO...
I GUESS...
...
BEFORE, I WAS HAVING A TOUGH TIME BECAUSE I FELT LIKE I WAS LYING WHEN I CALLED MYSELF A UNIVERSITY STUDENT...
...
BUT NOW...
"I'M NOT LEARNING ANYTHING FROM ART SCHOOL ANYWAY."

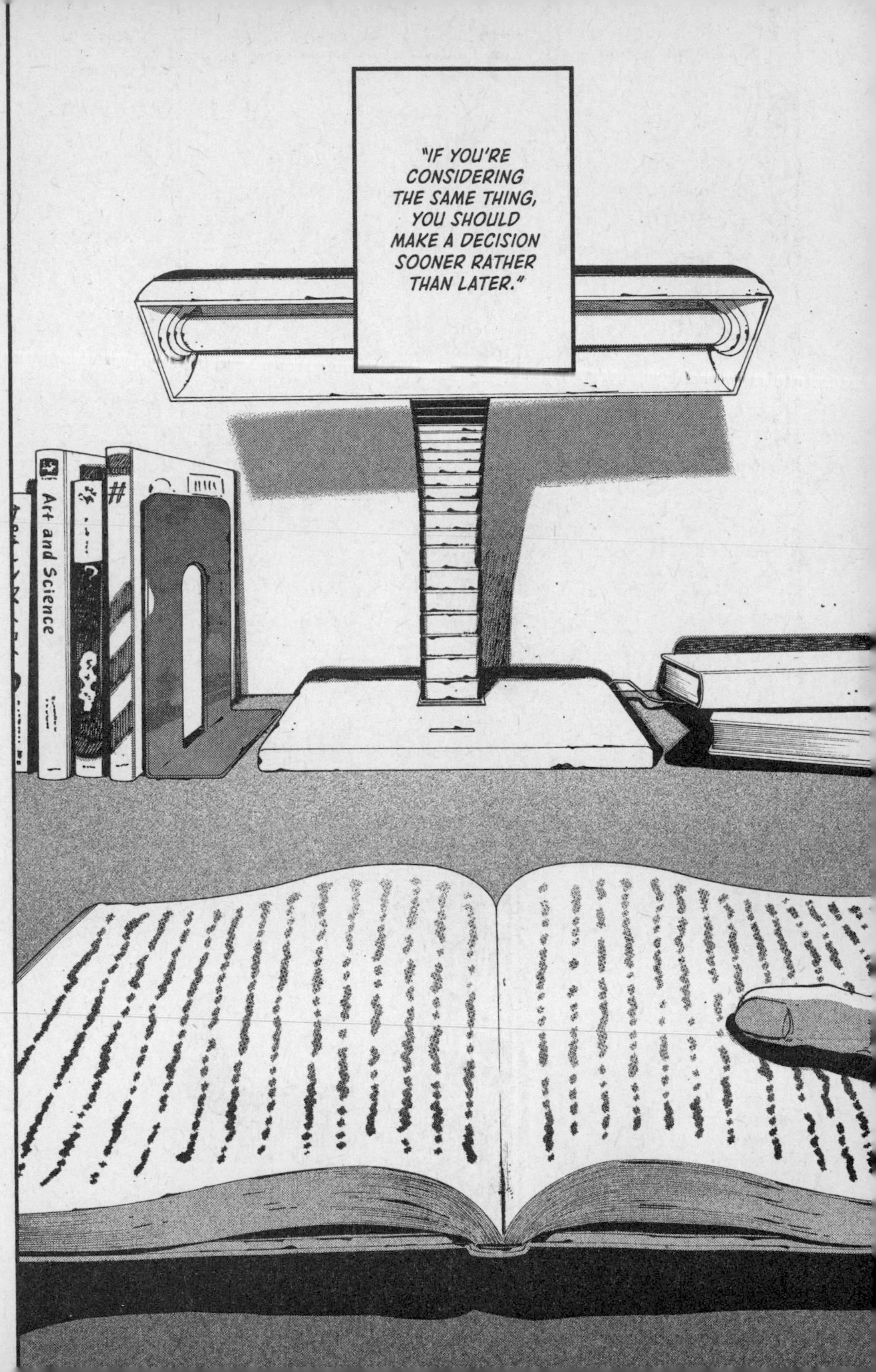
"IF YOU'RE CONSIDERING THE SAME THING, YOU SHOULD MAKE A DECISION SOONER RATHER THAN LATER."
Art and Science

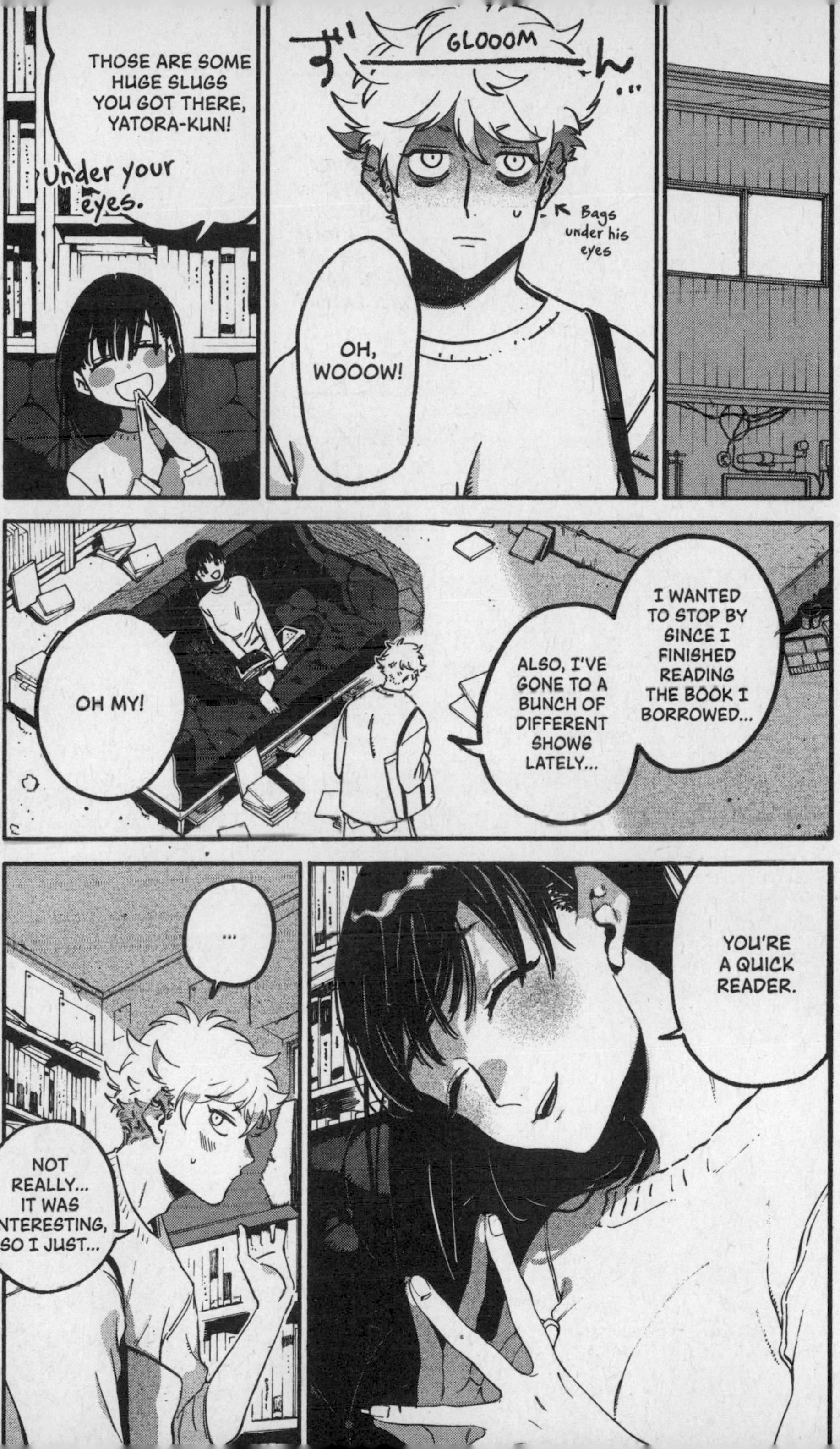
ず
GLOOOM
ん...
Bags under his eyes
OH, WOOOW!
THOSE ARE SOME HUGE SLUGS YOU GOT THERE, YATORA-KUN!
Under your eyes.
I WANTED TO STOP BY SINCE I FINISHED READING THE BOOK I BORROWED...
ALSO, I'VE GONE TO A BUNCH OF DIFFERENT SHOWS LATELY...
OH MY!
YOU'RE A QUICK READER.
...
NOT REALLY... IT WAS INTERESTING, SO I JUST...

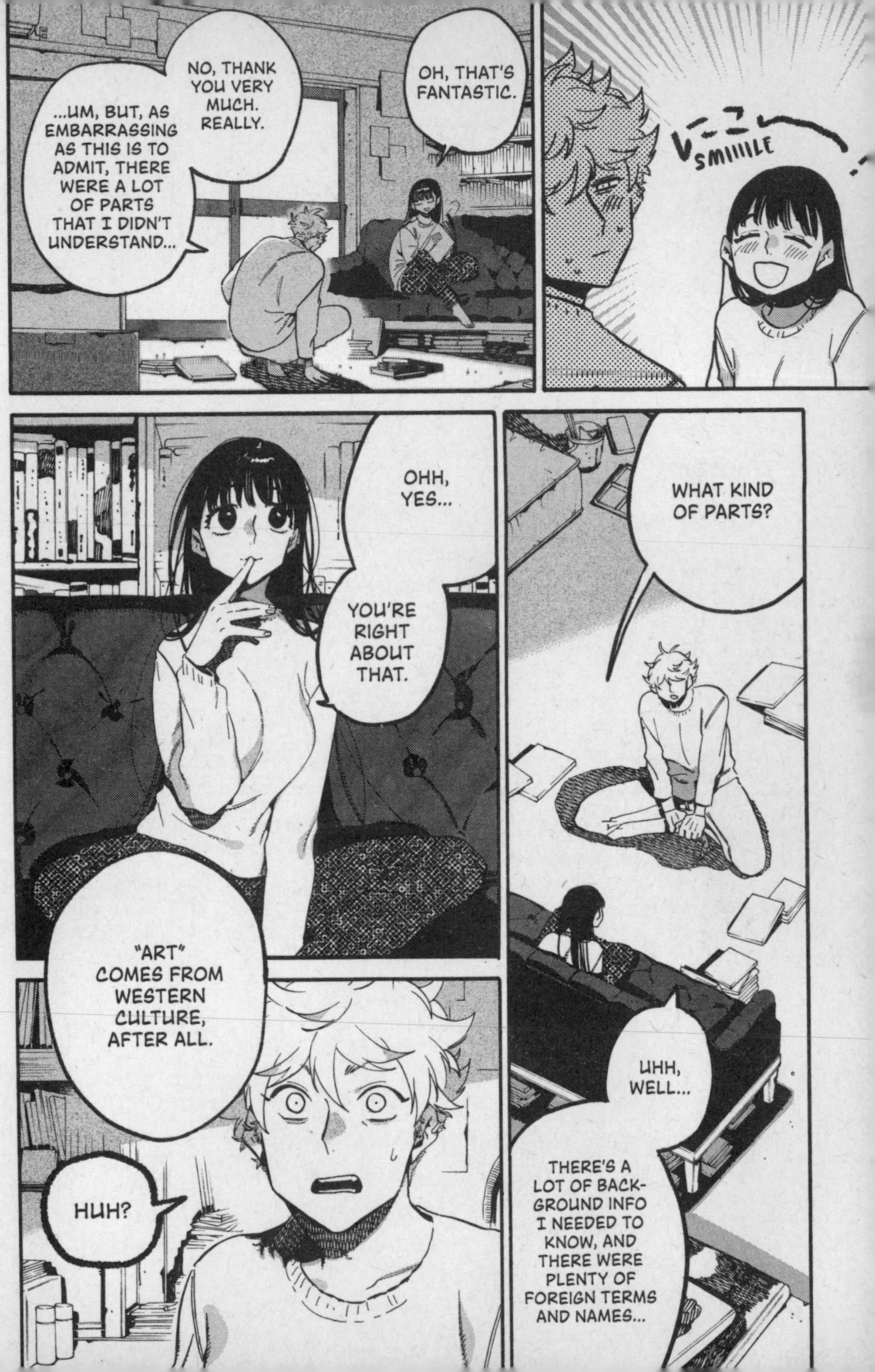
SMIIIILE
OH, THAT'S FANTASTIC.
NO, THANK YOU VERY MUCH. REALLY.
...UM, BUT, AS EMBARRASSING AS THIS IS TO ADMIT, THERE WERE A LOT OF PARTS THAT I DIDN'T UNDERSTAND...
WHAT KIND OF PARTS?
UHH, WELL...
THERE'S A LOT OF BACK-GROUND INFO I NEEDED TO KNOW, AND THERE WERE PLENTY OF FOREIGN TERMS AND NAMES...
OHH, YES...
YOU'RE RIGHT ABOUT THAT.
"ART" COMES FROM WESTERN CULTURE, AFTER ALL.
HUH?

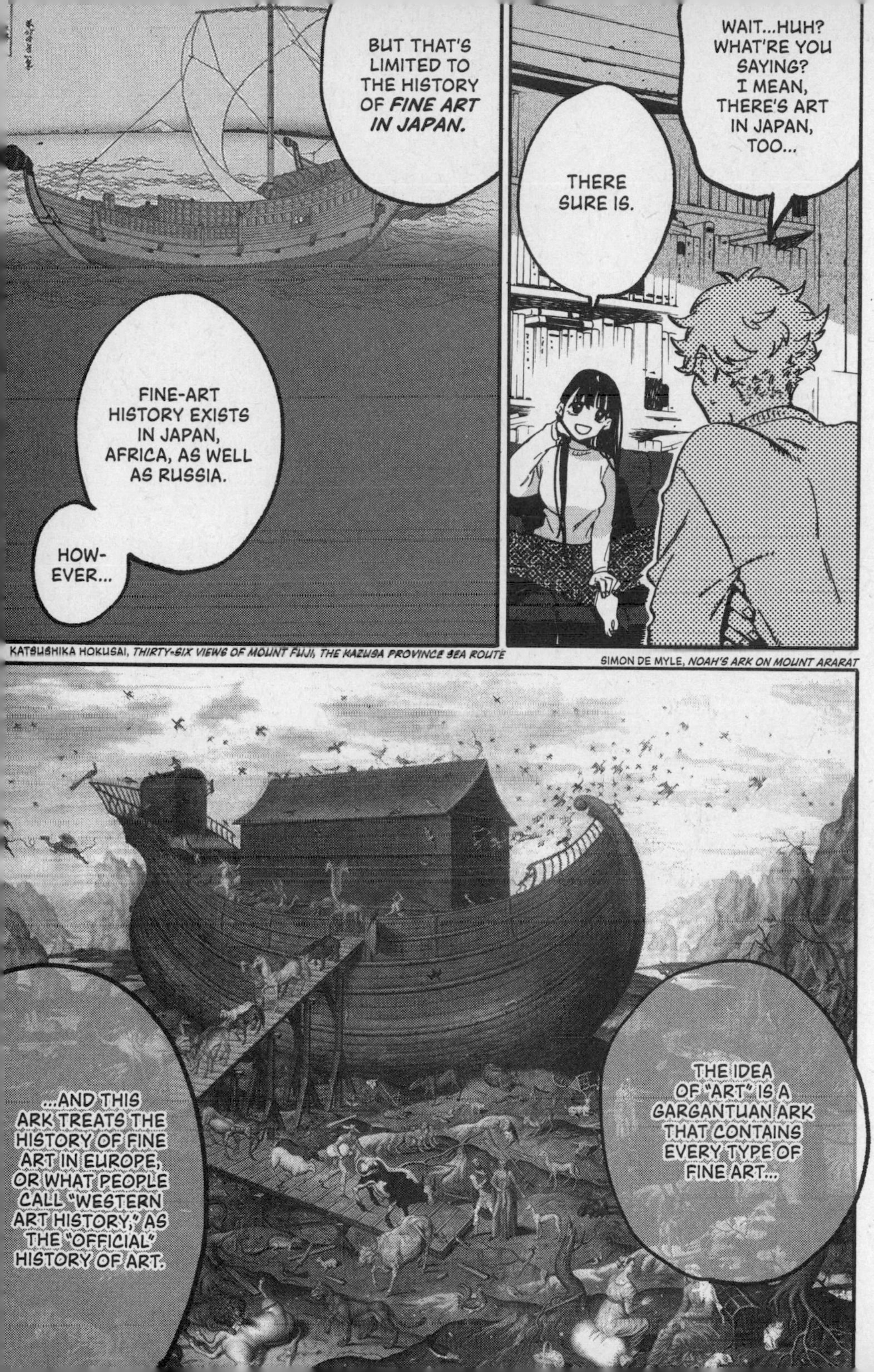
WAIT...HUH? WHAT'RE YOU SAYING? I MEAN, THERE'S ART IN JAPAN, TOO...
THERE SURE IS.
BUT THAT'S LIMITED TO THE HISTORY OF *FINE ART IN JAPAN.*
FINE-ART HISTORY EXISTS IN JAPAN, AFRICA, AS WELL AS RUSSIA.
HOW-EVER...
KATSUSHIKA HOKUSAI, *THIRTY-SIX VIEWS OF MOUNT FUJI, THE KAZUSA PROVINCE SEA ROUTE*
SIMON DE MYLE, *NOAH'S ARK ON MOUNT ARARAT*
THE IDEA OF "ART" IS A GARGANTUAN ARK THAT CONTAINS EVERY TYPE OF FINE ART...
...AND THIS ARK TREATS THE HISTORY OF FINE ART IN EUROPE, OR WHAT PEOPLE CALL "WESTERN ART HISTORY," AS THE "OFFICIAL" HISTORY OF ART.

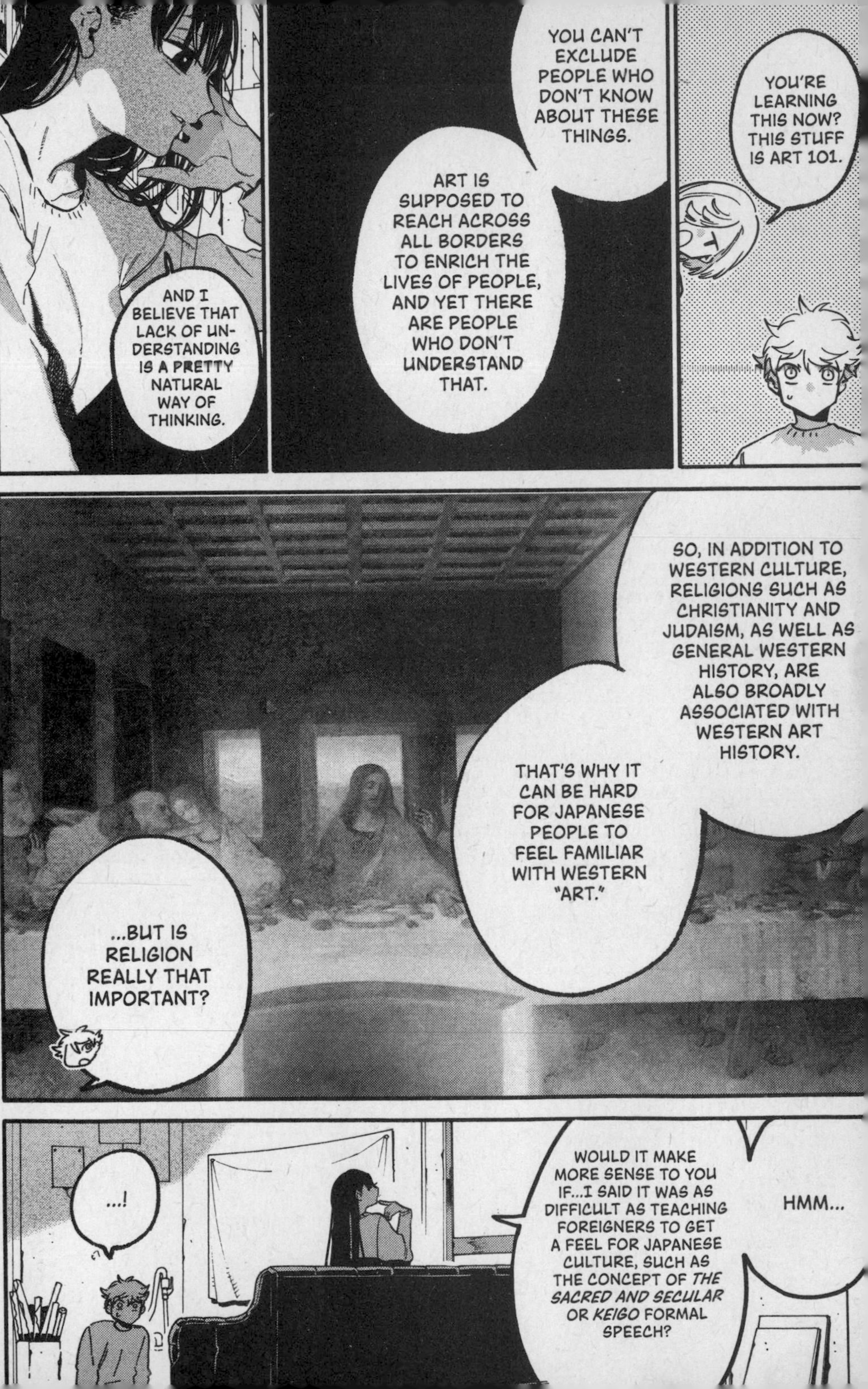
YOU'RE LEARNING THIS NOW? THIS STUFF IS ART 101.
YOU CAN'T EXCLUDE PEOPLE WHO DON'T KNOW ABOUT THESE THINGS.
ART IS SUPPOSED TO REACH ACROSS ALL BORDERS TO ENRICH THE LIVES OF PEOPLE, AND YET THERE ARE PEOPLE WHO DON'T UNDERSTAND THAT.
AND I BELIEVE THAT LACK OF UN-DERSTANDING IS A PRETTY NATURAL WAY OF THINKING.
SO, IN ADDITION TO WESTERN CULTURE, RELIGIONS SUCH AS CHRISTIANITY AND JUDAISM, AS WELL AS GENERAL WESTERN HISTORY, ARE ALSO BROADLY ASSOCIATED WITH WESTERN ART HISTORY.
THAT'S WHY IT CAN BE HARD FOR JAPANESE PEOPLE TO FEEL FAMILIAR WITH WESTERN "ART."
...BUT IS RELIGION REALLY THAT IMPORTANT?
HMM...
WOULD IT MAKE MORE SENSE TO YOU IF...I SAID IT WAS AS DIFFICULT AS TEACHING FOREIGNERS TO GET A FEEL FOR JAPANESE CULTURE, SUCH AS THE CONCEPT OF *THE SACRED AND SECULAR* OR *KEIGO* FORMAL SPEECH?
...!
LEONARDO DAVINCI, *THE LAST SUPPER*

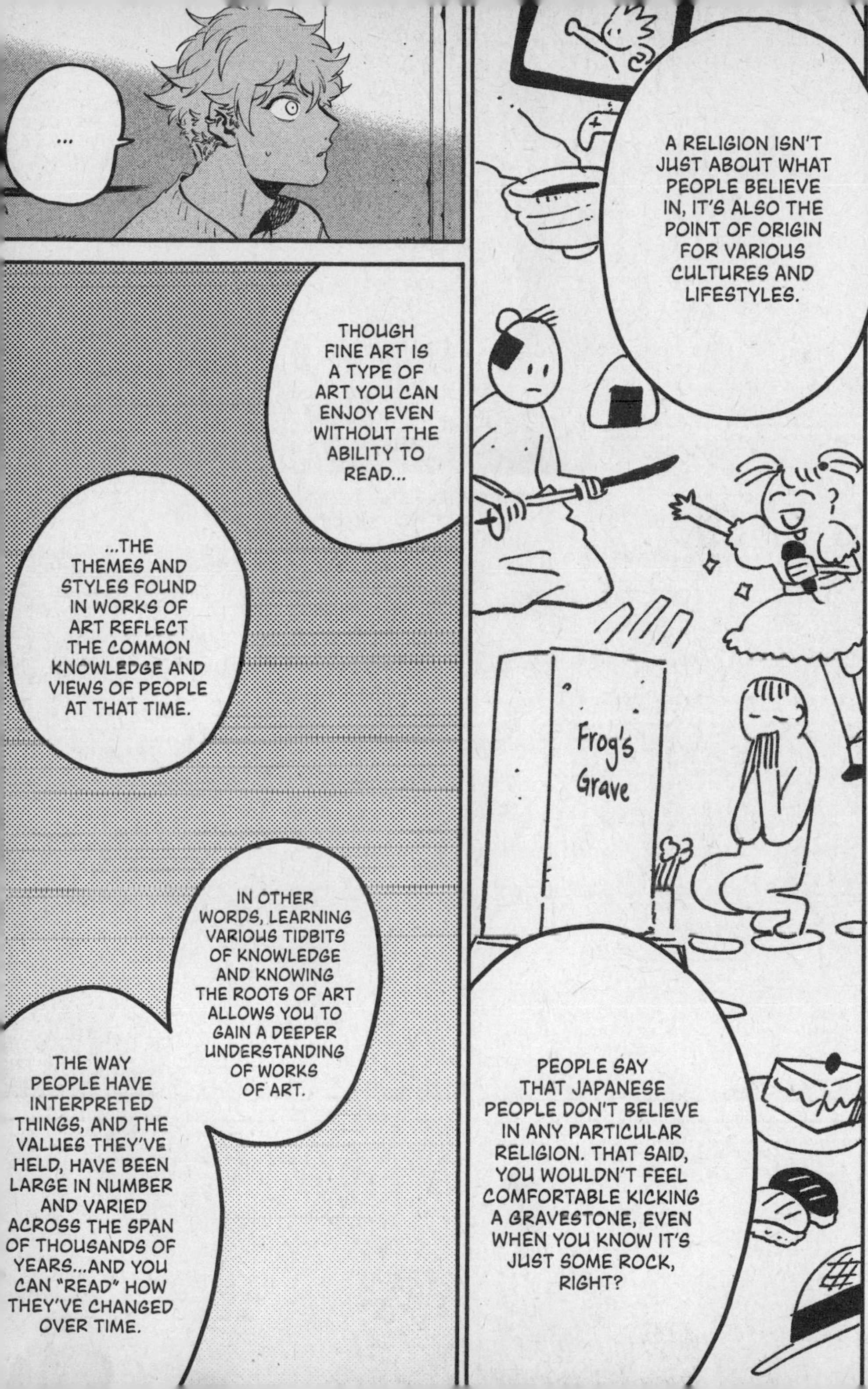
A RELIGION ISN'T JUST ABOUT WHAT PEOPLE BELIEVE IN, IT'S ALSO THE POINT OF ORIGIN FOR VARIOUS CULTURES AND LIFESTYLES.
Frog's Grave
PEOPLE SAY THAT JAPANESE PEOPLE DON'T BELIEVE IN ANY PARTICULAR RELIGION. THAT SAID, YOU WOULDN'T FEEL COMFORTABLE KICKING A GRAVESTONE, EVEN WHEN YOU KNOW IT'S JUST SOME ROCK, RIGHT?
...
THOUGH FINE ART IS A TYPE OF ART YOU CAN ENJOY EVEN WITHOUT THE ABILITY TO READ...
...THE THEMES AND STYLES FOUND IN WORKS OF ART REFLECT THE COMMON KNOWLEDGE AND VIEWS OF PEOPLE AT THAT TIME.
IN OTHER WORDS, LEARNING VARIOUS TIDBITS OF KNOWLEDGE AND KNOWING THE ROOTS OF ART ALLOWS YOU TO GAIN A DEEPER UNDERSTANDING OF WORKS OF ART.
THE WAY PEOPLE HAVE INTERPRETED THINGS, AND THE VALUES THEY'VE HELD, HAVE BEEN LARGE IN NUMBER AND VARIED ACROSS THE SPAN OF THOUSANDS OF YEARS...AND YOU CAN "READ" HOW THEY'VE CHANGED OVER TIME.

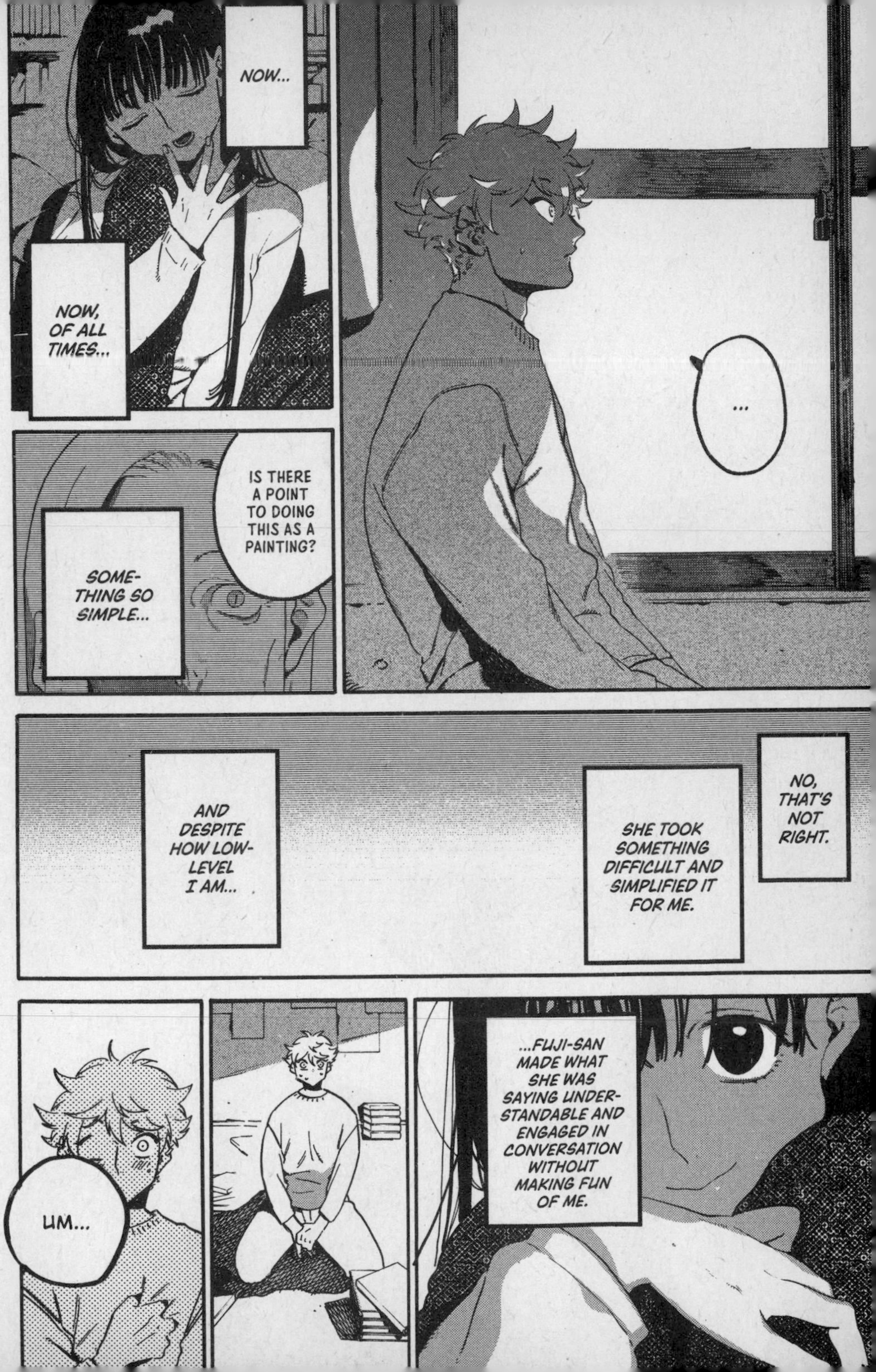
...
NOW...
NOW, OF ALL TIMES...
IS THERE A POINT TO DOING THIS AS A PAINTING?
SOMETHING SO SIMPLE...
NO, THAT'S NOT RIGHT.
SHE TOOK SOMETHING DIFFICULT AND SIMPLIFIED IT FOR ME.
AND DESPITE HOW LOW-LEVEL I AM...
...FUJI-SAN MADE WHAT SHE WAS SAYING UNDERSTANDABLE AND ENGAGED IN CONVERSATION WITHOUT MAKING FUN OF ME.
UM...

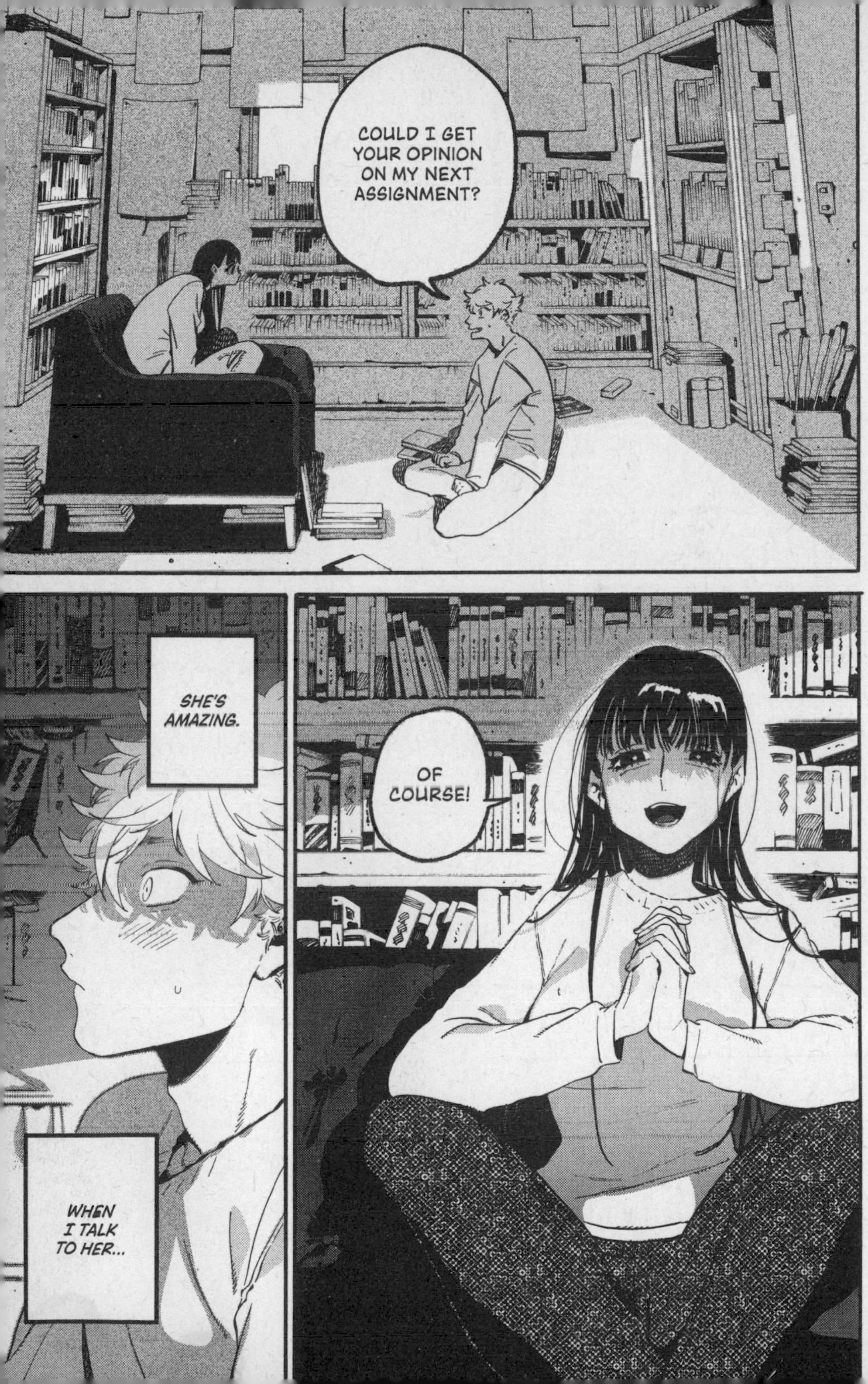
COULD I GET YOUR OPINION ON MY NEXT ASSIGNMENT?
OF COURSE!
SHE'S AMAZING.
WHEN I TALK TO HER...

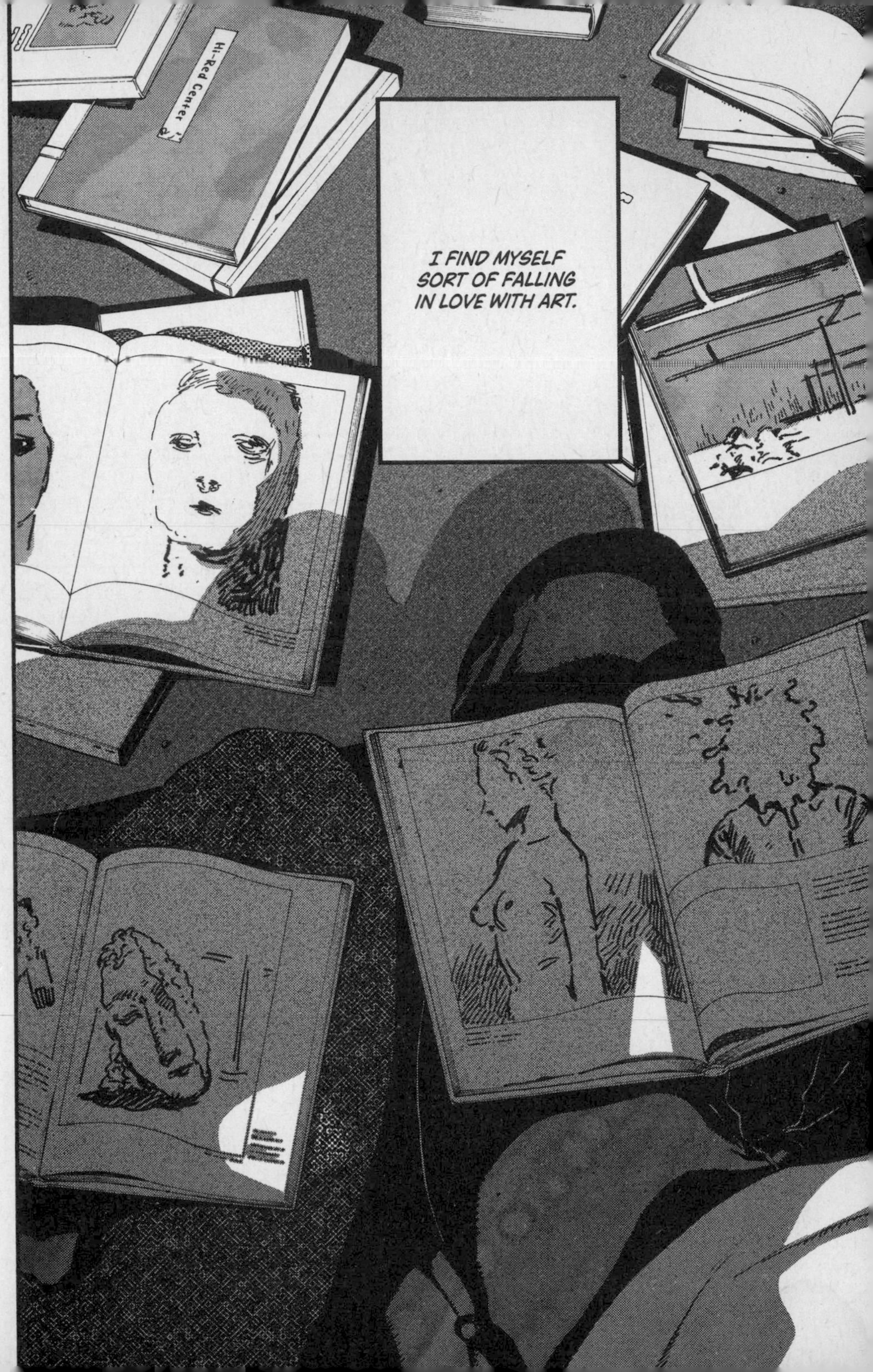
Hi-Red Center
I FIND MYSELF SORT OF FALLING IN LOVE WITH ART.

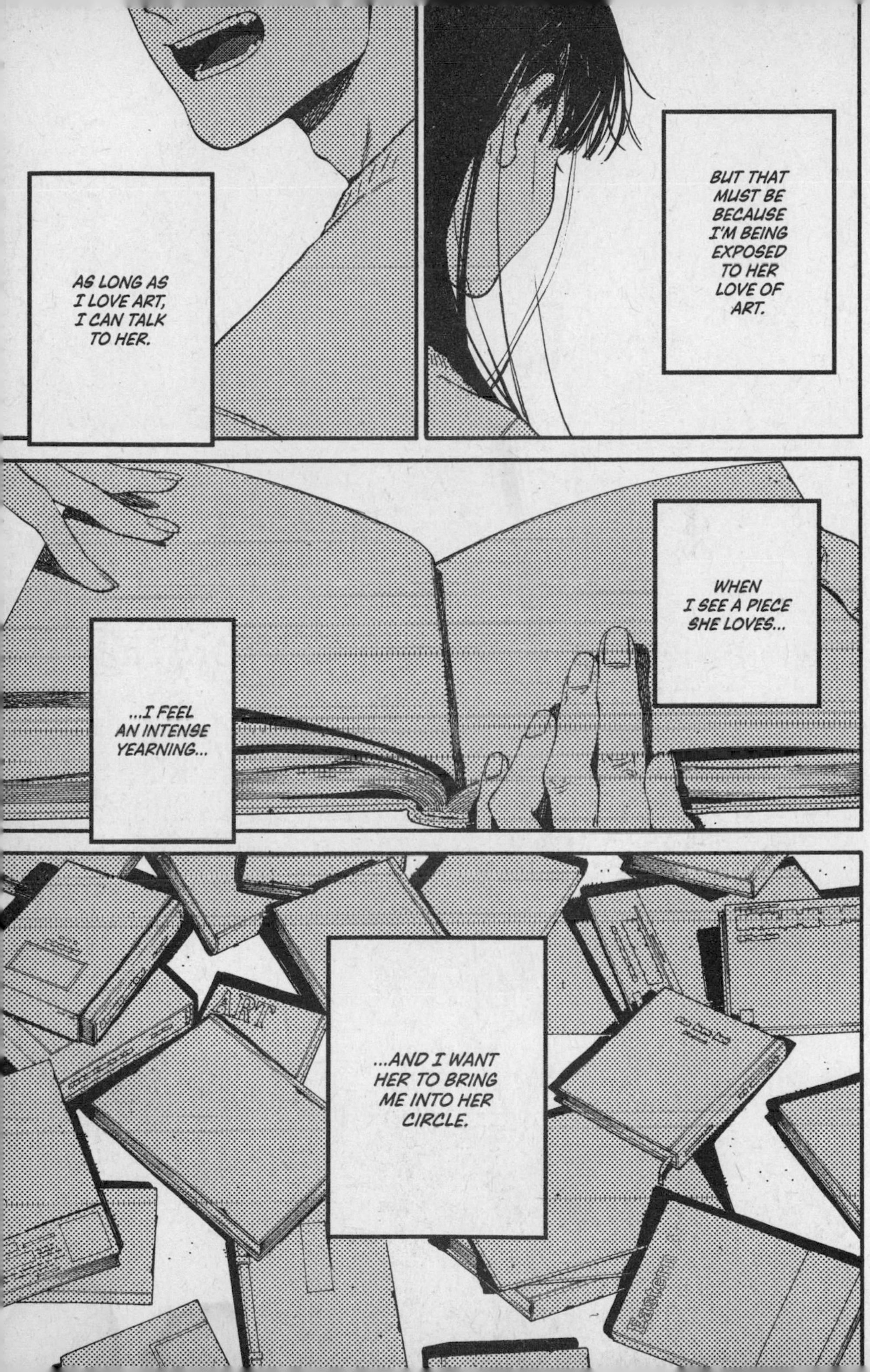
BUT THAT MUST BE BECAUSE I'M BEING EXPOSED TO HER LOVE OF ART.
AS LONG AS I LOVE ART, I CAN TALK TO HER.
WHEN I SEE A PIECE SHE LOVES...
...I FEEL AN INTENSE YEARNING...
...AND I WANT HER TO BRING ME INTO HER CIRCLE.

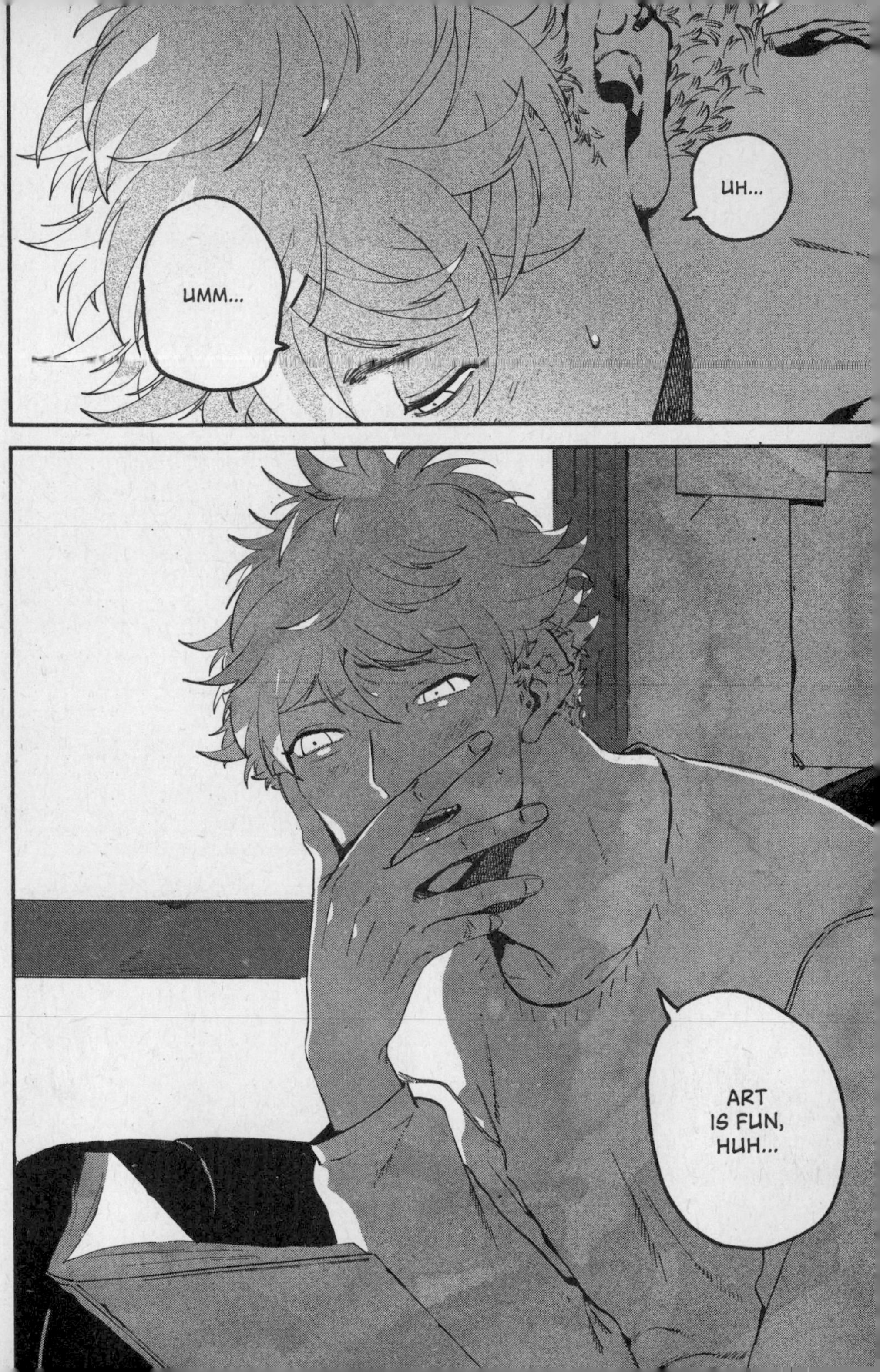
UH...
UMM...
ART IS FUN, HUH...

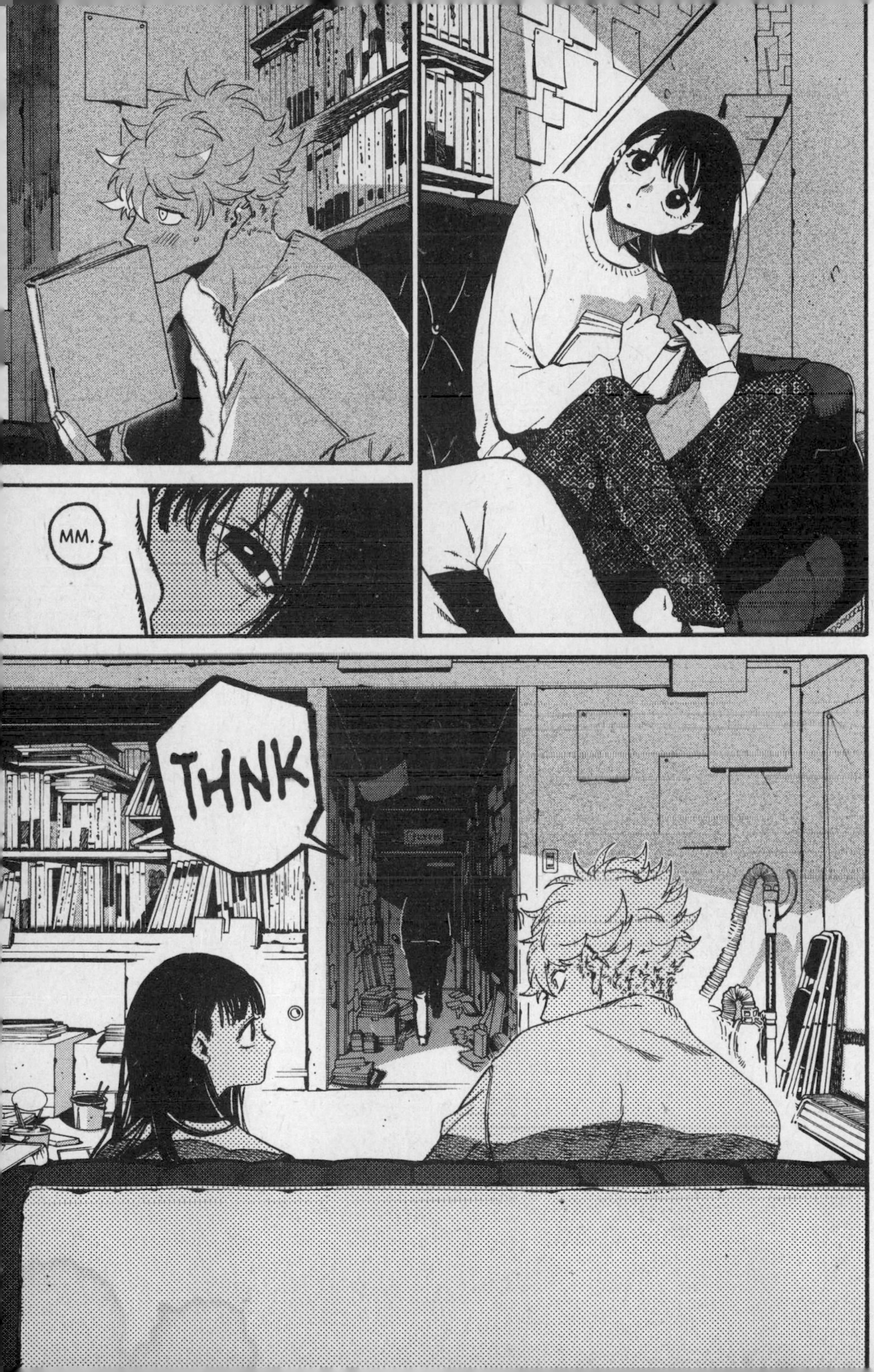
MM.
THNK

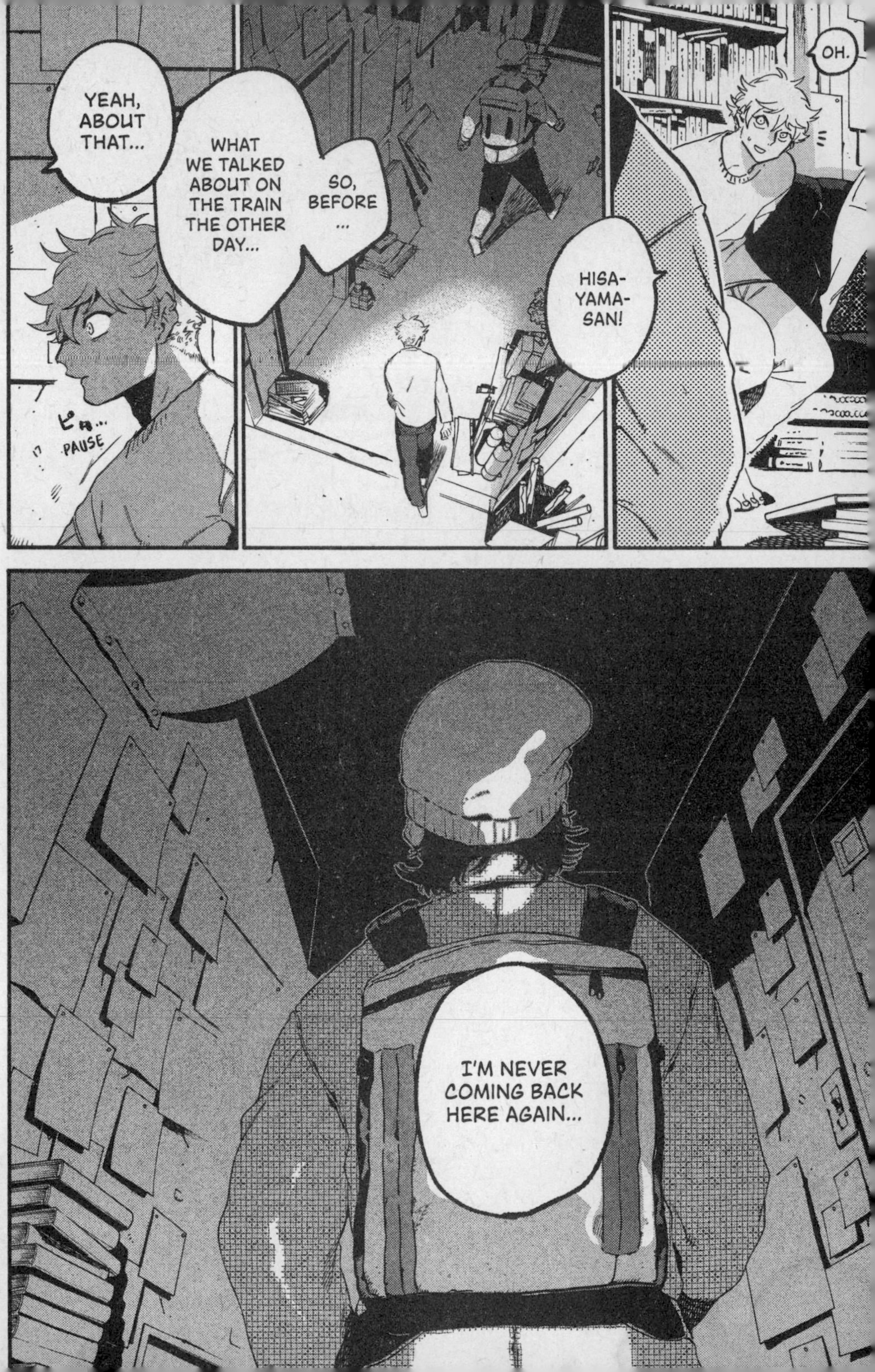
OH.
HISA-YAMA-SAN!
SO, BEFORE ...
WHAT WE TALKED ABOUT ON THE TRAIN THE OTHER DAY...
YEAH, ABOUT THAT...
PAUSE
I'M NEVER COMING BACK HERE AGAIN...

STROKE 52 END

He's got that intense battle-manga drive...

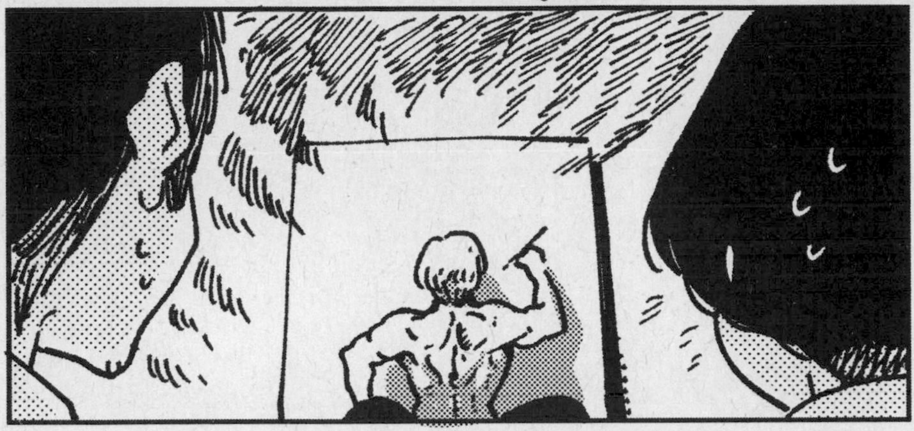

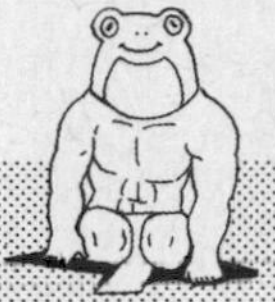

Blue Period was created with the support of many people!

Special Thanks

Thank you so very much!

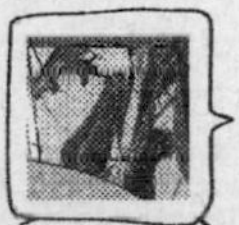

Meguru Yamaguchi-sama
Thank you for collaborating with me on the anime in addition to everything else! Please allow me to join you for a meal when I go to America someday!

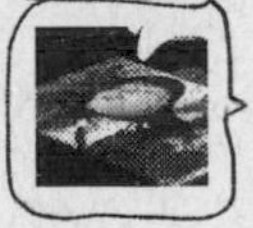

Makoto Aida-sama
Thank you for letting me borrow your precious piece...! I've been hoping to have something of yours in my manga ever since the talk we did before, so I'm so glad this could happen.

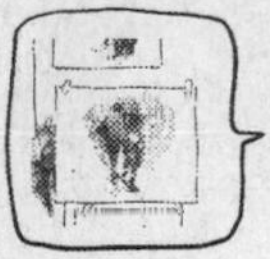

Tamana Moteki-sama
I'm always grateful to you! You continue to contribute such awesome paintings. Your landscapes are one thing, but I also love your paintings of people, Tamana-chan... Thank you very much! Let's keep doing this!

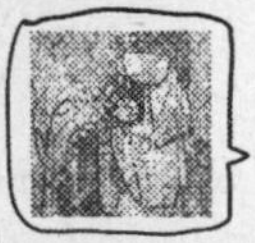

Ikuo Masumoto-sama
Thank you so much for responding so willingly despite a request that was so close to the deadline. Please allow me to see you in person sometime...!

Research Cooperation: Thank you so much to Yoichi Umetsu-sama, and Shinjuku Ophthalmologist (Ganka) Gallery!

We'll be holding a *Blue Period* exhibition!

The stage play was also awesome!

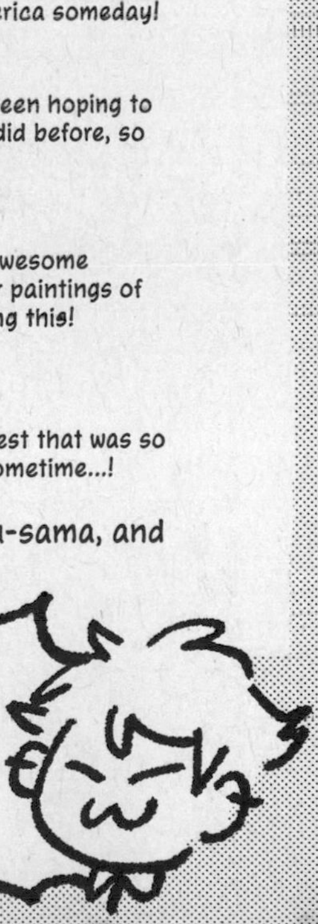

THE LEADER OF NO MARKs
FUJI-SAN...
...IS ODDLY KNOWL-EDGEABLE.
SHE'S ODDLY UNREFINED.
SHE'S ODDLY PURE.
AND ODDLY POPULAR.

THE MEMBERS OF NO MARKs (1)
TAKADA-SAN IS...
...ODDLY INTO TOKU-SATSU.
SHE'S ODDLY UNFRIENDLY.
HMPH
ぷ
SHE'S ODDLY BOSSY.
Take a bath!
Eat some food!
Change your clothes!
Have some snacks!
SHE'S ALSO ODDLY SWEET...
...ONLY WHEN IT COMES TO FUJI-SAN.

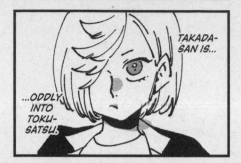

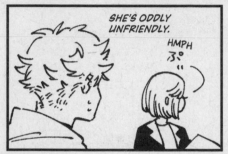

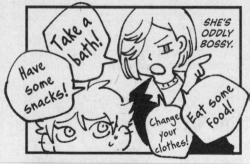

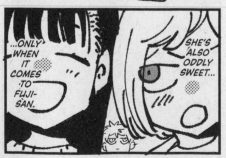

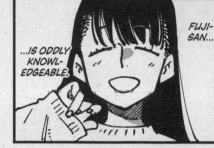

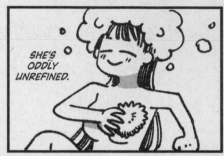

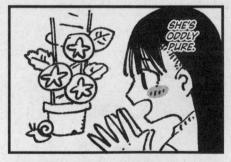

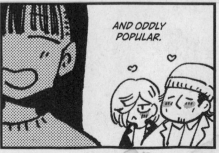

THE MEMBERS OF NO MARKs (2)

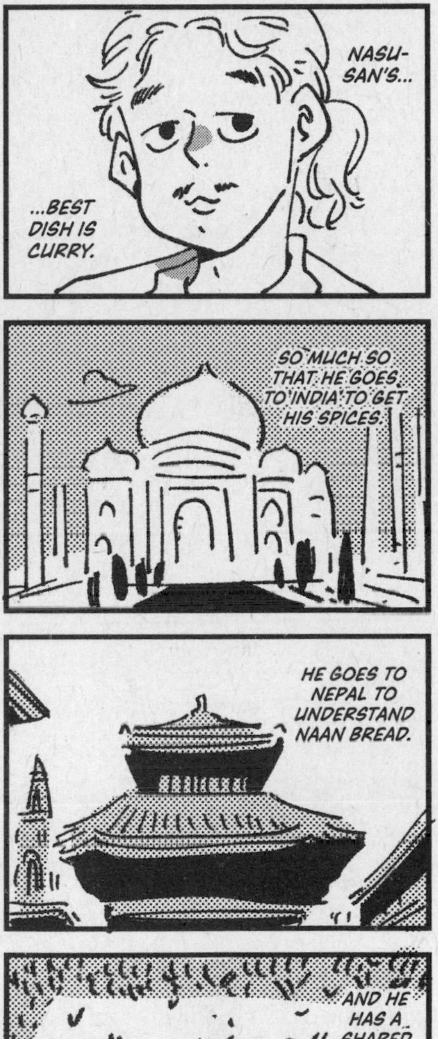
NASU-SAN'S...
...BEST DISH IS CURRY.
SO MUCH SO THAT HE GOES TO INDIA TO GET HIS SPICES.
HE GOES TO NEPAL TO UNDERSTAND NAAN BREAD.
AND HE HAS A SHARED RICE PLOT TO PRODUCE RICE.

THE MEMBERS OF NO MARKs (3)

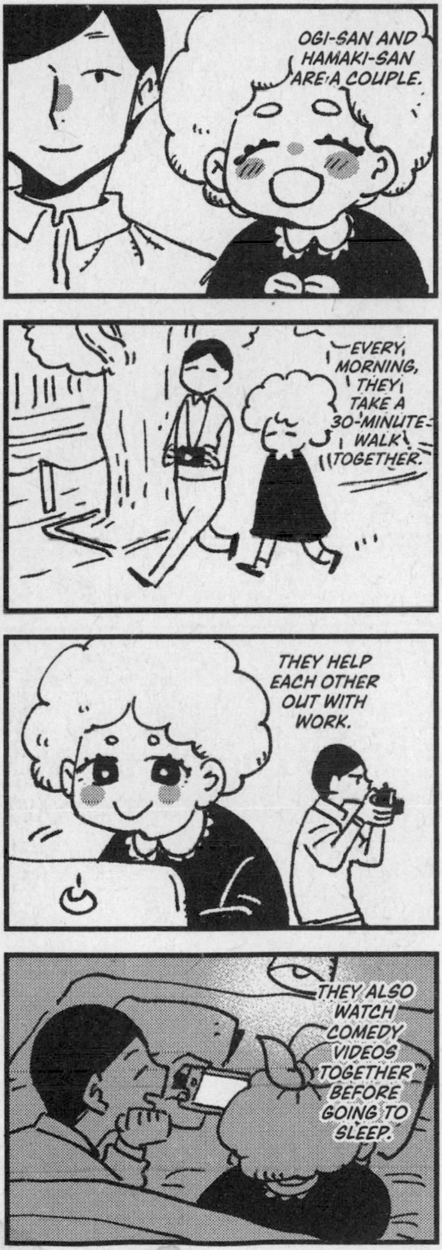
OGI-SAN AND HAMAKI-SAN ARE A COUPLE.
EVERY MORNING, THEY TAKE A 30-MINUTE WALK TOGETHER.
THEY HELP EACH OTHER OUT WITH WORK.
THEY ALSO WATCH COMEDY VIDEOS TOGETHER BEFORE GOING TO SLEEP.

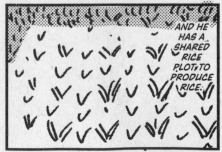

TRANSLATION NOTES

Ketchup spaghetti, page 21
The dish that Professor Inukai dislikes is actually known as *Napolitan* (or *Naporitan*), a Western-influenced pasta dish made with ketchup in place of the standard tomato sauce. Additional ingredients include bell peppers, onions, button mushrooms, Japanese-style sausage, or bacon (typically processed, pre-cooked, and with a ham-like texture). Cafés and restaurants that serve *Napolitan* typically boil the pasta, let it rest, and then reheat it with the other ingredients before being served.

The origin of this dish is unclear, but many people believe it was invented in the 1950s in Yokohama at the New Grand Hotel. And despite a name derived from the Italian city of Naples, *Napolitan* is said to have been inspired by dishes American soldiers would eat during the occupation of Japan.

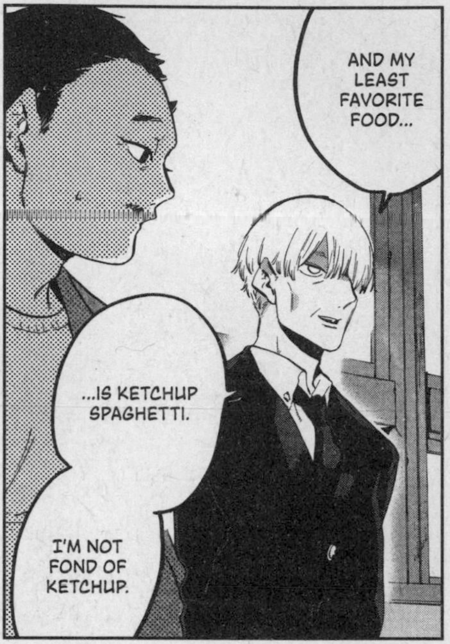
AND MY LEAST FAVORITE FOOD...
...IS KETCHUP SPAGHETTI.
I'M NOT FOND OF KETCHUP.

Washi paper, page 30
Washi, also known as Japanese paper (and often mistakenly referred to as "rice paper"), is a traditional paper made from plant fibers. Most washi paper is made from mulberry (*kozo*) bark, but other varieties are made from the bark of the Edgeworth chrysantha (*mitsumata*) bush or *ganpi* shrub.

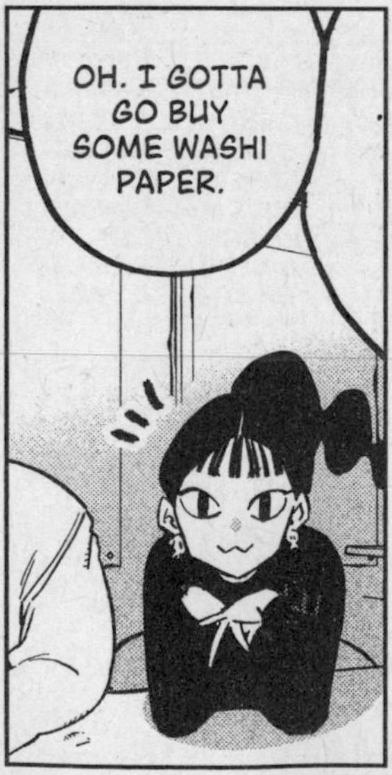
OH. I GOTTA GO BUY SOME WASHI PAPER.

The Moon Over the Mountain, page 105

The Moon Over the Mountain (also known as *Tiger-Poet* and, in Japanese, *Sangetsuki*) is a short story by Atsushi Nakajima. Like many of his works, this story was based on a Classical Chinese story from the Tang Dynasty. The story is about a civil servant named Li Zheng whose monstrous pride turns him into a tiger. He passes the civil servant exams and is able to do well in his job, but feels the job is beneath him and quits to pursue his true passion, poetry. Unfortunately, he can't make ends meet as a poet, and he returns to his civil servant job, taking a lower position than before. This badly hurts his pride and drives him mad, eventually turning him into a tiger that still retains his human mind but is unable to write, which is a hellish existence for Li Zheng.

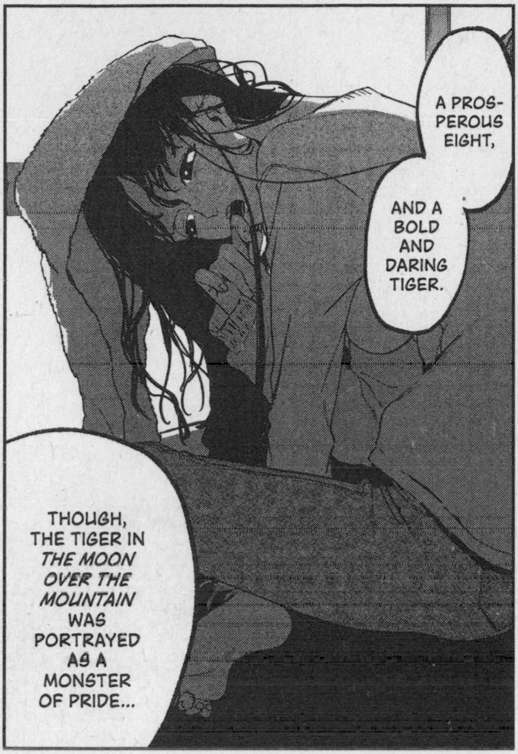
A PROS-PEROUS EIGHT,
AND A BOLD AND DARING TIGER.
THOUGH, THE TIGER IN THE MOON OVER THE MOUNTAIN WAS PORTRAYED AS A MONSTER OF PRIDE...

The sacred and secular, page 182

Hare and *ke* is a concept of dual temporalities most often used in Japanese folklore studies. Though there are several interpretations, *hare* can refer to "good weather," or a positive turn in the weather, and are sacred days of celebration, ritual, festival, change—essentially, they are extraordinary days. Special attire, dishes, manners, and access to sacred locations may be associated with *hare*. On the other hand, *ke*, which is thought to refer to "qi" or "food," represents ordinary daily life. These distinctions can be fluid and have changed over time.

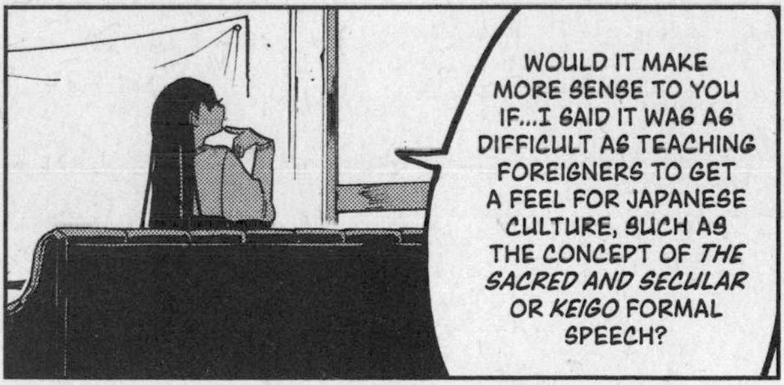
WOULD IT MAKE MORE SENSE TO YOU IF...I SAID IT WAS AS DIFFICULT AS TEACHING FOREIGNERS TO GET A FEEL FOR JAPANESE CULTURE, SUCH AS THE CONCEPT OF THE SACRED AND SECULAR OR KEIGO FORMAL SPEECH?

A Kodansha Comics Trade Paperback Original
Blue Period 12 copyright © 2022 Tsubasa Yamaguchi
English translation copyright © 2023 Tsubasa Yamaguchi

All rights reserved.

Published in the United States by Kodansha Comics, an imprint of Kodansha USA Publishing, LLC, New York.

Publication rights for this English edition arranged through Kodansha Ltd., Tokyo.

First published in Japan in 2022 by Kodansha Ltd., Tokyo.

ISBN 978-1-64651-567-7

Printed in the United States of America.

www.kodansha.us

9 8 7 6 5 4 3 2 1
Translation: Ajani Oloye
Lettering: Lys Blakeslee
Editing: Haruko Hashimoto
Kodansha Comics edition cover design by Matthew Akuginow

Publisher: Kiichiro Sugawara

Director of publishing services: Ben Applegate
Director of publishing operations: Dave Barrett
Associate director of publishing operations: Stephen Pakula
Publishing services managing editors: Madison Salters, Alanna Ruse, with Grace Chen
Production manager: Emi Lotto
Logo and character art ©Kodansha USA Publishing, LLC